A STEP TOO FAR

A STEP TOO FAR

Written by

Ross Martyn

June 03, 2010

THE CHOIR PRESS

First published in the United Kingdom in 2022 by
The Choir Press

ISBN 978-178963-241-5

The writing of this script is of its time and was written between the years 2006 and 2011. This is a disclaimer in that I am not responsible for any errors of issues, legal or otherwise contained in this writing which is or may be out of date and may now be seen as using culturally offensive terminology in the year of publication. I wish to emphasise that this writing is in the nature of fiction. As the author is now deceased, is no longer able to clarify his views.

M. Martyn

To my beloved parents,
Bill and Betty Martyn

List of characters

No. of Characters	Initials	Full name	Last name	First name	Sex	Age	Dwarf/Genhance Country Club	Background
1	AB	Anthony Barrett	Barrett	Anthony	M	52	–	Anthony Barrett is an attendee at the lecture Bill Horowitz presents at the Royal Society on 14 May 2013.
2	**Admin**	High Court administrator	High Court	Administrator	M	56	High Court	Administrator in the High Court who deals with injunctions
3	AG	Amerjit Ghuman	Ghuman	Amerjit	M	20	Student	Amerjit Ghuman (together with his girlfriend Sambhi Khangura) catch a lift with Max Lyford and have a discussion on "Schindler's Lift" (vs. "Schindler's List").
4	ALB	Angus Le Bon	Le Bon	Angus	M	63	CC	Member of the Country Club (CC). Is not a member of the GPA Ethics Ruling Committee – but attends (in the gallery) the Hearing of the Ethics Ruling Committee – that Ivan brought on.
5	AUD	Audience	Audience	Audience	–	–	Dwarves	During Ivan Henry's speeches to the Dwarf Associations (AKA Small Persons Association) he is questioned and hackled by the audience (Aud).
6	AW	Andrew Watts	Watts	Andrew	Me	24	Dwarf	One of two close friends with Ivan Henry (the other being Robert Walker).
								Works as an actor. He graduated from the Royal Academy of Dramatic Art (RADA) and is currently an active member of the Royal Shakespeare Company.
								Often comes across as dumb, but occasionally shows amazing flashes of brilliance.
								He is a dwarf and is 4'2" tall. Suffers from the achondroplasia form of dwarfism.

No. of Characters	Initials	Full name	Last name	First name	Sex	Age	Dwarf/Genhance Country Club	Background
7	BG	Barry Green . CHANGE TO BARRY GREENSLADE	GreenSLADE	Barry	M	53	GPA	Barry has advance balding – with a comb over, reasonably unattractive, and a closet gay. He is o.k. at his work, but realises that, at 53, he is never going to get another promotion – so, there is no need to try too hard at work. Wears standard Civil Service brown and beige. Pleasant enough guy – just a wee bit too effeminate.
8	BH	Bill Horowitz	Horowitz	Bill	M	38	BDW	Worlds leading genetics lawyer. A Jew who has married a Catholic (Cynthia Horowitz). Together they have a disabled son (Samuel). He is very energetic, warm, personable and very likeable. He like to work on assignments that 'make a difference'. He is a partner in the law firm Bradbury, Dywer & Waldron (BDW). His grandparents were saved from the Nazis by Schindler (i.e. they were on the Schindler's list).
9	BM	Bruce May-CHANGE TO BRUCE MAYNE	Mayne	Bruce	M	9	Genhance	One of the genetically enhanced kids doing work experience at the law firm Bradbury, Dywer & Waldron (BDW). His father is Trevor Mayne.
10	BN	Bernard Newman	Newman	Bernard	M	47	GPA	Bernard is a little slow, but sort of harmless. He takes everything very seriously and pays close attention to everything that is said – taking notes readily. However, he can be painful, as he does take everything so literally - and cannot be directed to 'see the bigger picture'. Has a habit of referring back to his notes to make his point.
11	BT	Ben Thomas	Thomas	Ben	M	53	Publican	Ben is the Publican of 'The Grapes' Pub at 76 Narrow Street, Limehouse, London, E14 8BP. His regular patrons include Gough Rutherford, Mark Hardwick, Elaine Kellaway and Ivan Henry – and is familiar enough with them to know their names.

No. of Characters	Initials	Full name	Last name	First name	Sex	Age	Dwarf/Genhance Country Club	Background
12	CB	Chris Braithwaite	Braithwaite	Chris	M	65	CC	Key member of the Country Club (CC) and the owner of the Claydon House Mansion – where the CC often meet.
13	CD	Clarissa Dalloway	Dalloway	Clarissa	F	52	High Court	Clarissa Dalloway is Judge Frederick Rogers Secretary. This is a play on Virginia Woolf's novel "Mrs.Dalloway" (i.e. the characters full name was Clarissa Dalloway). In the spirit of Woolf's novel, Clarissa thinks she's 18 – but is actually 52.
14	CH	Cynthia Horowitz	Horowitz	Cynthia	F	40		Bill Horowitz's wife and the mother of Samuel (their mentally retarded son). She is a Catholic and has PhD in Psychology.
15	DK	Doris Keyes	Keyes	Doris	F	52	GPA	Personal Assistant to Max Lyford.
16	DM	Douglas McCauley	McCauley	Douglas	M	52		Douglas McCauley is the husband of Judy McCauley. They have a seven year old daughter, Heather, who is genetic enhanced (a genhance) – who is doing work experience at the Bradbury, Dywer and Waldron law firm.
17	DT	Duncan Thomilson	Thomilson	Duncan	M	48	Royal Society	Duncan attempts to by-pass protocol and security by not registering before going into the RoyalSociety's Seminar room - where Bill Horowitz is about to give a lecture.
18	EA	Elizaveta Alekseev	Alekseev	Elizaveta	F	35	Rubliov Museum	A Junior Attendant (Jane Kemp) at the London Annex of the Andrei Rubliov Museum of Early Russian Art challenges Jon Raney to produce his life membership – as she is new and does not recognise him. The senior attendant (Elizaveta Alekseev) recognise Jon - and instructs Jane to let him through.
19	EK	Eileen Kellaway – CHANGE TO ELAINE KELLAWAY	Kellaway	Elaine	F	26	GPA	Eilaine works for the GPA as a social researcher. She is Jewish and a good work friend of Ivan Henry, Gough Rutherford and Mark Hardwick. She is shortish, being 5'1", and is constantly on the edge.

No. of Characters	Initials	Full name	Last name	First name	Sex	Age	Dwarf/Genhance Country Club	Background
20	FR	Frederick Rogers	Rogers	Frederick	M	65	CC High Court	Frederick is a High Court Judge and a member of the Country Club – albeit, on the cusp of being a dissident member of the club. Father of Gough Rutherford. But he left his wife and Gough when Gough was only 5 years old. While he is approaching seventy, he is still a handsome man with a square jaw line, high cheek bones and arched eye brows
21	GK	George Kelvin	Kelvin	George	M	38	GPA	George is an unrecognised genius – capable of assimilation of information with perfect recall – and the ability to quickly synthesis the information can arrive at new insights. While he may be a genius, he has appalling social skills, is arrogant – does not shower regularly nor maintain the usual level of personal grooming expected of professional office workers.
22	GO	Greg O'Leary	O'Leary	Greg	M	25	Dwarf	A legendary aggressive dwarf – whom many others find him threatening and abrasive. He is very well built up – the result of many hours per day spent doing weights at the gym. Typically, he wears leather clothing, complete with leather hat, has a Denis Lillee moustache, thick gold chains, and wears Goth type rings on his fingers, his ears, nose and eye brow are all pieced. Part of the (true) legend surrounding Greg, is that he stars in extreme SM dwarf porn videos. He has two close dwarf mates, Peter Giles and Paul Firth.
23	GR	Gough Rutherford	Rutherford	Gough	M	25	GPA	Gough Rutherford works at the GPA as a social researcher and is good work mates with Ivan Henry, Mark Hardwick and Eileen Kellaway. His father left home when he was five years old. Natural Comedian, white Caucasian, 6 foot tall. Black hair like 'Sideshow Bob' (from the Simpsons' ,i.e. very fuzzy), always laughing and playing practical jokes. Many of his comments/jokes are politically incorrect – which he knows and plays on. He is either liked or hated by his work colleagues. Mildly above intelligence, mild attitude problem, degree in sociology and ethics. Is a through and through Londoner with strong Cockney accent.

No. of Characters	Initials	Full name	Last name	First name	Sex	Age	Dwarf/Genhance Country Club	Background
24	**G-Rcep**	GPA Receptionist	–	–	F	22	GPA	The receptionist at the GPA's other offices (at the Gherkin). She is the receptionist positioned on the ground floor.
25	GS	Geoff Stapleton – CHANGE TO GARY STAPLETON	Stapleton	Gary	M	43	GPA	Gary, while not a genius, is never the less highly intelligent. He is a warm caring sort of a guy with an odd sense of humour – albeit, humour that others can 'just' grasp. He is highly diligent and has a strong work ethic – in as much if you are given instructions - then you execute them to the best of your ability.
26	**Guard**	Guard	–	–	M	28	High Court	Guard at the High Court – who directs Max Lyford in Scene 56
27	GZ	Gordon Zhou	Zhou	Gordon	M	7	Genhance	Gordon is a genetically enhanced kid – who is doing work experience at the Bradbury, Dywer and Waldron law firm. His parents are Mingzi Shou and Xium i Zhou.
28	HC	Heather McCauley	McCauley	Heather	F	7	Genhance	Heather is a genetically enhanced kid – who is doing work experience at the Bradbury, Dywer and Waldron law firm. Her parents are Douglas and Judy McCauley
29	HL	Harry Laughlin	Laughlin	Harry	M	38	Professor	Professor Harry Laughlin is consulted during a news article on Sky News in regards to the phenomena of Mothers having more children – once their former children are removed from them by Social Services. The Name Harry Laughlin is the name of a hard core Eugenics activists in America – during the 1920-1950.
30	HSP	Hye Soon Park	Soon Park	Hye	F	8	Genhance	Hye Soon is a genetically enhanced kid - who is doing work experience at the Bradbury, Dywer and Waldron law firm. Her parents are Jung Ho Hyun and Jin-Sook Park.

No. of Characters	Initials	Full name	Last name	First name	Sex	Age	Dwarf/Genhance Country Club	Background
31	IH	Ivan Henry	Henry	Ivan	M	23	Dwarf	Ivan has the lead role in the script. Ivan is 4' 4" Tall – which is the average height of dwarves suffering from Achondroplasia. He is a Dwarf activist, which includes being the President of the 'Little Person's Association'. A private mission of his is to change the name of the organisation back to the 'Dwarves Association' – as there is nothing wrong with being a dwarf, in fact, it is something to be proud of. He works as a social researcher at the GPA – where he is good work mates with Mark Hardwick, Gough Rutherford and Elaine Kellaway. He is married to Sandra Small. They live together in an apartment in Croydon (in which they have recently moved into – when they moved to London). They met at Leeds Metropolitan University while students (Ivan's degree is in Sociology). For work reasons they moved to London shortly after graduation. Ivan found a job with the Genetic Protection Authority as a social research scientist and Sandra found work as a legal researcher with a large legal firm Bradbury, Dywer and Waldron. They moved to London in late October 2012 – and both Ivan and Sandra started work in early November 2012. Ivan's mother is Valentina Henry (Russian decent) – formally Valentina Tikhonov, but she changed their (hers and Ivan's) to Henry upon moving to the UK Ivan's father, Igor Tikhonov (Russian decent), was also a dwarf, a celebrated clown in the Moscow circus. However, Igor and Valentina escaped from the USSR (with Ivan - aged 5)- but Igor was killed in the process.

No. of Characters	Initials	Full name	Last name	First name	Sex	Age	Dwarf/Genhance Country Club	Background
32	IT	Igor Tikhonov	Tikhonov	Igor	M		Dwarf	Igor is the father of Ivan Henry – and was the husband of Valentina Henry. He was a dwarf suffering from achondroplasia. he was 4'5" tall. He was a celebrated clown in the Moscow Circus and a noted traditional Russian and theatre dancer. His stage name was "Igor the Great". Igor was shot dead during the family escape from the USSR – however, his wife Valentina and son Ivan managed to escape safely. Once in the UK (after the escape from USSR), Valentina and Ivan changed their surname name from 'Tikhonov' to 'Henry'.
33	JB	Jasmine Bannered	Jasmine	Bannered	F	32	Police	Chief Inspector in the Metropolitan Police Force.
34	JC	Josephine Cartledge	Cartledge	Josephine	F	29	BDW	Bill Horowitz's secretary.
35	JHH	Jung Ho Hyun	Ho Hyun	Jung	M	63	BDW	Jung Ho Hyun is the father of Hye Soon Park – and the husband of Jin-Sook Park. Hye Soon Park is a genetically enhanced kid doing work experience with the Bradbury, Dwyer and Waldron law firm.
36	JK	Jane Kemp	Kemp	Jane	F	22	Rubliov Museum	Jane is a Junior Attendant at the London Annex of the Andrei Rubliov Museum of Early Russian Art. She challenges Jon Raney to produce his life membership - as she is new and does not recognise him. The senior attendant (Elizaveta Alekseev) recognise Jon – and instructs Jane to let him through.
37	JL	Joel Lawrence	Lawrence	Joel	M	40	BDW - US	He is a colleague of Bill Horowitz – based in the NY office of BDW.
38	JM	Judy McCauley	McCauley	Judy	F	31		Judy is the wife of Douglas McCauley and the mother of Heather McCauley. Heather is a genetically enhanced kid doing work experience with the Bradbury, Dwyer and Waldron law firm.

No. of Characters	Initials	Full name	Last name	First name	Sex	Age	Dwarf/Genhance Country Club	Background
39	JP	Jeff Portwood	Portwood	Jeff	M	36	GPA	Jeff Portwood works for the GPA as a social researcher/administrator. He is not very bright and a little dull. He laughs a lot, but doesn't get many jokes. Tells the odd stupid/kid jokes – at which he is the only person who laughs. Very dedicated to job, attention to detail, procedures and process.
40	JR	Jon Raney	Raney	Jon	M	45	GPA	Jon is the Director (below the CEO) of the GPA – and the boss of Ivan Henry. He has a very practical/pragmatic approach to his work – whilst still insisting on excellence. Hates Bullshit. He can pick up the main point of all issues, but has a lot of difficulty getting his section or his superiors to understand the problems/issues. Will only extend himself if there is a 'real' issue at hand. Less significant issues are delegated down and not afforded much of his time. Strong disrespect for authority and corporate culture/protocol BUT – does know what 'must' be done and 'when' – and does it.
41	JSP	Jin-Sook Park	Sook Park	Jin	F	34		Jin-Sook Park is the wife of Jung Ho Hyun and mother of Hye Soon Park. Hye Soon Park is a genetically enhanced kid doing work experience with the Bradbury, Dwyer and Waldron law firm.
42	KS	Kharechka Solovyou Solovyou	Solovyou	Kharechka	F	7	Genhance	Kharechka is a genetically enhanced kid doing work experience with the Bradbury, Dwyer and Waldron law firm. Her father is Nikanosha Solovyou and her mother is Poliusha Solovyou.
43	LC	Laurie Coulson	Coulson	Laurie	F	42	BDW	Laurie is a very competent lawyer with Bradbury, Dwyer & Waldron (BDW). She is the lead defence counsel that supports Sandra Small (originally) and the GPA. She is originally from Liverpool. At 18, her boyfriend 'Tony Bland' was seriously injured in the Hillsborough football stadium disaster in Liverpool – which led to him being in a Permanent Vegetative State (PVS). The High Court later ruled that food/water should be withheld from Tony to allow him to die. She has always been bitter about this decision.

No. of Characters	Initials	Full name	Last name	First name	Sex	Age	Dwarf/Genhance Country Club	Background
44	LS	Larry Stockton	Stockton	Larry	M	47	BDW - US	He is a colleague of Bill Horowitz – based in the NY office of BDW.
45	LTD	Lord Thomas Denman	Denman	Thomas	M	68	CC GPAERC	Lord Thomas Denman is the Chair of the GPA Ethics Ruling Committee that oversees the 'Hearing' and presents the hearing's ruling. Additionally, he is a member of the Country Club.
46	MB	Matthew Brown	Brown	Matthew	M	52	High Court	Matthew Brown Is a official of the High Court who serves injunctions in person. His life has not lived up to his expectations – particularly in regards to his career progress. He now derives sinister pleasure from delivering bad news by personally delivering legal injunctions on unsuspecting members of the public. He is relatively short, being only 5'5" tall.
47	MH	Mark Hardwick	Hardwick	Mark	M	28	GPA	Mark Hardwick works for the GPA as a Social Researcher. He is good work friends with Ivan Henry, Gough Rutherford and Elaine Kellaway. Warm and caring. Will extend himself to cater for the needs of others. Very smart and competent. Is a through and through Londoner with strong Cockney accent.
48	ML	Max Lyford	Lyford	Max	M	58	CC GPA	Max Lyford is the CEO of the GPA and also a very influential member of the Country Club. He is approx 5'4" tall. Max is Jon Raney's Boss. Max is a complete autocratic prick, self interest drives him to the total exclusion of all other considerations, including the most fundamental ethical issues, departmental directives.
49	MS	Morgue Staff			M	45	Morgue	Morgue Staff – guides Judge Frederick Rogers around the morgue.
50	MZ	Mingzi Zhou	Zhou	Mingzi	M	33		Is the father of Gordon Zhou (a genetically enhanced kid) and husband of Xiùm i Zhou.

No. of Characters	Initials	Full name	Last name	First name	Sex	Age	Dwarf/Genhance Country Club	Background
51	NA	Nathan Alderman	News	Anchor	M	46	Sky News	This is the Anchor Man for Sky News.
52	NC	Neville Cheng	Cheng	Neville	M	28	Police	Inspector in the Metropolitan Police Force.
53	NH	Norma Hudson CHANGE TO NOELENE HUDSON	Hudson	Noelene	F	47	GPA	Noelene is blind (and has been from birth), very unattractive and overweight. She is near useless at work – being employed in prior governments, there was an initiative to hire disabled people – and now she cannot be fired. She does not in anyway attempt to be independent or contribute to the work section.
54	NS	Nikanosha Solovyov	Solovyov	Nikanosha	M	54		Nikanosha Solovyov is the father of Kharechka Solovyou (a genetically enhanced kid) and the husband of Poliusha Solovyou.
55	OW	Oscar Williamson	Williamson	Oscar	M	71	CC	Oscar Williamson is a regular member of the Country Club.
56	Pass	Passenger	Passenger	Passenger	M	23	Plumber	This is the Passenger in a Plumber's pick-up truck. The driver is also plumber – and the father of the passenger (i.e. a father and son plumbing team).
57	PF	Paul Firth	Firth	Paul	M	22	Dwarf	Paul is the first of two dwarves that accompanies Greg O'Leary (the aggressive dwarf) when they 'storm' the High Court (the other dwarf is Peter Giles). From his appearance, it is evident that he spends a lot of time doing weights at a gym - as he may be short, but he is very solidly built. His attire shows off his body – i.e. loose fitting singlet showing his biceps and chest. He is ornated with a number of aggressive (or dark) tattoos – including several on his neck.
58	PG	Peter Giles	Giles	Peter	M	19	Dwarf	Peter is the second of two dwarves that accompanies Greg O'Leary (the aggressive dwarf) when they 'storm' the High Court. Like his friend Paul Firth, it is apparent from his appearance that he spends many hours a day pumping iron at the gym. He has a tight fitting T-shirt that shows off his well developed body. He has many piercings and tattoos together with a two to three day growth.

No. of Characters	Initials	Full name	Last name	First name	Sex	Age	Dwarf/Genhance Country Club	Background
59	PR	Pat Rushworth	Rushworth	Pat	M	47	BDW	Pat Rushworth is the senior partner of the prestigious law firm Bradbury, Dwyer and Waldron. He is Bill Horowitz's boss. He is 6' 6" and quite overweight. He has a razor sharp intellect and uses sophisticated derogatory wit to cut people down when they are 'not up to the mark'.
60	PS	Poliusha Solovyov	Solovyov	Poliusha	F	44		Poliusha Solovyov is the mother of Kharechka Solovyou (a genetically enhanced kid) and the wife of Nikanosha Solovyov.
61	Rabbi	Rabbi	Rabbi	Rabbi	M	68		Rabbi is Bill Horowitz's Rabbi. He is an immigrant from the former USSR. While in the USSR, he once went to the Moscow circus – and saw Igor Tikhonov (an acclaimed clown in the circus) who is the late father of Ivan Henry.
62	Recep	Bradbury, Dywer & Waldron Receptionist	Bradbury, Dywer & Waldron	Receptionist	F	23	Bradbury, Dywer & Waldron	Receptionist at Bradbury, Dywer & Waldron.
63	Recp	High Court Receptionist	High Court	Receptionist	F	55	High Court	High Court Receptionist – who obviously is friendly with Frederick Rogers.
64	Rgstr	Registrar	–	Registrar at the Royal Society	F	42	Royal Society	The Registrar at the Royal Society – first takes a phone call from Ivan Henry in scene 17. Then in scene 18, encounters Ivan attempting to gate crash Bill Horowitz's presentation to the Royal Society.
65	RW	Robert Walker	Walker	Robert	M	24	Dwarf	Dwarf – suffering from achondroplasia. Robert is one of two close friends of Ivan Henry (the other being Andy Watts). He is a chartered accountant. Very stable and sensible person. Wears round glasses – a little like "Doc's" – from Disney's Snow White and the seven dwarfs. He lives in his own terrace house at: 15 Durban Road West Ham (now Newham) London E15 3BW (very close to the West Ham train/tube station).

No. of Characters	Initials	Full name	Last name	First name	Sex	Age	Dwarf/Genhance Country Club	Background
66	SDG	Sir David Griffiths	Griffiths	David	M	56	GPA Ethics Ruling Committee	He is one of the three members of the Genetic Protection Authority's 'Ethics Ruling Committee' (GPAERC) that preside over the hearing that Ivan Henry brings before them. He is NOT a member of the Country Club, however, the other two officials who preside over the Hearing are members of the Country Club.
67	SG	Security Guard	Security	Guard	M	28	Royal Society	The Royal Society Security Guard notices Ivan attempting to sneak into Bill Horowitz's presentation into the Royal Society (scene 18) – and escorts Ivan to the door – ejecting Ivan from the Royal Society's premises.
68	SH	Samuel Horowitz	Horowitz	Samuel	M	7		Sam Horowitz is the son of Bill and Mary Horowitz. He suffers from what was formerly called 'Hallervorden-Spatz Syndrome' which has been renamed 'Neurodegeneration with Brain Iron Accumulation' (NBIA), which make Samuel severely mentally retarded.
70	SJPB	Sir John Poo Beresford	Beresford	John Poo	M	72	CC GPA Ethics Ruling Committee	Member of both the Country Club and the GPA Ethics Ruling Committee (GPAERC). Has a very big nose.
71	SK	Sambhi Khangura	Khangura	Sambhi	F	19	Student	Sambhi Khangura (together with her boyfriend Amerjit Ghuman) catch a lift with Max Lyford and have a discussion on "Schindler's Lift" (vs. "Schindler's List").
72	SL	Susanna Ling	Ling	Susanna	F	27	Sky TV	Susanna is a Social Welfare reporter with Sky News.
73	SM	Sebastian McKibben McKibben	McKibben	Sebastian	M	61	CC	Sebastian is a regular attendee of the Country Club meetings. Note: the name McKibben is from the author: Bill McKibben who wrote "Enough" which I rate.

No. of Characters	Initials	Full name	Last name	First name	Sex	Age	Dwarf/Genhance Country Club	Background
74	SRLD	Sir Ronald Lawe-Davies	Lawe-Davies	Ronald	M	74	CC	Sir Ronald is a regular attendee of the Country Club meetings.
75	SS	Sandra Small	Small	Sandra	F	24	BDW	Sandra is the leading female of the script. She is normal heighted (5'5") and the wife of Ivan Henry (a dwarf) - whom she becomes pregnant to. She looks, just a little, like Disney's Snow White character.
								She grew up in a small village, Ripon, in North Yorkshire. She moved to Leeds to go to the Leeds Metropolitan University. She is the first person in her family to get a University education or to move out of Yorkshire.
								While at Leeds Metropolitan University, where she completed a Sociology degree, she met Ivan.
								They both moved to London in late October 2012 – and both Ivan and Sandra started work in early November 2012.
								Sandra works as a Legal Clerk (as a legal research officer) at a prestigious law firm: Bradbury, Dywer & Waldron (BDW).
								Sandra, now climbing through the ranks of a Big Law Firm social/professional circles, wants everything to be perfect – a trait that was not evident when she was a free and easy student, where she met, fell in love and married Ivan.
								Now, she is becoming slightly embarrassed about having a dwarf as a husband – and she is subject to the odd jibe at work. She reads far more into these jibes than is intended. To help with her career – she has started doing her Masters in Sociology at the University of East London (UEL). She believes she has a promising career at the Law Firm.

No. of Characters	Initials	Full name	Last name	First name	Sex	Age	Dwarf/Genhance Country Club	Background
76	TC	Tanya Coleman-CHANGE TO TESS COLEMAN	Coleman	Tess	F	36	GPA	Tess is a public servant at the GPA. She is a little dim witted coupled with being incredibly boring and a stickler for blindly following procedures. She is assigned the role of QA manager of a GPA a legal case – as the CEO knows that she will blindly enforce every letter of every procedure/standard. In her spare time, she is a long distant swimmer. She is mildly over weight (size 16) and 5'2" tall.
77	TG	Tall Guy	Tall	Guy	M	39	–	The 'Tall Guy' attends Bill Horowitz's presentation at the Royal Society (scene 18). In the scene, he turns around and walks back to where he came – and immediately trips over Ivan – who had been 'tailgating' him. He also appears in scene 22 – when Ivan runs after Bill Horowitz, and inadvertently runs into the Tall Guy.
78	TM	Trevor May-CHANGE TO TREVOR MAYNE	Mayne	Trevor	M	51		The father of Bruce Mayne, who is a genetically enhanced kid doing work experience at Bradbury, Dywer and Waldron.
79	TO	Theresa Olmsted	Olmsted	Theresa	F	43	BDW	Theresa is the only female partner in BDW.
80	VH	Valentina Henry	Henry	Valentina	F	56		Valentina (normal heighted, Russian decent) is the mother of Ivan Henry – and was the wife of the late Igor Tikhonov (who was Ivan's father and was also a dwarf). The three of them escaped the USSR when Ivan was a young child – but Igor was killed during the escape. Upon settling in the UK, she changed her (and Ivan's) name from 'Tikhonov' to 'Henry'. Ivan was 5 years old when she escaped from USSR. Valentina managed to smuggle out of the USSR some important religious icons, which now affords her a reasonably comfortable lifestyle. To help her climb within the Anglo/Russian community, she wants her son (only child), daughter-in-law, and any future grandchildren to be 'just' so perfect. This is a little difficult having a dwarf as a son (and possibly future grandchildren).

No. of Characters	Initials	Full name	Last name	First name	Sex	Age	Dwarf/Genhance Country Club	Background
81	VI	Viral Inspector	Viral	Inspector	F	28	Health Department	Viral Inspectors (VI) do random samples of public places – and check everyone there for avian flu vaccination. It is a crime not to be inoculated for avian flu, and the VI's do a simple test to determine if a person has been inoculated or not.
82	VP	Veronica Peritina	Peritina	Veronica	F	27	BDW	Veronica is Pat Rushworth's secretary
83	WN	Wigburg Nussbaum	Nussbaum	Wigburg	M	38	GPA	Wigburg has German parents and was born in Germany, but migrated with his family to the UK when he was 9. He is an out of the closet gay – who is a butch gay. He is quite intelligent, but very intense, and does not 'get' humour. Due to his intenseness and lack of humour, as well as always trying to prove that he is right, he does not have that many work friends.
84	XZ	Xiùm i Zhou	Zhou	Xiùm i	F	28		Xiùm i Zhou is the mother of Gordon Zhou (a genetically enhanced kid – who is doing work experience for the BDW law firm) and wife of Mingzi Zhou.
85	YL	Young Lawyer	Young	Lawyer	M	27	BDW	YL is an up and coming lawyer at BDW – who (in scene 2) whispers to his mate that the new 'genetics revenue stream' should enable him to buy a new Porsche for his girl friend – as he hates her driving his.

Biography for Ross Martyn

Ross Martyn was born in 1962 and raised on a 22,000 acre wheat and sheep farm in Mullewa, Western Australia. He was a mischievous and inquisitive child in a large family of six where he developed a playful sense of humour.

At age 20 he left for a back backing adventure to Europe which included a three month bus tour through the Middle East, Pakistan, India and Nepal. Along his travels, his observations of peoples and their cultures deepened his continuing studies of philosophy and religions. It reaffirmed his belief that all individuals have the right to be equal and respected.

With his wife and two daughters he moved to the UK in 1996, settled in Kent where he relished family life and enjoyed a successful career in London.
He passed away in 2018, aged 55.

Scene 1 – The monument to the first Great Fire of London

8:30am, Monday, 6 May 2013

Setting: The City of London and London Bridge.

The scene slowly fades in from dark – with the sound of Vivaldi's Spring – which slowly lowers as the sound of early morning traffic rises (noises preceding the visual).

The visual slowly comes into focus – opening up over the Thames at high tide – looking towards London Bridge during a Monday morning peak hour with thousands of city workers crossing London Bridge on their way to work.

Gradually Vivaldi's Spring lowers as the sound of traffic becomes the dominant sound. It is a bright spring day and there is a perceptible skip in everyone's step as they walk from London Bridge mainline train station, across London Bridge, into the City of London.

As human traffic crossing London Bridge comes more into focus, the sound of The Proclaimers' 'I'm Gonna Be (500 Miles)' fades in.

The pedestrians cross in their thousands. The camera zooms and briefly focuses on random individuals – which highlights the diversity of London – their class, physicality, dress, dress colouring, ethnicity, facial expression, professionalism and demeanour/poise. All, however, walking across that bridge purposefully – with a hint of a smile on their face – as they enjoy the glorious spring sunshine on their way to work in the greatest city on Earth.

The view of the pedestrians crossing the bridge is interrupted as a red bus passes, which has a poster health advertisement down its side:

> *Avian Flu vaccination – it is compulsory.*
> *Get vaccinated, or be fined or die – whatever comes first.*
> *UK death toll remains lowest in Europe. Keep it that way.*

The camera follows the bridge to the City and pans around to bring into focus 'The Monument'. As the camera traverses the monument – text comes onto the scene:

> *The Monument – designed by Sir Christopher Wren and Robert Hooke. Built between 1671 and 1677 to mark the Great Fire of London of 1666.*
>
> *It is 202 feet tall, which is the distance from its base to the bakery in Pudding Lane where the Great Fire of London started. The Great Fire destroyed 80% of the city, including St. Paul's Cathedral and 13,200 houses. Amazingly, only six people died in the inferno.*
>
> *As terrible as the Great Fire of London was, it did however rid the city of the deadly diseases that gave rise to the bubonic epidemics – known as 'The Black Plague'.*
>
> *The Great Fire of London was a horrific price to pay for disease control. Was it worth it?*

The text clears – and new text is displayed:

> *There are no bakeries in Pudding Lane now, only office blocks. It is here [the camera now focuses on a building on the corner of Monument Street and Pudding Lane], where this non-descript office building now stands, that the Great Fire started.*
>
> *This story is about the Second Great Fire of London.*

The camera zooms in on the office block [where the fire started] – and continues to zoom into a window until the camera peers into a conference room – with a meeting in full swing.

Scene 2 – The Authority's Monday morning meeting

8:45am, Monday, 6 May 2013

Setting: The Genetic Protection Authority's (GPA) conference room.

Max Lyford is at the head of the conference table, reading from his prepared meeting agenda.

The following are sitting around the conference table: Ivan Henry, Gough Rutherford, Tess Coleman, Jeff Portwood, George Kelvin, Gary Stapleton, Noelene Hudson, Wigburg Nussbaum, Bernard Newman, Barry Greenslade, Jon Raney, Elaine Kellaway and Mark Hardwick.

There is a close up of Max – showing him speaking very firmly, authoritatively and autocratically about the new management initiative that is to be introduced to the authority.

ML … we are the Genetic Protection Authority. The work we do here, the decisions that we make here, the investigations and research that we do here, and by we, I mean each and every one of us, the government policies we formulate, the regulations that we develop, is critical, let me repeat, is critical, and just to emphasis the point again – IS CRITICAL – to the welfare, the survival, and the genetic health of our community and for all humanity. NOT only for our generation, and our children's generation, but for the welfare of thousands of generations to come.

As Max speaks, the camera pulls back to show all those at the meeting around the board room table. As Max continues, the camera goes around the table providing a close up of all those sitting around the conference table, showing their general expression as follows:

Gough Rutherford – Shows no interest at all in Max's update, but nevertheless smiles as he throws mint wrappers at the blind Noelene Hudson – and achieves the desired result of annoying her.

Tess Coleman – Dumb, slightly confused expression – but paying keen interest.

Jeff Portwood – Frowning, seriously showing keen interest and taking copious notes.

George Kelvin – Bored, day-dreaming, passing barely audible farts as those each side of him show a degree of suspicion.

Gary Stapleton – General acceptance of speech, thinking of policies/procedures to support directive – making notes on how he can develop/introduce new policies/procedures to support the directive.

Ivan Henry – Attempting to show interest – swivelling in his chair – taking the occasional note.

Noelene Hudson – Doesn't want to be there, and annoyed by the wrappers (or whatever it is – is it an insect?) being thrown at her.

Wigburg – Leaning back gazing at the ceiling – heard all this shit before.

Nussbaum – Expression: let's get it over with and leave.

Bernard Newman – Very interested – constantly nodding in agreement.

Barry Greenslade – Non-committed look, very public service brown/beige clothing.

Jon Raney – At head of table next to Max Lyford. He knows it's all shit, but also knows that they have to listen to the directives, and in his role as 'second in charge' after Max, he has to support Max, regardless of how erratic he may be and regardless of his own thoughts on the matter. He carefully watches others at table for their body language, to size up what politic/opposition he will face in implementing the initiatives.

Elaine Kellaway – 'Why am I here' expression. Notices wrapper being thrown at Noelene – passes an almost inaudible giggle – then gives a reprimanding look to Gough. Then temptation gets to her and she throws one herself.

Mark Hardwick – Smiling at Gough's actions, and by his expression encourages him to continue to throw wrappers at Noelene. He has a wonderful, warm smile, tempered by a sense of mischievousness.

4

ML   To ensure that we fulfil our obligations, our commitment, our duties to the electorate, to the people, to humanity now and for generations to come, we HAVE to, WE HAVE TO, WE SIMPLY HAVE to ensure that we are making the right, the correct, the absolute optimum decision on each and every case put to us – and – to emphasise the importance of our role – which I know you're all acutely aware of, but I'm going to state it again – THE human SPECIES SIMPLY CANNOT AFFORD FOR US TO MAKE A SINGLE MISTAKE.

To help ensure we always make optimum decisions, and to mitigate humanity and ourselves as a whole from the risk of us making a mistake – we need to introduce a quality assurance management system.

The group around the table hear the key words 'Quality Assurance' then visibly and just audibly sigh – as in 'here we go again, another bloody management initiative'.

ML   A QA system will make us both more efficient and more effective. It will increase the quality of our decision-making process. Further, it will provide us with a robust management trail which will enable us to trace our steps through all the procedures, research and thought processes that lead us to make each of our assessments and rulings. This will also enable us to have the necessary documentation available – should we ever be challenged on any of our decisions, assessments or rulings. And, I cannot emphasis just how important this is, given the very litigious world we live in …
[*After looking around the table and catching everybody's eye in turn – he continues*]
This is not just good for us, it is also good for the department as a whole, for our minister, for the government, for the Parliament, and most importantly for the homo sapiens species.

Max's voice keeps babbling in the background as the camera pans around the table – showing increasing boredom by those present (except for Gary, Tess, Jeff and Bernard, who continue to hang off every word – while Jon continues to keep an eye on the reaction of each of those present). Mark signals Gough to have a beer at lunch time (after the meeting). Gough – confirms, signals back that they should go to the strip bar. Mark then signals Ivan for a lunch time drink, who, while a little surprised by the offer, accepts. Gough then, while Ivan isn't looking, signals a questioning/disapproval sign to Mark about inviting Ivan. Mark dismisses Gough's concerns, signalling with hands and facial expression that 'he's okay'. Gough, via facial expression, reluctantly concedes that it's okay to bring Ivan along.

Noelene Hudson is attempting to get out a wrapper that fell into her bra. A general look of unease/disgust is reflected in most attendees' faces – but a quite mischievous grin of accomplishment spreads over Gough, Elaine and Mark's faces at Noelene's difficulties.

ML   Does anyone have any questions?'

JP   [*Sticks his hand up and is immediately and firmly kicked by Elaine – to signal him to 'shut the fuck up'.*]

ML   [*Gives a disapproving frown.*] Yes?

JP   I think a QA system is just what we need. I've heard so much about them, I mean a lot of my friends in other departments have introduced them, and one of my mates is a QA consultant and is earning a fortune.

        But, they haven't talked about making better decisions – can a QA system do this?

ML   Are you trying to take the piss Jeff, heh? Jeff knows best does he? Well Jeff, how about you come up the front and tell us how to manage the development, the protection, and the continued evolution of our species – heh, think you're up to it do you?

        Well, Jeff, if you know so much about QA systems, I want you to deliver an outline, if you like a high-level game plan, of how QA can be applied to our work for next Monday's meeting. Your plan needs to show all the necessary steps, deliverables and milestones that's required for us to be QA certified by the end of October this year.

        Now do you feel so smart?

Jeff nods his head – with a shocked/disappointed/disturbed look.

ML   Jeff, if I was you, I'd write that down in your diary right now – Okay.

        [Looks to Elaine] Elaine, can you type up the minutes of the meeting and have them circulated by tomorrow lunch time?

EK   [Stunned look – she was not expecting to have to type up minutes, and therefore didn't take any notes. She nods with a mild scowl] Okay.

ML   Noelene – for God's sake, compose yourself. You might be blind – but the rest of us are sighted – and we don't want to be punished for this privilege by having to see you undress yourself in public.

The camera scans around the table – showing everybody slightly embarrassed for Noelene, even Mark and Gough look down, still with a slight smile, while Noelene eventually finds the wrapper and composes herself.

ML   Okay, unless anyone else wishes to raise any other business, the meeting is finished.

As Noelene finishes composing herself, everybody starts to leave the meeting, and the camera fades out.

Scene 3 – Bradbury, Dywer & Waldron's Law Firm – Monday morning meeting

9:00am, Monday, 6 May 2013

Setting: Bradbury, Dywer & Waldron (BDW) legal firm's board room for their weekly meeting

At the head of the table is the head partner (Pat Rushworth), giving a strategy update to the management team. Around the table are a dozen lawyers – which includes only three women. All the men are dressed in dark charcoal pinstriped suits, white shirts, cuff links, all impeccably dressed. Two of the women, Laurie Coulson and Theresa Olmsted, are likewise impeccably dressed in conservative, but expensive, corporate attire. The third woman, Sandra Small, in comparison to the others at the meeting, particularly the other two women, appears somewhat 'drab'. Further, while her hair is well groomed, it is long, and her makeup is clumsily applied.

Sandra is a legal research clerk, who has been invited to attend the meeting due to her research work. Being invited to the partner's Monday morning briefing meeting, she 'feels' as though she is on the edge of being part of the firm's 'in crowd'.

PR   With the introduction of the new Family Law Acts, the New Tenancy agreements, the new Real Property Act, and the revision of the Provision of Legal Services Act, many of our bread and butter lines of business have dried up – or at least hardly worth pursuing as there isn't a decent profit margin in doing the work, i.e. now that it is no longer restricted to the legal professions and anyone and everyone can and is doing these lines of pseudo-legal work, the rates have collapsed.

Therefore, we have to open up new business lines. Fortunately, in this day and age with such rapid change, more opportunities are opening than closing. I think the most fruitful out of these can be summarised as follows: satellite insurance disputes; native title land disputes with oil companies; auditor litigation; negligence torts relating to inaccurate data provided by online service providers; media litigation; disputes between parents/scientists/pressure groups and the Genetic Protection Authority.

Now, I've asked several of you to do a little research into the above areas. Today I have asked Bill to present his assessment on genetic law and disputes with the Genetic Protection Authority. So, over to you Bill.

BH   Thanks Pat. I've been looking into the issues surrounding the legalities associated with artificial insemination, surrogate parenthood, incubators, embryo freezing storage and eventual use, cloning, embryo genetic testing and the like.

The whole point in these matters, is that there are very few common law cases establishing precedence on these issues. There is the Genetic Protection Authority, and their governing 'Ethics Ruling Committee'. God help us if our genetic future is entrusted to those fuckwits. [He looks up to the girls and apologises.] If our evolutionary future is entrusted to the GPA, then I suggest the evolution of our species has just come to a grinding halt – and now we're heading for devolution.

Slight chuckle from audience on hearing the last line – more on its delivery and timing than content.

BH   Now, notwithstanding the unfortunate situation that future generations have been burdened with, i.e. having to live with the consequences of the decisions made by our friends at the GPA – together with their governing Ethics Ruling Committee – the current situation is certainly opening up tremendous opportunities for high fees for the current generation of homo sapiens currently present in this office. AND, better still – as far as I'm aware, none of us here have defective genes (Bill has a slight embarrassed hesitation as he glances in Sandra's direction, and continues) – at least not as a consequence of the decisions made by our friends at the GPA.

If our driving objective in this office is to generate high fees – all I can say is 'Thank God for childless couples, scientists, drug companies and of course, my personal favourite – the Genetic Protection Authority'.

I'll briefly outline our position on each of the above three target groups:

Childless couples: I expect the revenue from poor childless couples will grow exponentially through to 2020 when it is projected to bring in thirteen million euros a year in revenue. Just to avoid any confusion, when I said poor childless couples, I mean poor as in unfortunate.

Our target of course is 'rich childless couples'. As I'm sure you would agree with me – I really don't think we should be in the charity business of helping poor couples have kids – who can't pay our fees.

No other big firm is in this market yet – and we are already starting to get a solid reputation in this arena. As such, I think that the projected thirteen million euros a year by 2020 is conservative.

Targeted childless couples fall in to the following four broad groups; first, one of the partners has died – and the other wants to have their deceased partner's child. The second, a couple's child has died – and the couple want to give birth to a clone of their deceased child. The third, couples suing fertility clinics – as the child born is not what they ordered. And lastly, couples wanting designer babies, i.e. blue eyes, blond hair, good at music, et cetera.

Now, for scientists, they fall within three broad categories: those trying to protect their genetic research intellectual property through patents and other means – these essentially fall into the company category. Next we have cases where a scientist research has been banned or restricted due to a decision or ruling made by the GPA or the Ethics Ruling Committee and other such wonderful organisations trying to halt certain areas of research and development.

Then there are those scientists wanting to carry on certain areas of research into human genetics, reproduction, animal transplants et cetera – which the GPA has or is about to have gazetted as illegal.

With drug companies, broadly speaking, there are three target areas of law in which we are actively building the firm's franchise, namely drug companies attempting to patent their genetic research. Those trying to market their genetically modified products. And those defending themselves from litigation from the ill effects of their genetically modified products.

This brings us to cloning. While we don't have any cases yet, we expect to start advising on cloning, specifically, for people wanting to clone themselves or their loved ones for spare parts.

Now the whole point of the matter – is that childless couples, scientists and corporates have a passion, a ruthless drive to get their cases heard, so that they can have children, conduct their embryo experiments, patent their modified genes or grow a new organ.

To this end – money is no object. AND, there's more. The best part about this is that, aside from ourselves, nobody knows how to deal with those mental dwarfs at the GPA …

With the mention of 'dwarves at the GPA', there ensues slight embarrassed giggles from the meeting attendees. Bill looks up and realises his faux pas and then gives a general apology.

BH   Sorry, no pun intended.

The camera turns to Sandra, who has a facial expression of several conflicting emotions – hurt/offence/embarrassment/shock – but says nothing. Her body language clearly shows her discomfort.

BH   … nor how to deal with those clowns on the GPA Ethics Ruling Committee. So, all in all, we are well placed to pick up the lion's share of the cases going to dispute.

Because this is such a new area, nobody knows the rules. We have already built a reputation in this area – we should be able to do some serious billing. On each assignment we should be able to charge in excess of twice our scheduled fees.

Cheers erupt with the news of the over recovery – the camera pans around the table with everybody smiling and clapping.

YL   This will be good little earner. I need to buy my girlfriend a new Porsche; I hate her driving mine.

Sandra overhears the comments and again is confronted by conflicting emotions – desire to be in the same league as the lawyers and yet disgust of such overt decadence.

The camera fades out while on Sandra's face – still displaying the anguish of her conflicting emotions.

First Insert Scene

Insert Scenes

This is the first of many 'insert scenes' similar to the inserts in *When Harry Met Sally*, where there were a series of scenes of couples discussing to a camera how they met, married etc. With all these insert scenes the relevance of them were not apparent until the last scene which was of Harry and Sally describing how they met – which in fact describes the film.

In this script, the inserts are of school children reciting literature from elite early twentieth century intelligentsia. The setting is at an opulent manor, where it is apparent that the pupils are from a private preparatory school gathered for a school exercise. All the children and their attendant parents are impeccably dressed in conservative, but still beautiful clothes.

The children are on a one-foot-high stage and one-by-one come forward and recite their piece of literature. The parents are all standing in the room listening to the kids and all clap dignifiedly as each finishes their reading. The whole gathering is not overly formalised; the kids are relaxed, confident and speak brilliantly. The adults are relaxed and chatting with each other between readings.

The room itself is large with a number of doorways, members occasionally strolling in and out, making light chat between recitals, all adding to the semi-informality of the event.

During the first insert scene, the camera slowly pans around the whole room – ending with the stage banner in view with the first speaker underneath confidently reciting his reading. The banner reads 'Early Twentieth Century Literature Appreciation Society'.

Camera fades in at the conclusion of each reading.

Insert Scene – 1

> The new ethics will hold life to be a privilege and a responsibility, not a sort of night refuge of base spirits out of the void; and the alternative in right conduct between living fully, beautifully and efficiently will be to die.

For a multitude of contemptible and silly creatures, fear-driven and helpless and useless, unhappy or hatefully happy in the midst of squalid dishonour, feeble, ugly, inefficient, born of unrestrained lusts, and increasing and multiplying through sheer incontinence and stupidity, the men of the New Republic will have little pity and less benevolence.

Anticipations by HG Wells

Scene 4 – A pint and a bite for lunch

12:30pm, Monday, 6 May 2013

Setting: A lunchtime setting at the garden bar of the Anchor Pub, a lively London pub overlooking the Thames, predominantly young male patrons, all quite rowdy. The patrons are dressed in attire reflecting the middle to lower echelons of Civil Service office hierarchy. Gough, Mark and Ivan are sitting at a small round table with half-empty pints of larger.

IH   So, what did you think of Max's speech this morning?

MH   It's all shit. How the fuck is a bloody QA system going to improve our 'decision making process'? I mean, every week Max comes in with some other management initiative he's read in the Dilbert comic strip – it is a very sad fact that he hasn't caught on to the fact that Dilbert is a bloody comic strip, not a new-age management manual.

I mean, the protection of our genes is entrusted to us, we are the professionals, we make professional judgments, we formulate sound guidelines, we're sensitive to the cases presented to us, we evaluate the evidence, the pros, the cons and arrive at good fucking conclusions – and make a recommendation, a decision, a regulation or policy accordingly.

As Mark continues to talk – a public transport ferry passes the pub as it travels down the Thames. It has a health advertisement down its side:

> *Avian Flu vaccination – it is compulsory.*
> *Get vaccinated – or be fined or die – whatever comes first. UK death toll remains lowest in Europe. Keep it that way.*

MH   A QA system is not going to do anything, I mean nothing at all, to aid this process, nothing to help manage the protection of our genetic heritage. All it's going to do is swamp us in paper work – especially if Portwood has carriage of the bloody project.

The general noise level of the pub abruptly rises – with loud jeering. The camera pans back to show a woman's long, sexy legs walking down the top the bar. Gough and Mark stop talking and look up to admire the show. The camera pans over to Gough's face, with his mouth wide open with delight.

GR   Now, that's what I call genetic perfection. What we should be using the QA system for is to ensure she is cloned a thousand times over. I mean, if we got enough copies of her, we could start a 'Miss Eleven' franchise.

            But, that, I'm afraid is fundamentally wrong, we cannot even consider such a preposterous proposition – we don't need any QA system to accurately clone her over and over and over again.

The three boys break out in light laughter and more jeering.

MH   I think you're right – with her the possibilities are endless. Without her even knowing it – she could conquer the world. More so than any chief, king or emperor ever. I mean who needs a harem these days to spread your genes widely and thoroughly?

GR Signals the stripper over, and presses €20 into her revealing bra when she bends down. As she bends down, her face and body is shown for the first time – and she is absolutely stunning, cool, in total control and very athletic.

Ivan obviously enjoys the show, but is more reserved – and slightly disapproving. A little tormented by his conflicting emotions.

IH   Well, whether we like it or not, we got to put up with a QA system …

GR   Shut the fuck up, this is not the time to discuss a fucking QA system.

They return their gaze to the stripper as they bring their glasses up to their mouths.

The camera pans up to the stripper as she is walking away down the bar, and fades out with a loud jeer as she takes her top off, but the camera only sees her back.

Insert Scene – 2

Life is more vivid in the dandelion than in the green fern, or than in the palm tree, Life is more vivid in a snake than in a butterfly
Life is more vivid in a wren than in an alligator
Life is more vivid in me, than in the Mexican who drives the wagon for me.
Reflections on the Death of a Porcupine by DH Lawrence.

Scene 5 – Lunch and an offer Sandra can't refuse

12:30 pm, Monday, 6 May 2013

Setting: Bill Horowitz, Laurie Coulson and Sandra Small all dining alfresco at the upmarket Chop House restaurant at Butler's Wharf on the bank of the Thames. It is a beautiful sunny day overlooking the river and the restaurant is full of beautiful well-attired professionals.

The three are all sipping their glass of Amberley Estate, Margaret River, Chenin Blanc – commenting on bouquet, clarity etc.

Tide: Fully in

BH   Not bad, I've never missed with Amberley Estate. They've consistently made a superb Chenin Blanc.

The waiters arrive with the meals, all fantastic looking nouvelle cuisine, big beautiful plates with small decorative servings.

The plates are placed on the table. Bill looks down at his plate, which includes a small serving of rice. He shakes his head and asks the waiter abruptly:

BH   Is that crayfish I see in the rice?

Waiter No sir, it's crabmeat – caught this morning in Newlyn, Cornwall.

BH   Look – I asked when I ordered NOT to include any shellfish – can you take this back and get me another plate? And please hurry, as I've got to leave here in 30 minutes.

The waiter looks a little disgruntled, but takes the plate politely – and assures the next plate will be served soon.

BH   Please start – don't wait until Giuseppe gets my meal right.

[Bill then turns to Sandra] Anyway Sandra, Laurie and I have been speaking – which is why we invited you to lunch today, so that we have an opportunity to discuss our thoughts with you.

Your research into emerging legal markets was – well, how shall I put it – on the one hand brilliant. You managed to identify a field of law that the rest of us missed or ignored, and managed to provide insights into this area, which can form the basis of further research and training to ensure that we become the recognised leaders in this field.

As Bill talks – a public transport ferry passes the pub as it travels down the Thames. It has a heath advertisement down its side:

> *Avian Flu vaccination – it is compulsory.*
> *Get vaccinated – or be fined or die – whatever comes first. UK death toll remains lowest in Europe. Keep it that way.*

BH   So – thank you. I know at this morning's meeting I appeared to take all the credit for the hard work you've done. But before you jump to this conclusion – remember that 'you were there' at the meeting to witness what I was presenting. It is very rare, let me repeat that, it is very rare for legal clerks to attend our management meetings. The rare time a clerk is present at our meetings, everybody knows that it is the clerk who has done much of the leg work for the research being presented. So, be assured that your good work has been well recognised – and believe me, I cannot emphasis this point too strongly.

While Bill was praising Sandra she had a quite awkward, surprised, somewhat embarrassed (not able to accept complements easily) smile on her face.

BH   On the other hand – and please take me the right way here – your work was shite.

Sandra's facial composure – together with body composure – shatters with Bill's comment on 'shite'. After ending his sentence on 'shite', Bill stops speaking and picks up his glass to sip his wine – slowly swirls it in his mouth with his eyes closed – and mutters 'wow that's exceptional'.

BH   Sandra, I know you went to Leeds Polytechnic …

SS   You mean 'Leeds Metropolitan University'.

BH   Whatever … graduating with a degree in sociology, and now you've started your masters in sociology at the East London Polytechnic …

SS   [*Resentfully interjects*] You mean 'the University of East London'.

BH   Whatever … and that you have only been with the firm for six months *[deliberately pauses – then looks straight into her eyes]* – but this does not excuse you from presenting me with the crap you wrote about on potential genetic law issues.

      [Pauses while he has a sip of wine] The reason I ran with your paper and invited you to the meeting – is because it contained one gem – you identified a wonderfully brilliant and original idea that could potentially make the firm millions. Unfortunately, I had to dig through a mountain of shit to dig out that one ruby. Thank god it was worth the dig – well I suppose time will tell whether it was worth it or not.
      Now, as I said, Laurie and I have been speaking about you – and your career with us specifically. This is what we think of you so far – you're very dependable and reliable, you are willing to put in the hours when required, and you're capable of brilliant original, which is your biggest strength. However, your written expression is awful – absolute shite. And while I'm suffering from a bout of honesty – your attire also leaves a lot to be desired. Any questions – or shall I continue?

SS   *[Shakes her head in almost disbelief – and stammers, beginning to feel self-conscious of her dress]* No, go ahead.

BH   Laurie – am I presenting our conversations correctly, or do you have anything to add?

LC   Bill you're picking up the streams of thought that we've had – missing a little on the diplomacy and specifics. But hey, on a glorious day like this, I don't think we need to get bogged down in detail, so please carry on.

The waiter arrives back at this point with a new dish. Bill eyes it very carefully and asks 'Are you sure there is no shellfish in this? The waiter replies, 'I checked with the chef personally, sir.'

While the waiter and Bill were talking and diverting Laurie's attention – Sandra downs her glass of wine and fills it back up.

BH   So Sandra, as I said, Laurie and I have been discussing you and I've also talked to several of my colleagues, and basically we have to make a really hard decision about you. And, it's really tough. In fact it's so tough, I thought the only way I can make the correct decision – is to get you to make it for me.

Sandra had been sipping her glass up to this point, and now gulps hard when Bill put the last sentence to her – and her state of anxiety markedly increased.

BH   As I've, said we've got to decide on your future at Bradbury, Dywer & Waldron. We have two choices – well, more correctly, you've got two choices.

Bill pauses – engages her eyes – then in slow deliberate movements has some of his meal – never wavering from his engaged eye contact with her.

Sandra's chest is visibly pounding and she is blush red. To defuse the gaze somewhat, she takes another sip of wine and also has a mouthful from her plate – but does not break the gaze.

SS   Well Bill, are you going to tell me what the choices are?

BH   Yes. Your choice is [long pause] to either leave the firm ... today ... [He breaks gaze and has another mouthful of his lunch] ... or get yourself a decent education.

SS   [Indignantly] What do you mean get 'a decent education'. What the hell do you think I've got? I've got a degree and I'm completing my masters. So I have a decent education – and I'm already improving upon it. So, what the hell do you mean 'Get a decent education'?

BH   Good question – I raised this same question with Pat ...

SS   [Cuts into Bill's sentence – in an astonished indignant tone] You've discussed this with Pat... what the hell is this?

BH   Of course I raised this with Pat ... we are making a very important decision here. Anyway, in my discussions with Pat ... if you decide to stay with us ... you'll be required to complete a law degree. That is, a proper, law degree.

SS   A proper law degree? Can you be a little more specific – does the Open University count?

BH   Oxford.

Bill then puts his head down and starts eating again – making small comments on the meal.

SS   [Totally stunned] Oxford! I can't afford to take time off to study, and I can't afford the course anyway. And there's another tiny problem, getting in – you just derided the degree I have, so do you really think Oxford is going to accept me into their law school?

BH   We know your current constraints and circumstances. That's why I talked to Pat. If you say yes, that is, you want to stay with Bradbury, Dywer & Waldron, then yes, we'll get you into the law school. Well actually, Pat put through a call while I was in his office, and well … you're already in, that is, should you decide to accept the offer.

        Secondly, we'd sponsor you. If you agree, you'll be on the same salary that you're currently on, which I know isn't brilliant, but hey that's life as a legal clerk. And, we'll also pay your tuition fees. And we'll only require you to be in the office for twenty hours a week.

        Thirdly, if you say yes, then Laurie will take you out after we finish this meal and buy you some decent clothes so that your attire is more in line with our corporate culture. And, while my bout on honesty continues – don't dress like this again!

        Lastly, if you agree to stay with Bradbury, Dywer & Waldron you will need to have a makeover. Personal appearance is so important in this vanity-obsessed age. Again, Laurie can help and advise you on this.

Laurie and Bill both lean forward over the table and stare at her, watching every smallest movement in her face and body, visibly applying emotional pressure on her.

LC   Well Sandra, what's your decision – would you like to stay with Bradbury, Dywer & Waldron?

Dazzled/dazed/stunned by both the sustained onslaught of verbal abuse and the unbelievable offer she has just been made, she picks up a glass of water and hastily sips it, using the pause to try and compose herself. She closes her eyes for several seconds, opens them and gazes at the river and Tower Bridge. She slowly and nervously places the glass down.

SS   Do you ever listen to any of Sixto Rodriguez? The lyrics to one of his
        songs has the phrase, 'A monkey in silk is a monkey no less'.

BH   We could sit here all day and night discussing philosophy – and
        Rodriguez's anti- establishmentarian views – but we're not going to. We
        want that gem of a brain of yours. However, for better or for worse,
        rightly or wrongly, politically correct or not, Bradbury, Dywer & Waldron is
        only prepared to accept 'cut' and 'polished' gems. The 'cutting' can be
        done at Oxford and the polishing – well a couple of grand and a bit of
        guidance from Laurie can help with the polishing. This should bring you
        in line with the Bradbury, Dywer & Waldron's corporate image. But since
        you're inclined to quote Rodriguez – I will as well:

        *And you want to be held with the highest regard It delights you if he's
        trying so hard
        And you conceal your ordinary ways
        With a smile or a shrug of some stolen cliché.*

        Sandra, take this opportunity. Then you won't need to 'smile or shrug off
        some stolen cliché' to be held in the highest regard. But the choice is
        yours.

        Anyway, it's been nice sitting here and speaking with you, but I have to
        go now *[looking at his watch]*. So, stay here and talk it over with Laurie,
        there is plenty of time to decide. I'm back at the office later today at 4:30,
        so let me know then.

SS   [Composing herself – and realising what a fantastic opportunity she has
        just been offered] Bill, thank you for your very generous offer and you
        vote of confidence in me. Yes of course I'll stay. Thank you, thank you
        very much.

BH   [Big warm smile comes across his face] Excellent, I'll catch you back at
        the office, but use the rest of today to attire yourself – and get your
        makeover some time this week. [He pulls €5,000 cash out of his pocket
        and passes it to Sandra] This should help with your new wardrobe.

[Turns and walks off.] Bon appétit.

Scene 6 – Ivan's commute home

6:00pm, Monday, 6 May 2013

Setting: Ivan's commute from his work, via London Bridge railway station to the East Croydon railway station to his apartment.

Within the offices that Ivan works in – the scene fades in on a clock that is rapidly approaching 5:30pm. As the second hand reaches the '12' at the top of the clock (signifying that it is now 5:30pm) the camera pans across the office to Ivan's cubical. Ivan looks up and sees that it is 5:30, looks down at his watch to confirm the time, then spends a few seconds tidying his desk before he jumps up, grabs his oversized briefcase (aircraft maximum-sized cabin case) and walks to the elevators, saying his goodbyes to his colleagues, who are also on the cusp of leaving.

The camera picks him up walking out the front door of his building and joins the peak hour rush of city workers leaving the office. He heads towards London Bridge and starts walking over it. As in the morning rush, the volume of human traffic crossing London Bridge is enough to shake the bridge to its foundations.

During his crossing of London Bridge, several buses pass – one of which has the public health advertisement:

> Avian Flu vaccination – it is compulsory.
> Get vaccinated – or be fined or die – whatever comes first. UK death toll remains lowest in Europe. Keep it that way.

Ivan pushes his way through the passengers to get on a train from London Bridge Train Station, which is difficult for him due to the crowds. He keeps hitting his head on other standing passengers' briefcases and knapsacks. The bags and cases left on the floor also make it difficult for him to navigate – as other passengers are mostly ignorant of his presence and of the difficulty he has in such circumstances.

He eventually finds a place to stand and takes out a book from his briefcase to read War Against the Week: Eugenics and America's Campaign to Create a Master Race, by Edwin Black. He opens the book up to page 279, to the start of Chapter 15 'Hitler's Eugenic Reich'.

The scene fades out then back in with the train coming to a halt. Several minutes pass without the train moving – or any announcements as to why the train has stopped. Eventually, an announcement comes over the PA system informing the passengers that 'there is a points failure' which is holding causing delays to all trains in the area.

Some time passes before the train starts to move again, only to stop a short time later with the eventual announcement from the driver that 'they have been delayed again – this time due to signal problems'.

Some time passes before the train starts to move again. The scene fades out and back in with the conductor announcing that 'The next station will be East Croydon'.

As the train arrives at East Croydon train station, Ivan packs his book back into his briefcase and manages to get off the train just as the doors are closing. As he jumps off (now or never situation) he first trips on the platform (as there is a gap between the train and the platform), and then stumbles straight into a public bin, which causes him to fall back flat on his behind.

He composes himself, stands up and picks up his oversized briefcase, then, mustering any dignity he has left, starts his walk home.

On his way home, he has to walk up some steep stairs, which is difficult due to their steepness and the size and weight of his briefcase.

He walks up the front path of a block of units, enters a security code for the front door, walks through the door, checks the mail – which is awkward as the mail box he is checking is above his head. He enters the lift and immediately opens the emergency phone box in the lift. A very pissed-off expression rolls up his face, as you see him retrieve a broken 18' ruler from the box.

Looking very disgruntled, he uses the longest piece, while standing on his briefcase, to press the button for floor 20 – the highest number he can reach, obviously wanting to go to floor 33.

He exits the lift, and has to walk up the remaining flights of stairs, which is difficult with his big briefcase.

He eventually arrives at apartment 33, stands on his briefcase, takes out his keys and opens the door, swings the door inwards to the lounge room, and shouts out:

IH   I'm home, honey.

Scene 7 – Ivan arrives home

7:30 pm, Monday, 6 May 2013

Setting: Ivan and Sandra's apartment.

The scene cuts over immediately from last scene where Ivan just arrived home.

Camera opens on the bathroom mirror with Sandra standing just in front of it, looking downwards into the basin. From the mirror image, it is evident that she has had a full makeover – and looks much more elegant. As she hears Ivan, she looks up with a bit of apprehension into the mirror, in a wee bit of a fluster looks back down into the basin, madly trying to hide something. She finished wrapping a small object (size of a toothpaste box) and then a quizzical look rolls down her face, quickly followed by sense of knowing, and places the object on top of the vanity cupboard – nicely out of sight.

She walks into the lounge room with a bit of a staid look (although smiling – albeit put on) and walks up to Ivan.

Ivan jogs up to her, throws the briefcase onto the floor, jumps on top of it to time with Sandra's arrival, whereupon they kiss 'hello'.

As this is happening, the noise of a mainline train comes into perception, and gradually gets louder as it gets closer, then eventually gets softer as it passes and travels further away.

SS   You're late – I was expecting you a half hour ago

IH   Apologies – the train was delayed, again. First due to failed points, then later due to signal problems.

       Hey, did you get your hair done? It looks very nice!

SS   Yes, I thought I would give myself a bit of a treat. What do you think?

IH   Yes, it suits you – you look very nice.

SS   Oh, thank you. I'm glad you like it. And how was your day?

IH   It was okay, Actually, I went out with the boys for lunch …

SS   Oh that's great, who was there? Who invited you?

IH   Mark and Gough – we went to a pub and had a couple of pints. You know, I really started to feel as though I was … well you know … you know.. (awkwardly) being part of the … well …

SS   Yes?

IH   Well, becoming part of … you know, accepted as one of the boys.

SS   Really (delighted). Cool, so what did you do? Where did you go? What did you talk about?

        Were any others there besides Mark and Gough?

IH   Nobody else was there, we just talked shop. At this morning's meeting, Max said that we have to introduce a quality management system and was a real prick about it – so what's new there …

SS   What's with a QMS – what's that got to do with managing and protecting our genetic heritage?

IH   [In a sarcastic voice – imitating Max] It will help us to make better – no not better – make optimal decisions all the time when …

There is a knock on the door.

SS   I'll get it …

IH   Who would that be? We're not expecting anybody are we?

SS   Yes – your mum – sorry I was going to tell you but you got home late, and I didn't get a chance to tell you before now as I was on calls all day and didn't have a chance to phone you. I asked her over for tea tonight – I thought we'd get an M&S takeaway …

IH   WHAT … why?

Sandra opens the door and warmly greets Valentina.

SS   Hi – good to see you at last. How are you?

VH   Lovely to see you too, my dear, I'm fine. Must say it has been a fantastic day, and look at you – you look wonderful. Corporate life obviously agrees with you.

Ivan gets up and walks towards the door to greet Valentina as she comes into the apartment – they give each other civil, but not warm, looks at each other.

IH   Hi Mum, nice to see you. So, you found our place okay then?

VH   [A little patronizingly – with a discernible Russian accent] Nice to see you to my dear – ooh yes. Sandra emailed me a lovely map of Croydon that made it so easy to find. So, how have you been … now that you're a 'working man'?

IH   Yea – I'm fine – and yeah, work is good. I'm with a really good bunch of guys …

SS   Valentina – I'm really sorry, I wanted to cook you something really special as a sort of 'welcome back from Russia and welcome to our place' … but I got caught up at work on a big assignment and only just got in. So, I don't want to insult you, but would you be offended if we get an M&S meal for tonight, there's an M&S just down the road in the high street.

VH   While I love your cooking, dear, I understand what a tough place these law firms are now and, if you want to succeed, well you just got to put in those hours. So darling, a lovely M&S will be fine. But, Ivan, couldn't you have got off a little early – I mean that circus you're with doesn't require you to put in any more than the 35-hour week does it? I mean, we are talking about the Civil Service.

IH   [Very curtly] It's not a circus – and what I do – what we do – protects humanity from itself, we're the guardians, the protectors of our gene pool. If we, if I make a wrong decision … then the consequence will be felt for generations to come. I mean, we're it. We're what stand between what we know as humanity and … and well something potentially very non-human.

VH   Oh – good, I'm so pleased there won't be any more genetic deformities in our family … [realising she had crossed the line – starts to backtrack] I mean, your poor cousin Ulga having a baby with spina bifida – how terrible – poor girl went through hell and back with that deformed little baby.

IH   We're not a culling service. We don't pass judgment on unborn children conceived in natural ways. We're there to prevent unauthorised manipulation of genes, so people like you can't go off and clone yourself.

SS   Well it's so nice to see you two talking and enjoying yourselves – is a stroganoff okay with everyone? If so I'll nip down to M&S and pick it up.

VH   A stroganoff sounds lovely.

The scene fades out with Sandra picking up her car keys and walking out the door.

Scene 8 – Dinner with mamma – and the unfolding of the test

8:00pm, Monday, 6 May 2013

Setting: Ivan and Sandra's apartment.

Valentina, Sandra and Ivan are all sitting at a small round table, neatly laid out with napkins and placemats and nice (but not expensive) matching crockery and cutlery, with wine glasses filled and a bottle of [Margaret River] Clairault 2007 Chardonnay wine on the table. All eating – but from the amount of food on their plates it is apparent that they have only just started their meal of Marks & Spencer's stroganoff and rice.

Again, as the scene progresses, the noise of mainline trains can be heard to approach then disappear.

VH   Sandra, before I forget, I have been given two tickets to *Les Misérables* for Saturday week – the eighteenth of May. Would you like to come with me? – as it really is a superb production.

SS   Oh thank you so much – I've always wanted to go, but we've never gotten around to it. So, yes I would love to join you. Perhaps we could meet early and have a meal beforehand?

VH   Excellent, I'll give you a call on the day to arrange where we'll meet. Perhaps we can have dinner beforehand?

Anyway, Sandra, tell me how your job is going? Have you settled in yet? What areas of research are you delving into?

SS   Well, we're err, [almost audible gulp – as she doesn't want Ivan to know that she has been advising her firm on matters relating to the GPA], we're trying to forecast new growth areas in law. Law and social issues are changing so rapidly now that it is very difficult to see which areas are the potential long-term growths as opposed to the issue of the moment.

VH   So – what areas do you think are the growth areas?

SS   Well, pension disputes, elderly care and inheritance, dispossessed tribal people suing governments and big mining companies … you know … that sort of thing.

VH   Really, how interesting … and what's your involvement?

SS   Well, err umm I model social scenarios and try to determine the impact on the status quo – due to a shift in power, caused by a change in legal rights, between the various interest groups. The bigger the shift in power, then the more people that are impacted by the change – or proposed change – will be either advocating or opposed to the change. Obviously, a percentage of the impacted people will be prepared to legally defend their position. If we are ahead of the curve on determining the legalities of the various positions – then we stand to get more clients than our competitors. More clients, more fees, better bonuses.

IH   What – so social justice is not a factor in your legal forecasting?

SS   Sadly – or not so sadly – no it isn't. I mean we're not a charity are we? Also, it's up to the government to create the climate and legal framework, change the relative power between interest groups to create justice. Lawyers can't create it. They just assist in the execution of government policy and justice.

IH   Only if there is money in it!

SS   Well I suppose that's why there's Legal Aid.

IH   And Legal Aid is really going to stop the illegal logging of a rainforest in Malaysia, is it?

VH   Well my darlings, this is exciting stuff – so much more interesting than discussing the great days of the Cold War with my friends – but you must excuse me while I go to the powder room.

Valentina gets up and walks off – and the camera fades out on her as she walks down the passage.

The camera fades back on Valentina coming back, walking very sternly, very aggressively back to the table [while the other two are eating oblivious to her stern looks and aggressive walk] holding something in her hand – clutching it out in front of her.

VH   Please tell me what this is [as she holds the object out over the table and waves it aggressively in front of their faces]? What do you think you're doing? Who do you think you are? [At this point she throws the object onto the table.]

Ivan is completely dumfounded, glancing alternatively between his aggressive mother, the object just thrown on the table and Sandra, trying to figure out what's going on.

SS   WHAT do you mean 'who do we think we are' – the question is who the fuck do you think you are going through my private things, my toiletries, you have no right, no right, NO FUCKING right at all!

VH   [Very restrained, cold and calculating] I have every right, as you are well aware. But enough for now – I take it from Ivan's dumb expression that he doesn't know [as she eyed him off and noted his dumbfoundment] therefore, let's stop discussing this now until I can talk to you in private. He does not need to be involved in our private conversation.

SS   [Reticently] No we won't discuss this, either now or later, as it none of your damn business.

IH   [In a relaxed – barely veiled sarcastic voice] I'm sorry, I missed something in the last conversation, so may I ask – WHAT THE FUCK IS GOING ON? WHAT ARE YOU TALKING ABOUT? AND DON'T TREAT ME LIKE A PIECE OF SHIT ON THE SIDE OF THE PAVEMENT.

Ivan, in a very agile and sudden movement – that is so quick that it looks like a single move – jumps up onto his chair, and dives across the table and, while he is still in mid-air, grabs the object that came to rest just in front of Sandra. His momentum keeps him airborne and once he reaches the other side of the table he completes a somersault and lands gracefully on his feet. The manoeuvre is so perfectly executed it looked like a practiced stunt.

IH   See Mamma, I still have some of Papa's circus blood in me.

Ivan studies the object quizzically while the other two look on in semi-stunned embarrassed. His eyes light up abruptly in astonishment. He gives his head a disbelieving shake and looks at it again, eyes wide open.

He lifts his head very slowly, in a state of many mixed emotions: shock, disbelief and deep hurt. He looks long and hard at SS. He tries to detect tell-tale signs in her face for her action – trying to get some feedback as to what it all means and what her words and actions meant. Slowly he starts to speak.

IH   You're pregnant?'

SS   [Shouting] How would I fucking know? I haven't had a chance to look at the fucking thing yet [at which point she shows signs of emotional discomfort/regret]. Apparently I don't have any rights to privacy in this fucking apartment.

IH   I've had a chance to look at it – and it's blue – you're pregnant!

SS   [Tears now starting to form] Oh no, I don't want this, not now, not now, NOT FUCKING NOW!

IH   You weren't going to tell me?

SS   [Sobering up] Of course I was … [She gets cut off by a fierce look from Ivan – as in 'don't you dare bullshit me now'. She pauses, looks down in shame with tears starting to roll down her cheek.] … No I wasn't – not just now at any rate.

       Please excuse me …

Sandra walks off down the passage and out of sight – followed by the sound of a slamming door – then door locks being bolted.

The camera pans down and brings Ivan and Valentina into focus – both staring in a state of shock in the general direction of the passage that Sandra just disappeared from – and in the case of Ivan, his expression is compounded by a general sense of bewilderment.

The camera fades out on their silent mixed emotional expressions.

Insert Scene – 3

We want fewer and better children … and we cannot make the social life and the world- peace we are determined to make, with ill-bred, ill-trained swarms of inferior citizens that you inflict upon us.

The introduction to Margaret Sanger's The Pivot of Civilization *by HG Wells, 1922*

Scene 9 – Advanced pregnancy test: shopping

7:30am, Wednesday, 8 May 2013

Setting: Sandra's morning commute to work.

During Sandra's morning commute to work, she ducks into a Boots pharmacy and checks out the range of pregnancy and DNA testing products.

She eyes them all very discerningly – reading the labels intensely. She eventually chooses the 'Three in One Tester: Pregnancy, Parentage and Genetic Health Check'.

She takes it to the counter, pays for it (by keying in her PIN on her mobile phone), then continues on her way to work.

Scene 10 – Advanced pregnancy test: results

7:30pm, Wednesday, 8 May 2013

Setting: Sandra's Evening Commute Home – Then in Sandra and Ivan's apartment.

After her day at work, Sandra commutes home.

Ivan is in the kitchen, standing on a portable step, chopping up some vegetables – evidently preparing the evening meal.

Sandra reaches their apartment and unlocks and opens the front door. She walks in and as she passes the kitchen, she looks in and sees Ivan, where they exchange civil, if strained, greetings.

SS   Hi.

IH   Nice to see you too.

SS   I have to finish writing a report. I'm going to the study to log on, so that I can finish it at a decent hour.

IH   Well, I'll see you later.

SS   Sure – when will dinner be ready?

IH   Whenever.

SS   Okay, give me a call when it is ready.

IH   Sure.

Sandra disappears down the passage and enters the study.

She sits down at her desk, grabs her handbag, searches through it until she finds the device she bought from Boots in the morning.

She opens the box, takes out the instructions and reads them intensely.

SS Voiceover:

> The triple test device collates information stored on NHS medical files, The International Gynaecological and Paediatric database, the National Registration for Births, Deaths and Marriages, the Home Office, the National DNA database, the Genome Project and the GPA database of identified genetic abnormalities.
>
> The results returned from the test are:
>
> - 100% accurate pregnancy tester.
> - Whether the mother, father or child have any of 62 gazetted genetic abnormalities defined by the GPA and is automatically updated with any additions or amendments made by the GPA.
> - Whether the mother, father or child have any of the 1075 genetic abnormalities identified by the Genome Project.
> - The biological mother of the child.
> - The biological father of the child.
> - The surrogate mother of the child.
>
> Instruction for use
>
> - Plug the sensor into the USB port of a computer connected to the internet.
> - Log on.
> - Enter the UserID and password provided within the envelope within the pack.
> - Follow the instructions to enter your personal details.
> - Once prompted by the on-screen instructions, with the pink sensor, remove protective cover, and prick end of the mother's thumb with the exposed needle.
> - With the blue sensor, prick the end of the father's thumb with the exposed needle.
> - The above databases will be searched, and the results will be available within approximately four minutes.

After reading the instructions, Sandra removes the sensors from the box and plugs them into the USB port, then logs onto the website.

She follows the instructions:

> Please enter the assumed biological mother's full name – as registered either on her birth certificate, marriage certificate or passport.

Sandra enters her name.

Please enter the assumed biological mother's date of birth.

Sandra enters her birth date.

Is the carrier of the child the same person as registered above as the biological mother – please select 'Yes' or 'No'.

Sandra clicks on 'Yes'

Please enter the assumed father's full name – as registered on his birth certificate, marriage certificate or passport.

Sandra enters Ivan's name

Please enter the assumed father's date of birth.

Sandra enters Ivan's date of birth.

Please remove the protective cover from the pink sensor – and prick the end of the mother's thumb with the exposed needle sensor.

Once done – please hit the enter key.

Sandra removes the protective cover and with a degree of apprehension, she pricks the end of her thumb – then presses the enter key.

Please remove the protective cover from the blue sensor – and prick the end of the father's thumb with the exposed needle sensor.

If this is not possible – then please click the on-screen button 'Skip Paternal Blood Test'.

Otherwise, once the father's thumb is pricked – please click the enter key.

Sandra ponders for a moment, puts her face in her hand in despair – shaking her head – not knowing quite what to do. She pauses for a minute. Her strength and determination return and her demeanour straightens with a new sense of resolve.

She gets up and walks to the kitchen where Ivan is still chopping vegetables.

SS   I just need to get a glass of water

IH   Sure.

Sandra goes to the cupboard and retrieves a glass. She waits until Ivan is on the cusp of making his next slice of a pepper, and with impeccable timing purposely reaches past him to pick up the water jug, and in doing so firmly knocks his elbow.

Ivan brings down his knife, and as he is knocked his thumb is pushed into the 'cutting line' and he drives the knife into his thumb.

IH   Fuck, what was that for? Jesus, you made me cut my thumb. Fuck that hurt!

SS   Oh, Ivan, I'm so sorry. It was an accident; I was just getting the water. Here, let me help. I'll get you a plaster. First, you need to stop the bleeding.

Sandra reaches for a tissue and grabs Ivan's bleeding hand and wraps the tissue around his thumb.

SS   Okay, I'll be back in a second – I'll just get a band-aid, I'm sure there are some in the bathroom vanity unit.

Sandra swiftly walks out of the kitchen and soon returns with a band-aid where she has already taken it out of its protective wrapper.

SS   I am so sorry. Okay take the tissue off, and let me stick this on.

As she says this, she helps Ivan remove the tissue, where she keeps it in her hand. She then applies the band-aid.

IH   Thanks for your help, but you should be more careful around people using knives – that could have been serious!

SS   Yes you are right – I should have been more careful. I am sorry. Are you okay now?

IH   Sure, I guess I can continue with the cooking.

SS   Okay, then if you don't mind, I'll continue with my report.

IH   That's nice, you stab me then you fuck off.

SS   I didn't actually stab you – and it was only a small cut. Look, you're not bleeding anymore.

IH   Whatever. Sure, just go back to you report. I'll be fine here by myself.

SS   Thanks. And, I am sorry. I really didn't mean to bump you and make you cut yourself.

IH   Just go and finish your report – okay.

SS   Okay.

Sandra returns to the study, picks up the blue sensor, takes the protective cover off, then wraps the bloodied tissue around it – then she presses the enter key on her computer.

A screen appears advising that the analysis will take approximately four minutes.

The screen has a status and information bar – which informs the user of the various data and checks that are being conducted:

- *Assessing pregnancy.*
- *Assessing NHS medical records.*
- *Checking International Gynaecological and Paediatric Database.*
- *Checking the Register of Births, Deaths and Marriages.*
- *Checking the Home Office records.*
- *Checking the National DNA database.*
- *Checking the Genome Database.*
- *Checking the GPA's database of genetic abnormalities.*

After the above messages, a screen is displayed:

> *Analysis successfully completed. Press enter key to display results.*

Sandra is startled by the notice and clearly does not know what to do – whether she should go ahead and press the enter key to get the results. After a prolonged pause with a great deal of visible anxiety, Sandra eventually reaches over to the keyboard and presses the enter key.

A new screen appears. 'Test Results':

Pregnancy:
Positive – the mother is pregnant

Pregnancy Duration:
Conception took place between 7:37pm and 11:19pm on
Saturday, 23 March 2013.

Natural Birth Term of Pregnancy:
The current projection for a natural, full-term birth is 14-Dec-2013. This
will be a gestation period of 266 days (38 weeks). This is 14 days less
than the average of 280 days (40 weeks).

Medical Status of pregnancy:
There are no known severe medical conditions associated with the
pregnancy.
Health of Mother:
Satisfactory.
Health of Foetus:
Satisfactory.

Click 'Next' to view parental information

Sandra reaches for her PDA, flicks through her calendar until she sees the entry
for 23-March-2013 and looks at the entry for 'Weekend at Bath'.

SS   Fuck it, the weekend at Bath. Fuck, fuck, fuck.

She regains her composure somewhat, then clicks on the next button and the
following information is displayed:

Sandra Small, the assumed biological mother, is the biological mother.
Sandra Small, the assumed carrier mother, is the carrier mother.
Ivan Henry, the assumed biological father, is the biological father. Click
Next to view results of the genetic tests.

Sandra clicks on the next button

Click Next to view genetic results for Sandra Small.

Sandra clicks the next button

> *Genetic Test Results for Sandra Small:*
> *GPA Gazetted Genetic Conditions:*
> *None Detected.*
> *Other Genetic Conditions Detected:*
> - *Factor V Leiden.*
> - *Haemochromatosis.*

> *Click next to view genetic results for Ivan Henry.*

Sandra sits up and studies the screen. She gets out her smartphone and types the two genetic conditions listed for her into the notes application.

Sandra clicks the next button.

> *Genetic Test Results for Ivan Henry:*

> *GPA Gazetted Genetic Conditions: None Detected.*
> - *Other Genetic Conditions Detected:*
> - *Achondroplasia.*
> - *Hereditary nonpolyposis colorectal cancer.*
> - *Cerebral Autosomal Dominant Arteriopathy with Subcortical Infarcts and Leukoencephalopathy (CADASIL).*

> *Click next to view genetic results for the unborn foetus.*

Sandra is again surprised to see what has been revealed by the test – and types the last two listed conditions into her PDA.

After she finishes typing in the last two genetic conditions into her PDA, she stares at the screen with a heightened sense of trepidation. She draws in a deep breath, closes her eyes momentarily to gain her composure – opens them, grabs the mouse and places the cursor on the next button – then closes her eyes again before she clicks.

Slowly she opens her eyes to read the screen:

> *Genetic Test Results for the Unborn Foetus: Sex: Male*
> *GPA Gazetted Genetic Conditions: None Detected.*

Other Genetic Conditions Detected:

- *Factor V Leiden*
- *Haemochromatosis*
- *Achondroplasia*

She runs her finger down the screen, first shuddering as she sees 'Factor V Leiden', cringes further when she sees 'Haemochromatosis', then, as her finger reveals 'Achondroplasia', she crumbles and starts sobbing in her chair.

The scene fades out and, when it fades back in, her demeanour has changed from being a sobbing wreck to that of a woman possessed of sheer rage. She gets up and storms out of the study and marches down the corridor to the kitchen.

From a bowlful of eggs, she picks one up and throws it at Ivan.

SS   You fucking little cretin. You just had to forget your fucking condoms when we went to Bath didn't you? I hope you're fucking pleased with yourself! Not only have you got me knocked up – but you got me knocked up with a fucking midget.
You just couldn't help yourself could you? Let's get Sandra knocked up so that she can spew out more fucking midgets. Well congratulations.

IH   [Wiping egg from his face with a tea towel] Sandra, please calm down. What is all this? I didn't know that you were having an embryo genetic test.

SS   Well I have – and bingo, you scored big time. I'm carrying your fucking midget son.

IH   Sandra, why are you so upset? You married one, and I think I'm okay, so what is the problem with having a dwarf for a son?

SS   Don't be so bloody ignorant. There is a gulf of difference between marrying a dwarf and having one as a child. One is choice – which to be blunt, is reversible. The other isn't a choice, and it is not reversible. Well, at least not reversible once, and if, it is born.

IH   What are you saying? Calm down, I think we need to speak about a few things.

SS   No, I really don't want to speak to you at the moment. I'm going out. Sandra heads towards the door.

IH   Where are you going?

SS   To see some friends.

IH   [Unintentionally insensitive] I didn't know you had any friends in London.

SS   Fuck you too lonely boy.

With this, Sandra storms out of the apartment and slams the door behind her.

Ivan is left dumbfounded. He takes a seat and places his face into his hands accentuating the stress that he is feeling. After a few moments, he looks up, as though he just remembered something. He looks down at his thumb, thinks for a moment, then jumps up and walks down the passage to the study.

He enters the study, and notices the tester packaging. He picks the packaging up and looks at the diagram on the bottom of the box and notes the illustration of the USB sensors. He looks at the desk and sees the sensors that are plugged into the computer.

He approaches the computer, and is alarmed when he sees the blue sensor wrapped in his bloodied tissue. With this, he jumps up onto the desk chair and sees the screen detailing the genetic condition of his unborn child.

While he is not alarmed with the diagnosis that the embryo has achondroplasia – he shows considerable concern over the diagnosis of Factor V Leiden and Haemochromatosis.

He then realises there are 'Previous' and 'Next' buttons at the bottom of the screen. The camera fades out as a scene of betrayal and alarm crosses his face as he sees his own results – realising that Sandra had purposely cut him to get his blood – so that she could run the tests without his knowledge.

Insert Scene – 4

Now the world proposes to interrupt the terrible austere laws of nature which ordain that the weak shall be trampled upon, shall be ground into death and dust.

Confessions of a Young Man *by George Moore.*

Scene 11 – Another Monday morning team meeting at the GPA

9:00am, Monday, 13 May 2013

Setting: GPA offices.

The scene is repetitious of the opening morning scene of the city workers crossing London Bridge, the scene shows Ivan, along with thousands of others, walking over the bridge in order to get to work.

Like the opening scene, all have a perceptible skip in their step – with the exception of Ivan, who looks decidedly glum.

The scene advances to the GPA conference room, where the Monday morning staff meeting is in progress. Jeff Portwood is just finishing his presentation on his proposed implementation schedule for a quality management system. Jeff totally lacks confidence and presentation skills. He is nervous, laughs inappropriately, constantly 'ums' and 'ers' and his message is all but lost on his audience. Max resumes control.

ML   Jeff can you see me in my office at 2:30 this afternoon? I think we need to have a wee discussion on your proposed pathetic approach.

       Now, turning to another matter entirely, I've asked Jon [*referring to Jon Raney*] to give us a presentation on 'cloning and growing foetus in such a manner as they grow into a specific organ – e.g. the heart'. Jon, are you okay to present now?

JR   [*Very confidently and authoritatively*] Yes, thanks Max, my pleasure.

       Today's issue is, like all issues we have to deal in and judicate on, drenched in ethics vs. technology vs. emotional complexity.

       As you are all very much aware, the technology now exists to make a clone of ourselves so that the genetic makeup, the genetic material of the clone, is identical to our own. Further, we have the technology and the means to be able to modify the growth behaviour within our cloned foetus. This enables us to, well, safely and reliably grow ourselves a new heart when our current ticker starts to give up the ghost. There is no waste or anything, we don't have to cut the new heart out of a foetus or baby, or wait for someone to die. We simply place an order for new heart, donate a couple for raw genetic material, wait, say, 60 days, and bingo there it is – a brand new heart. Perfect isn't it?

So what could be ethically wrong with this? No one is hurt, no one dies – all just good clean fun isn't it?

Or is it? As you're aware, identical twins are also genetically identical. So, since one twin is essentially a clone of the other is it alright to, say, modify the growth pattern of one of the twin foetus so that only one child is born, and as a bonus to him, he will be delivered with a whole host of spare parts thanks to modifying the growth pattern of his twin sibling?

Somehow, even though we now have the technology to do the above with identical twins – I don't think society would approve or allow this to happen.

If society wouldn't allow the normal growth pattern of a twin to be modified, in order to be used as spare parts for his identical twin, would society allow growth modification of a clone for the same purpose? After all, the difference is far from black and white. In one instance the cloning takes place when both parties are very small and in the womb, the other when one party is mature and outside the womb. Aside from that, the process and issues are conceptually the same. Both 'spare parts' start as a single living cell that could grow into a complete living person, or should I say 'the development' of both possibilities start from a single cell.

With natural twins, society's expectation is that both parties have equal right to life, assuming that they're both healthy. Does this change if/when an artificial twin is created? I suggest not. Regardless of when a twin is conceived either simultaneously as happens naturally, or staggered as happens with human intervention, the principle remains the same – both have the same right to life.

Therefore, in the upcoming debate over the use of cloning techniques to deform the natural growth pattern of an embryo in order to produce a spare part for patients – we need to formulate a position on this issue, which reflects the reality of the situation. The situation is that after being banned and outlawed in the UK since 1807 – 200 years or so later – we, the self-proclaimed 'enlightened' era, are bringing back, in a brand new and horrific form, slavery.

NH   Jon, when will this technology be available? As I would like to order some new eyes?

Insert Scene – 5

Universal Education has created an immense class of what I may call the New Stupid. Beyond the Mexique Bay by Aldous Huxley.

Scene 12 – The gazette

10:30am, Monday, 13 May 2013

Setting: GPA offices – and Jon Raney's office at the GPA

Ivan is at his work desk looking very perturbed. After a while, he gets out of his seat and walks down an office corridor, where after a bit of a walk he reaches an office, peers in and softly knocks on the open door. Jon Raney looks up from a journal that he is reading, looks a little surprised to see Ivan at his door, but signals him in anyway. Ivan walks into Jon's office, pauses momentarily, then turns and closes the door behind him. Jon's expression acknowledges the gravity of the visit by this act – and signals Ivan to sit.

IH   Jon, I think I have a problem. I need your advice on a private matter.

JR   Sure, Ivan, I'll be glad to help. What's up?

IH   Well … [he sits puzzled trying to formulate words to express his problems, but the pregnant pause grows to a long awkward silence as he sits uncomfortably in his chair, alternating between looking up to Jon and down to his own chest].

JR   What's up Ivan? Whatever it is, it's obviously important. Therefore, just start at the beginning and we can work through it.

IH   Well – you know that I am married.

JR   Yes, I remember her from the office Christmas party. Sandra isn't it? Nice lass if I remember correctly.

IH   Yes she is, we met at Leeds Metropolitan University – and moved down to London together after we graduated.

A long pause transpires.

JR   Well Ivan, tell me, what has Sandra done?

IH   She's pregnant [as Ivan says this his voice croaks with tortured emotion and he looks down to hide his emotion and avoid Jon's gaze].

JR   Congratulations, Ivan! ... But this obviously is causing you some grief ... So what is the problem?

Another long pause transpires.

IH   [Looking down] Sandra wants to terminate the pregnancy.

JR   [Leans back in his seat, brings his hands up to his face as in realisation of the full magnitude of what the issue, the BIG issue, is.] Yes.

IH   [Ivan looking up at him angrily] She wants to abort my child.

JR   [With a high degree of empathy in his speech, Jon continues] Ivan, Sandra isn't the first woman to pursue this line of action – so what's the issue, what is different between Sandra and the other women who pursue their right to choose?

IH   [Snidely] You know what the issue is, you know why this is different ...

JR   Ivan, you have come here and asked for my advice. Until I know the full story I will not be able to provide you with any advice. And believe me, I won't make any assumptions as to what your particular circumstances are. So, tell me clearly what your problem is – because I am not going to speculate.

IH   She wants to terminate the child because ... it will be ... it will be a dwarf.

JR   [Showing genuine empathy] Ivan, I understand that it would have been difficult for you to come to me for advice on this matter. But, before we proceed, can I ask whether you have discussed this matter with Sandra? Have you let her know how deeply you feel about the child, and her reasons for wanting the termination?

IH   Jon, I guess they're fair enough questions, but at the moment we are not really communicating.

JR   Well, as difficult as it may be, I strongly urge you to ... to ... to do whatever is necessary to start communicating, to start a dialogue with Sandra, so that she is aware of your feelings – and conversely, so you become acquainted with her views on the matter. While I am happy to offer my advice, from your perspective, you should be trying to resolve this matter between yourselves.

IH   Jon, good advice under normal conditions. But, look, now I'm sleeping on the couch and we do whatever we can to avoid each other – work late, start early, go out, etc. And, if we ever get caught together in the same room at home, then one of us immediately exits. As much as I would like to sit down with Sandra and work this out together, it just isn't going to happen.

JR   Sorry to hear that Ivan, it must be very difficult for you.

IH   Yes. So, I feel isolated and yet I need some advice on this matter. So, apologies for bringing you into it, but I feel I had no alternatives.

JR   Okay I still think you would be better served by sitting down with Sandra and discussing this matter and working it out collectively.

IH   Jon, you're not listening, it isn't going to happen. That's why I'm here in your office. You're right, it wasn't easy for me to approach you, and now you're making it more difficult by making light of my situation, advising me to essentially kiss and make up.

JR   Apologies, I was not making light of your situation. Taking a longer term view of the situation, I think it would be in your best interest to resolve this matter between Sandra and yourself. However, if this is not going to happen, then, yes I can provide you with advice, inasmuch as what you're seeking relates to the GPA Act and associated regulations.

IH   Sure, that's why I'm here.

JR   Okay. Now Ivan, I don't want you to think that I'm a prick. But, I'm now going to ask you some tough questions which will make me look like a prize arsehole. However, for me to understand what the issue is – so that I can give you the advice you're seeking – I have to ask you these questions ... okay?

IH closes his eyes and slowly nods his consent.

JR   Now ... should the child be born ... some sections of the community, even large sections... would consider that being a dwarf would be a disadvantage to the child ...

IH   IT'S NOT A FUCKING DISADVANTAGE. I'M ONE AND I'M FUCKING FINE, I'M OKAY, being a dwarf is not a fucking disadvantage – do you understand?

JR   Ivan. Two things. Firstly, you agreed that I could ask the tough questions – is this still okay?

IH   very agitatedly nods his consent.

JR   Secondly, you have to understand the difference between 'your knowledge' of being a dwarf and all that goes with it, and the 'public perception' of what being a dwarf is like. These are potentially two very different views.
        Now, what I was asking was whether you were aware that a large part of the community would consider it disadvantageous to be a dwarf. So, again, at the risk of sounding like a prick, do you understand that such public perception *may* exist?

IH   No, I fucking don't.

JR   Ivan. Please try to separate what the public *may* perceive from *why* they may hold this perception – and whether or not, based on your own first-hand knowledge and experience, whether the public perception is valid. Okay?

IH   Nods In agitated agreement.

JR   Now, do you accept the position that … that society, generally, *may* perceive it a handicap to be a dwarf – or at least a disadvantage?

IH   IT IS NOT A FUCKING HANDICAP OR A DISADVANTAGE!

        JR looks sternly at Ivan. IH is agitated and moves restlessly in his seat – he nods his acknowledgement.

JR   Now Ivan, tell me so that I can hear it.

IH   Yes Jon – I accept that society *may* have a false perception that it is disadvantageous to be a dwarf.

JR   Ivan, now, from the emotion and direction of our conversation, I take it that you're not in agreement about having the pregnancy terminated.

IH   No, I'm not in favour of having the pregnancy terminated. It's as much my child as hers, and I think I should have an equal say as to whether or not the pregnancy is terminated.

If the sole reason for terminating the pregnancy is due to it being a dwarf, then I oppose the basis for making this decision as being a dwarf is not a disadvantage. It is not a handicap and it is not a disability – regardless of what the public may think, what she may think.

JR   I understand. Now what is it that you specifically want to ask me in regard to … to your current dilemma?

IH   Well, what's our position on abortion?

JR   What do you mean – my personal view – or something broader?

IH   What is the GPA's position on abortion – does it favour abortions or not?

JR   Mmmm. The GPA does not exactly have a position on abortion – you should know that. The GPA's position, or more correctly its mandate, is to protect and advance the genetic heritage of the homo sapiens species. So, the issue of abortion is at the very margin of the GPA's remit. In essence abortions are still the personal choice of expectant parents.

IH   What about forced abortion, you know culling, when a foetus is showing signs of genetic abnormality?

JR   The GPA does not exactly have a position on this issue – it is too close to the abortion issues which, as I just mentioned, is at the margin of the GPA's remit. However, we do have a remit to reduce the risk of and the number of incidences of the transmission of genetically defective material from one generation to the next.

IH   So what does that mean – do we enforce abortions where it has been determined that a foetus is genetically abnormal?

JR   No, as I just mentioned, that is too politically sensitive – at the moment at any rate. We – we as in the GPA and the government – hope to achieve such a position by 2020. So over the next seven years or so, we are charged with developing and maintaining an educational programme in order to change the attitude of the public, to the point they will support genetic screening and forced termination – based on reliable evidence of a genetically defective embryo or foetus.

IH   What's the position, or, sorry, the practice now?

JR   All newly expectant mothers are encouraged to have a 'Genetic Health' test on the embryo they are carrying within twelve weeks of conception. If abnormalities are detected, after more tests are undertaken to confirm the finding, the evidence will be presented to the expectant parents. They will then be encouraged and supported to have the pregnancy terminated – to avoid bringing a child into the world that is genetically defective.

IH   And if they refuse?

JR   Well that is their choice, at least at the moment. However, our counselling to such parents is quite persuasive, as we do have a 94.5% success rate.

IH   So, what do you mean by 'their choice'? Do both parents need to agree to the termination?

JR   Good question. The GPA does not affect the rights of either expectant mothers or fathers in relation to pregnancies where there are no signs of genetic defects in the embryo or foetus. In such cases fathers do have their common law rights over the life of their unborn children.

However, in cases where genetic defects are identified in an embryo or foetus, the GPA Act alters the rights of expectant fathers. Perhaps, 'altered' is not the correct word – 'extinguished' better describes the rights of expectant fathers in these circumstances.

IH   Sorry, I don't understand?

JR   In cases of normal pregnancies, both the mother and father have rights over the unborn child, obviously the mother has more rights than the father, but still, the father does have some residual rights as to the plight of the unborn child, including rights over the termination of a pregnancy – or not as the case may be.

However, where the unborn child has been assessed as a carrier of a defective genetic disorder, in these circumstances the GPA Act extinguishes the rights of the expectant father to prevent the pregnancy from being terminated.

IH   Are you telling me that the GPA extinguishes the rights of fathers to save their unborn children from termination?

JR   Only in cases where genetic defects are identified in the embryo or foetus. In all other cases fathers continue to have the same rights as they always had.

IH   So then, what is the definition of a 'genetic defect'?

JR   Ivan, you know the answer to this yourself. According to our statute, we can only consider something genetically defective if the defect has been sufficiently defined to allow: reliable detection, or if the defect or condition will be a significant impediment to the child once born, whether in childhood or adulthood.

IH   Are dwarfs considered as genetically defective?

JR   Not exactly, but this area of the GPA legislation is a little tricky. So, let's go through it together. Now stay with me, and don't get emotional about this, just listen and understand the 'process' and avoid thinking about the reason, logic or justice of the process okay?
[He eyes Ivan as he says this – and waits for an acknowledgement.]

Now, we both work at the GPA, so you're well aware of this process, but now you will be viewing the process from a different angle, so you are going to have to read it with a different perspective than previously, okay?

The GPA act classifies all embryos as falling into one of three categories. The first category is where the embryo shows no sign of any form of genetic abnormality. In other words, there is every reason to believe the baby will be perfectly normal. In these cases, the pregnancy and embryo is clearly outside the interest and reach of the GPA.

Although this is not my area of knowledge, I know fathers do have some rights over the plight of their unborn child. I suspect that a father, in order to exercise his right, would have to place an injunction on the mother to stop her doing anything that is deemed 'unnatural', i.e. to stop her having an abortion. But again, this is not my field of knowledge, so you need to consult a lawyer to get specific advice.

The second category is where the embryo has a specific genetic condition, and the genetic condition has been formally gazetted as a 'genetic defect'. In this scenario, the state encourages and supports parents to have the pregnancy terminated. However, by law, it only requires the mother to agree to the termination. This is because, as I mentioned a minute ago, the father's rights over the unborn child are extinguished.

The third and final category is where the embryo's genetic makeup will determine that, as a child or as an adult, it would be three standard deviations from the accepted 'human norm'.

The same rules apply for this third category as in the second category, the state encourages the parents to terminate the pregnancy, and the fathers' rights over the unborn child are extinguished.

IH   What an outrageous piece of legislation. Who the fuck drafted it? And what Nazi regime passed the act through Parliament?

JR   I understand your frustration, but I don't know how the legislation was drafted or passed.
        That was a little before my time.

IH   Well, what do I do now, in order to save my baby?

JR   Realistically, I think you have a tough ride ahead of you. In order to prevent the termination of your unborn child, you have to get through the following three hurdles. First, confirm that achondroplasia is not a gazetted genetic disorder – you do suffer from achondroplasia don't you?

IH   [In an indignant tone] I do not suffer from any disease. I may have achondroplasia – but I do not suffer from it.

JR   Apologies for my insensitivity. Shall we continue?

IH   [Nods] Sure, keep going.

JR   Okay, I don't believe achondroplasia is gazetted, but let's check to be sure.

Jon goes to the shelves behind his desk and brings out the 'Consolidated Gazette of Genetic Disorders'. He brings it back to the desk and puts it in the middle of the desk so that they both can read it. Jon looks up the index and runs his finger down it.

JR   Good, achondroplasia is not gazetted as a genetic disorder. So, to put it in blunt terms, you're not genetically outlawed!

IH   Jon, this whole system is just so, so fucked. I mean, I have the achondroplasia form of dwarfism which, perhaps you may know, is the most common form of dwarfism. But what about the 200 odd other forms of dwarfism, like: cartilage-hair hypoplasia; chondroectodermal dysplasia; congenital adrenal hyperplasia; De Morsier's syndrome; diastrophic dysplasia; Ellis-van Creveld syndrome and the Laron's form of dwarfism?

Are these forms of dwarfism 'genetically outlawed' – and which prick is making the decision as to who's genetically defective? Whoever is making these decisions may not be genetically defective, but they are certainly morally defective.

JR   Ivan, I don't need a lecture in genetic ethics, not for the moment at least. Currently we are talking about you and your problem. Achondroplasia is not gazetted – therefore you've made it though hurdle number one. Now – shall we continue, or do you wish to resume your lecture?

IH   Jon, I'm sorry, I'm just really pissed at the moment, and unfortunately I'm taking it out on you. I have no right … I think I should go …

JR   NO – not yet. Let's work through this, as far as we can at least, then you should have a framework from which you can develop your … strategy … your position. Now, we know your particular condition, achondroplasia, is not gazetted, so you've got past the first of the three hurdles. Now for the second hurdle – that is where the embryo's genetic makeup determines that, as either a child or an adult, it will be three standard deviations from the accepted 'Human Norm'.

While it's part of the Genetic Protection Act, no guidance has been issued as to how to interpret or measure this criterion. Further, there haven't been any court hearings relating to this particular section of the Act, therefore there isn't any case law or guidance offered by the courts.

So, it is not clear whether the test relates to physical, mental or emotional attributes. The answer is unknown, it could relate to any or all of these human attributes.

IH   Shouldn't it be based on capacity, ability and humanity – not some arbitrary physical attribute?

JR   Ivan, you may be right, I don't know the answer. But, the way it is written, it's open to interpretation. Therefore there is a risk that a judge, if it were ever to go to court, would interpret the act in a very literal sense, confining the act to physical attributes.

IH   That's fucking outrageous. So what you are saying is that I'm genetically defective, that I don't have a right to reproduce? Don't give me this shit it would be an injustice on a grand scale if this is the case.

JR   Ivan, I told you at the start that I have to be a prized prick to give you any worthwhile advice. I'm sorry but this is the case. Remember, if you were to make an application to the GPA's Ethics Ruling Committee – or even the appeals court to adjudicate on this matter, you would be facing similar lines of inquiry during those hearings – but, may I suggest, the line of questioning would be put forward in a far more brutal manner.

Now, as I said – there are no guidelines on how this section of the act is to be interpreted. So, if it is interpreted as applying to physical attributes – in a very literal sense – then, possibly you would have a problem. I don't know off hand what the average human height is nor the standard deviation from the average human height – nor for that matter, your height.

BUT, for the sake of this discussion, suppose for a minute that your unborn child is projected to be shorter than three standard deviations from the average height of the population, AND a court took a very narrow physical interpretation of this section of the act – then, in order to prevent the pregnancy being terminated, it would require Sandra to resist or defy the GPA's encouragement to have the pregnancy terminated.

In this scenario, if a court were to rule that your unborn child fell outside the three standard deviation rule, based on the child's projected height as an adult, your paternal rights over your unborn child would be extinguished. If the mother of a defective embryo wished to terminate the pregnancy, then it is enshrined in legislation that this is her decision alone, and the father has no legal right to be involved or to change the decision.

Ivan gets out of his seat and approaches Jon's desk.

IH   This is a violation of basic human rights, liberty and decency – how dare you, how dare the fucking GPA sentence my child to death, merely on the basis that he is short in stature? What an insidious, disgusting and immoral organisation do you run? Hitler would be proud of you … you fucking fascist bastard.

JR   Ivan – don't shoot the messenger, I'm trying to help here. Now sit down … and let's explore the possibilities, how the Act can be interpreted differently, or what other options are open...

IH   Fuck off, Jon. I now understand what this organisation is all about and how we all are part of the machinery to cleanse our society, our gene pool, our species of genetic diversity of all people who are a little different from the rest, a little different from the norm.

        You know, in ages past, in the unenlightened age, people who were a little different were locked up in asylums, bell towers, freak shows or circuses. Now in our enlightened age society is much more accepting, more accommodating – by just making sure freaks are killed before birth. I hope you're proud of yourself and of your job.

Ivan then storms out of the office – slamming the door behind him. Jon leans forward rests his elbows on the table and sinks his face into his hands – in deep hurt and sorrow for Ivan.

He then looks up – grabs a post-it note and writes something on it. He gets up and walks out the door, chases Ivan down the corridor, catches him.

JR   Ivan – look, you are going to need help, good help. Take this number. He's as good as you can get … call him okay?

IH   What – are you going to sue me because I called you a fascist? You Nazi bastard … go and rot in hell.

JR   Ivan … I don't give a shit what you call me, and no I'm not going to sue you. You need a lawyer, a good lawyer, to help you save your unborn child. This guy is your best chance – call him and use him. And do it now – because if you wait, even a few days, your opportunity to do something about the plight of your unborn child will be lost.

Now it's up to you. Good luck, because you're going to need all you can get.

Ivan looks at Jon still with pent up rage – grabs the post-it note, turns and walks down the corridor.

Insert Scene – 6

> *Again I say that all we deem sublime in the world's history are acts of injustice; and it is certain that if man does not relinquish at once, and forever, his vain, mad and fatal dream of justice, the world will lapse into barbarism.*

Confessions of a Young Man *by George Moore.*

Scene 13 – Ivan – A good coffee and a bad phone call

11:30am, Tuesday, 14 May 2013

Setting: Hays Galleria.

Ivan is sitting at table by himself outside a coffee shop inside Hays Galleria – reading a copy of the Annotated Genetic Protection Act – With Case Studies *by Dr S. Plice. A voiceover begins with Ivan speaking the words he is reading:*

IH   [Voiceover] Where embryonic genetic testing indicates the embryo will develop into a person that will be three standard deviations from the accepted human norm, the parents are to be encouraged to terminate the pregnancy.

Should the parents agree to terminate the pregnancy, the state shall cover all medical costs associated with the termination and pay compensation towards any reasonable expenses incurred by the parents and compensate the parents for any loss of income arising from terminating the pregnancy.

Should the parents not agree to terminate the pregnancy, the following penalties shall be levied on the parents and the subsequent child:

The paternal rights of the embryo's father will be extinguished – preventing the father from exercising any statute or common law rights over the embryo and/or pregnancy; the removal of all state support and aid for the entire life of unborn and born child from the moment of diagnosis through to the death of the child; including: pre-natal care, birth, post-natal care, medical support for the life of the child, education and training for the life of the child, social benefits and social welfare for the life of the child, state-funded housing for both parents and the child, funeral and burial costs of the child.

Notwithstanding that the father had his paternal rights revoked, the father and mother of the child shall be jointly responsible for all costs associated with the child for the full life of the child, including but not limited to any costs defined above.

For the full duration of the life of the child, should the state incur any costs whatsoever in relation to the child, the state shall take action against either or both parents to fully recover these costs. The recovery of costs shall include the sale or liquidation of any asset, including: bank accounts, shares, cars, houses (both primary and secondary), chattels, pension or any other current or future asset whatsoever.

After reading the above, Ivan utters to himself:

IH   Holly shit – they're serious about encouraging terminations.

Ivan closes the book and stares up into space for a while. Then an expression dawns over his blank face – showing that he has just thought of a 'good idea'.

He reaches into his pocket and pulls out the post-it note that Jon Raney gave him an hour or so earlier. He reads the note 'Dr William Horowitz'. A voiceover starts with Ivan reading:

>*Dr William Horowitz, Dr William Horowitz, Dr William Horowitz.*

He looks up trying to recall where he has heard this name before. A memory fades into the screen:

>*Sandra and Ivan are at the Leeds Metropolitan University. Sandra is opening an envelope and pulls out the letter. She screams with excitement and shouts 'I've got an interview with Bradbury, Dywer & Waldron – I'm meeting Dr William Horowitz on the fifth of Feb for a job interview.'*

A second recollection comes drifting onto the screen:

>*Sandra and Ivan are sitting at their dining table in their Croydon Apartment where Sandra is animatedly talking about her great new job – and going on and on about how great her new boss 'Bill' is.*

The scene fades back on with Ivan sipping his coffee – and pondering:

IH   Dr William Horowitz, Dr William Horowitz, Dr William Horowitz – okay Bill, let's give Billy Boy a phone call shall we.

The camera fades out as Ivan is typing numbers into his mobile.

Scene cuts over to the secretary at the law practice taking the call

A female voice slowly fades into the scene, followed by a visual of a secretary taking a phone call … the first distinguishable words heard are:

JC   Sorry sir, I didn't catch your name. I'm sorry, before I can make an appointment for you. I have to be able to inform Dr Horowitz who his client is. As such I do need your name to make an appointment with Dr Horowitz …
No, sorry Dr Horowitz is out now, so you cannot speak to him directly …
No, I don't know when he will be back …
No, I don't know his mobile number. No – nor his pager number.
Actually, I am a good secretary – I make sure Dr Horowitz knows whom he is meeting when he sees his clients.

Scene cuts back to Ivan at Hays Galleria

IH   [Shouting down the phone] Well I hope you get a fucking promotion for being such a good little secretary.

He then throws the mobile onto his table, which bounces off and lands on the paving. The back of the phone comes off – and he then groans.

IH   Damn, now I'll have to re-key-in all my numbers.

He then pauses and thinks for a moment. A very slight sense of mischievousness comes across his face.

Insert Scene – 7

> *Going to work is a misery and a tragedy for the great multitude of boys and girls who have to face it. Suddenly they see their lives plainly defined as limited and inferior. It is a humiliation so great that they cannot even express the hidden bitterness of their souls. But it is there. It betrays itself in derision. I do not believe that it would be possible for contemporary economic life to go on if it were not for the consolations of derision.*
>
> The World of William Clissold *by HG Wells*

Scene 14 – Sandra and Valentina do lunch

12:30pm, Tuesday, 14 May 2013

Setting: Café Rouge at Canary Wharf

Setting: Valentina Henry and Sandra Small are sitting at a table outside Café Rouge at Canary Wharf on a spectacular sunny day, overlooking one of the now unused docks that has ducks leisurely swimming around on it. Sandra is dressed in a very flattering corporate suit. The remains of lunch dishes are on the table, making it obvious both have finished eating. Sandra's knife and fork are randomly placed on the dish, with the remaining food dotted around the plate. Whereas Valentina's knife and fork are placed neatly together with her remaining food neatly moved to the right-hand side of the plate. There is a bottle of Xanadu Semillon Sauvignon Blanc on the table, which is approximately half full.

VH   [voice fades in] … It's absolutely gorgeous, darling, you do look magnificent, your clothes, your shoes, your bag, your hair – well, you really have come of age, what a stunning daughter-in-law I have.

SS   Valentina – thanks, yes I really like the outfit. I needed a new wardrobe, so I thought what the heck, let's go all the way, and while I'm at it, I thought why not check into a beauty salon and go for a complete makeover. So, this is the result – a new me.

VH   It certainly is a new you. It demonstrates your exceedingly developed sense of professional attire and style. And darling, that salon was worth every penny you spent, even if did cost you hundreds of euros – which I can safely assume it did? [Look at Sandra for acknowledgement].

SS   Yes, I agree it was worth it, regardless of the cost. Anyway, thanks for agreeing to have lunch with me. I was apprehensive that you wouldn't accept my invitation after the other night. I'm really embarrassed and really sorry. I want to apologise for what I said and the way I behaved. I was totally out of order.

VH   [*Nods her acceptance of her apology*] Of course, Sandra – we're family and family always forgive and forget.

SS   I just feel very emotionally distraught at the moment, and I really don't know where to turn or what to do … and ever since I've known you, well you've been like the mother I never had.

VH   Sandra, thank you, darling … and I've always looked upon you as the daughter I never had.

SS   It's just that now, [stumbling for words – or lacking confidence to express the words] well – I'm not sure of the appropriateness of having you as a confidant, when what I'm divulging is about your son – and the advice I'm soliciting … well … you know.

VH   What darling, what do I know …?

SS   Well … [emotion boils up to the face, eyes redden and voice goes croaky] I don't want to put you in a position where the advice I'm seeking … is at odds with …

VH   My advice is at odds … with what, darling?

SS   Valentina, look, I think we had better forget this conversation, as I don't think it would be right to put you in this position – I really should have thought about it before …

So, tell me how is the Russian icon exhibition progressing?

VH   Please! We, and I don't think I'm being modest when I say mostly 'I', have secured artwork from Daniil Chyorny, Dionysius, Vladimir, Smolensk, Kazan and Czestochowa – and most importantly, from the master himself, none other than Andrei Rubliov. This will be the most significant exhibition of Russian iconic art to ever be exhibited outside of Russia. Do you know, for all but five of the exhibits, this will be the first time they have travelled outside Russia – including eight works by Rubliov himself. This really is a great honour for us, and for that matter, London.

Anyway, Sandra, while I'm touched by your interest in Russian iconic art and the exhibition. I also know that your interest in Russian iconic art is not the reason you invited me out for lunch.

Valentina pauses while she composes herself.

VH   Sandra, you are very aware that I treat you as my own daughter, so you have every right to ask me what any daughter would ask of her mother. Now, what is the problem … I presume it has something to do with your pregnancy … is this right?

Sandra puts her face in her hands and starts sobbing uncontrollably. She eventually manages to splutter out …

SS   It's just that I don't need this now, not now, not now.

VH   Of course, darling, you don't need to throw away your career just now, I understand.

SS   You know, I'm really doing well at work – they've offered to put me through Oxford … and I don't know if I can do it if I also have to look after a baby and keep working.

VH   They've done what? What did you say? What's this about Oxford? Why haven't you told me this before?

SS   I was going to when you came around for dinner the other night … but the evening sort of fizzled out, and I haven't spoken of it since.

VH   So sorry, darling … tell me more, who, what, when is this Oxford all about?

SS   The firm has offered to pay for my tuition fees for Oxford, keep me on my current salary and only require me to come into the office twenty hours a week.

VH   That is truly magnificent. Congratulations … I'm so proud of you.

SS   Thank you.

VH   That is quite an achievement. I must say that I really didn't think your grades were good enough for Oxford … They have seen your grades, haven't they?

SS   [Curtly] Thank you for being so honest. Yes, they have seen my grades – and yes they still want to interview me.

VH   Well, that is good news – it can prove so disappointing when one is riding on a false hope – only to fall off and hit the ground with a thud. So, you have received an official invitation for the interview?

SS   Yes, in fact a week today, next Tuesday at 2:30.

VH   Fantastic, when would you start – should your application be successful?

SS   In October – the start of the academic year.

VH   Well, that is good news. Let's hope the interview goes well – I'll be praying for you.

      So, presumably, it won't be long now before you're a partner in the firm?

SS   Well it is going to take me seven years part-time to complete the LLB – and that is if I'm accepted. And somehow, I don't think that they'll make me a partner before I finish.

VH   But … at least you're on the path, you're climbing up that old corporate ladder … this really is fantastic news. What does Ivan think about it?

SS   I haven't spoken to him about it as yet. After you left the other night, we had a big fight … and we have hardly spoken to each other since then.

      I've been waiting for the right moment to tell him – so that he too will be excited for me. But, now, when we do speak, it is only to fight.

      To make matters worse, the other night, after I confirmed my pregnancy using another pregnancy test, we had another huge fight and he's been sleeping on the couch in the lounge room ever since.

      So, I'm yet to tell him about Oxford.

VH   Oh dear. The fights, presumably they're about the pregnancy. So, is this what you want to talk about?

SS   [Turning her head/eyes downwards with the weight of sensitivity] Yes.

VH   Ah ha … so … [enticing Sandra to speak].

SS Ivan wants to proceed with the pregnancy!

VH But why?

SS I don't know – I mean it's not like we can't have kids later – you know, after I've at least had some sort of career, or at least managed to climb a couple of rungs up the ladder. To have a child now could just wreck all my career aspirations, not to mention this opportunity that work has just given me.

VH Absolutely, Sandra. But tell me, is it just for career reasons you wish to terminate the pregnancy … or are there any other reasons?

SS [Starts to sob and a sense of embarrassment flashes across her face] Well also … the baby … well it is going to be a … no, it's alright, I can't say. The baby is fine.

   No – it is just for the sake of my career – I mean, as you said, I'm now just starting to take the initial couple of steps up the corporate ladder, and it would be a pity to climb back down now. All I want is to be able to take step after step after step – without crashing back down to the ground. Without my family ridiculing me, saying:

> *'You thought you were better than us didn't ya, going to university, going to London, working at a law firm, well look at you now – all knocked up and nowhere to go. You're nothing. You're no better than us. You're nothing'.*

VH Yes, you have mentioned in the past that your family are not very supportive of your career or your move to London. That certainly creates a challenge for you – to succeed in life in spite of your family rather than because of them.

   However, I sense there is another reason that you are considering a termination … [pauses and carefully, powerfully and strangely maternally engages Sandra eyes].

   The other reason you're thinking of terminating – is it because of the baby will be a dwarf?

Sandra breaks down crying and nods in confirmation – turning her head to avoid Valentina's gaze.

VH   You know, it's not easy having a child that suffers from achondroplasia – it can make things very difficult. For me it was hard enough having a husband who suffered from it. But Igor was well respected in Russia; he was one of the top clowns in the Moscow Circus and a respected theatre dancer, so a degree of stature was bestowed upon him, upon us.

Ivan was understandably very poor at sport, however, he did enjoy Circus School and his Russian dancing. And, I don't know where he got it from, but he was always very keen on his debating – I always put it down to part of his short man syndrome.

SS   Tell me about his debating! At university he'd be up all night preparing and studying for the college debating championships. If that's not enough, he brings his debating skills into our relationship, every argument, every fight is a challenge for him to win on pure intellectual reasoning. It drives me mad.

VH   Yes, I know what you mean – his need to win every argument certainly drove me half insane over the years.

There is a bit of a pause while both Sandra and Valentina reflect for a moment.

VH   You know, he always idolised the father he never had. I guess this is why he tried to follow in his footsteps. But, while he was a good circus performer and quite a good dancer, he was a long way short of perfection. So, unfortunately, he was never going to make it professionally, as to have a career in the arts does require perfection.

However, there is a big difference between having a dwarf child and having a dwarf for a husband. With a child, it's so different, so much harder. Of course you heart goes out to the poor child, all the taunts they get at school, never being selected in any of the sporting teams. The other kids tend to shun your child.

All this makes it so difficult as a parent. Your child is never invited to other kids' places, birthday parties – and also, as a parent, you get left out of the school social scene. When you are invited, the hosts feel awkward or embarrassed about the manner in which they are to approach and treat your child.

And, what's different about having a dwarf child, as opposed to a husband is that, it's a product of yourself – and friends and strangers alike make hurtful inquiries about your own... your own purity, health or hereditary. It is very, very difficult not to get upset about such spiteful inquiries and implied accusations.

If you want my advice, if I had my time over again, I'd terminate any pregnancy where the foetus showed signs of achondroplasia – or any other form of dwarfism!

SS   So – why did you have Ivan, why didn't you abort your pregnancy – I mean you were in the same position as I am in now?

VH   I didn't have someone to advise me like you have – and there were no tests available at the time. Even if there were tests available, I just didn't realise how *difficult* it was going to be to raise a dwarf child.
You don't have the same disadvantages that I suffered. If you don't want to rely on my thoughts and opinions, then I will give you some contacts that have also had to suffer the same experiences as I endured.

As Valentina is talking, under the table, Sandra takes out a mobile phone dials a number – which makes her other mobile phone that is on the table ring. She answers the ringing mobile – pretending it is an important call from the office …

SS   [*Abruptly – and standing suddenly*] I really have to get back to the office. Thanks for meeting me for lunch … I really appreciate your support, not to mention having a lovely lunch.

VH   Okay, bye darling, have a good day – and don't forget, we're seeing Les Misérables this Saturday, that's the eighteenth of May. So be prepared for a good night out!

SS   I've got to go, and yes I will give you a call about the theatre. Must run – bye.

Insert Scene – 8

Of people – mainly women – who use the theatre as an uncritical escape from their daily lives. Suburb-dwellers, spinsters, schoolteachers, women secretaries, proprietresses of teashops, all these, whether bored with jobs or idleness, go to the theatre for their regular dream-hour off. The same instinct leads them which makes many hospital nurses spend all their savings on cosmetics, cigarettes and expensive underclothes.

Louis MacNeice.

Scene 15 – Ivan finds Bill's mobile number

1:00pm, Tuesday, 14 May 2013

Setting: Sandra and Ivan's apartment.

Ivan is flicking through the bill file and comes across a British Telecom bill. He pulls it out and goes through all the dialled numbers – noting all the mobile phone numbers that appear on the statement.

As he is doing so, the sound of mainline trains can be heard approaching and then passing by. A memory fades onto the screen:

> *Sandra and Ivan are in their flat – and Sandra looks up at the clock and shouts 'Oh shit, I was meant to have a report to Bill at 10:00am. He's going to be really pissed – I better phone him and let him know that I won't have it ready until 1:00pm.'*
>
> *[Ivan] What are you talking about? This is Sunday – and we're going to the 'National Summer Exhibition' to see a little art and get our weekly fill of culture.*
>
> *[Sandra] Oh Ivan, look, I'm really sorry – but I gotta get this report out – sorry I thought I'd told you. [As she is talking she is dialling Bill's number on the landline.]*

Memory fades out and Ivan is scrutinising the phone bill – he notes a call made to a mobile number on a particular date at a certain time – 'Bingo – this is it'.

Scene 16 – Bill's pint is rudely interrupted

1:00pm, Tuesday, 14 May 2006

Setting: Coq d'Argent Roof Top Pub

Bill is drinking with work colleagues at the ultra-trendy rooftop pub, Coq d'Argent, drinking with five others from his office – including Laurie Coulson, Theresa Olmsted and three of the male partners that attend the Monday morning strategy meetings. Bill's in the middle of telling a great story, recounting Laurie's and his lunch with Sandra Small.

BH   … and then I said to her, 'and don't dress like that again'.

As Bill delivers this punch line, the six of them all burst out laughing.

LC   You should have seen her – her composure just collapsed – it was incredible.

TO   Bill, whatever your other virtues are – that is, assuming you have any – your shock therapy tactics are untouchable.

       God, I still remember when you took me out for that dreaded lunch, what a nightmare.

Male 1 Yes, Bill has quite the touch. It takes the military years to break down soldiers before they rebuild them into fighting machines. But Bill accomplishes this complex psychological exercise over a lunch.

They all giggle at this last remark.

At this point Bill's mobile phone starts ringing. Bill steps out of the circle of colleagues to take the call.

BH   Hello, Bill Horowitz …

       Yes that's right, I'm Dr Horowitz …

       Sorry, I don't have my diary on me – could I ask you to phone my secretary to book a meeting …

What do you mean she wouldn't schedule a meeting … Why can't you give your name … or place …

Look – I'm really sorry, but I'm really busy. If you would like to meet me – then please phone my secretary and make an appointment, okay? Thank you and goodbye.

With this, Bill terminates the call and rejoins his colleagues.

Scene 17 – Ivan finishing phone call to Bill Horowitz

1:05pm, Tuesday, 14 May 2013

Setting: Sandra and Ivan's apartment

After Bill hangs up on Ivan, he looks dismayed. He remains seated at the dining table in his apartment. On the table is a journal titled 'Journal of British Genetic Law'. Ivan, despondently, picks it up and starts flicking through it. One of the article titles he notes as he flicks through is 'Genetic Screening – Reintroduction of the Survival of the Fittest?' On reading this he picks the journal up and chucks it across the room in anger/disgust. As it spreads out on its way across the room an insert fall out onto the table – advertising a seminar titled 'Genetics, the Law, and your Rights to Immortality'. The flyer has a picture of the presenter 'Dr William Horowitz'.

After a few moments Ivan's gaze into nothing breaks with him slowly becoming conscious of the flyer – after a while he picks it up to view. The flyer reads:

> *Dr William Horowitz, Europe's leading expert in genetic and reproductive law will be holding a free seminar at The Royal Society, 6-9 Carlton House Terrace, London, SW1Y 5AG on Tuesday, 14 May 2013, 6:30pm to 8:30pm.*

IH   [Muttering loudly] Damn.

Ivan types the listed web address into his mobile phone and a webpage near instantly displays the following:

> This seminar is now fully subscribed, we therefore apologies that we are unable to accept your RSVP to attend.

He then phones the number provided. The scene skips ahead with the recipient of Ivan's call responding to Ivan's unheard question:

Rgstr   I'm sorry, sir, but this is an extremely popular seminar, and unfortunately we are unable to accommodate any more attendees. We simply do not have the room to cater for them.

IH   Please, I'm sure you could squeeze in just one more delegate – it is really important that I'm at the seminar. I thought my secretary had booked it, and just now I realised that she hadn't made the booking – thus this phone call. So, please, can I ask you to see if there are any cancellations, or whether I can just stand at the back of the forum? I really do not need to have a seat.

Rgstr Sir, I'm really sorry, but we are well oversubscribed, and we have a long list of people already on our waiting list – should there be any cancellations.

IH   Well fuck you [and throws the phone on the table].

Insert Scene – 9

> *I suppose that by nature, these people would not be so very much more depraved than the ordinary African black fellow. Their essential hideousness comes, I take it, from their essential and abominable hypocrisy.*

The Secret Glory *by Arthur Machen*

Scene 18 – Ivan attempts to gate crash Bill's presentation

6:00pm, Tuesday, 14 May 2013

Setting: the Royal Society

The scene opens from the outside of the Royal Society building, with academics, scientists and the odd corporate making their way up the stairs into the foyer.

The scene then moves inside to the foyer of the building, where it is evident that the evening's event is picking up momentum with groups of colleagues milling around and talking together with a number of delegates queuing to be processed at the registration desk.

Delegates are registered by producing their written invitation together with proof of identity, whereupon they are given their name badge. In the background a person (Duncan Thomilson) attempts to bypass the protocol by walking straight through to the seminar room, but is discretely stopped by internal security and asked to register:

SG   Sir, I am sorry, but only registered delegates can be admitted to the seminar room. Can I ask you to go to the desk and register?

DT   [Disgruntled, as his plans to bypass security were foiled] Oh, okay.

Duncan walks to the registration desk and explains his plight to the registrar

DT   I'm Duncan Thomilson and it appears that I have lost my invitation. However, I did register online and I do have some personal identification on me.

Rgstr Mr Thomilson, I must apologise. For security reasons, only delegates with a written invitation can attend the seminar. So, if you do not have your invitation with you, unfortunately, we will not be able to admit you into the seminar.

DT   Well, you are expecting me, look you have my name badge already printed and waiting for me to collect it. Look, here's my driver's licence, that must satisfy your security requirements, doesn't it?

Rgstr   Mr Thomilson, as I said, only delegates with their written invitation will be admitted to the seminar. If you do not have your invitation with you, then you will not be admitted. Do you have any other questions?

DT   [Realising he is not going to win this argument] No, no more questions. Thank you for your time.

In conceding defeat, Duncan, turns and sulks away towards the building's front door. In the background, Jon Raney can be seen registering. Ivan enters the foyer and looks around – clearly a little phased by the opulence, prestige and reputation of the Royal Society's building – together with all the very well-attired corporate delegates. Ivan is dressed in a suit, but, notwithstanding his short stature, it is obviously a cheap and tacky suit together with a tacky unironed shirt and tie.

Ivan observes the registration protocol for a minute or so – then notices a delegate (that is yet to register – as he is talking to a colleague near the entrance) who has a leather writing folder in his arms with his name etched into it in gold, 'Anthony Barrett, Life Extension Corporation'.

Ivan then walks up to the registration desk and attempts to register:

IH   Hi, I'm Anthony Barrett from the Life Extension Corporation and I'd like to register for this evening's seminar.

Rgstr   Can you show me your invitation please?

IH   Apologies, I was not aware that I had to bring my invitation with me.

Rgstr   I'm sorry sir, it was very clearly written on the invitation that in order to complete your registration and attend the lecture, you would have to produce your written invitation.

IH   Apologies, I must confess that I did not read my invitation that closely.

    However, as you can see – I am invited – see there is my name badge [pointing the name badge already printed for Anthony Barrett].

Rgstr   Yes, I am aware that a name badge has been pre-printed for a Mr Anthony Barrett. However, our security rules require all attendees to produce their written invitation and proof of identity to register and attend a seminar.

Therefore, unless you can produce your written invitation, I will have to ask you to leave.

IH   [With raised voice.] Look, you can see that I have been invited. There is my name tag. What banal security policy do you have that cannot recognise your own name badge? Now, can I please ask you to do the common-sense thing and pass me my name tag and let me in?

At this point, due to the raised voices, a security guard becomes alerted to the conversation, moves closer to the desk and listens into the conversation, in anticipation that he may need to become more actively involved in the situation.

Rgstr   Sir, our security procedures are designed to protect all attendees and staff of the Royal Academy. They are not designed to make up for the lapse in your personal organisation ability.

As such, if you cannot produce your invitation, I must ask you to leave.

IH   Look, this is ridiculous. You know that I'm invited – so what's the problem.

Rgstr   Sir, either you show me your invitation right now – or leave right now. Otherwise, I will call security – understand? [As she says this she gives a quick glance in the direction of the security guard that had been listening to the conversation – both Ivan and the security guard saw and understood the meaning behind the 'glance'].

Ivan turns and walks out the entrance. He then attempts to hide himself within a group of six who, having already completed their registration, are all walking into the seminar room together. Ivan worms his way into the centre of this group and is successful in passing the security guards at the entrance to the seminar doors. Just when it appears as though he has made it into the seminar room, a tall guy (TG) immediately in front of him says to the others:

TG   We've lost Jayne. I'll go back and get her.

As he turns around and starts to walk back he trips over Ivan and they both end up on the floor.

TG   I am so sorry, I did not see you there. Please let me help you up.

While Ivan doesn't say anything, he glares at the tall guy with a fierce look.

IH   Arsehole

The security guard that had witnessed Ivan's encounter with the registrar now sees Ivan and approaches him.

SG   Sir, you are to leave the building now. I shall escort you to the door.

The scene ends (fades out) with Ivan exiting the building with most of those still in the foyer area looking on with a degree of bemusement.

Insert Scene – 10

There goes on a rapid increase of low-grade population, undersized physically and mentally, and retarding the mechanical development of civilisation.

The Open Conspiracy: Blue Prints for a World Revolution *by HG Wells*

Scene 19 – Juxtaposition scenes: Bill warms while Ivan shivers

6:30pm, Tuesday, 14 May 2013

Setting: the Royal Society

These two juxtaposition scenes contrast: Bill giving his presentation to an appreciative audience and Ivan waiting outside in the cold and drizzle.

Outside: The camera has picked up on Ivan (rear view) as he walks outside the door of the Royal Society. He turns around and gives the 'fuck you' one-finger salute to the security guard – but really to the establishment. He walks to the side of the entrance steps – just inside the shadow (of the light from inside the building) and, in an act of defiance, pisses on the steps.

Inside: The camera cuts from Ivan pissing to the pouring of Champagne into Bill's glass – the focus then broadens to encompass Bill talking with his 'admirers'. Bill warmly and energetically talks to his admirers, thoroughly enjoying the pre-presentation drinks and the general ambiance. Bill chats in his usual charismatic manner with a large smile and enthusiastic discussion. As he talks the camera pans around those listening. From their expression it is obvious that they are 'enchanted' by Bills energy.

Outside: *The camera cuts over to Ivan, who is finishing his piss and reaches down and attempts to find his zip end to zip himself up. As he fumbles with his zip, arriving delegates give him very disapproving looks.*

Inside: *The camera focuses on Bill as he swirls the Champagne and smells it – then brings the glass up to his lips.*

Outside: *Ivan finally finds the end of his zip and, with a quick jerk, zips up his trousers.*

Inside: *Bill swirls Champagne in mouth and visibly and audibly swallows.*

Outside: *Ivan turns to view and scowl at the disapproving onlookers and spits in their general direction.*

Inside: Bill turns to engage in conversation with a small waiting party behind him – with the obvious delight of those in the party.

Outside:

IH Haven't you ever seen a man take a piss before [and proceeds to give them a one-finger salute].

Inside:

BH I've never been in such good company before – why, it is so good to see you all [and proceeds to warmly shake their hands].

Outside: Ivan turns and starts to walk down the stairs – head and shoulders stooped.

Inside: Bill turns and walks up the stairs to the lectern – full of confidence and charm.

Insert Scene – 11

> *To learn plainly to hate mankind,*
> *to detest the spawning human being, That is the only cleanliness now.*

> *A Letter to: Mr Waldo Frank from DH Lawrence*
> *15 September 1917*

Scene 20 – Bill delivers to the Royal Society

7:00pm, Tuesday, 14 May 2013

Setting: the Royal Society

BH   I cannot tell you how much I enjoy coming to the Royal Society – whether to enjoy the great company one always finds here, to listen and be challenged and educated by presenters or, like on this occasion, to come and share a few of my thoughts on the urgency of advancing the genetics programme.

I think you will all share my belief that we live in the time foreseen by Confucius – when he cursed his nemesis with the now famous phase 'may you live in interesting times'. However, to me, it isn't a curse, it is a blessing. I ask you, if time travel were possible, would any of you seriously consider, voluntarily, travelling to another time to live – to live forever – for the rest of your life? I know I wouldn't. I admit, I'd love to be a time tourist – going back and seeing the events in history that got us to this point. The leaving of the Garden of Eden, the great flood, the exodus, the building of Solomon's Temple etc.

But, time tourism would be a little like leaving London for a holiday in the Seychelles. The Seychelles is a great place to visit and relax, but I always want to return home to London to live. I always want to return to London, not just because it is the greatest city in the world, but because this is where all the action is – this is the leading city in the world for genetic research, medical diagnosis based on genetics, ethical and philosophical genetic debates and, of course the leading genetic legislation, regulator and regulations. With all this action in London, who would want to live anywhere else?

Call me a chronocentralist if you like. However, if I had the ability to time travel and live in any era – past, present or future, I'd always return to the twenty-first century to live my life out – more specifically, even if I had a choice, I'd still live my life over the exact period that the current laws of physics and relativity demand that I do. The reason I call the twenty-first century home is not because there hasn't been, or won't be, other fantastic eras to live in, but because this century will prove to be the greatest century in the history of the homo sapiens species – both past and future.

Why, you may ask, do I say this century will be the greatest ever, past and future, for us, for our species, for homo sapiens? You may dismiss my assertion as pure arrogance, as we have no idea what future centuries hold in store for us humans. You may well assert that there must be a better century somewhere in the future to live in.

It is true that I don't know what future centuries hold for us – but, I am very confident they will not hold a candle to the seminal advances that this century will make in the advancement of our own species. To explain this, let me put my assertion into perspective – first by giving a flying overview of the history of our species – then speculating on future advancements.

So, to start at the very beginning: Our planet is 4.5 billion years old. Life started on Earth around 4 billion years ago. About 2 billion years later – something fantastic happened –sex was invented. Yes, that's right, it was not invented in the seventh decade of the twentieth century – nor during the dot.com boom of the first decade of the twenty-first century. Before sex, new varieties of organisms could only arise from the accumulation of random mutations – the selection of changes, letter by letter, in the genetic instructions. Evolution must have been agonizingly slow. With the invention of sex, two organisms could exchange whole paragraphs, pages and books of their DNA code, producing new varieties ready for the sieve of selection. This created the environment where organisms were selected by other organisms to have sex with in order to exchange the DNA in their offspring. The fit had more offers than the unfit. Those organisms that found sex uninteresting – or weren't selected by others to have sex with, well, they quickly become extinct. This is as true, not only of the microbes of two billion years ago, but equally of the complex society that we find ourselves living in today. As the late great Carl Sagan observed, even today, we humans also have a palpable devotion to exchanging segments of our DNA.

While life has been on this planet for 4 billion years and for 2 billion years these life forms have been having sex – complex life forms have only been around for about 540 million years. By complex life forms, I refer to the development of the first homeotic genes that evolved during the Cambrian explosion, a time of free experiments in body design. It was during the short period of the Cambrian explosion that at least 19, and perhaps as many as 35, of the 40 known phyla made their first appearance on Earth.

Jumping several hundred million years of evolution history, between five and seven million years ago – our ancestors split off from the chimpanzee – and pursued their own evolutionary path. Looking at this event as a time-mark in Earth's life history, this event came in the last 0.2% of the history of life on Earth.

Around 100,000 years ago, Adam and Eve were born, the man and woman in Eastern Africa, who all people on Earth today can trace their ancestry back to. Around 85,000 years ago, the first migration out of Africa took place, when some adventurers crossed the Red Sea at the Gate of Grief, whose descendants went on to conquer every other continent on Earth.

The first complex civilisations came into existence with the Sumerians, between the Tigress and Euphrates rivers around 6,000 BC, in what is now Iraq.

The Sumerians are the fathers of civilisation. They are the ones that developed agriculture, skill diversity and specialisation, the written word, government and bureaucracy, money, maths, accountancy and all that is required to have a successful metropolis.

So we have the Sumerians to thank for changing us, as a species, from subsistence farming cave dwellers that lived in communities defined strictly by family or tribe. They taught us to be cosmopolitan, possibly even to be 'politically correct' – God bless them. They gave us so much, including bronze, the wheel, iron mongering, modern building techniques and architecture together with the development of many of the religious fables we still hold closely to – including genesis, the great flood and many others. However, their biggest contribution, including the development of the wheel, is to teach us to live with each other and to respect each other – to be civilised.

The next event that changed us in the way we as a species thought of ourselves was the Egyptian civilisation. Even today, none of us can fail to be awe struck when we see the pyramids, to gaze in disbelief at their stunning jewellery, their tombs, the row of awesome statues in the Valley of the Kings. Their belief and obsession in the afterlife taught us how to be proud, how to be grand, how to conquer nature, how to engineer on a grand scale. Today, all of us are still proud of these achievements. Still, today their efforts, their civilisation moves us, and we all share in the collective pride of their achievements.

The next gift we received was from the little known, little recognised Ionian civilisation that made a colossal contribution to humanity. These are the guys who developed and gave the world the concept and practice of the 'experiment'. Today, our 'scientific method' has its foundation in experimentation. Unfortunately, this gift was to be not only ignored, but also scorned upon for some 2,000 years. It wasn't until Kepler and Galileo unwrapped the beauty of this precious gift that the Ionian method of science took root and thrived – of course, if it hadn't we wouldn't be here tonight discussing genetics.

Then of course we have the Greeks. In the context of my discussion, trying to identify and define events, practices and knowledge that fundamentally changed our view of ourselves, I say Ancient Greece's contribution is immense, encompassing architecture, literature, math, science and of course philosophy. It's pretty impressive, 2,370 years after it was first published, Plato's Republic is still in print. I'd be chuffed if anyone can remember this lecture by the time you get home tonight. Aristotle had such an impact on science and maths, that his textbooks were still being used in universities as 'the text' 2,200 years after his death.

So in what way did the Ancient Greeks change our outlook on ourselves? Well, the Alexandria library is where we humans first collected, then seriously and systematically studied, all knowledge of the world. The Greeks taught us that we were intelligent; they taught us to be passionate about learning, knowledge and scientific discovery.

The Romans' contribution was one of scale. The Romans taught us that we can all live as one nation, one big, big nation in harmony and peace. Sure, for most of the Roman Empire they were at war somewhere in the world, but these wars were at the fringes of its empire. The heartland, the conquered areas, remained for the most part in peace – aside from the short incident with our friend Spartacus.

After the Romans, what was the next development that fundamentally changed our view of ourselves? Looking at history, nothing really flies off the page until we come across the works of Copernicus, Kepler and Galileo. These three gentlemen did change our view of our place in the world – or more correctly, our place in the wider universe. Between them, by maths, theory and observation conclusively established that the sun is at the centre of our solar system – not us – not the Earth. From this point on we, as humans, became aware that the universe was not built for us, not built around us. We became aware that we were merely a part of a larger, more complex system.

Since the three aforementioned gentlemen, we've had a bit of a rush when it comes to individuals making discoveries which fundamentally redefined our relationship with ourselves, the wider world and to the wider universe. I will spare you the details, but briefly, the guys that I think have had the biggest impact are:

- Newton – who not only recognised gravity as a force, but was able to accurately measure it across space. As an aside, he also gave us Principia and, every school kid's favourite, calculus.
- Darwin – who crushed our creationist view of the world.
- Nietzsche – who first articulated as a concept what the works of Galileo, Newton, and Darwin were suggesting but never made explicit – yes it was Nietzsche who said 'God is Dead', long live the superman. Asking each of us to become responsible for our own lives, our own decisions, our own destiny – not to baulk at these responsibilities by passing them onto an intangible God.
- Freud and Jung who showed us that there is more to our minds than just conscious thought, and demonstrated the existence of the collective unconscious.
- George Lemaître – who gave us the Big Bang Theory.
- Hubble – who showed us just how big our universe is, its limits and our place in it.
- Einstein – who redefined the nature of our universe – 'Matter is not matter anymore'.
- Heisenberg – who, with his Uncertainty Principle, single-handedly blew away the concept and philosophy of Determinism. Thus we now know nothing is certain – in essence everything is up for grabs.
- Crick and Watson – who cracked the DNA code – the secret to life. In doing so, again it challenged or shattered religious concepts as what it is to be human. We're human, because our DNA states we are, not because of divine intervention.
- Hawking – who showed us that we live in one of an infinite number of universes, further shattering the concept, religious or not, that God created only this universe, for our development and enjoyment. The fact is that there are zillions of universes out there – so why is ours so special? Why does our universe get God's favour? And if other universe end in destruction – why can't ours?

As you can appreciate, we have come through some wonderful ages of discoveries, great science, philosophy and maths, that have cumulatively defined our 'Woustanchow' the German word for 'view of the world'. And now each of us lives every day with this collective view of the world. Each and every one of us lives, perceives and believes our world and our universe to be the model defined by the above giants. Without these giants we would not have this model of the universe – nor understand our place in it. Without this model, we all would still be thinking Earth was flat, that the sun revolves around the Earth, that the universe was static. Without the model created by these geniuses, as far as our view of the world goes, there would be nothing that distinguished us from cavemen who lived 50 thousand years ago.

So, with the above developments and discoveries, each of which fundamentally and permanently changed our view of ourselves within our universe – if you will – the universe of universes – why am I here tonight proudly telling you all 'this' is the golden age, that this is the age I would choose to live in – if I had my choice of any age?

The answer is simple – but I'll use an analogy to answer it, so here goes.

If we had the opportunity to communicate with another intelligent life form from another solar system, say by radio communication, in order for us to assess their level of maturity – both as a civilisation and their level of intellectual and technological advancement – we would ask them four questions:

- Where are you from? Which Darwin answered for us.
- Where are you now? Which Copernicus, Kepler, Galileo, Hubble and Hawking answered for us.
- What defines you as a species and an individual? Which Crick and Watson answered for us.
- What powers your sun? Which Einstein answered for us.

If they replied that God created them; or that they are at the centre of the universe; or that astrology or some other form of metaphysics defines their individuality or their species; or their sun was powered by means other than nuclear fusion, then we would know they have not reached the level of maturity, the level of knowledge and technological development, that we have.
The above are the four benchmark questions that we would use to assess the maturity of another intelligent life form.

However, life forms more advanced than us would ask us a few questions in response, namely:

- Where are you going?
- How are you going to get there?
- What will you be?

Why these three questions?

For the same reason as we asked our four questions. We would be asked these three questions so that the more advanced form of intelligence could assess our state of knowledge, maturity and technological advancement – in comparison to theirs.

But why these three questions specifically? What have they got to do with our level of maturity as a technologically advanced life form? The answer lies in the mortality of planets, solar systems, stars and galaxies and ultimately our universe.

Take Earth. If, as improbable as it sounds, each nation adopted, introduced and enforced the most stringent planet-friendly policies and practices, our planet will still die. In a few billion years our sun will deplete its hydrogen fuel supply and start expanding. As it expands, it will eventually engulf Earth. If not before, at least at this point in our planetary life cycle there will not be a single living cell left on our planet. Therefore, even with the most wildly optimistic forecasts, we cannot live on this planet forever. All the environmentally friendly policies and practices will merely allow us to live on this planet longer – but certainly not forever.

As such, the three questions that will be put to us will be designed to determine the extent to which we realise the mortality of our planet and the provisions and contingencies we've made to overcome planet-threatening events.

Many of you here tonight may be thinking – sure, the planet won't last forever, but, hey, we're not in any immediate danger. So if we can't answer these three questions, so what? It doesn't make us cosmic rednecks. Essentially, many of you will be thinking, why waste precious resources developing planetary or species contingency plans when we don't need them?

Well – you're wrong. You are so very wrong. There have been many, many instances in which we as a species have been close, so very, very close to being taken out – either at a planetary level or a species level. I'll briefly reflect on a few near misses that we've had, kicking off with just a few species-threatening events, which naturally includes our genetic ancestry:

- We are descendants of apes, which almost became extinct 15 million years ago when they faced competition from the better designed monkey.
- We are descendants of primates, which nearly became extinct 45 million years ago when they faced competition from the better designed rodents.
- We are descendants of synapsid tetrapods, a group of reptiles that almost became extinct 200 million years ago when they faced competition from the dinosaurs.
- We are descendants from limbed fishes, which almost became extinct 360 million when they faced competition from the better designed ray-finned fishes.
- We are descendants from chordates, a phylum which very, very nearly became extinct when they faced competition from the brilliantly successful arthropods – 500 million years ago.
- And of course before that we descended from the roundish-flatworm that existed some 530 million years ago, when we all in danger of being used for fishing bait by a higher life form – fortunately for us, neither fish nor the higher life form existed at the time.

Now a few planetary threatening events:

- Approximately 600 million years ago, the Earth was nearly completed covered in snow and ice – only the odd 'pool' of uncovered sea water here and there kept life on the planet from complete extinction.
- The brutal and sustained volcanic activity that managed to break the Earth free from the snowball effect released so much carbon dioxide into the atmosphere that it was 350 times the level we experience today, i.e. about thirteen percent of the atmosphere. Now, that's what I call a greenhouse – an atmosphere that we humans could not survive in.
- The Permian–Triassic extinction event, also known as the 'Great Dying' occurred approximately 251 million years ago, which killed off 96% of all marine species and 70% of terrestrial vertebrate species and is the only known mass extinction of insects. This was caused by a giant meteorite.

- The Cretaceous–Tertiary mass extinction was caused by a ten kilometre meteorite hitting the Yucatan Peninsula in Mexico about 65 million years ago, where it gouged out a crater about 180 kms in diameter. The impact killed 99% of all life and 75% of all species – including of course the dinosaurs.
- An asteroid fragment, about 100m diameter, hit Arizona about 20,000 years ago, leaving the one kilometre wide 'Arizona Meteor Crater'. Again, if this was bigger or hit a populated area – then it could have had a devastating impact.
- At 7:17am on 30 June 1908 a meteor hit the Tunguska forests of Siberia, unleashing the equivalent energy of a 15 megaton nuclear bomb, which flattened more than 800 square miles of forest – equal to about 60 million trees. Witnesses described 'deafening bangs' and a 'fiery cloud on the horizon'. However, in asteroid terms, it was a relatively small player, only around 50–60 metres in diameter. If it had hit a city, the death toll would have been enormous. If it had been much bigger, it may well have had a global affect. In fact it did – the impact spewed so much dust into the atmosphere that the reduced light caused global temperatures to be measurably lower for the subsequent two years.
- In 1972, a 1,000-ton object skimmed tangentially through Earth's atmosphere over the Grand Tetons in Wyoming, USA, and then skipped back out into space like a stone skipping off water. It was photographed by tourists and detected by Air Force satellites. Had it continued on into the atmosphere, it could have caused a Hiroshima-scale explosion somewhere over Canada.
- In total, there have been about 60 meteorites with diameters in excess of five kilometres that have hit the Earth in the past 600 million years. The smallest ones have left craters 95 kilometres wide. Any of these impacts had the potential to wipe us out a species or possibly sanitise the whole planet.

While none of the above quite took out our planet – some went dangerously close. To illustrate how close, let's check what our neighbours have experienced:

- Mars still bears the scars of three massive celestial impacts – the Hellas, Isidis and Argyre craters. They have diameters of 2,000, 1,000, and 630 km across. The Hellas crater is 5 km deep. The meteorites that caused these are estimated to be 100 km, 50 km and 36 km in diameter respectively. The meteorite that caused the Hellas crater penetrated the Martian crust and continued into the planet's interior magma – causing such stress and shock waves that it created the Tharsis Bulge on the opposite side of the planet.

- In addition to these three monster craters, Mars has more than 3,000 craters greater than 30 kms – dozens of which are in excess of 250 kilometres.
- Had any of these meteorites hit Earth, rather than Mars, Earth would be as barren and lifeless as Mars is now.
- More recently, between 16 and 22 July 1994, 21 fragments of comet Shoemaker-Levy 9, some of which were in excess of 2 kilometres in diameter, slammed into Jupiter. The largest fragment, fragment G, released the equivalent energy of 6,000,000 megatons of TNT – or 750 times the world's nuclear arsenal. The resulting impact created a dark spot over 12,000 km across – easily large enough to swallow the entire Earth. If fragment G had hit Earth, rather than Jupiter, it would have sanitised all life on Earth.
- Closer to home, on the 25 June 1178, five people in Canterbury witnessed a meteor hit the moon. The impact of the meteor, as we can now ascertain, created the 22 km wide 'Giordano Bruno' crater. Again, if this meteor hit Earth, rather than the moon, you would be spared having to listen to me tonight.

While the above list is far, far from a comprehensive account of all life-threatening events – it does go some way to illustrate that, looking back over the last half billion years or so, we have had some very, very close calls.

But we needn't dwell on the past – because we've survived it, we're here. Now that we are here, in this room, at this time, on this planet – is the game won? Are we now safe? Will we now live forever? Will no bad times return?

Of course not. Planetary threatening events are part of cosmic life. Take a star in our neighbourhood, a white dwarf called 'HR 8210'. Soon it will explode in a supernova. Unfortunately it is only 150 light years away – which is well short of the 160–200 light years thought to be the minimum safe distance from a supernova. When it explodes the high-energy electromagnetic radiation and cosmic rays that will hit us will destroy our ozone layers within minutes – giving little chance of life surviving on our planet. Fortunately for our generation – 'soon' in astronomical language means within the next few hundred million years. But put this in perspective, the Cambrian explosion only happened 540 million years ago.

An event that may be closer to us on the time horizon is the accelerating deterioration in the strength of the Earth's magnetic field. Should the current rate of deterioration continue, by 3000 to 4000 AD, the dipole field will have collapsed. Our protective magnetic field is already 35% weaker than it was 2,000 years ago. Once the dipole field collapses, then the solar winds emanating from the sun will pound the Earth and, over time, strip away our atmosphere. In the absence of an atmosphere and oxygen, our mother Earth will no longer support life.

Returning to the threat of asteroids, based on the findings of the Spaceguard program, NASA predicts that there are more than 20,000 large, potentially dangerous objects that pass in close proximity to Earth and, given the proper circumstance, any one of these asteroids could threaten or severely impact our existence. Sooner or later, one of these babies is going to hit us and take us out. To quote Carl Sagan again, 'It is a statistical certainty that we will be hit by a killer asteroid sometime in the future.'

However, there is an even more imminent danger, namely manmade disasters. While there are many, many examples of 'near' manmade mass extinction events, I'll cite just four here:

- During the height of the 1962 Cuban missile crisis, Robert Kennedy, the then attorney general, opined to his brother, the President John F. Kennedy, that there was a 50 percent chance that the crisis would lead to an all-out nuclear war. As the attorney general and the president's most trusted advisor, more than anyone else, he must have had the best intelligence on the situation. For our continued existence to be subject to the outcome of a throw of a coin – is inconceivably scary.
- On 26 September 1983 – the Soviet's missile detection computers wrongly identified a US nuclear missile attack. The error was caused by the alignment of sunlight on high-altitude clouds and the Soviet's early warning satellite. Given the intelligence they received from the satellite, the Soviet's procedures and training required a retaliatory attack to be launched. If it wasn't for the defiance of a single man, Colonel Stanislav Petrov, who refused to issue the order to counter-strike, we'd all be dead now.
- Later in 1983, on the 2 November, NATO commenced a ten-day nuclear war simulation exercise codenamed Able Archer 83. The exercise involved heads of state and raising the Nuclear Military Alert

from DEFCON 5 to DEFCON 1 – which put the nuclear arsenal at ready to launch status. However, no one thought to tell the Soviets of the war game and the exercise proved so realistic that the Soviets thought it was for real. They believed the only way they could survive a NATO strike was to make a pre-emptive strike and as such they put their huge array of nuclear arsenal on 'launch status' – primed for a pre-emptive strike. The CIA later reported that the Soviets had armed nuclear-capable aircraft which were 'readying for a nuclear strike'. Fortunately, the Able Archer exercise finished just in time to stop this accidental nuclear war.

- On 25 January 1995 again the Soviet early warning system identified a missile attack from off the cost of Norway. They were aware that this single missile, if launched from a US submarine, could split into eight separate nuclear strikes over Moscow within fifteen minutes. This was escalated to President Boris Yeltsin, and for the first time ever the presidential 'nuclear briefcase' was activated in readiness to launch a retaliatory attack. The military monitored the missile until they were just two minutes shy of the procedural deadline to launch a retaliatory attack in response to an impending nuclear attack on Russia. Fortunately in the final minutes, they determined that the missile was heading out to sea and was not a threat to Russia. The missile turned out to be a high-altitude experiment – which the Norwegians had informed Russia of weeks earlier – but this had not been communicated to the appropriate guys in the military.

Each of these four incidents took us perilously close to an all -ut nuclear war. As ghastly as the Cold War was, during this time there were really only two trigger points – the Soviets and the US, arguably both of which were reasonably stable and sensible. And yet even with only these two trigger points, over the course of a 33-year period we had four instances which took us to the brink of a manmade mass extinction which, in comparison, would have made the Yucatan meteorite mass extinction look like a little global delousing.

In the post-Cold-War world, there is an ever increasing number of trigger points, arguably many of whom are not so stable and sensible. The contenders for starting a nuclear war now include the United States, Russia, the United Kingdom, France, China, Israel, India, Pakistan, Iran and North Korea.

It is often said that if the 1908 Siberian meteorite had landed during the height of the Cold War – due to the ferocity of the ensuing explosion – it would have been deemed a nuclear attack, which may well lead to an all-out nuclear war. If a Siberian-sized meteorite was to land in any of the ten nuclear armed countries today, their military may well think that they have been subjected to a nuclear attack. From which they may conclude that more missiles are on their way. In this situation, their military procedures probably dictate 'Launch Retaliatory Strike'. If they do not have someone at the helm like Colonel Stanislav Petrov, it will be goodbye world.

Even without a meteorite event, there is enough instability within the ten nuclear armed countries to become very, very nervous about the prospects of a nuclear war. Let's face it, with only two stable trigger points – we went to the very brink of a nuclear war on four separate occasions. Will we be so lucky over the next 50 years?

Now, even if the impossible happens and we miraculously escape being hit by a killer asteroid, escape being killed by supernova radiations, we weather the solar storms brought on by the collapse of our protective magnetic field, we reverse global warming and we avert an all-out nuclear war – even if we do all that – our planet will still die. If nothing else, our planet will die of solar system old age. In about 7.5 billion years' time, the sun will start to exhaust its nuclear fuel supply, expand and slowly consume Mercury, Venus and then Earth.

Obviously, before this happens, the heat from the expanding sun will sanitise all life from our planet.

This brings us back to the line of questioning put to us by our extra-terrestrial cousins, designed to determine our awareness of our cosmic fate. In short, if we don't build planetary contingency plans, our species, our heritage, our life, sooner or later, will die.

So let's return to the three questions that the more advanced intelligence put to us – and give our state of preparedness to answer them:

Astronomers have now identified in excess of 300 extrasolar planets, and more are being discovered every week. So far, only one has been identified as a 'Goldilocks' planet – i.e. it is not too hot, not too cold, not too big not too small, not too wet, not too dry. The planet, Gliese 581C, may prove habitable, but chances are that it won't, as once we learn more about it; it may have no water, or is covered in water; it may have no soil, or poisonous soil; it may not have any oxygen, or its atmosphere may be toxic, or a thousand other factors that could make it inhospitable to us sensitive earthlings. However, the discovery of Gliese 581C is important – as it is the first planet discovered that has the 'potential' to support us. Now we need to find hundreds, if not thousands of others, so that eventually we identify one that is hospitable for us humans. By mid-century, we may well have identified a planet that has the potential to support life as we know it. So, within the next 40-odd years, we should be able to answer the first question; 'Where are you going'?

But clearly we cannot answer this question at the moment.

The second question: how are you going to get there?

This probably is the toughest question. The sheer magnitude of space, the distances involved make this an engineering nightmare – but I must emphasise it is an engineering nightmare, not an engineering impossibility.

To travel to Gliese 581C, the only planet we've identified so far that has the potential to support life as we know it, is a 20.4 light year one-way trip.

To date, the fastest we have propelled an object was the Helios II probe sent to observe the sun. On 17 April 1976, it reached a speed of 241,350 km/h. If we were to travel at this speed to colonise Gliese, the mission would take approximately 91,000 years to reach its destination. Even if we were to travel in excess of four times this speed at 1 million km/h, the trip would still be a 23,000 year one-way trip.

The only option available to us in regards to propulsion for this distance and duration is nuclear fusion energy.

Aside from the development of the hydrogen bomb, it has proved incredibly difficult to actually harness and use fusion energy in a controlled manner. However, the Joint European Torus facility did have some success. In 1997 it produced a peak of 16.1 MW of fusion power during a fusion burn sustained over half a second.

In June 2005, the construction of the experimental reactor, the 'International Thermonuclear Experimental Reactor', or ITER for short, was announced, which is being designed to have a 500 second burn. After ITER, which incidentally means 'The Way' in Latin, the third generation fusion generator, DEMO, is to be designed to both (a) produce more energy than it consumes; and (b) to operate on a continual basis.

Notwithstanding, the significant progress we have made in the design and development of fusion generators, realistically, we will not have a generator capable of continuous energy production, in excess of what it consumes, for at least another 50 years.

However, in the context of the question 'how are you going to get there?' a 50-year time horizon is just acceptable, i.e. we will get to our new planet by the use of a nuclear fusion reactor, even if we are 50 years away from developing such a reactor.

In his 1991 Spitzer lecture, Carl Sagan put it a little more eloquently with:

Every time you look up at the sky, every one of those points of light is a reminder that fusion power is extractable from hydrogen and other light elements, and it is an everyday reality throughout the Milky Way galaxy.

Thus, indeed fusion energy is 'The Way'.

This brings us to the third and final question: what will you be? What does this question mean? What will we be? Human of course. What a stupid question. Except for the fact that humans as we know them, in all probability, will neither survive the 23,000 year trip to this other planet nor the planet itself once our spaceship lands.

This is the paradox. To survive the death of our planet – we have to travel to another. But, we will neither survive the trip to the other planet nor the new planet's hostile environment once we get there. So how do we survive?

To survive, we have to send someone else – someone non-human – who can survive a near eternity travelling to the new planet then thrive in the planet's toxic atmosphere and environment.

But why would we, as humans, expend all the resources required to get to another planet, only to save someone else, to save another species. I mean the whole idea is to save us, save our own species right? Not something else, not a cucumber, not my pet dog Rover, not some really intelligent chimpanzee. If for no other reason, a cucumber, a dog, a chimpanzee wouldn't know how to control the spacecraft and certainly wouldn't be able to colonise the new hostile planet once it arrived. And besides, if cucumbers want to survive the next mass extinction, then they can build their own spaceship.

This brings us back to the paradox. To survive the death of our planet we have to leave home. But it can't be us that leaves – because we are too fragile to survive both the trip and the new home. And, no one else is up for the job.

It is solving this paradox that makes this, our age, the most exciting age ever to live and work.

The four questions we put to the extra-terrestrial intelligence were about the past – self- discovery, self-consciousness and about awareness of the laws of the universe.

Conversely, the three questions they put to us, particularly the last question, are about the future, about self-development, about self-control, about seizing the controls of cosmic fate and steering it in any direction we desire – or possibly the 'direction we must travel'.

This age, the age that you and I live in now, is the age of cosmic self-determination. How we step up to the plate to fulfil the challenge laid down to us by this imaginary superior extra-terrestrial intelligence that asks us these three forward-looking questions will define this age, will define our age, as the golden age of science and more importantly the golden age of all humanity.

To solve the paradox, we have to redefine what it is to be human. We need to redefine humanism, because we want to save humanity by colonising other planets, without killing us by sending us on death trips or deadly planets.

The reason why our age is the golden age, is that we, the people alive today, the people in this city, the very people in this room, will redefine 'what it is to be human'. Once redefined, we collectively will advance all humanity to new levels of existence.

I put it to you, the best genetic minds in the world assembled at the Royal Society tonight, what is it that makes us human?

The answer to this question is the solution to the paradox I highlighted previously.

And the answer is of course – 'our genetic uniqueness defines us as human'. We have been shaped, sculptured, engineered, tried and tested over 4 billion years of genetic evolution on Earth. The social natural selection process working hand-in-hand with the environmentally imposed survival-of-the-fittest obstacle course has evolved those first self-replicating molecules into the complex 100 trillion-plus cell structure that today we call 'human'. It is the genetic code, the genetic heritage, the genetic fingerprint in each one of us, in each of our cells that defines me, defines us as humans. The genetic code in each of us distinguishes us apart from all other life on this planet.

While we may share 98.7% of our genetic code with our closest relative, the chimpanzee, it is the 1.3% difference that distinguishes us as human. This slight difference is what allows us to think, through deduction and induction, to discover the laws of nature, the laws of the universe, the ability to design and build spaceships to carry us to far away solar systems.

Can I ask – who broadly agrees with the answer I just gave?

Bill scans the lecture theatre and notes broad acceptance from those assembled, evidenced by slight nodding.

Well, I say bollocks to the above argument, the above answer. That definition has been used ever since Crick and Watson discovered our DNA! I say genetics is not what defines us as human. Why do I say this to a bunch of highly educated and opinionated genetic professionals? Let me explain: when you have a child, are you worried whether the child has your ears, your nose, your feet or your smile? Do you disown the child because it has a genetic disease? No we don't, not as parents and not as a society. We adopt and respect all children that are born into our midst.

In some cases, those born into our midst are less 'genetically' human than our cousin the chimpanzee. I'll illustrate this anomaly with a few examples. Conjoined twins are genetic oddities; their genetic code is far removed from what we define as fitting the human genetic model of 23 chromosomes.

To cite a few other examples:

- Children with Down syndrome have three, not two, copies of chromosome 21.

- Women with Turner's Syndrome only have a single X chromosome – and no Y chromosome.
- Men with XYY Syndrome – as the name suggests, have a single X chromosome and two Y chromosomes.
- Men with Klinefelter's syndrome have two X chromosomes and a single Y chromosome.
- Women with Triple X syndrome – have three copies of the X chromosome.
- Women with Tetrasomy X syndrome – have four copies of the X chromosome.

In each of the above cases, in genetic percentage terms, arguably, it makes them less genetically human than chimpanzees.

However, we as humans make no distinction over the humanness of conjoined twins, Down, Turner, XYY and Klinefelter's syndrome children and all other children. To us, each and all of them are rightly and properly treated the same – as fellow humans. Note that I did not say 'treat them as though they were human'. I said that we see them as fellow humans, we understand and respect their humanity.

Why do we do this when, in strictly genetic terms, they are less human than a chimp? It is because what defines us as humans is not based on genetics.

What defines us as humans is not our DNA. What defines us as humans is in our values, in our beliefs, in our culture, in our dignity, in our pride, in our ingenuity. While certain of our children may be genetically further away from humanity than a monkey, providing they share in our value system, they are human and we unquestioningly see and understand their humanity.

It is understanding that our values, our beliefs, our culture is what defines us as humans, that will enable us humans to make the voyage to distant suns, to distant solar systems, to distant planets.

To survive the trip to a new planet, then to survive the elements awaiting us at our destination planet, we will have to re-engineer our genetic structure to cope with the hardships that we will encounter. This re-engineering process will make the next generation of humans more genetically removed from us than a chimp. But, providing that our new children share our beliefs, our values, our hopes, our aspirations – then they will be as human as anyone in this room.

What we as the human race wish to preserve is our humanity defined by our feelings, emotions, thoughts, inventions, ambitions, religions and values.

Would a Muslim care that the captain of the ship going to the new Earth is weak and feeble on Earth, but has the capacity to live for 500 years in zero gravity – providing the captain observes Ramadan?

Does the Christian care that the captain of the landing party can sleep for a century at a time in zero gravity, and is capable of breathing toxic air in an atmospheric pressure of 50 atmospheres while experiencing force 10 gravity – providing the captain believes in the Immaculate Conception?

Does the quantum theorist care how deformed any of the colonising party may appear – providing they understand the Heisenberg's Uncertainty Principle and that $E=MC2$?

Does the Englishman care that our travellers' system will allow them to digest tree bark, bones and teeth – providing they understand the rules of cricket?

Does the politician care that our new children will have redundant hearts, lungs, brains and reproductive organs – providing they understand the principles of segregating the state from church and segregating the legislator, from the enforcer, from the judiciary?

Does the economist care that each member of the colonising party will be designed to be self-sufficient and have the ability to self-fertilise, providing they understand the laws of money supply and Adam Smith's invisible hand?

Does the accountant care that the mathematical ability of the crew and landing party will be on par with a super-computer – providing these guys understand the principle of the double-entry accounting system?

Does the comedian care that the crew members 6th sense of kinaesthesia is a thousand times more sensitive than ours – providing they can deliver punch lines?

The point is that to survive we have to genetically engineer life forms that are capable of surviving the trip with the necessary talent and resources to colonise the new planets. These life forms will be more removed from us – genetically speaking – than apes. But, providing they still hold our values and beliefs, our feelings, our sense of humanity – they still will be human.

This is how we as humans will survive the inevitable destruction of our own planet – by allowing our values, beliefs and feelings to live on in our new child called eternity.

For our new child eternity to be born it is up to us – the very people in this room – to work, to explore and to create our child, our saviour.

What we do here and now, what each of us do in this room, today, tomorrow and during our lives – what we do will shape the lives of generations to come. When I say 'generations to come' I mean every generation which will follows us – thousands and thousands of generations. We, the very people in this room, will indelibly alter the course of human evolution and, with it, humanity's chances of universal survival.

When I say it is up to us to work, I mean to work now, not the next generation of geneticists, not after we all get together at next year's annual genetic engineering conference, not after your submission for funding is approved, not after Parliament provides guidance, law and direction for interventional human advancement, not after the Genetic Protection Authority's Ethics Ruling Committee comes to grips with the reality of what's facing us, NO, I MEAN NOW.

Personally, I don't think any of us should be at this lecture, including myself; we all have work to do, each one of us, whether we are involved in genetics, bio-nanotechnology, planetary ecosystems, or, like me genetic law. We, the people in this room, collectively have the responsibility to advance and save our species – to save human kind.

It is this challenge that faces us NOW, not tomorrow. It is our response to this challenge which will set this age, this generation, the people in this room, the biggest the most important page in the history of humanity – because we will develop, we will create the means, we will create the ability, we will create the children which will survive our planet, survive our solar system, survive our sun so that we as humans can live forever.

No other generation in the history of humanity – past or future – has ever, or will ever, make such a contribution to science, to our species, our humanity, our world – as we in this room will do.

This is why I choose to live in this age – the age when we take the first steps in becoming masters of the cosmos. Now – get to work. Thank you and God bless you.

There is a standing ovation for Bill at the end of his presentation

Insert Scene – 12

It is our business to ask what Utopia will do with its congenital invalids, its idiots and madmen, its drunkards and men of vicious mind, its cruel and furtive souls, its stupid people, too stupid to be of use to the community, its lumpish, unteachable, and unimaginative people? And what will it do with the man who is 'poor' all round, the rather spiritless, rather incompetent low-grade man, who on Earth sits in the den of the sweater, traps the streets under the banner of the unemployed, or trembles – in another man's cast-off clothing, and with an infinity of hat- touching – on the verge of rural employment?

These people are in their descendent phase. The species must be engaged in eliminating them; there is no escape from this.

A Modern Utopia *by HG Wells*

Scene 21 – Bill leaves his admirers

9:00pm, Tuesday, 14 May 2013

Setting: The Royal Society – looking into the foyer

Bill is surrounded by admirers all listening to every word he says. As always he is warm, sociable, charismatic and enigmatic

Bill   Yes I know law isn't a science – pity, as I always loved science and scientists. The search for truth is what it is all about: demystifying the universe. Taking the explanation of phenomenon out of the hands of the gods of old and defining phenomena by scientifically developed and verifiable natural laws. Knowledge is a truth – but the truth is knowledge.

However, I chose law as I was appalled by how scientists today are so inhibited in their quest for truth by bureaucracy, regulations, laws, funding proposals, the media, ethics committees etc, etc, etc. I thought my biggest contribution to science would be to clear a path through these obstacle courses so that others – scientists – could continue with their quest.

If I help just one scientist in overcoming these barriers to reach their quest to discover a truth, a natural law, then I will know that I made the right career path. My choice will then be vindicated. However, hopefully, I will help many scientists overcome these artificially imposed barriers, so that they can concentrate and focus on what matters – science, not bureaucracy.

Anyway guys, I have a traditionally created child at home, and I need to get back to the co-creator of the child, otherwise, like the new generation of children I spoke of in the lecture, I too will be sleeping under the stars tonight.

Bye and God bless.

Bill turns from his admirers (on somewhat of a high) and proudly strolls out of the foyer through the front doors and down the stairs.

As he was talking to his admirers he was facing the camera with the front door visible behind him – as he turns to walk out – he turns his back to the camera – heads straight for the door – walks through them – and starts descending the stairs when the camera fades out.

Scene 22 – Ivan confronts Bill

9:15pm, Tuesday, 14 May 2013

Setting: The Royal Society

The camera fades in on a frontal of Bill as he is descending the stairs outside the Royal Society – still proud and high with his coat flowing behind him.

Another camera picks up a disgruntled Ivan leaning against a car in the slight drizzle, clearly uncomfortable being outside for so long in the cold. He notices Bill exiting the building and puckers himself together, runs his hands though his mop of damp hair to try and bring a little composure to his 'look'. He keeps Bill firmly in his sight and with the concentration and focus of a hunting dog sets off after his prey.

The camera cuts back to Bill still descending the stairs with his beautiful cashmere coat rising up so that it gives the image of a cape – him being a superhero.

The camera cuts back to Ivan, who has him lined up in his sight, with a deadly determined look on his face, getting a swagger up as he walks faster and faster towards his target.

Bill reaches the bottom of the stairs, pauses momentarily to take a deep breath, as to enjoy the evening air – drizzle and all – then starts off again with purpose and authority in his steps. Just as he starts off he hears a muffled 'Dr Horowitz, Dr Horowitz, Dr Horowitz' (spoken by Ivan). Bill slightly cocks his head with a quizzical face to try and hear whether or not it was his name being called. Bill figures it wasn't – and sets off again.

The camera cuts back to Ivan – who now starts to trot. A look of desperation starts to show as he sees Bill turn and continue after nearly hearing his name called. He then breaks into a sprint, with his head down and 'going for it'. As he builds up his speed he bumps into the same tall guy (TG) who tripped over him in the foyer (prior to the lecture).

TG   What the fuck – you again!

Bill hears the commotion, slightly turns his head in the direction of the noise, glances out the corner of his eye and gives an expression of first mild curiosity, changing to a dismissive expression. He straightens up and continues to proudly walk on.

Ivan picks himself up off the ground.

IH   And fuck you again.

Ivan gets up, turns, and runs after Bill.

IH   Dr Horowitz, Dr Horowitz, Dr Horowitz – I need to speak to you.

Bill hears the call, and a very quizzical expression rolls over his face (as who could be calling me at this time of night – on a street). He continues walking but turns his head to see who is calling him. All he can see is other guests who are walking away from the building – none of whom appear to be calling him. He frowns, showing his uneasiness at not being able to identify the person calling him. He continues to walk and slowly straightens his head to look forward.

Ivan, comes out from behind others (who were walking between him and Bill) and keeps running towards Bill.

Bill reaches his car and raises his key to remotely unlock it – still showing slight signs of unease of not knowing who was calling him. As he starts to open his car door.

IH   Dr Horowitz, Dr Horowitz, Dr Horowitz – I really do need to speak to you. Please wait, please do not drive off – not yet.

Again Bill searches for the owner of the voice, but sees nothing, clear signs of anxiety are now visible on his face as he again looks around.

Ivan emerges from behind a trash can – running up to Bill – again shouting:

IH   Dr Horowitz, Dr Horowitz, Dr Horowitz – please wait a moment – just one moment – I need to speak to you urgently.

Bill, now annoyed, turns to identify the voice – just in time to witness Ivan trip over a raised street paving slab and career into his BMW 8 series car door that he had just opened. The door hits Bill, which causes him to drop his brief case, flinging open and sprawling all its papers and contents over the footpath.

BH   What the fuck is going on here and who the fuck are you?

IH   Dr Horowitz – here let me help you pick up your papers, I am so sorry about that.

BH   It's okay, I can pick them up myself. Now what's your problem? Why are you shouting at me in the middle of a street at 9:15 on a dark, wet night?

They are now both crouching down collecting Bill's papers.

IH   Dr Horowitz, I have a big problem and you're the only one that can help me. I need to speak to you urgently.

BH   Well – here is my business card – please phone my secretary and book an appoint–

IH   I've already tried that. She wouldn't book an appointment for me …

BH   I find that very hard to believe. I'll have a word with her in the morning to expect a call from you, and I'll instruct her to book it in the first slot I have available. Now what's your name, so that I can pass it on to her.

IH   That's the problem – I can't tell you.

BH   What – that's ridiculous, why can't you tell …

IH   I can't – and I can't tell your secretary either.

BH   [A look of realisation comes over his face] Look, I can only assume you're the guy who called me on my mobile earlier today – like then, like now, if you want to see me, please make an appointment through my secretary. Thank you and goodbye.

IH   Bill, I mean Dr Horowitz, please just give me fifteen minutes to tell you what is happening to me. If after that you don't what anything to do with me – then fine, I won't bother you again. But, if you want to hear more, then I'll tell you my name and make an appointment – but please, just give me 15 minutes first.

BH [Bill sighs – and shows signs of 'pissed offness' and concedes defeat] Look, tomorrow I will be in Canary Wharf for several meetings. [He pulls out his Google phone and keys in several strokes] There is a gap in my calendar from 2:30 to 3:00pm. If you can make it to Canary Wharf at this time, I'll buy you a coffee. This is a take it or leave it offer.

IH Excellent. I'll be there. Where shall I meet you?

BH At Zizzi – near the waterfront by the Four Seasons Hotel. Remember – 2:30pm sharp. I won't wait if you're late.

IH 2:30 – see you tomorrow. Thank you.

Insert Scene – 13

No one can question, on the streets of London, the contrast between the Piccadilly gentleman of Nordic race and the cockney street vendor of the Neolithic type

Madison Grant, Trustee of the American Museum of Natural History, 1936

Scene 23 – Banter at the GPA

10:00am, Wednesday, 15 May 2013

Setting: The GPA Office

The scene fades in to a general office cubical scene at the GPA – with the usual sense of complacency that is normally associated with government departments. People walking aimlessly and slowly around the office, and small groups of people clustered together in idle chitchat.

The camera slowly and meanderingly brings Ivan into focus, who is sitting at his cubical flicking through his copy of the Annotated Genetic Protection Act. The camera zooms in on the chapter heading 'Termination of Embryos with Gazetted Genetic Disorders'. Ivan starts to read this chapter, then starts to flick through the next few pages until he comes to a page headed 'The Three Standard Deviation Rule'.

Ivan's facial expression shows obvious extreme interest as he focuses in on text below the heading. Just as he starts to get absorbed by the book – he is startled when Gough sneaks up behind him [with Mark Hardwick following Gough] and slaps him on the back with loud morning greeting designed to startle.

GR   Good morning, Ivan. Good to see you hard at work already – looking for a promotion are we? Want to climb that old public service ladder do we?

As he says this he deliberately glances down at a small foldout stepladder at the side of Ivan's cubical.

GR   Or are you just making up for pissing off yesterday without telling anyone where you were going? I like that in a man. Don't like work, then just fuck right out of here, no questions, no explanations, just get the fuck up and get the fuck out – that's the way to do it!

IH   Fuck off Gough, I'm not in the mood to be fucked around with at the moment.

GR   Oooohhhh – touchy, touchy, touchy …

MH   Ivan – are you okay?   What's up?

GR   The problem is he's not up enough – he's just low!

Mark turns and gives Gough a stern look – which gets Gough to back off.

MH   Ivan, look we're going down the pub for lunch – come with us. A beer
       and a good strip show will make you feel better.

IH   Thanks, but I'm going out for lunch.

MH   Okay – what time?

IH   Two-thirty.

MH   That's not lunch, that's an afternoon snack. Come on – come to the pub
       with us.

IH   Thanks – I'll think about it.

*At this point Elaine Kellaway walks up and stops next to Mark to join [uninvitedly]
the conversation.*

EK   So, who's going to the pub for lunch?

She eyes off the others – waiting for a response – until Mark concedes.

MH   Yes we're going to 'The Grapes' pub for lunch – we'd love to invite you,
       but I think they may have strippers there, and, well, we don't want to
       offend your modesty …

GR   Offend her fucking modesty … It is more likely that she would offend the
       strippers' modesty.
       Fuck, I'm surprised I haven't seen her up on the catwalk.

EK   Gough, one day you are going take a step too far and you're going to
       piss someone off who will want to extract revenge – so just cool it okay?
       Mark – look I don't mind strippers, so if you're okay can I join you?

MH   Well, if you don't mind, but I don't want you to be lodging an 'Offensive
       Act' claim against me once we return.

EK No, look I'm fine. Besides if I don't get out today, I'll go insane. The three guys look up to her to explain herself

EK Oh – well tomorrow is Shavu'ot.

She pauses and looks at their non-comprehending blank faces.

EK Shavu'ot is a Jewish religious holiday, so I'll be in the Synagogue for most of tomorrow afternoon and tomorrow night.

IH So, do you get tomorrow off as a religious holiday?

EK No, unfortunately, I have to take rec leave – just to spend the day in the Synagogue.

GR So, why do you bother, is it that much better than a day in the office?

EK Don't go there – otherwise we'll be here all day discussing the thousand and one ways Jewish matriarchs subject their offspring to emotional blackmail.

So, let's just go to the pub for a pint – and I'll allow you guys to gawk at the strippers, providing you don't mind if I keep my back to them. I'll just enjoy the pint.

MH Cool, deal done. So Ivan, are you in?

IH [With a despondent conceded expression on his face agrees] Oh, okay.

GR Well you don't have to come, I'm sure the Annotated Genetic Protection Act is better company than us [as he snatches the book off Ivan, reads the cover, then throws the book back on the desk].

IH Gough, give me a fucking break, okay? I've got a lot of shit happening at the moment.

GR Touchy, touchy, touchy

EK So, done, we're all going to the Grapes for lunch.

As Elaine says this, Jeff Portwood starts walking towards them, obviously wanting to join in the conversation, as he suspects that they may be discussing 'going out to the pub' (as written all over his face by his stupid smile). He is keen to join them and have the invitation extended to himself.

Gough is the first to spot Jeff coming towards them, so as Elaine is finishing her last sentence he gives the rest of the group a 'warning cough' and signals with his eyes in the direction of Jeff coming towards them. They all look up in unison at Jeff, and without uttering a single word disband their assembled little group and walk away from Ivan's desk [with the exception of Ivan – who remains seated].

As they disperse, a glum look spreads over Jeff's face as he realises, yet again, he's been left out of an office outing, and the camera fades out.

Insert Scene – 14

> *I would never like to have children from a person who has Jewish Blood.*
> *Carl Jung*

Scene 24 – Laurie offers a little personal advice

11:00am, Wednesday, 15 May 2013

Setting: Bradbury, Dywer & Waldron's Offices

The scene opens at the offices of Bradbury, Dywer & Waldron – Laurie Coulson is sitting at her meeting table in her office, providing directives to an unseen staff member. As the directions continue, the camera slowly pans around the table to the staff member, revealing Sandra Small as the other meeting attendee.

LC   We have just received instruction from Mr Pauling to go ahead with the injunction on Mr Bragg in his ongoing dispute over who was the first to isolate the genes responsible for 'perfect pitch'. So, after you file the injunction, you will need to immediately contact the scientific journal 'Cell' and instruct the editor that she is legally obliged to pull Mr Bragg's paper from the summer volume of the Journal.

SS   Sure, I will get onto it straight away.

LC   Excellent. Do you have any other questions or comments?

SS   No, it all is quite straightforward. As I said, I'll get straight onto it.

LC   Sandra, if I may, can I inquire as to how your other half took the news about your, how shall I put it, your new study commitments?

SS   Yes, he was very pleased for me.

LC   He does realise that this is a significant commitment from yourself – and that, to a large extent, it will affect his life as well?

SS   Oh, yes, we did discuss all the ramifications.

LC   So, how did he respond when you broke the news to him?

SS   [A little caught unawares for this line of questioning]. Ahh … sorry, what were you asking?

LC   Nothing really, I was just inquiring how your other half took the news. Men can be a little odd at times – if not all the time. And, some men might feel uncomfortable about their partner's gaining ground on them – or even passing them in the career race.

SS   No, no, he is very supportive.

LC   Hmmm. That's good to hear. I was in a similar situation once, albeit a long time ago. While it might not sound like it, I'm a Scouser, yes, yes – I'm from Liverpool. My many years in London have now mostly drowned out my accent. I too was offered a place in Oxford to study law. Back then in 1989 it was nearly unheard of, a comprehensive school student getting an offer from Oxford.

      I desperately wanted to go, but my boyfriend refused to countenance the idea. Tony thought I was overstepping my position, he thought that I believed I was better than him, that I was belittling him. It was a load of rubbish.

      Anyway, we had a massive row over it. I was sure it was just a bit of the old male ego that had been put out of place. I thought it was just temporary – and that after a while he would rationalise the situation and that he would eventually support and move south with me. But, it never happened.

SS   So, what did happen?

LC   He went off to a football match with a bunch of mates … [with a hint of choking and a barely perceptible 'watery eyes'] and, well, he never spoke to me again.

SS   Did you try and speak to him?

LC   Oh yes, boy did I try. I spoke and spoke and spoke. But, he never once spoke back to me.

SS   Laurie, I am so sorry to hear that. What about now, are you in touch with him?

Long pause.

LC No. Tony died a few years later, or more correctly he was killed. So, I never did have the opportunity to tell him just how much I cared about him, how sorry I was about the way I treated him – or how much I loved him. He just stopped talking to me – and then he eventually died on me.

SS Oh my God, I had no idea. Were the killer – or killers – ever caught and brought to justice?

LC Well, yes and no. There is no dispute over who the killers are – so in a sense, they have been caught, or at least identified. But, no, they have never been brought to justice. They just carry on with their lovely lives as though Tony was nothing more than an object of interest – or possibly an object of debate.

Anyway, that all was a very long time ago, and the world and I have moved on. But, the whole dreadful experience had made me far more mindful of what can happen to relationships when one partner appears to be accelerating their career. It does not always make for happy families!

Long pause.

So Sandra, be honest with me. Have you told Ivan?

SS [Shocked by confrontational question] Sorry, what are you asking?

LC Sandra, you haven't told Ivan have you?

SS [Looks down] No, not yet … we're sort of going through a difficult time at the moment … and by raising Oxford with him … well, it will just make things more difficult.

LC Sandra, what you have is a fantastic opportunity. Take it with both hands and never let it go.

SS Yes, yes, I will – I mean I am.

LC Well, a big part of grabbing the opportunity, is securing the support of your other half. If you don't have Ivan's support, then it will prove very, very difficult – and I mean that in every sense of the word. It will be difficult to study, it will be difficult to work and most of all it will be difficult to maintain a working relationship with Ivan.

SS   I know. You know, things used to be so easy between us. At university, we were both free spirits – life was so much fun. We were both into art, poetry and music. We met at the Leeds Met Renaissance Society. Ivan was heavily into Giotto – and he always wanted to travel to Italy to see his frescoes in Assisi, Padua and Florence. He always maintains that the only redeeming trait that he inherited from his mother was a passion for art. Mind you, her taste is pretty esoteric, namely medieval Russian religious icons.

My passion was far more mainstream renaissance, you know, Michelangelo and Leonardo da Vinci. As soon as we graduated we got married and went to Italy for our honeymoon before moving down to London. We spent a month in Italy – travelling from city to city spending day after day admiring the great works of the renaissance artists. Even though neither of us can speak much Italian, we still had a truly fantastic time.

LC   So, what was the highlight of your art fest?

SS   You know, even after a month in Italy, everyday visiting different museums, galleries, churches and cathedrals, nothing prepared us for the last gallery we visited – the Sistine Chapel.

When we went into the Chapel, both of us were totally awestruck. Neither of us spoke for at least ten minutes. We were just gazing, almost in a trance. Then I broke the silence – the Judith and Holofernes Pendentive, even though I'd seen so many photos of it in numerous books, I still could not believe how perfect the fresco was – the composition was sublime. In photos, it can be hard to make out Holoferne's decapitated head, but when you're in the Chapel and see the real McCoy, there's no mistaking it – it's definitely a head on a plate.

LC   Sandra, it sounds like you and Ivan have something really special between you. If you want my unsolicited advice, then nurture and protect it. Don't take what you have for granted. Many divorced couples would have gladly stayed together, if they just had what you have.

If I had my time again, then, well I would have been more considerate to Tony's sensitivities. Of course, I still would have gone to Oxford, but I would have been more tactful in trying to change his mind to join me.

Who knows, if I had been less of a bitch about it, maybe he would never have gone to that football match, and just maybe he would never have stopped talking to me.

SS   Laurie, thanks for the advice. But, we are experiencing some turbulence at the moment, so I don't want to pour fuel onto the fire at this stage.

I will find the right time to tell Ivan about Oxford, but now is not the time.

LC   Okay, but be careful and remember, to have a happy family you must be so very careful not to jilt their precious little egos – they are just so sensitive!

Now, I guess this is the time for us to get back to work. So, you had best get that injunction issued.

SS   Not a problem, thanks for the chat and advice.

Scene fades out with Sandra collecting her papers and walking out of Laurie's office.

Insert Scene – 15

How exasperating it is to see the kind of people who constitute the mass of foreign visitors to Rome. As sure as ever the English language fell on my ear, so surely did I hear words of ignorance or vulgarity! Impossible to describe the vulgarity of most of these people. Many of them are absolute shop-boys and work girls. How in heaven's name do they get enough money to come here? … Every day I saw people whom I should like to have assaulted.

What business have these gross animals in such places? A letter to Eduard Bertz from George Gissing.

Scene 25 – The GPA friends lunch at the pub

12:15pm, Wednesday, 15 May 2013

Setting – The Grapes Pub, 76 Narrow Street, Limehouse, London, E14 8BP

The camera is inside the pub and pans around showing the office patrons – all drinking pints and reasonably rowdy, but the 'show' is yet to start. It pans up to the front door to witness the entry of Mark Hardwick, Gough Rogers, Elaine Kellaway and Ivan Henry. Gough and Mark stroll confidently into the pub, which is obviously familiar territory for the two of them. However, Elaine and Ivan hesitate as they enter to get their bearings and size up the pub. This creates several metres of space between Gough/Mark and Elaine/Ivan. It is at this point the publican behind the bar spots Ivan and Elaine – and doesn't identify their connection with Gough and Mark due to the several metres distance between them. As he spots them he glances down at his watch in obvious annoyance – then glances back up to Elaine and Ivan.

The barman (Ben Thomas) rushes up to Elaine and Ivan, looks at them with his annoyed expression as he taps his watch.

BT   What fucking time is this ah?

        You were meant to be here fifteen fucking minutes ago. Now – the dressing room is through the back there, just to the left of the stage. Now grab your kit, get changed and get the show rolling within 5 minutes okay? Or I'll phone your agency and I swear none of you fuckers will work here again.

Elaine's and Ivan's faces drop to a state of shock, unable to comment or respond to the publican. After a long pause the publican shouts at them:

BT   Get the fucking Fairy and Leprechaun show started.
        eeeeeeeeeeeeeeeeeee

        As the publican shouts this the camera brings into focus the flyer for the week's entertainment – which shows 'Wednesday, 15 May 2013 – the fairy stripping leprechaun show, featuring the 'Blond Fox' and 'Mike the Midget'.

Gough overhears the conversation and has spotted the flyer, walks over to Ben and Elaine/Ivan and tells Ben:

GR   Ben, I saw this show last Tuesday at the Cucumber and Sandwich – and they're fucking brilliant. The little blond is a hot number I can tell you – you did well to get these two here.

He then turns to an even more stunned Elaine and Ivan and continues:

GR   Come on guys, get a move on, I can't wait to see your fairy eating routine again.

With this Elaine stamps on Gough's toe as hard as she can with the sharp point of her high heeled boots.

EK   Gough, I'm telling you – one day you're going to take a step too far!

At this point, Mark approaches the scene with a broad smile on his face.

MH   Sorry Ben, these are some of our friends from work, they're not your act.

Ben looks at Mark for a 'confirmation expression'.

MH   Sorry Ben, they're friends. [He points out the window] I think those guys might be your act.

The camera pans up to the window to focus on a short lady dressed in a stunning fairy outfit, with a dwarf dressed in a green leprechaun suit.

Ben looks down to Elaine and Ivan.

BT   Ohhh, sorry guys, I've obviously made a bit of a mistake. I'm really sorry about that.

There is a silent pause as everyone feels uncomfortable and nobody knows what to say – then Ben continues.

BT   Tell you what, for you four drinks are on me this lunchtime – and I'll throw in a seafood platter. I'd like to stay and chat, but I gotta get the act up and running.

Ben flies out of the door to start bollocking the 'real act'.

The scene cuts over to the four of them at a table on the balcony of the pub, directly over the river. There are four freshly poured beers on the table [no empties on the table – indicating this is their first round]. There is a big seafood platter in the middle of the table. They all raise their glasses and say the customary 'cheers' and sip their pints.

GR   This is not so bad – a little innocent misunderstanding and Ben lays on free beer and a seafood platter. Makes being insulted worthwhile – doesn't it?

EK   No it doesn't, that was totally out of order what he said to us – who the fuck does he think I am? And, as yet, I haven't received an apology from you. Besides, I can't eat anything from the seafood platter.

GR   Come on Elaine, chill a little. No need to get so worked up over an innocent misunderstanding and a little joke that you won't eat Ben's free lunch. It's not like you can send your portion back!

EK   It was a wee bit more than a misunderstanding and a little joke! Besides, the reason I'm not eating the free lunch is because I'm Jewish, not because I wouldn't accept a free lunch from that arsehole.

IH   What's being a Jew got to do with not eating lunch?

EK   The platter is made up of shellfish. Jews can't eat shellfish [she looks around the table – they all got dumb expressions]. Look, in the Old Testament, the book of Leviticus states that we can only eat seafood that have fins and scales. Shellfish don't have fins or scales – so I can't eat them.

GR   In that case, I've just lost interest in converting to Judaism.

EH   Somehow, I don't think your revelation is a great loss to our cause!

Elaine looks over at Mark, who (unusually) hasn't been involved in any of the conversation – and is looking a little pre-occupied and melancholy.

EH   Mark, are you okay? You don't seem your normal chirpy self. What's up?

MH   Nothing much ... well, it's my old man's birthday today. I sent him a card and phoned him up this morning – but we have so little in common aside from discussing the shit weather and the cricket score. Barely talk. I always try and have a chat and a laugh, but it is never appreciated. I always get the impression that Dad's relieved when I have to go or hang- up.

You know, a place like this, sharing a pint, a joke, a yarn and a bit of a show – this is where I'd like to bring my old man – just to sit, chat and enjoy the occasion. But he still treats me like a kid, and if I brought him to a place like this, even to a pub without a show, he would grimace his disapproval the whole way through the encounter.

EK   Well, you know, relationships with parents can go through periods of strain – or even indifference. But, over time, you get through these dull periods. Something changes, someone gets married, has a kid, divorces or dies. It is at these times families come together – and it's these times when we rejoice, sorrow or mourn with our family that makes all the dull times worthwhile.

Your relationship with your dad may be dull at the moment – but, believe me, it will not always be like this.

MH   Well, what a little therapist you have turned out to be. I guess you're right. But, sweet Jesus, how many years of penance do I need to serve before I get a reprieve? Speaking of self-imposed penance, have you seen your old man lately Gough?

GR   No mate, never. Not even for his birthdays – which if I remember correctly, is in a few weeks' time.

IH   Why's that? Don't you know where he is?

GR   Yeah I know who he is and where he is – the bastard.

EK   What's the problem with your old man?

GH   The bastard left me and my mother when I was only five years old. I haven't seen him since.

EK   How do you know where he is then?

GR   He keeps writing to me.

EK   How and what does he write to you about?

GR   He remembers my birthday and Christmas.

IH   Is this recent then – that he's been writing to you for Christmas and birthdays?

GR   Not exactly recent.

EK   So for how long has he been writing to you?

A very long pause – with the other three increasingly eyeing him for a response, with Gough looking increasingly downward to hide his emotional expression.

GR   He's never missed sending me a letter and present since he left me – every fucking birthday, every fucking Christmas.

EK   And you've never responded – you've never contacted him?

GR   Fuck him! Where was he when we needed him? I'll tell you where he was, career and social climbing. Had to make it big time didn't he? Having a wife and kid hindered his rise – so fuck us – he kicked us out of his life so that he could study more, work more and get more promotions. To me he may as well be dead. In fact I'd prefer that so I'd stop receiving those fucking presents every birthday and Christmas.

IH   So what is he?

GR   A lawyer or something. He left when he was studying for his bar exams.

EK   You know, Gough, you really should try and get in touch with him – at least give him the opportunity to explain and defend himself. At least give him the chance … because, time eventually runs out for all of us and there comes a point where we can't reverse past decisions – then we're stuck with those decisions for life. It drove my mother nearly insane, as she hadn't spoken to her father for two years prior to him being killed in a car crash. Now her apologies and forgiveness mean nothing. She can't shake the guilt she feels for not saying goodbye – and that he may have died not knowing that she really did love him. I tell you it drives her crazy, which in turn she takes out on me, which drives me crazy.

IH   My old man died for me, coincidently when I was also seven. He was a clown in the Moscow Circus. He and my mother tried to escape the USSR so that they could give me a better life. My mother made it – but my father was shot. What a fucking joke. Your old man left you so he can get a better life, mine gets killed trying to give me a better life.

You're bitter and twisted that your old man's still alive. I'm bitter and twisted that mine isn't.

I tell you what, Elaine's right. If you've got a father – particularly one that cares and wants to see you, judging by your birthday and Christmas presents – you should see him.

I'd give anything to see my father again. I'd far prefer to have a shit life in Moscow with my dad than a great life in London without him. And the irony is, I've got a fucking shit life here, and I'd probably have had a pretty decent life in Moscow – as Russia, despite all its short comings, still supports the arts, and I could have followed my father into the Moscow Circus or the theatre.

Well that's all gone now. My career in the arts is a non-starter. At least I've got salvation with my career at the Genetic Protection Authority. [Last sentence said in a sarcastic tone.]

MH   Gough, I think they're right, you should at least see your father once and give him the opportunity to explain himself. If after that you still think he is a shit head – then that's fine, you've tried. But who knows, maybe, just maybe, it will turn into something [long pause as Mark's facial expression changes from serious and sombre to excitedly attentive] … but at the moment, I don't give a fuck, as the fairy is about to strip [the noise level in the bar goes up and the fairy – followed by the leprechaun – appears].

Insert Scene – 16

A marriage which is devoted entirely to mutual understanding is bad for the development of the individual personality; it is a descent to the lowest common denominator, which is probably something like the collective stupidity of the masses.

Carl Jung

Scene 26 – A pee and straight talk

1:00pm, Wednesday, 15 May 2013

Setting: The Grapes Pub, 76 Narrow Street, Limehouse, London, E14 8BP

This follows the strip scene – in as much as the Fairy and Leprechaun act has just finished and both Ivan and Mark go to the pub toilet. The camera is in the toilet as the two walk in – the two are both discussing the good merits of the act along the lines:

MH   Fucking hell, that lucky little shit. Fancy getting to do that to the fairy. And getting paid to do it. Fuck, I'd pay to do that to her.

IH   Tell you what, seeing acts like that, well, it's got me thinking, if this job at the GPA goes pear shaped then, fuck it, I'll get a job in a strip show playing a leprechaun, I'm not proud.

The conversation goes along these lines as the two walk past the camera – and they approach the urinals. Mark walks straight up to his and pulls his fly down and gets ready to start his business – but Ivan has a distressed expression roll over his face as he surveys the facilities available and realises there are not any 'kid height' urinals available' and all the booths are engaged.

IH   Fuck I hate this, with all the equality laws, employment laws and disadvantaged access rights legislation, anyone who is deaf, blind or in a wheel chair can get anywhere and do anything – have purpose built toilet cubicles in every public toilet in the country – but, if you're a dwarf, well fuck it, nobody lowers the height of the urinals so that we can have a piss.

Ivan checks out what's available in the toilet room – and notes there is a large unopened bag of toilet rolls (say holding twenty rolls or so). He turns to Mark and asks:

IH   Mark, look can I ask you a favour? Can you get that parcel of toilet papers down, so I can stand on them and have a piss?

MH   Woo, just hold on a minute. It's not that easy to stop in mid-stream.

IH	Oh man, I'm fucking busting.

MH	Okay I'll do the equivalent of Moses parting the water – by stopping the water in mid-stream.
There we go, slowing, slowing, slowing – stopped. Now, what did you want me to do?

IH	[Pointing to the bag of toilet papers on top of a cupboard] Can you get those down – so I can stand on them and have a piss?

Mark obliges by dragging the bag of toilet rolls down. Ivan then drags them to the spare urinal adjacent to Mark's, clambers on top, and then starts his business.

IH	Mark, do you know who Gough's father is – or at least, does Gough know?

MH	From the odd comment he has made to me, I think he's quite senior in the legal profession.

IH	Who is he?

MH	I'm not sure, Gough has only given me a few hints. Maybe he's a QC or something. My guess is this is part of Gough's problem with his father – his father being quite successful and prominent – that Gough may feel, I don't know, that his father will judge him, and that Gough is frightened of being rejected a second time round. The first time his father walked out on him scarred him deeply, and I don't think he wants to risk lifting his emotional guard in case he is hurt again.

IH	Jeez Mark, I didn't know you were a shrink.

MH	I'm not, but I did study how to be a 'Sensitive New Age Guy' so I can spin bullshit to pick up a little tottie on a Saturday night. [This is said both as a joke (which is funny and they both laugh at) but also to dismiss or hide Mark's acute sense of how relationships work].

IH	I still don't understand it. If you've got a father, you should at least try and see him and try to form a relationship with him. If you don't owe it to your father – then you at least owe it to yourself. To just leave that sense of hollow inside that constantly gnaws at your sense of identity and belonging, constantly the same question going around and around. Why did you do it? Why not just stay in the USSR and be alive. Fuck – it couldn't have been that bad. If I had a father then at least I could attempt to start filling in that hollow.

MH   Ivan, if you found out that your old man was still alive in Russia and was at the top of his profession, and the darling of the theatre, the darling of St Petersburg, and that he just faked his own death just to rid himself of his family obligations so he could enjoy the single life of a celebrity – would you really contact him? If it became apparent that he dumped you and your mother just so that he could, well, enjoy himself, without ever trying to make contact with you, would you really call on him to help fulfil your hollow? Wouldn't you be risking making the hollow a little fucking bigger?

Ivan turns bight red and is about to explode with a ranting response when Mark stops him with:

MH   I know that was an unfair question, it was a piece of insensitive rhetoric, and I didn't intend you to answer it. But, note the feelings this invoked in you – then you may have a sense as to how Gough feels about his father.

I guess what I'm saying is – let Gough work out his problem with his father himself – as he's probably not overly receptive to well-meaning advice on the issue.

Ivan, now taken aback, catches himself from exploding and turns his head down in distress, feeling that Mark unjustifiably (or cruelly) used his father to make a point that could have been made more tactfully. So he walks off from Mark without saying another word, leaving the bag of toilet paper rolls in front of the urinal.

IH   So Gough's the only one with feelings around here is he? Well fuck you too.

MH   Ivan, give it a rest – you don't have to make everything an issue – just calm down a little.

With this Ivan does a loud fart and continues uninterrupted as he walks off.

Insert Scene – 17

I hate common humanity. The oafish crowd which tramples the ground whence my cloud- capped pinnacles might rise. I am tired of humanity – beyond measure. Take it away. This gaping, stinking, bombing, shooting, throat-slitting, cringing brawl of gawky, under-nourished riff- raff.

Clear the Earth of them!

Star Begotten *by HG Wells*

Scene 27 – Bill meets Ivan for coffee

2:30pm, Wednesday, 15 May 2013

Setting: Canary Wharf – Near the Four Seasons Hotel

It is a glorious summer day. Bill is sitting at a table outside the Zizzi Restaurant at Canary Wharf riverfront (at the back of the Four Seasons Hotel) sipping a glass of water with ice and a few slices of lemon in a relaxed disposition reading one of Ashley Brilliant's books I May Not Be Perfect – But Parts of Me Are Excellent, *clearly amused by the content.*

Another camera shoots from the bottom of the stairs leading down to the waterfront, shooting upwards at Ivan awkwardly descending the stairs, again carrying a briefcase that is too big for him, while on his mobile phone. Ivan is obviously talking to one of his mates:

IH   Andy, are you still on for the pub this Saturday? … Ah good, we'll be able to watch the Arsenal/Spurs match. Rob said he's still up for it – so it should be a good afternoon. Excellent, see you Saturday at the Narrow Pub. Bye.

As Ivan arrives at the bottom of the stairs the camera lets him walk past then follows him, now shooting the back of him walking towards the restaurant. At this point the camera picks up the stunning scenery of the river and then swings around the corner (with Ivan) which shows Ivan approaching Bill at the table.

Bill looks over his book and sees Ivan approaching. He stands up and extends his hand to shake hands with Ivan. Ivan has to swap his big briefcase from his right hand to his left then awkwardly extends his hand over the table, which requires him to press against the table in order to reach up and shake hands.

BH   It's good you could make it, particularly on a fine day like this. Isn't this fantastic? I just hope tomorrow is a fabulous day like this …

Ivan and Bill exchange glances – with Ivan asking the unspoken question – 'What's special about tomorrow?'

BH   Ah, well, I've got the day off tomorrow – so I just hope that it's like this so that I can enjoy it. Mind you, I'll be indoors for most of the afternoon.

IH   I'll be in the office – so it hardly matters what the weather is like. Anyway, thank you for seeing me Dr Horowitz … I really appreciate it.

BH   I told you I'd buy you a coffee, but you know, I haven't had lunch yet, and on a day like this – well I'm up for it – so can I buy you lunch instead? And please call me Bill.

IH   No, thank you. I'm fine, I just need a little of your time – as I said just fifteen minutes.

BH   If I remember correctly you gave me the option of continuing the conversation – with your name – should I find the first fifteen minutes worthwhile. So I'll take a chance and exercise my option now. So what would you like for lunch – and you don't even have to tell me your name after fifteen minutes.

IH   Thank you – this is very generous – but all I wanted …

BH   NO – please don't insult me by turning down my offer – lunch okay? [Pauses and looks at Ivan forcefully, seeking his consent – and receives it. A waiter arrives.] The risotto – does it have any bacon in it?

Waiter No sir, there isn't any bacon in the risotto.

BH   Any shellfish in the risotto?

Waiter Yes sir, it has clams and cockerels.

BH   In that case – for the appetiser I'll have the ricotta crepes – there isn't shellfish or bacon in these are there? [Gets a shake of the head from the waiter] Good.

For the main – could I have the Trota al Cartoccio?

Waiter One Trota al Cartoccio with no bacon and no shellfish. Excellent.

The waiter turns to Ivan to order. Ivan is somewhat caught out – as he hasn't had a chance to study the menu.

IH   I'll have the same.

BH   No, come now, we're not in a rush – take your time to order what you like.

As Ivan is hastily reading the menu – the camera pans down on the menu, which shows there is no English – just the Italian names for the dishes. The look on Ivan's face shows that he isn't really sure what he is ordering.

IH   [Looking quickly over the menu] I'll have the [poorly pronouncing the Italian dishes] Zuppa di Pesce for the starter – and the Ravioli al Prosciutto Panna for the main – thanks.

As he orders – it is evident that Bill does understand the names of the dishes and mildly lifts his eyebrow – unseen to Ivan, who is looking at either the menu or the waiter as Ivan has to resort to pointing his order on the menu so that the waiter can understand the order.

BH   Okay start talking – what's this big problem that you have which requires you to phone my secretary, my mobile phone – and I'm curious to find out how you got my mobile number as no one in the office gave it to you – and to eventually bail me up at nine at night after giving a lecture at the Royal Society – which you obviously knew about but, judging from how wet you were last night, didn't attend. And during this whole episode keeping your name a secret. I must say, it is all very odd behaviour.

      So – shoot – what's up?

IH   Well I don't know where to start …

BH   Considering the extraordinary means you've gone through to speak to me this isn't a good start – particularly if I renege on my offer and hold you to just 15 minutes.

      Now tell me your fucking problem.

IH   Well – you may have noticed that I have a genetic condition.

BH   Good call on my observational powers – yes I have noticed.

IH   To me, I don't have a choice on the matter – that is, if I want a life. The only cure for my disease is suicide. And to be quite frank the life I have is a fucking sight better than the alternative.

BH   No shit – Mr Brilliant says something of this [raising his book for Ivan to see].

'The task I've been given seems absurd – to wait here on Earth until I no longer exist'.

IH   [More or less ignores Bill's comment] And, to me, I don't think anyone else should be able to make that decision about my life. I mean, I'm happy enough, independent enough, smart enough to get through my life all by myself. So I'd feel pretty shafted if at some point – somebody was to say:

You know the achondroplasia form of dwarfism – Jesus that must be a shit disease to have. It must make the lives of those that suffer from it downright awful.

Tell you what we'll do. To improve their lives – we'll eliminate the disease by going out and killing all the dwarfs that have it. We could deploy the same tactics as the Canadians use during their annual baby seal cull, just pick up a big baseball bat and club them all to death. And, while we're at it, we'll improve the lives of all dwarfs by killing off all other forms of dwarfism.

That will make us all happier, a better world, and save all those poor dwarfs from their horrid disease. What nice guys we are for taking time out of our busy lives to help those less fortunate short-ass midgets.

And I'd feel worse if those that said it had power and authority to just do it – and started a campaign to kill us all off.

BH   What – are you paranoid or something? I can't believe that anyone, whether in authority or not, is talking about having a dwarf cull. Where the hell did you get this shit?

IH   The Genetic Protection Authority.

BH   Look, I know the GPA and the Ethics Ruling Committee are a bunch of fuckwits – but come on, they aren't about to go on a dwarf clubbing spree.

IH   No – not exactly.

BH   Not exactly – what then?

IH   As you are probably aware, the GPA gazettes genetic diseases.

BH   Yes – during the monthly 'GPA Genetic Disease Determination Committee' meeting genetic disease submissions are put forward and the committee either agrees to – or rejects – the need to gazette a disease.

IH   Any idea of the implications of a disease being gazetted?

BH   Yes – the state encourages the termination of all pregnancies where a gazetted genetic disease has been identified in the embryo or foetus. Further, the rights of the father are revoked – so, it is the sole discretion of the mother as to whether or not to terminate the pregnancy.

      This is one of the few, if not the only area of genetic law that the GPA appears to have got right. Essentially, this process has dramatically reduced the number of crippling genetic diseases in our society, for instance: Parkinson disease; spina bifida; cystic fibrosis; Huntingdon's chorea; osteoporosis – not to mention numerous cancer and heart diseases.

      So, in all, the implementation of this policy has had significant benefits to society. And, before you start waving your finger at me – I know achondroplasia is not gazetted, as I've had reason to look it up recently. So I assume this isn't the issue you want to discuss.

IH   Who gives you – or anyone else the fucking right to determine who should be born or not. Take Huntington's disease, it's a gazetted genetic condition. If the genetic word CAG is repeated 39 times or more on chromosome 4 then you get Huntington's chorea; if it is repeated 35 times or less then you don't get the disease.

      So in order to cure the disease we terminate all unborn children that have CAG replicated more than 35 times on chromosome 4. If there are only 39 replications the first symptoms of the disease starts at age 66 and you don't get full-blown dementia until you are 75.

      So, we kill the foetus, because if the foetus was born then at age 75 they will get dementia. I think that's a wee bit fucking harsh. Chances are the poor guy wouldn't have lived to 75 anyway – so he would never have suffered.

BH   What if there are 50 repetitions, then the guy loses his mind at 27 and probably passes the disease onto his kids. I bet his wife and kids are ecstatic about all descendants going insane in their mid-twenties. And you sit here and tell me nobody has a right to stop this crippling disease being passed on from one generation to the next. Well, I think just a few families who have to live with the disease year in year out, for 10, 20, 30 years, then see the same symptoms appear in their kids may just disagree with you.

Anyway – at a guess, we're not here to discuss Huntington's Chorea, so let's get back to your problem.

IH   The other plank of the Genetic Protection Act is that any embryo that is determined to be three standard deviations from the 'Accepted Human Norm' is deemed to be genetically defective. Does this mean that I'm genetically defective? Does this mean that I'm not allowed to have kids – merely because they also will be dwarfs?

BH   I see what you're driving at, but I think you may be missing the point. I apologise in advance for being blunt and insensitive, but I suspect you want to hear my legal views on the situation and that you haven't come to me for emotional counselling.

There are many genetic disorders – only a fraction of them have been identified, and only a fraction of these have actually had their genetic roots isolated.

We no longer live in a Darwinist world of 'survival of the fittest', which effectively kills off bad genes before they are passed onto the next generation, as for the past 100 years or so, due to medical intervention and social policy, we have passed a huge baggage of genetic diseases from one generation to the next. Each successive generation multiplies and amplifies the number and severity of all these genetic disorders. All this without abate.

Now we have the means to stop suffering in future generations – not only for those that may have inherited the disease, but also to all those who have to care, pay and tend the sufferers. In many, many cases the carers are co-sufferers, as it wrecks their lives as well.

To use an example that I assume that you would be familiar with – the Cornelia de Lange form of dwarfism? Symptoms typically include delays in physical development before and after birth, malformations of the hands and arms and mild to severe mental retardation. Many infants and children with the disorder have an unusually small head, distinctive malformations of the limbs, such as unusually small hands and feet. Infants have feeding and breathing difficulties; an increased susceptibility to respiratory infections; heart defects; delayed skeletal maturation; hearing loss; and other physical abnormalities. This condition can be passed from one generation to the next – yet this genetic disorder is not gazetted. Those who suffer from it live in a high degree of pain, are usually incapable of holding down a job, and need constant care. It is a massive burden on their parents and siblings and, later in life, their partners and children.

Given this, now that we have the means to stop this crippling disease being passed to future generation – then shouldn't we try? If it isn't stopped, then potentially millions in future generations will inherit this destructive, painful and crippling disease when it could have been prevented.

So, by using the three standard deviation rule, this disease could be eradicated within one or two generations. Otherwise, well, it will be with us for hundreds of generations – crippling thousands or possibly millions of future lives.

Then of course there is a safety valve on such decisions: the state only encourages the abortion of such diagnosed embryos – it doesn't mandate it.

IH   So Bill, you think I'm genetically defective and that I should be thrown out of the human reproductive programme due to the filth of my genes – those dirty disgusting genes you see in me. I'm surprised you're game enough to sit at the same table as me, in case achondroplasia proves to be genetically contagious.

You know, my father was also a dwarf. He was the top clown in the Moscow Circus, a great man, a legend in his own lifetime. When I was seven years old, he and my mother attempted to escape from the USSR. You know why? So they could build a better life for me – not them, my father was in the arts, a celebrity, and the Soviets looked after their artists. By Moscow standards he had status and wealth. They attempted their escape in the hope of giving me a better life.

For his merits, his best intentions and ambitions for me – he was shot dead on the night of the escape. However, my mother managed to escape with me in check. He was a great man. Some of my mother's Russian friends remember him both as the great clown 'Igor the Great' and as the wonderful man and the father he was to me.

He was my father – and he passed his genes on to me. I have no complaints. I love my father for all that he was, and for all that he passed onto me. I'd be born a dwarf a million times over just to have him as my father one more time.

And you sit across the table from me and tell me I have no right to exist, as my father was short. That's his only crime, my only crime – that we're short. Unlike what you're advocating, the Soviets didn't kill him because he was short – they killed him because he was attempting to defect to the West, attempting to bring me a better life. What a fucking win he had; he gets killed trying, then his unborn grandchild gets killed because he will be a dwarf just like his grandfather.

How the fuck can you live with yourself?

BH   I'm sorry, I offended you. I was more than a little insensitive. Now, what is this about your father's grandchild – are you referring to your own child?

At this point the waiter arrives with the first course and places the ricotta crepes in front of Bill. Bill closely examines the dish – then asks,

BH   This isn't crabmeat is it? [Pointing to some *white* thing on his plate.]

Waiter Yes sir, I believe it is crabmeat – the chef says that it adds flavour and texture to the crepes.

BH   Look – I specifically asked you whether the dishes had shellfish in them – you said no – and now I find crabmeat in the crepes.

Waiter It is crabmeat, sir – not shellfish.

BH   I cannot eat any seafood aside from fish okay? So – please take this away. I'll have some of that [pointing to Ivan's soup] providing there isn't any non-fish seafood in it.

The camera focuses on Ivan, who is obviously observing the exchange between Bill and the waiter with a sense of contemplation travelling across his face – a voiceover comes from his work colleague, Elaine, from earlier in the day 'It's the Shavu'ot Jewish holiday tomorrow – so I won't be at work – I'll be in the Synagogue all afternoon', followed by Bill's earlier comment about his day off tomorrow. Then a voiceover from Elaine Kellaway explaining 'Jews can't eat shellfish'. Then Ivan focuses on Bill's current argument with the waiter about not being able to eat seafood.

IH   You're a Jew.

BH   [Startled]. What? [Replying in disbelief that he made' the statement – not disbelief of the 'substance' of the statement].

IH   You're Jewish.

BH   Sorry, I'm a little lost by your revelation and the thread of this conversation. Presumably you either follow a faith or don't, which in any event wouldn't cause me to stand bolt upright and shout he's an atheist or a Christian or a Hare Krishna – or whatever you happen to be.

IH   There is a big difference isn't there? Your people have suffered genocide – merely because of what you are.

I can't reconcile how somebody who has been persecuted, eradicated and subject to genocide now advocates the persecution of someone else – regardless of whether it's based on faith, nationality, colour or genetic disorders.

BH   [Raising his voice.] Who are you to draw parallels between Hitler and his 'Final Solution' and the genetic advancement of humanity – which has nothing at all to do with either faith or race.

IH   Your people were persecuted because of what you were – what you are. You were persecuted due to the faith you inherited from your parents, your religious name. I'm being persecuted because of what I am, what I inherited from my father – my dwarf gene. Jews were killed due to their inherited name, dwarfs are to be killed due to their inherited gene. Sorry Bill, but I can see a wee bit of a parallel here.

BH   There is no parallel. Nazis indiscriminately killed Jews as an act of hatred, as an act of genocide. It had no compassion, no intent of human

135

advancement – the sole intent was to kill Jews, to wipe them off the planet – there was nothing, nothing at all noble about their cause.

Whereas, the three standard deviation clause, together with the Genome Project is specifically designed to stop diseases, to stop suffering, to stop crippling disease being passed onto future generations. It is a noble and just cause.

IH   Really? Prior to the war, prior to the 'Final Solution', as part of their eugenics programme the Nazis forced the sterilisation of 400,000 people in Germany. In the most part, this wasn't directed towards any particular faith, Jew or otherwise, but towards 'the feeble minded'. After the war started, in an 18-month period, 70,000 of these already sterilised feebleminded people were sent to the gas chambers – just to free hospital beds for wounded soldiers.

With the Nazis, they sterilised those they thought were genetically deficient in the name of eugenics, which was philosophically based to advance the human species – based on the Galtonian creed. Later they sped up the process of genetic cleansing by just killing them– killing them of course after they were born.

It was in a later phase of the Nazi eugenics programme that they started their mass murdering based on faith and nationality. But they never stopped killing the feeble minded and the disabled. Not that it is recorded, but chances are that they gassed dwarfs for being disabled.

BH   You ungrateful, self-centred, conceited, selfish little shit. I give up my time to come and listen to your problem, to offer my help – and you call me a fucking Nazi.

Do you know that those bastards killed most of my family? Do you know what my parents had to go through to escape the Nazi regime? They came to this country with nothing, nothing, absolutely nothing. Their minds fucked up from the trauma and horrors they were subjected to. The Nazis were ruthless, torturing, murderous, genocidal bastards, without a compassionate bone in their body, no feelings, no humanity – just full of twisted, macabre, sadistic hatred.

Those bastards weren't interested in the advancement of our species – they were just interested in power, cruelty and self-obsessiveness. They were ruled by negative hate, stopping at nothing to gain and keep power then ensuring no one else was around to share or challenge it.

The Genome Project, together with the three standard deviation rule, is here to advance us all. To make us a stronger species. To stop unnecessary suffering in future generations. The Genome Project is a project of love, respect and admiration of humanity – not one of hatred and disrespect.

You are way, way out of order for comparing the Genome Project with the eugenics of the Nazis.

IH   If I'm reading you right – you deplore the eugenics of the Nazis but advocate the killing of those you think are genetically deficient – before they are born.

When the Nazis first came to power, this was their exact position. In 1933, they defined nine categories of defectives to be sterilised – which included 'hereditary body deformities'. This sounds perilously close to your beloved three standard deviation rule.

So, I'm sorry Dr Horowitz – the difference is a little lost on me. You're telling me what the Nazis did was bad, but what you're advocating is good. The only difference I see between you and the Nazis is one of timing. They killed after birth, you kill before birth.

Thanks for the meal – but I made a mistake, I didn't need to speak to you, and I certainly don't need or want your help. I hope you sleep well at night – as no doubt Hitler did.

Ivan gets up from the table and leaves without saying another word. Bill sits in his seat steaming with anger – as Ivan walks away Bill shouts after him:

BH   Fuck you.

Ivan keeps walking but raises his finger behind him – giving Bill the one-finger salute.

Insert Scene – 18

The health of the race is paramount. The will of the eternal creator and the iron logic of nature both decree that the weak or diseased should be destroyed, that defectives should be prevented from breeding, and that miscegenation should be banned, since it generates cross-breeds and mongrels, who are inevitably inferior.

Mein Kampf *by Adolf Hitler.*

Scene 28 – Bill at home with an unsympathetic wife

7:30pm, Wednesday, 15 May 2013

Setting: Bill and Cynthia Horowitz's Kitchen at their Home

The scene opens with Bill talking to his wife [Cynthia Horowitz] at home in their kitchen.

BH   You won't believe what happened to me today. You know how I told you about this guy, this dwarf kept trying to see me yesterday. He phoned the office, he phoned my mobile, then he bailed me up at my car as I was leaving the Royal Society – the whole time refusing to give his name.

CH   Yes Bill, I remember. Weren't you going to meet him today for a coffee?

BH   Yeah, well, Dave at genetics for Life Corp cancelled our meeting, as he was called to an emergency meeting with their market analysts after they reported a profit warning – so as I had spare time between meetings I offered the midget lunch …

CH   Honey – they're 'small people', not 'midgets'

BH   No, this guy is definitely a fucking midget – he lost his claim to sympathy, respect and political correctness.

CH   Why, what did he do to upset you so much?

BH   That self-centred, selfish little shit called me a Nazi. Me of all people, being called a Nazi, by who? A fucking midget. Imagine that, the day before Shavu'ot, I'm accused of being a Nazi.

CH   Bill – please don't use language like that.

BH   I'm sorry, but this guy really pissed me off …

CH   Why did he call you a Nazi? What on Earth did you do to provoke such an outrageous insult?

BH   You know the Nazis butchered, tortured, killed nine million people in their concentration camps, six million of them Jews – then this little shit compares me to one of them. Can you believe it? Can you imagine what my parents would have done if they heard this little shit?

CH   In which way … how … did he compare you to the Nazi's?

BH   Haven't you been listening? He compared me to the Nazis because I was able to explain to him the philosophy behind the Genetic Protection Authority's three standard deviation rule. The little fuckwit.

CH   Bill – enough of that language. But how? There must have been some discussion leading up to this accusation.

BH   I'm looking for a little support here, so can you forget that you're a doctor of psychology for once and have a conversation with me as husband and wife – not as doctor and patient? You know all the work I've done over the past ten years, building the practice, building my profile, leading discussion forums, advising governments, reviewing research grant allocations, making statements to both a Parliamentary elect committee and to the US Congress on genetics, law and ethics. I'm now the most experienced, respected and called upon lawyer in the world on genetics – and a dwarf calls me a Nazi. Upon which you ask me to explain myself, as though I'm at fault.

CH   Bill, I'm not your mother – I'm your wife. If you want unconditional sympathy without ever being challenged on anything, then you need to have a séance and speak to your mother. If you want to engage in an adult dialogue to assess and understand the cause of this outburst, this accusation, so you can deal with it and cool down a little – then let me ask an occasional question.

BH   I'm not in the mood to have to defend myself to anyone, particularly my wife, who I thought could, just for once, show a wee bit of consideration – if not sympathy.

Where's Samuel?

CH   He's in the games room.

Bill exits the kitchen and walks aggressively away.

Scene 29 – Bill plays with son Samuel

7:45pm, Wednesday, 15 May 2013

Setting: Bill and Cynthia Horowitz's games room at their home

Bill enters a large games room, which has tiled floor, a pool table, table tennis table and a large number of assorted toys.

BH   [Walks through the doors] Hey Samuel, my man, howz my main man?

SH   Daddy, Daddy, Daddy!

Samuel, Bill's seven-year-old son, comes running up to Bill flat out and jumps on him with full force – taking the wind out of Bill.

BH   Samuel, a little slower, Samuel, you don't want to hurt Daddy do you?

Bill picks Samuel up. The father/son scene is one of obvious love on both sides, Samuel with a wide open smile, but not cognisant of his own physicality keeps hitting Bill (his way of showing affection), putting Bill in great discomfort. Bill then placed in the difficult emotional predicament – does he keep holding his son to show affection, love and warmth, or does he put his son down to spare himself the not inconsiderable pain associated with Samuel's constant punching?

BH   Samuel, Samuel, SAMUEL – settle down – please don't hit me any more [waving his finger in Samuel's face].

Samuel stops for a second. Another wide open smile ripples across his face, and he re-commences his punching routine again, shouting Daddy, Daddy, Daddy, Daddy. One of his punches connects, causing Bill's glasses to fly off and smash on the floor – and causing Bill an obvious degree of pain.

BH   That's it Samuel, down now, come on, Samuel, get down now.

Bill puts Samuel down on the floor, with wide, angry protests from Samuel, wriggling like mad and clutching onto Bill so that he can stay in Bill's arms. After a struggle, Bill eventually gets Samuel down on the floor. Samuel starts screaming uncontrollably, first jumping up over and over again onto Bill attempting to clutch hold of Bill's neck – so that he can be held – then after a while, when this doesn't work, Samuel throws himself onto the floor and starts shouting hysterically, banging his fists against the floor as Bill crouches next to him to say some soothing words. He quiets down – only to start crying and hitting his head against the tiled floor.

BH   Samuel – stop that, stop it, stop hitting your head, goddamn it. Stop it, remember what happened last time you did this? You had to wear that helmet for a month. You don't want that again do you?

Samuel continues with his crying and head hitting

BH   Oh fuck, fuck fuck [He picks up Samuel, and then stands up to stop him hurting himself]. Come on, Samuel, be a good boy and stop crying – Daddy loves you – you know that don't you heh? Daddy loves you very much. There's no need to cry and hit yourself.

Samuel's crying slowly starts to subside as he is consoled by Bill, now Samuel resting his head on his father's shoulder with Bill slowly and lovingly stroking his head.

BH   Good boy, good boy, good boy.

BH   Would you like a game of table tennis hey? Samuel starts hitting Bill again – still sobbing.

BH   Samuel – hey, you know what a good table tennis player you are – don't you want to beat Daddy, hey?

Samuel's face lightens up, illustrating a dramatic mood change – as a smile ripples across his face and he throws his head back and shouts:

SH   Beat Daddy. Beat Daddy. Beat Daddy – I can beat Daddy, I can beat Daddy.

Samuel jumps off Bill with a sudden jerk – without any forethought as to his own safety or how he is going to land. He catches Bill by surprise, who doesn't let go of Samuel's legs. This results in Samuel's top half swinging away from Bill – but as his bottom half is still being held by Bill his head arches in a circle downwards to the floor. As he swings down he gets into a bit of a panic and kicks hard with his legs to free them, again taking Bill by surprise, causing his grip to slip. The end result of this manoeuvre is Samuel lands head first onto the tiled floor.

142

Samuel again starts screaming and going hysterical. Bill's expression is one of absolute despondency/grief. He kneels down, again trying to pacify Samuel, taking him and holding him in his arms, stroking him and repeating soothing words of comfort:

BH   Samuel, it's okay, you'll be fine, it's okay you will be fine ...

Bill starts to examine Samuel's head for any damage bruising, and notices a slight trickle of blood. A close up of Bill's face shows the expression of 'fuck' (without saying the word).

At this point Cynthia walks in and asks:

CH   What the hell is going on – what have you done to Samuel?

Samuel forces himself from Bill's arms and goes screaming to his mum.

SH   Mummy, Mummy, Mummy – Daddy hit me, Daddy hit me, Daddy hurt me.

        Cynthia takes Samuel in her arms and consoles him.

CH   Mummy's here, it will be okay, it will be okay.

Samuel's shouting subsides into sobbing – while he imposes a strangle like grip around Cynthia neck.

The camera cuts across to Bill, who shows an expression of absolute despair as Cynthia gives him a reprimanding look.

Cynthia turns and carries Samuel out of the room.

CH   Come with Mummy, hey? We'll go to the kitchen and get you a nice ice-cream, hey – would you like a nice ice-cream?

As she turns and carries Samuel away, Samuel increases his grip on her by curling his legs around her waist and linking his feet together.

CH   Samuel no, don't squeeze Mummy, it hurts Mummy – don't squeeze me, don't squeeze me, STOP HURTING MUMMY.

Samuel on being reprimanded by his mummy – starts to chuck another tantrum.

SH   Mummy don't love me, Mummy don't love me, Mummy don't love me.

CH   Samuel, of course Mummy loves you. Bill, can you call Dr Docerty and ask him to make an immediate house call to look at Samuel's head?

The scene fades out with Cynthia walking away with Samuel still shouting – with Bill in the sideline with a look of anguish.

Insert Scene – 19

The world is no place for the bad, the stupid, the enervated. Their duty – it's a fine duty too! is to die.

When the Sleeper Wakes *by HG Wells*

Scene 30 – Bill and Cynthia have dinner

8:30pm, Wednesday, 15 May 2013

Setting: Bill and Cynthia Horowitz's dining room at their home

Bill and Cynthia are seated at a formal dining room setting, with well-set table and a bottle of wine on the table [Lenswood 2000 Pinot Noir – Australian]. The two eat in silence for a while, with obvious tension in the air. Bill sips his wine, swirls it around in his mouth, an expression of delight breaks through his previous stern expression as he savours the taste. As he swallows he closes his eyes and a barely audible 'mmmhh' sound can be heard. He puts down the wine, with the attitudinal change still visible in his face then comments:

BH   So, do you think Samuel's getting any better?

CH   What?

BH   Well – is Samuel improving?

CH   Improving from what?

BH   I don't know, is he developing, is he learning – is he maturing?

CH   Bill, how many times do we have to go over this? Samuel has Hallervorden-Spatz Syndrome.

BH   How many times have I asked you? Please do not honour those two Nazis bastards by referring to Samuel's condition by their name. The name of his condition, as you are very well aware, is 'neurodegeneration with brain iron accumulation'. NBIA will suffice.

CH   Okay, he has NBIA, not 'Hallervorden-Spatz Syndrome', but changing the name doesn't change the condition. You of all people should know this. NBIA means he has a genetic defect on his X chromosome – making him retarded. He isn't going to improve.

This is it – this is what we have – this is Samuel. He isn't going to be a lawyer, he isn't going to be a doctor and he isn't going to be a scientist. He will need care for the rest of his life. But he is our son, we love him and he loves us. This is what's important, not our career aspirations for him. Just because he isn't going to follow in your footsteps as a world-renowned lawyer doesn't make him any less of a son or any less of a human being.

BH   I thought the new diet might have helped. Part of his condition is that his body isn't producing some of his developing hormones, and well, with the new diet there was the possibility of improvement.

CH   As the specialist said, this was a long shot, and any improvement would be minor even if it did work. So let's not get too optimistic about the diet. Now, tell me about your meeting with the dwarf.

BH   Cynthia, look I've had a rough day already, I don't need to have a psychoanalysis session at the moment. I mean, all that I've done in the legal arena and in public debate has been for the promotion of genetic research and development for the betterment of us all, to improve both the life of us, and to reduce unnecessary human suffering.

There isn't anything sinister in what I have done, nothing untoward, nothing to be embarrassed about and certainly nothing that requires me to defend myself against accusations of being a Nazi.

CH   Bill. I agree with you. You are rightly proud of the work you've done and are doing. And believe me, I'm very proud of your achievements too. You are a very exceptional person. But, every view is legitimate, and in order to understand the cause of these accusations, you need to explore the reasons why someone else may not view your work in the same light as you and I do. So why did he come to you for help, what did he think you could do for him, what changed his mind, and then why did he turn against you? Let's start with the first – why did he come to you?

BH   Cynthia, please give it a break. I'm really not in the mood for psychoanalysis. I've got my own shrink – and I can save these discussions for my next shrink session.

CH   Bill, I've never seen you so edgy over a client meeting before, and we both know that it's a hazard of your profession to be accused and insulted in the harshest of terms. Being accused of something undesirable is nothing new to you – so why are you taking the dwarf's comments so much to heart, why are you letting his comments upset you so much?

BH   Cynthia, again – please give it a break, okay? I think we both can understand the difference between being called an 'arsehole' and being called a Nazi. For fuck's sake, many of my family were wiped out by them. Now, not only do I have to suffer the indignity of being called a Nazi by a dwarf, I have to explain myself to my wife. So, please, can we end this conversation?

CH   Sure. [A long pause] Bill, why do you speak about him the way you do?

BH   What?

CH   You know, the way you refer to him 'a dwarf'.

BH   What do you mean – I told you he didn't tell me his name.

CH   There are lots of people that you talk about that you don't know their names – you normally refer to them as 'this guy', a prospective client, a delegate, a witness et cetera. When you talk about these guys – you don't emphasise their alias as you have done with 'the dwarf'.

BH   Jesus Cynthia, can you shut the fuck up? How many times do I have to ask? Quit with the psychoanalysis – I don't need it at the moment and I certainly don't need it from my wife.

CH   Sorry. To change the subject, did I tell you that Amelia and Guedeo have invited us around for a dinner party on Saturday, 22 June? It should be a nice evening. Five other couples have also been invited, but I haven't been told of the guest list yet. You know what they're like, always trying to pull surprises.

BH   Sounds good. Do they still bottle their own salsa?

CH   I don't know – I haven't asked recently.

BH   Well I hope so – they sure make a mean lasagne with it. Anyway, I'm off to my study; I have to prepare some briefing notes for a case tomorrow.

Scene fades out with Bill walking out of the room.

Insert Scene – 20

The world exists for exceptional people. By extending educational opportunity, it aims to select and develop the exceptional. No longer will they be lost in the crowd, marrying 'commonplace wives' and becoming commonplace workmen and second-rate professional men. No longer will they be waste as the driftage of superfluous pollen in the pine forest is waste.

The New Machiavelli *by HG Wells*

Scene 31 – Bill gets introspective

10:00pm, Wednesday, 15 May 2013

Setting: Bill Horowitz's home study

Bill is sitting in his home study – screwing up bits of blank paper (out of his printer tray) and slam dunking them into his waste paper basketball net. The tension, frustration of the day's events very evident in his facial expression and his stress-related time-wasting antics with the waste paper.

BH   [Talking to himself like this as he slams each ball of paper through the net] Little shit – how could that midget call me a Nazi? The little prick deserves to be a midget. I buy 'duck disease boy' lunch, and the prick doesn't have the decency to give me his fucking name.

       Fucking Nazis killed for the sake of killing, indiscriminate killing of selected races and religions – Poles, Gypsies, Jews, Catholics, Masons. He didn't pick out people based on their genetic conditions …

Bill then stands and walks across the room and muses at his bookshelves, goes along the titles, first coming across the title In the Name of Eugenics by Dan Kevles. He stops and stares at it and starts to take it out of the shelf, when he spots another book nearby:

       THE REICH GOVERNMENT, *translated from Third Reich originals. Covers economics, social welfare, law and legislation plus several short profiles of political leaders.*

This obviously catches his attention, and he takes this off the shelf and starts to flick through the pages.

Bill starts to furiously flick through the book, using speed reading techniques of running his index finger down the centre of the while walking back to his desk.

Bill finds something in the book that makes him slow down to a stop. Bill then does a voiceover as he reads the following passage from the book:

       It did not take Germany long to implement its eugenic vision. The first law was decreed July 14, 1933: Reich Statute Part I, No. 86, the Law for the Prevention of Defective Progeny. It was a mass compulsory sterilisation law. Rüdin was the co-editor of the official rules and commentary on the law.

Nine categories of defectives were identified for sterilisation. At the top of the list were the feebleminded, followed by those afflicted by schizophrenia, manic depression, Huntington's chorea, epilepsy, hereditary body deformities, deafness and, of course, hereditary blindness. Alcoholism, the ninth category, was listed as optional to avoid confusion with ordinary drunkenness.

The Reich announced that 400,000 Germans would be immediately subjected to the procedure, beginning January 1, 1934. (War Against the Weak, page 299).

BH [Talking to himself] Fucking Nazi bastards. How could they sterilise those poor innocent people, just because they were a few cents short of a euro? Arseholes!

Bill then flicks though more pages – and comes across the following passage:

Sterilisation had begun January 1 of that year. Within 48 hours, the Reich Interior Ministry's eugenics expert announced that the list would include a vast cross-section of the population – from children as young as ten to men over the age of 50. The ministry added that the first to be sterilised would not be residents of 'institutions,' but those who were 'at large'. Quickly, the procedure became known as the Hitlerschnitte, or 'Hitler's cut.' During 1934, the Third Reich sterilised at least 56,000 individuals – approximately one out of every 1,200 Germans. (War Against the Weak, page 304)

BH [Talking to himself] What arseholes – thank God they didn't have access to the genome database – otherwise they would have gone ballistic in rooting out state-decreed unallowable diseases …

Bill stops in his tracks, starts to look very distressed, and perspiration beads from on his forehead and he loosens his tie.

BH Ah fuck this!

He throws the book though the basketball hoop – in which the book is too big to fit through, causing the whole device, together with the book, to crash into the wastepaper bin. He then walks over to a cabinet, opens it up and pours himself a large scotch [from a bottle of 'Black Bowmore 1964'] and downs the lot in one.

He walks out of the room, slamming the door behind him. Camera fades out on closed door.

Insert Scene – 21

If I had it my way, I would build a lethal chamber as big as the Crystal Palace, with a military band playing softly, and a Cinematograph working brightly; then I'd go out in the back streets and main streets and bring them in, all the sick, the halt, and the maimed; I would lead them gently, and they would smile me a weary thanks; and the band would softly bubble out the 'Hallelujah Chorus'.

A letter to Blanche Jennings *from DH Lawrence*

Scene 32 – The dwarf luncheon

11:45am, Saturday, 18 May 2013

Setting: The Narrow Pub

The camera pans around a quite trendy English pub on the Thames – which has a big TV screen currently on a Sky Sports channel – until a table comes into focus that has two empty and two half-filled pint glasses on it, with two dwarfs around it enjoying the game on the TV. The two guys are chatting to each other.

AW   Hey, there's short-ass.

RW   So he's arrived at last [as he glances down at his watch].

IH   [Ivan walks up to the table and shakes their hands] Good to see you guys. Sorry I'm late, I've had a bad couple of days, and well, I slept in. Has the game started?

AW   Yes, about 10 minutes ago. Good to see you too. What are you drinking?

IH   No, it is my round – what are you drinking. Redback? [Gets a nod from Andy and Rob]. Okay, three Redbacks it is.

The scene fades out as Ivan goes up to the bar to order a round of drinks – then fades back with him empty handed at their table.

IH   Sorry guys, they've run out of Redbacks. What would you like instead?

AW   What a piss-poor pub! We should have gone to the Castle.

IH   What's so stellar about the Castle?

AW   At the Castle there's beer that's worth the climb,
And wenches who will give you a good time,
And pretty cudgel-play, you'll find.

Ivan and Rob both stare at Andy asking 'What?' with their expressions.

AW   Goethe, Faust Part One.

RW   Well, that's nice to know, but as it happens, I'm not much into cudgel-play – whatever it is.

Ivan, if there's no Redback, I'll have a Corona.

AW   I'll have a Brugs Wit.

IH   Sure.

The scene fades out on Ivan walking to the bar and fades back in with all of them sitting at the table with several rounds of empty pints on their table. They are obviously more relaxed and boisterous. Cheers are heard around the pub as some of the patrons throw up their arms in delight. 'YESSSS' – resulting from the final whistle of the Arsenal/Spurs game – where Spurs won 2-1 at the Emirates Stadium.

RW   You fucking beauty – on the Spurs!

AW   Top game – coming back 0-1 at half time, talk about precious.

Rob and Andy turn to Ivan for his similar encouraging comments on Spurs performance – but Ivan's mind is elsewhere, with a deep-in-thought expression on his face.

RW   Ivan – top game or what ah? I tell you, the best thing that has happened to football in a hundred years is the introduction of 'the Summer Tournament'.

What do you think of their chance of getting in the Champions League now ah?

IH   What?

RW   The fucking game. Spurs, you know – are they going to get into the Champions League?

IH   Really, who gives a shit, it's only a fucking game.

AW   Heh, heh, heh – we're talking football here, the beautiful game. The mighty Spurs are going to win the Championship League, the very first year they've been in it.

IH   Well good for them – I hope they enjoy it.

RW   Are you okay? I mean, what the hell is your problem?

IH   Nothing … I don't know, I've got a few things on my mind, and football doesn't actually figure on my list of 'what's important' at the moment.

RW   When did this happen? When we coughed up €120 each to see the mighty Spurs play AC Milan it seemed pretty important to you then!

There is a prolonged silence as Rob and Andy wait for Ivan's response. As the silence endures, Ivan's level of discomfort with the silence steadily increases.

RW   So … you gonna tell us?

IH   Tell you what?

RW   What is more important than football?

IH   Well, Sandra's pregnant.

AW&RW [Excitedly] Excellent news, congratulations.

AW   So, how long have you known? When's it due, and holy shit, your mum must be over the moon?

IH   It's not good news – maybe it should be, but it's not.

AW   Why? Is there a problem with the baby, with Sandra – what's the problem?

IH   I think Sandra wants to terminate the pregnancy. I'm not sure, but, well, yes I think she does. I think she wants to abort it.

RW   Why, what has she said? Did she say she wanted an abortion?

IH   Well, not directly.

AW   Well, mate, I suggest you ask her and find out.

IH   Thanks for the advice. But, it is a wee bit difficult as we're not talking and, well, it's got so bad between us that I'm sleeping on the couch in the lounge room.

AW   Oh, that must be uncomfortable. Can't you at least take turns to sleep on the couch?

IH   Yes, it bloody uncomfortable. But, as we're not talking, I can't ask her to take her turn on the couch.

RW   Ivan, sorry to hear that, it must make things difficult for you. If it gets too much for you sleeping on your couch you can always come over to my place and sleep in the spare bedroom.

IH   Rob, thanks, but hopefully it won't get to that stage.

RW   Sure, but the offer is always there. Now, what's all this about Sandra wanting an abortion?

AW   It is so she can advance her career? Continue her studies? What?

IH   You know – if that was the reason, to advance her career, I'd still be against the abortion, but could accept and support Sandra in her decision to terminate the pregnancy.

RW   So the reason Sandra wants to abort, there's something wrong with the child – Down's syndrome or something?

IH   Sandra's 24 – so there is only a 1 in 2,300 chance of the baby having Down syndrome – so NO, this isn't the reason, and as far as I'm concerned there is nothing wrong with the baby.

RW   So, you don't think there is anything wrong, but she does – and I suppose we're probably looking at a condition where the baby has a greater chance than 1 in 2,300 of having the condition in question.

IH   Yes – the baby had a one in four chance of having achondroplasia, a 25% chance of being like his grandfather, a 25% chance of being like Rob, a 25% chance of being like Andy and a 25% chance of being like his fucking short-ass father, yes like me.

      Yes, he had a 25% chance of being a dwarf – and boy he struck lucky. He's going to be a short-ass like the rest of us. So, fuck that, let's abort the little fucker. Let's kill the little midget and put it out of its misery right now – before he knows he's a dwarf. Before he's conscious of the fact that he shouldn't be alive.

The emotional delivery of Ivan's outburst stuns the other two. Neither knows what to say or do, so they both basically pick up their pints, have a sip and stare unfocusedly at the table in front of them. After an agonisingly long pause

RW   So, what are you going to do? Can we help you at all?

IH   Guys, you don't get it, this is not my problem.

RW   What? For something that isn't your problem, you sure seem a wee bit upset by it?

IH   You've missed the point. Of course it's my problem, but it's not 'just' mine.

AW   You mean Valentina, your mum is upset as well – of course!

IH   She's not a dwarf, so no it's not really her problem is it? And Jesus, she hardly wanted children of her own, so I don't think she's going to be too upset about the termination of a grandchild, a midget at that.

AW   I don't get where you're going here, who else's problem is it if it ain't either Sandra's or Valentina's?

RW   Andy, you're sharp as ever today. Don't you get it, the child's being terminated because it's a dwarf, it's being terminated because it's like you and me. We're not good enough to be born; we don't deserve a life because we're short-asses. Ivan's trying to tell us that it's also our problem, a dwarf problem.

AW   Hmmmmm.

        Get you gone, you dwarf;
        You minimus, of hindering knot-grass made;
        You bead, you acorn.

IH   What the fuck are you on about?

AW   A Midsummer Night's Dream, Act 3, Scene 2. Shakespeare didn't like dwarfs either – or at least Lysander didn't.

IH   Well, that makes me feel better – not only does my wife and mother hate dwarfs, but so did Shakespeare. Fantastic.

RW   So, Ivan, where are we – what's happened and what are you doing?

IH   It's worse than you think.

AW   What do you mean – how can it be any worse?

IH   You're not allowed to have kids, well at least not midget kids. Even if you want to have a child, to keep and love, you can't have it because it will have your dirty repulsive dwarf genes. You're the filth of the human genetic gene pool. Society has just started to put a few filters in to clean the pool up a little – and us filth will be removed, so the rest of society feel clean and healthy.

RW   Ivan, stop talking in riddles – and talk us through what has happened – slowly okay?

Ivan starts to relay the story to them – the filming of him telling the story fades in and out and just key words or phrases are heard as you see him passionately relaying what's happened to him up to now.

At the end of Ivan's relaying of his story:

RW   That's fucking outrageous. What the fuck is so wrong with us that we don't have the right to have kids. I mean does the Genetic Protection Authority want to rewrite all the fairytales as well and censor the dwarfs out of Snow White, Rumplestiltskin, Narnia and the Hobbit?

AW   Well what can we do, I mean … what can *we* do?

RW   For a start we can call a special general meeting of the 'Small Persons Association' [Ivan interjects to correct Rob and refer to it as the Dwarfs Association] and tell them what is happening – and see if they think this is all okay or whether they want to do something about it!

IH   Brilliant – I think they would be shocked. I'm sure they'd want to do something about this … about this … about being culled from the human race.

RW   Ivan, leave it to me to organise the meeting – I'll do it right now. I'll make sure all that can attend do attend. Now, as our guest of honour, I take it you will be giving the speech on the night [he looks up and Ivan nods back] – do you have a preferred date?

IH   [Brings out his phone, scrolls through his calendar]. Yes, Friday, the twenty-fourth of May.

RW   Sure that works for me. What about you Andy?

AW   [Checks his mobile] Yep – I can do the twenty fourth.

RW   Good. I'll just check the calendars of the other committee members [scratches a few squiggles into his mobile] they're all free except Greg – his calendar is blocked out for the day – maybe he is doing another one of those movies.

To be honest, I don't mind if Greg isn't there – he frightens the shit out of me. Why does he always have to be so aggressive?

IH   Agreed, I won't be crying if he can't make it. In fact, I'd be pretty happy never to see Greg or his two minders again. The three of them are just a bunch of sadistic arseholes who have nothing better to do than make sicko porn, work out and make life a misery for everyone they come into contact with.

Anyway, what about the associate members – what percentage are free to attend?

RW   [More squiggles] Looks good – 76 don't have any calendar entries that evening, so we might get a reasonable turnout.

AW   What a bunch of sad fucks, so many of them are free on a Friday night!

RW   You're free – you sad fuck! Anyway, I'll update everyone's calendar entry – I'll name the entry the 'Dwarf Genocide Project'. Attendance required to save your family.

IH   Where were you thinking of holding it?

RW   I'll figure that out later – I'll just put TBD under location.

IH   No, let's have it at the Institute of Directors.

RW   I'm not sure the association can afford the IoD

IH   Let's deal with the cost later – this is important – and the venue needs to suggest the gravitas of the situation.

RW   Okay I'll just check to see if they have a conference room available. [After some more interaction with his phone]. Yes, they have a room, and I'm just reserving it.

A few seconds later both Ivan and Rob have a 'beep' go off in their pockets – both pull out their phones, check and say 'I'm booked'.

At this point uniformed official-looking people simultaneously enter every door in the pub then stand immediately in front of the door, their positioning and posture deliberately preventing people from leaving. However, two of the members march into the bar. One takes out a microphone from his pocket and announces:

VI   We are the viral inspectors. Everyone in this pub is to be tested to see if you have been inoculated against avian flu. It will not take long, less than a minute per person. If you have been inoculated, after you have been tested you will be free to go about your business. If you have not been inoculated, you will be immediately arrested, taken to a police cell until tomorrow morning when you will be taken to the 'Viral Prevention Court' to be tried for posing a risk to the public. Furthermore, whether voluntary or otherwise, you shall be inoculated against avian flu.

        Now, can I ask you to form an orderly queue so we can start the testing? Once you have been positively tested, we will spray the back of your hand. You will not be able to leave these premises until your hand has been sprayed.

IH   [Looking to the others] Fuck, this is the second time in a week I've been tested. Look, I have to go soon, so I'm going to get to the front of the queue and get this over and done with so that I can leave. Anyway, thanks guys for listening to me and helping me out – it's much appreciated.

Ivan heads to the point indicated by the lead viral inspector and positions himself at the start of the queue. The viral inspector standing at the head of the queue pulls out a black electronic contraption from his pocket about the size of a mobile phone. He holds it in front of Ivan's face and instructs him:

VI   Please breathe onto the shiny disk at the centre of the viral immunity detector.

Ivan, familiar with the process, breathes heavily onto the shiny disk. After he finishes breathing out, there is a wait of about five seconds, at which time a green LED illuminates on the detector together with a single high pitched 'Beep'.

VI   Please put out you hand so that I can spray the back of it – which will allow you to leave the premises.

Ivan projects his arm with his hand facing downwards. The viral inspector takes out a canister and sprays the back of his hand – which does not make a visible mark.

Ivan waves to Andy and Rob and proceeds to the doors to exit. When he gets to the door, he raises the back of his hand to the viral inspector manning the door. The inspector scans the back of his hand with another electronic device which lights up with a green LED and makes a high pitched 'beep'. Upon testing positive to the hand swipe, the inspector signals to Ivan that he is free to leave the premises. On being given the all clear, Ivan leaves the pub and goes on his way.

Insert Scene – 22

> *This rich and abundant and ultimately aimless life, this tremendous spawning and proliferation of uneventful humanity! These individual lives signified no doubt enormously to the individuals, but did all the shining, reflecting, changing existence that went by like bubbles in a stream signify collectively anything more than the leaping, glittering confusion of shoaling mackerel on a sunlit afternoon?*

Marriage *by HG Wells*

Scene 33 – Bill casts suspicious eye on Sandra

10:30am, Monday, 20 May 2013

Setting: Bradbury, Dywer & Waldron offices

Sandra, very smartly dressed, is walking down a corridor at her law firm. As she walks down the corridors she passes a young Korean girl (Hye Soon Park – aged 8) that appears to be working very hard in a cubicle, then later passes a meeting room with four people having a meeting with a young Caucasian girl (Kharechka Solovyov – aged 7) dominating the meeting.

She arrives at an office with 'Dr Horowitz' on the name plate then looks to the secretary sitting outside his office (like a guard) and asks:

SS   Josephine, can I see Bill?

JC   I'll just check to see if Dr Horowitz has time to see you.

SS   I have an appointment!

JC   Yes, I'll just check to see if Dr Horowitz can see you.

Josephine uses the intercom and speaks to Bill, who confirms that Sandra can come in.

Sandra opens and walks through Bill's office door. The camera then pans around Bill's office, which is a large, very opulently appointed corner office with external windows on two walls. The walnut office furniture includes: a large desk, a meeting table with ten seats, filing cabinets, bookshelves and two chestnut sofas. Even with all the furniture, the office is still quite spacious. Bill is sitting at his desk, head down reading some case law on a recent genetic court case involving the patenting by a doctor of a patient's genes, after which the patient had to buy his own genes (but now part of a genetically developed medicine) back to get cured.

BH   Sandra, thanks for agreeing to see me. We haven't really spoken about your plans since our luncheon two weeks. I know from Laurie that you're keen to get ahead and take up our offer to support you studying at Oxford. But, as a little time has gone by since we last spoke on this topic, I thought I'd just touch base with you – and make sure everything is okay So – how are you readying yourself to embark on such a serious study program?

SS   Thanks Bill, all is very well. I can't thank you enough for the fantastic opportunity that you've given me. I really appreciate it!

BH   So, I understand that Corpus Christi College has set a date for your interview – in fact if my memory serves me correctly it must be tomorrow? [He looks to Sandra, who nods] Well, hopefully your enrolment will go through without a hitch.

SS   Well, I hope so.

BH   Sandra, don't hope for things to happen – make them happen.

SS   Sure. That's what I'm doing, I'm making Oxford happen.

BH   I know you have a husband, who also works [again there is an exchange of nods between them]. I know from my own experience it can be very difficult and very demanding when both you and your partner are working, and you have the additional heavy demand of study. It not only affects your own life and lifestyle, but also that of your partner's.

      So, what I guess I'm asking is whether you think you and your husband are both prepared and able to put up with the pressure, that both of you as a unit, will be subjected to?

SS   Funnily enough, I was having a similar conversation with Laurie last Wednesday. And, yes, Ivan and I are fine – he is as delighted as I am that I have this opportunity. And, as he readily admits, along with his mother, his job is not as demanding as mine. So, you know, he will be able to help to keep the household running.

BH   That's good, where does [pauses while he recalls the name Sandra just mentioned] Ivan work?

SS   [The question catches her by surprise – as she doesn't want to admit that Ivan works at the GPA, as this will give away the fact that her good ideas actually came from Ivan and were not necessarily her original ideas. After a detectable pause she goes on.] Oh, he is a civil servant at Whitehall.

BH   Well, there you go, there's someone who should definitely help shoulder some of the household pressures. What part of the Civil Service?

SS   [Again caught by surprise – and again after a detectable pause] Ah, with the MoD.

BH   Even better. I didn't think there were any MoD offices in Whitehall – what area is he in? Is he in the military or civilian part of the MoD?

SS   [Pause] He doesn't say, he maintains it's classified.

BH   Really? well maybe it's MI5.

SS   I don't know, he's taught me not to ask questions – as he can't give answers.

BH   Well, I suppose he has a point there. Well aside from the pressures of your two careers and your impending study programme – is there anything else in your lives that may inhibit you from reaching your goals?

SS   [Guardedly] Like what?

BH   I don't know, family, travel, money, sickness, babies?

SS   No. There is nothing out there that will stop me from reaching my goals.

BH   Excellent to hear. And, now tell me, what are your goals?

SS   [A little shaky] Well, first to graduate from Oxford with an LLB, then to become a partner at Bradbury, Dywer & Waldron.

BH   Excellent.

       [Pauses for a while]
       As you know I couldn't attend last year's Christmas party – as I was in the US giving evidence at a US Congressional select committee on human cloning ethics – but I understand your husband accompanied you to the Christmas party. Did he enjoy it?

SS   Yes, Ivan had a wow of a time. I suppose it showed him the contrast between the private and public sector work environments and workers. I think after speaking to some of the associates and hearing the hours they put in, it made him feel better about his own job. The pay may not be as good – but he has a lot more time off – including all his weekends. Moreover, it gave him an opportunity to show off his Cossack dancing.

BH   When I got back and caught up with all the office news, it was mentioned that you both appeared to have a good time – and, yes from all accounts, Ivan and Kharechka did put on an impressive impromptu Cossack dance. Apart from Josephine, who wouldn't know a good time if she fell over one backwards, everyone apparently had a good time.

Anyway, thank you for making the time to come and see me this morning and for being so positive about your opportunities.

Bill's Blackberry goes off – informing him that his next meeting is about to start. Bill looks at the Blackberry, then looks up to Sandra.

BH   Unfortunately, I have to jump onto a conference call now. So, thanks again and good luck with your interview at Corpus Christi tomorrow.

With this, he swings his chair around and starts typing in the conference call codes into his desk phone. Sandra gets up and thanks Bill and leaves.

The camera fades out as she closes the door behind her.

Insert Scene – 23

The spectre of famine, of the plague, of war, etc, are mild and gracious symbols compared with that menacing figure, Universal Education, with which we are threatened, which has already eunuched the genius of the last five-and-twenty years of the nineteenth century, and produced a limitless abortion in that of future time.

Confessions of a Young Man *by George Moore.*

Scene 34 – Bill investigates identity of Ivan

11:00am, Monday, 20 May 2013

As soon as Sandra has exited the office, Bill interrupts his conference call and uses the intercom to speak to his secretary, Josephine, asking her to come into his office. Josephine comes in and sits down opposite Bill at his desk. Bill has the conference call on speaker phone – he pushes the mute button [while others on the call are still talking] and starts to speak to Josephine.

BH   Josephine, can you liaise with corporate security and get the security file for those that attended the office Christmas party last year. Can you get them to email me the file – complete with their photos?

JC   Sure, I should have it this afternoon – by say 2:30pm. Is this okay?

BH   Yea, but the sooner the better.

JC   Okay, I'll see what I can do. Is there anything else?

BH   Yes – I don't want you to talk about this to anyone okay, and make sure the security guys get the same message. Tell them that if there's a hint that they were indiscreet over this request they're going to be out of a job.

JC   [Smiles at Bill] I'll make sure they get the message.

Josephine gets up and leaves. The camera pans back to Bill, who is in deep disturbed contemplation. The scene fades out with him getting up and staring out the window over the spectacular view of London – while the conference call continues in the background.

Scene 35 – The office Christmas party

1:00pm, Monday, 20 May 2013

Setting: Bill Horowitz's work office and BDW's 2012 Christmas party at the natural history museum

Josephine, Bill's secretary, knocks on Bill's office door. Bill looks up from his desk, where he is engaged in a conference call while eating his lunch, and signals her in. Josephine walks up to Bill and hands him a DVD – with the title written across the cover.

Bradbury, Dywer & Waldron 2012 Christmas party

Bill presses the mute button on his desk phone – with the conference call still ploughing on.

JC   Bill, is this what you were after?

BH   Actually, I asked for the security file photos – but, I'm sure that this will be even better.Did you discuss this with anyone?

JC   No, I was able to take a copy from the CCTV security system, so I didn't need to speak with anyone about it.

BH   Brilliant, once again you came through for me. Thanks a million. I can't leave this call, so can I ask you to put the DVD in the player [signalling to a media unit in his office] and hit the play button?

JC   Sure, do you want the sound muted?

BH   Yes, I only need the visual. Thanks.

Josephine walks over to the multimedia cabinet in Bill's office, inserts the DVD, presses a few buttons, then looks up to observe a ceiling partition opening, followed by the emergence of 60 inch LCD monitor that comes to rest a foot below the ceiling and two metres directly in front of Bill's desk. Once in its resting position, the monitor starts to display the DVD recording. Once the DVD starts to play, Bill looks up from his desk to watch it – but still fully engaged in the conference call.

The titles of the DVD roll, and then the video opens with pan of the venue, before the guests had arrived. The venue is the main foyer of the Natural History Museum – with all the tables and chairs arranged around the museum's centre piece – the full cast of a diplodocus dinosaur skeleton.

There is a 2.4 metre (8') high replica of a tyrannosaurus rex at the side of the entrance hall near the reception table. As guests approach the reception table to register – or stop to inspect the replica – the replica lurches out at them and in most cases causes a considerable (anticipated) fright to the guests. The replica then laughs or jokes – indicating that a person inside the replica is deliberately scaring the guest – all in good fun.

The DVD fades in and fades back out with the arrival of the first then subsequent guests – being greeted by the replica then hostess staff offering them Champagne. The DVD continues on in this mode – fading in and out to pick up the arrival of more guests. However, due to the noise, movement and number of people in the foreground and background – it is obvious not everyone's entrance was filmed.

After the non-exhaustive 'entrance scenes' are over, the DVD shows the guests starting to mill around and take their seats.

Once all the guests are duly assembled and standing at their tables, Pat Rushworth steps forward to make the obligatory office Christmas party speech.

At this point the scene ceases being a shot of the plasma screen – as the scene transforms into the scene at the actual Christmas party.

PR   I remember as a young lad how upset my mother was at one of my father's annual Christmas parties. He was in the Royal Navy at the time.

At one year's Christmas party, all personnel had to remain on the quay with their partners, until they were called on board. The calling went like this:

The first calling was *'Could all commissioned officers and their ladies please come on board.'*

The second calling was *'Could non-commissioned officers and their wives please come on board.'*

The third calling was *'Could all non-officers and their women please come on board.'*

My father was a rear admiral and Mother was a devout Christian. The unegalitarian announcements in reference to the partners, from ladies, wives, to women – offended my mother's Christian sensitivities. In her eyes, especially at Christmas, all partners should have been treated equally.

I learned a lot from this moment in my mother's life and the distress it caused her – and how a little Christian spirit, or at least a degree of consideration and humanity, can lead to greater harmony for all.

However, I have learned a great deal more from the UK Discrimination and Harassment Act – where I am now legally compelled to treat you all as equals [said as a joke, and elicits a small chuckle from the audience]. So in this spirit, I would like to welcome you all here tonight as equals to enjoy the food, the drink, the entertainment, and of course our collective company.

So, please raise your glasses for the festive season toast!

Everyone raises their glasses and makes a toast to the festive season.

PR   Well, you may have thought with that toast, you had heard the last of me, but it is not quite the case as I do have a few more observations and announcements, so, please bear with me for a while longer.

I raised the story of my mother for two reasons, the first, to emphasise the point that tonight at Bradbury, Dywer & Waldron, we are all equal – and we are all here to equally enjoy ourselves and one another. The second reason is to highlight the difference between the worlds my mother and, I believe I can speak for nearly everyone here, your mothers lived in – and the world that we live in.

There was a strong element of truth in my mother's Christian disposition – that we were all equal – or at the very least should all be treated as equals. That world has gone. Today, with the new genetic technology that is available, prospective parents can have their embryos genetically enhanced, for greater athleticism, musical ability, piousness, attractiveness and of course, intelligence.

With intelligence alone, it is now possible to raise the IQ of a child by twenty points, by undertaking a little genetic engineering on the embryo.

For better or worse, whether it is fair or not, only the ultra-wealthy parents can afford this luxury. However, it will not be a luxury for very long. If all your peers are boosting the IQ of their future offspring, then your offspring would be at a massive competitive disadvantage if you did not boost theirs. So we now see a clear trend, namely that the ultra-wealthy classes increasingly feel compelled to genetically enhance their kids, just so that their kids are not disadvantaged. This is a seismic shift. The genetic boosting of intelligence was once rarely done – those rare instances were done to give a kid a competitive advantage. Now parents boost their kids IQ just so that they're not at a competitive disadvantage.

Further, while at the moment the genetic IQ boosts maybe restricted to the kids of the ultra- wealthy, very soon it will be the domain of the wealthier class generally. It is now for me to state the obvious: the enhanced IQ genie is now out of the bottle – and it cannot be put back. The first batch of these new genetically boosted individuals, and I don't use the term 'batch' lightly, will be hitting the work force over the next ten or so years, assuming they start work at twenty – but who knows, maybe they will start at fifteen.

These kids will no doubt be able to make further enhancements to the human genome, which conceivably will give rise to a second generation of genetically enhanced kids – or, as I prefer to call them, 'genhance' with IQs of 200 plus. To put this in perspective, Einstein's IQ is estimated to have been somewhere in the region of 160 to 180.

Unlike our mothers' world, in this world, in our world, these kids' world, we are not all the same and we will not be able to treat everyone the same. The concept of Christian egalitarianism is obsolete.

Soon we will have one class of humans who will be able to solve the 'unified field theory' in the morning and write a musical composition rivalling Bach's sinfonias in the afternoon. The other class of humans will wait on their table. The chance of social mobility in this brave new world will be zero. And with every generation, the gap will widen and widen.

So, what does all this have to do with us and our office Christmas party?

Well, the companies that can attract these kids to work for them will likewise have a massive competitive advantage over their rivals. As more and more genhances are ready to join the workforce, they will increasingly want to work with other genhances, both so that they can be with their own types and because the company will obviously be more successful.

It is with this in mind that the firm has created a new charity for the benefit and wellbeing of the genetically enhanced. It is not that these kids need money – their parents have plenty of it. It is more for our firm to become far more involved with the kids – to be able to guide them so that their intellectual prowess is challenged and directed towards worthwhile pursuits. A key part of the charity is to provide them with intellectual challenges, here, at Bradbury, Dywer & Waldron – including work experience in our office. Ultimately, this will lead to an association between us, so that we will be a natural company for these kids to come and work for once they join the work force.

The first visible outcome of this aspect of the charity's programme is that five genhances will be starting work experience with us immediately after the festive season, commencing 2nd of January 2013. And, as a special treat for us all, I have invited these youngsters together with their parents to be with us tonight.

So, can you please welcome the first five genhances in the world to ever engage in work experience – together with their very proud, and shall I venture, very wise parents.

In no particular order, please welcome:

Heather McCauley, who is seven years old – and her parents, Douglas and Judy McCauley.
Hye Soon Park, 8 – and her parents Jung Ho Hyun and Jin-Sook Park
Gordon Zhou, 7 – and his parents Míngzì and Xiùměi Zhou.
Kharechka Solovyov, 7 – and her parents Nikanosha, and Poliusha Solovyov Bruce Mayne, 9 – and his father Trevor Mayne.

With each announcement the child, accompanied by their parent(s) comes on to the stage area, gives a slight bow of acknowledgement, and with each introduction there is loud enthusiastic clapping from the audience. As each child and parent(s) concludes their introduction, they step to the side to allow the next child/parent to come on stage. Once all of them have been introduced, they all walk confidently to the reserved spare table at the front of the museum – i.e. the best table closest to the staging area.

As they walk in union to the table, there is another bout of loud applause from all those at the function.

PR   Without further ado, please feel welcome and enjoy the evening.

Insert Scene – 24

The mass mind is debased because it is required to gravitate to a standard size to receive the standard idea. However, this stultifying process should be stepped up, because as the mass becomes more and more comatose, the few 'free intelligences' will be isolated and thrown into prominence, and this will create an intellectual caste system. Interbreeding within the intellectual caste may result in beneficial biological mutations. For though mankind as a whole will never be ready for civilisation, the isolated intelligent few may generate a new species of superior being

The Art of Being Ruled by Wyndham Lewis.

After the insert scene – the scene swaps back to the office Christmas party, picking up where it left off.

The scene then shows the usual movement as everyone gets seated and starts to chat – with the odd close up here and there.

The scene fades out and back in during the mid-point in the main course – with everyone in serious eating and drinking mode. During a pan of all the tables, Sandra briefly comes into focus and it is 'just' evident that someone is sitting beside her, but the flower arrangement on the table obscures the view of her partner. The scene then freezes – then starts to fast-rewind.

The scene swaps back to Bill, who has a remote in his hand. He starts to replay the last few seconds of the DVD and closely scrutinise the LCD monitor – particularly trying to determine who Sandra's partner is that is obscured by the flowers. Bill can't get a clear view – so he lets the DVD play on.

The scene fades out and back in at the Christmas party– with the band playing – composed of five Black musicians (a keyboard player, tenor saxophone, trumpet, percussionist and vocalist/guitarist). There are several couples up on the floor dancing – but most people are still eating, drinking and talking.

The scene fades out and in, with the floor packed with couples dancing to 'Shake a Tail Feather'. Within the pulsating crowd the dance floor, there are glimpse of Sandra dancing with a short person – but, due to the crowd, his facial features are never caught on the video. Included in the lively dancing is Hye Soon and Bruce Mayne dancing together – both fully getting into the spirit of the occasion and obviously enjoying themselves.

The scene fades out and back in – with an hour or so having past, around 10:30pm. The general demeanour of the guests is now less formal, with a number of the men having removed their suit coats and all notably more boisterous. There are not as many on the dance floor, but those dancing are 'getting into the music' of 'Rivers of Babylon'. On the dance floor are four of the five genhance kids – with Heather and Gordon dancing together and Hye Soon and Bruce still together.

The camera picks up on Kharechka, who is sitting at the table with the nine parents, who are all engaged in their own conversations, with Kharechka being left out of it and feeling uncomfortably alone.

Kharechka, feeling 'out of it' looks around for a dance partner – and looks towards the table where Sandra and Ivan are sitting, the camera picking up the back of Ivan and the side of Sandra.

Kharechka swallows hard, then nervously gets up and walks towards their table. She very apprehensively approaches Sandra and with an astounding degree of graciousness, asks whether she would be offended if she was to ask Ivan for a dance. Sandra is taken by surprise by the request, but after her shock, assures Kharechka that she is welcome to ask Ivan – but that it will be Ivan's decision not hers. Ivan witnessed the conversation with a degree of incredulousness, but due to the level of the music, was not able to follow the conversation that took place.

Kharechka then turns to Ivan and, again with a measure of grace that belies her young age, asks Ivan whether he would like a dance.

Ivan's incredulousness turned into astonished disbelief. However, Kharechka's maintains her inoffensive gracious pose, using her child femininity to devastating effect. After Ivan recovers from his shock, it was very apparent to him that he does not have a choice in the matter. He thinks for a second or so whether he should take offence to the position that he has been placed in – but realises that would get him nowhere. On realising he is trapped, rather than making a scene, he graciously accepts Kharechka's offer and accompanies her to the dance floor.

The scene fades out and back in on the dance floor with still a lively crowd on the dance floor, with all five genhance kids on the floor, Kharechka dancing with Ivan. However, it is evident that both Kharechka and Ivan are trained dancers as their style and rhythm are distinctly more refined than the rhythmic pulse of the dance floor crowd. The camera stays with them for a while where the two 'egg' each other on to ascertain the depth of each other's training, all while trying not to cause offence by upstaging each other.

The scene fades out and back in on the dance floor, which shows the dance floor with a crowd circled around the edge of the dance floor, all clapping and cheering the dancers in the centre – namely Kharechka and Ivan. The two of them performing a traditional Cossack dance – both with perfect step, timing and rhythm – it being evident that both are very much enjoying themselves.

At this point, the scene freezes. The scene swaps over to Bill in his office staring at the plasma screen in disbelief. He rewinds it back to the start of the Cossack dance and replays it – with the camera now including Bill watching the scene.

BH   Holy shit. It is Ivan – and boy he is quite a lad.

The scene fades out and back into the Christmas party – where now it looks to be the last dance or so of the evening with a number of couples on the dance floor moving slowly together to the jazz sound of John Coltrane's 'A Love Supreme'. Included in the slow dancers are Sandra and Ivan who, due to their size differential, are dancing awkwardly yet happily together.

With this the scene fades out.

Insert Scene – 25

The Negro's gift to the white world is jazz, an aesthetic medium of a sort of frantic proletarian subconscious. A barbarous, melancholy, epileptic folk music, worthy of a patagonian cannibal. It is degraded and degrading, expressing the mindless energy of the mass. It is the slum peasant and the city serf that rejoice in its gross proletarian nigger bumps.

The Apes of God *by Wyndham Lewis.*

Scene 36 – Bill meets Rabbi

9:30am, Tuesday, 21 May 2013

Setting: Outside: Blooms Kosher Deli

The scene opens with Bill having coffee with his rabbi at a table outside Bloom's Deli/Restaurant on Golders Green Road.

Rabbi Bill, it is so good to see you again – I'm delighted that with all your success, all your travel, your busy schedule – that you still have time to honour me with a visit.

BH I assure you, the honour is all mine. I am never, ever too busy to see you my old friend.

Rabbi Hey, I'm not that old, all my plumbing still works.

BH That's what I like to hear. I hope when I'm your age all mine is still working, and that I get to use it once in a while.

Rabbi Anyway Bill, what's up, what's on your mind? Why did you call me and ask me for coffee at such short notice?

BH Come on now, since when have I needed an excuse to have a coffee with you? I had some spare time and I thought of you, and this is what I get …

Rabbi Sure, sure, sure, but how can I help you?

BH That's what I like about you, never one for social pleasantries – you just dive in and keep fishing until you dig something up.

Rabbi I can't believe you said that [in a very indignant tone].

BH What – what did I say … [trying to get a handle on why the rabbi is trying to make him feel guilty over what he said – but nothing comes to mind].

Rabbi Such a gross mix of metaphors – dive in, then fish, how can you fish when you've just dived in, then dig something up, if you're either diving or fishing you ain't going to dig anything up.

BH Still sharp as ever – I should know better than even attempt to take you on.

Rabbi Yes, you should know better – now cut the crap and tell me what's up?

BH Well it's about a client. It's a little muddled as he refuses to give me his name, then he walked out on me before he actually became my client – and now he never wants me to speak to him again.

So, technically he is not my client, more an ex-prospective client whose name I don't officially know.

Rabbi Well, I never wanted you to speak to me, and you don't know my name. But you persisted and I eventually spoke back to you. And in the absence of knowing my name you just call me Rabbi. So you've been able to solve this sort of problem before.

BH Thanks for the vote of confidence. But it does get more complicated.

Rabbi Why, did your client marry a Catholic?

BH You'll never forgive me for that, will you?

Rabbi It's all right; I'm just winding you up – it's fun to watch.

BH The guy's a dwarf

Rabbi Cynthia's a dwarf, as well as a Catholic – and she's a guy? Hoolly doolly, I really should never have married you two.

BH Thanks Rabbi, but it is my ex-prospective client that is a male dwarf, not Cynthia. She's just a female Catholic.

Rabbi Okay okay – well, actually I'm not okay. I'm not sure I understand the situation. What's being a dwarf got to do with the issue?

BH Everything. But, it's worse …

Rabbi Worse than being a dwarf – is he also Catholic?

BH Can you quit the Catholic jokes?

Rabbi   You started it.

BH   I did not.

Rabbi   You married one.

BH   Shall I go on? [Gets a nod from the Rabbi.] He also came to our office Christmas party last year.

Rabbi   I can see you're going somewhere with this story – but unless he was one of Santa's elves at your Christmas party I'm afraid that the story is so far lost on me.

Bill pulls out his phone from his jacket pocket, flicks through the photos stored on his phone then passes the phone over the table to Rabbi. Rabbi gets the phone stares at it, then the camera zooms into it, which shows a photo of Ivan and Sandra taken on the dance floor during the office Christmas party.

BH   The little guy, I found out after a bit of an investigation is 'Ivan Henry', a dwarf suffering from achondroplasia.

Rabbi   I see – a dwarf. And the girl next to him – is that Snow White?

BH   Actually, her name is Sandra Small.

Rabbi   Good choice of surname. So, has she got anything to do with … whatever it is you're trying to tell me.

BH   Yes, she is one of my staff.

Rabbi   Aah, so it's starting to come together – you have a conflict of interest between your ex- prospective client, one that never wants you to speak to you again, and one of your staff that – that co-habits with him – or are they married – or divorced?

BH   They're married.

Rabbi   The obvious answer of course is not to take on the client, particularly as he never wants to see you again, which makes it a little easier for you. In fact, as he never wants to see you again, it would be hard to even get him as a client. But, I guess you have figured this bit out for yourself, so the story must be still a little deeper – so please go on.

BH   Well, not only are they married, but she is also pregnant.

Rabbi   Ooh. So, why would the little guy come to you if she's pregnant? He didn't give you his name, because then you would link it to Sandra and you would refuse to see him. But, as he didn't give you his name, you did see him. Then he must have told you about the pregnancy – obviously not naming the mother – seeking your help on some legal issue about the pregnancy, and you said something back to him that pissed him off so bad that he never wants to see you again. That must have been cracking advice!

         You obviously agonised over the incident, and wondered why he was so secretive about his name, that eventually you looked in your own backyard for the answer to his identity, finding he is the husband of one of your staff who I guess hasn't told you yet that she is pregnant.

BH   As I said before, still sharp as ever.

Rabbi   So the advice. Why would he come to you of all people – why not one of the other million odd lawyers in the country where his identity wouldn't have been an issue? Bill I don't read legal journals, but I do read the London Jewish Chronicle and the Hamodia, which have their share of gossip. They always refer to you as one of the world's foremost experts on genetic law.

         So why would a dwarf want to see the world's foremost genetic legal expert about his pregnant wife who, by coincidence, just happens to be one of your staff? Genetics is not my field of knowledge – as you are very well aware – but I'm going to go out on a limb and say that … what did you call it … achondroplasia [pauses and looks and receives a confirmation nod from Bill] is a genetic disorder.

Rabbi looks to Bill, who sheepishly nods to confirm Rabbi's correct understanding. Bill progressively feels more uncomfortable about being humbled by the rabbi in this way.

Rabbi   So, there must be a chance that the unborn child will also have achondroplasia?

         Bill nods again.

Rabbi   So why would he be seeing you, rather than her coming to see you about this issue? It must be for advice on the child – [Bill nods his confirmation] or Ivan's rights over the child?

Bill, again, nods his confirmation.

Rabbi   Maybe over Ivan's rights to either preserve or terminate the child's life – because it either is, or is not, a dwarf. My guess is that Ivan wants to protect his child's life, which Sandra is threatening because it's a dwarf.

BH   Rabbi, again, as ever – sharp and to the point – yes, yes you are right on the nail.

Rabbi   Now Bill, the next bit is where it hurts isn't it?

BH   [Squirms and shrugs] Just go on.

Rabbi   Your advice, what could that have been? What could have pissed him off so bad that he never wants to see you again? Your advice went beyond merely ranting the common twenty-first century mantra 'It's a woman's choice', because I can't see that upsetting the little guy that much – any lawyer is likely to recite the mantra, which therefore wouldn't have been that much of a shock to him.

Your advice must have included something about his genetic build – about the genetic build of his children. Did you question his right to have children?

BH   The bastard called me a 'Fucking Nazi'.

There is a long pause as the rabbi is obviously shocked and uncustomarily trying to catch up with the situation rather than being ahead of it.

Rabbi   Hmmmmm. Nazi. A procreating one at that. Boy, ho boy, ho boy – if your parents heard that heh? Maybe it's just as well they're dead, because that would have killed them. That is strong language. So why do you think he called you a Nazi?

BH   Give me a break, Cynthia tried the old psychoanalysis trick on me already 'why do you think …'

Rabbi   I have to start giving more credit to that Catholic wife of yours – she knows what's up.

So, how did you answer Cynthia?

BH   What? Didn't I just say …

Rabbi   Yes – but you haven't told me the answer. And until I understand what's troubling you – and I'm starting to get an idea – then I can't offer you any help: moral, spiritual, ethical or otherwise.

BH   You know that the 'Committee for the Prevention of Jewish Genetic Disease' in the US organises voluntary genetic tests for Jewish school children.

They do this because Jews, particularly Jews of Ashkenazi decent, are prone to two genetic mutations, namely the deletion of the 6,174th letter on gene BRCA2 on chromosome 13, and another mutation of gene BRCA1 on chromosome 17. Approximately 28% of Jewish breast-cancer cases under the age of 42 are attributable to either one of these two mutations. These tests help provide young ladies with an early warning of the risk they face of contracting breast cancer – which helps them to actively monitor their health and be active in seeking medical help if symptoms develop.

Also, when these genetic tests are done, the committee provides the children with an anonymous number. Later in life, when two Jews are considering marriage, they can phone the Committee for the Prevention of Jewish Genetic Disease, and tell them their anonymous number.

If both partners carry either of the BRCA mutations or other genetic diseases like Tay-Sachs or cystic fibrosis – the committee informs them. The partners then know that if they have children, there is a high risk of the children developing the genetic disease. In these circumstances, the couple usually either find other partners or adopt.

This voluntary process has all but eliminated cystic fibrosis from the American Ashkenazi Jewish population. I think this is impressive and has served humanity well – or it could do if everyone had these tests, not just American Jews. How can this be compared with Nazis?

Rabbi   It can't. Nobody is hurt, killed or forced to do something against their will.

BH   So why am I being compared to a Nazi?

Rabb   Your short friend is not an American Ashkenazi Jew and you are not offering him the same advice. So what advice did you offer him?

179

BH   You don't think the work that the Committee for the Prevention of Jewish Genetic Disease is worthy of praise, that it is adding or contributing to the welfare of humanity?

Rabbi Yes, I think it is noteworthy – it prevents the conception of children who otherwise could be born with a debilitating or terminal disease.

       But, what was the advice that you offered the short guy?

BH   I didn't offer him any advice, I merely offered him my interpretation of the Genetic Protection Act and the associated GPA Gazette of Deemed Genetic Diseases.

Rabbi My daily avid read of the Jewish Chronicle, unfortunately, has precluded me from reading the latest edition of the Genetic Protection Act and the associated GPA Gazette of Deemed Genetic Diseases. So, tell me what is your interpretation.

BH   It's not that simple, he took my interpretation out of context

Rabbi Hummm, not that simple and out of context. No doubt in comparison, the Torah is so simple it can't be taken out of context.

       I agree where you're going with this. It must be way too complex for a poor old rabbi to understand. No doubt, and rightly so, you are sitting there feeling embarrassed for me due to my soft, old, simple brain. Now you feel awkward, as you wanted to come to me for advice, but now you find that you operate in a sphere far above this poor old simple rabbi – and you now realise that I'm not capable of understanding your problem and I won't be able to give you the meaningful advice you were seeking. I'm so sorry for you.

       Now you must excuse me, I haven't finished reading the Hamodia and at this rate I won't get to finish it today, so I will be off. Thank you for the coffee.

BH   Rabbi, I'm sorry. Please sit. The GPA Act states that any embryo with a gene sequence that can give rise to a physical or behavioural condition that is three standard deviations outside the human norm, well the parents are to be encouraged to terminate the pregnancy. Further, the father loses all paternal rights over any decision the mother may make in relation to the termination of the pregnancy.

There is a long silence while the rabbi keeps eyeing Bill to continue to explain himself – but he doesn't.

Rabbi This is not the same as the work being done by the Committee for the Prevention of Jewish Genetic Diseases is it?

BH Yes it is – we're all trying to eradicate genetic diseases.

Rabbi I suppose the death squads in Bogota, Columbia that go around indiscriminately shooting street kids could base their rationale on the fact that they are just eradicating genetic inherited behavioural traits?

BH That's unfair; we are not advocating the killing of anyone.

Long Pause.

Rabbi 'We' [long pause]. That is such a strong word – 'we'. Not the undefined 'they', not the 'Genetic Protection Authority' but 'we'.

Bill, the Torah does have something to say about when life begins, and under what circumstances a pregnancy may be terminated. Under Jewish law, a Jewish woman may procure an abortion in a situation where her life is endangered by continuing with a pregnancy – or perhaps in a situation where the pregnancy poses grave danger to her own health. Other than these circumstances, abortion is prohibited.

The Torah says, 'Behold, I place before you today life and goodness, death and evil'. We are to clearly know the alternatives, and then, as the Torah implores us, we must allow our heads to guide our hearts and 'choose life'.

BH Rabbi, with all due respect, I really don't think you appreciate all the issues involved in this case.

Rabbi Maybe you're right – so can I ask you a few questions so that I can get a full appreciation of the issues at hand?

BH Sure – fire away.

Rabbi The young man who came to you – is he in pain?

BH Shakes his head.

Rabbi Will he be in pain later in life?

BH   Shakes his head.

Rabbi Is he a Mohel short of a Bris ceremony?

Bill looks up with a confused look.

Rabbi Is he slow?

Bill shakes his head.

Rabbi Is he in anyway disabled?

BH   Thinks for a bit then shakes his head.

Rabbi Is he a threat to anyone?

Bill shakes his head.

Rabbi Is he a social drop out, or a sponge on society?

BH   No.

Rabbi Does he have a job?

BH   Yes, he is a social research worker.

Rabbi Is there any reason to think he wouldn't make a good father?

Bill shakes his head.

Rabbi Is there any reason the GPA, society or you would want to stop him from
        having children – aside from the possibility that his children may also be
        short?

BH   You're missing the point again – we can now stop this genetic condition
        being passed to future generations. We now have the chance to rid
        society of this terrible genetic condition – and here you are saying to me
        that it's okay to keep inflicting this preventable disease on our children
        and their children.

182

Rabb   How can you classify this as a terrible disease? The guy who came to you works, is smart, is social and would be a good father. The only thing you have against him is that he is short.

So what! I tell ya, I saw a dwarf once back in Russia, the Moscow Circus. This guy, this dwarf was the funniest clown I've ever seen. The acrobatics, his clowning, his visual jokes, his horsemanship – unbelievable.

BH   Igor the Great?

Rabbi   That's him! How do you know about him?

BH   Just a lucky guess.

Rabbi   Bill, I can't tell you what to do, but I can certainly tell you what I think and what the Torah has to say on this issue – which I have now told you. But, before I go, can I ask you a couple more questions?

BH   Okay.

Rabbi   You mentioned before about genetic conditions that increase the probability for young women getting breast cancer?

BH   Yes, mutations on either gene BRCA1 or BRCA2.

Rabbi   Are these mutations evenly disbursed amongst the population at large?

BH   Anyone can have either of these two mutations – but the Ashkenazi Jews and Icelanders are particularly prone to this condition.

Rabbi   Thanks Bill, that's all I wanted to ask – thanks for the coffee, and say hello to that Catholic wife of yours. Bye.

BH   [Bill sinks in his chair as he realises the point that Rabbi was making]. Anytime, Rabbi, and thanks for the chat. It is very much appreciated.

Insert Scene – 26

One must feel sorry for the Jews – for it must be 'bitterly unpleasant' to be treated by everybody as an inferior.

But, one must feel even more sorry for the true-born Englishmen who find themselves in competition with Jews. It is a scandal that a man of the same blood as Chaucer and Shakespeare should, because his parents have not had the 'low cunning' to accumulate money, be obliged to abase himself before some offspring of an asiatic bazaar tout.

If we take such wrongs into account, we will understand that there is no need to hate Hitler just because he is impolite to Jews

Count Your Dead: They Are Alive, or a New War in the Making *by Wyndham Lewis.*

Scene 37 – Ivan goes DIY legal

10:00am, Tuesday, 21 May 2013

Setting: Genetic Protection Authority's library

Ivan is at his work, strolling down a corridor until he comes across the 'GPA Library'. He enters, goes to the legal section and climbs on a chair so that he can read and access the legal titles.

He keeps searching until he comes across the legal section – and, as he studies the titles, he selects and pulls the following titles off the shelf:

- *What Happens in a Law Court, Dan Lambeth*
- *Going to Court, Anne Peake, Olive Otway, Julia, Maria*
- *Law: Textbook, Alan Hosking*
- *Understand the Law 1: the Individual and Society, SCDC / Law Society*
- *The English Legal Process (Ninth Edition), Terence Ingman*
- *Introduction to the English Legal System (Second Edition), Martin Partington CBE*

The scene fades out on Ivan searching and selecting books, then fades back in on Ivan at a desk studiously going through the table of contents of each of the titles, turning to different chapters and reading intensely.

The camera fades out – and in – and out – with two piles of books gradually shifting from the 'unread' to the 'read' (with associated post-it notes highlighting selected pages in each of the read books). With each fade in, the lighting of the room changes due to the procession of the sun over the course of the day – illustrating the length of time Ivan has been 'hitting the books'.

The camera then fades in on him [with the adjacent window now black with the night] with all the books closed and him gazing upwards in an unfocused manner, deep in contemplation. He then snaps out of his meditation – and starts writing on a pad in front of him:

1) *Go to High Court and take out injunction on Sandra.*

2) *Request the GPA Ethics Ruling Committee for a hearing.*

The scene fades out as he continues to write up his list, then fades back in on his face, which shows a great sense of self-accomplishment, determination and pride.

The scene fades out then back in on Ivan as he gets up and starts walking to the library's exit door. He reaches the door and pushes on it – but it is evidently looked. A bit of a frown crosses his face and he looks up to read a notice on the door:

> *Library open from 9:00am to 6:00pm. Outside of these hours, a valid staff pass is required to operate the doors.*

Ivan checks his watch, showing that it is 8:00pm, which startles him, as he did not think it was this late. He retrieves his staff pass from his trousers pocket, swipes it across the card reader, waits to see the green LED displayed indicating the door has been unlocked, and pushes the door open. As he exits the library, he takes out his phone and makes a call – the conversation is blurred – but the following is just audible:

IH   It's Ivan … Yes, I'm going to the High Court tomorrow morning so, yeah, I'll meet you at the Edgar Wallace pub – it's opposite the High Court, in Essex Street, a little laneway off the Strand say at 9:30 tomorrow morning … Cheers and see you there.

Scene 38 – Ivan and friends meet before going to High Court

9:30am, Wednesday, 22 May 2013

Setting: Edgar Wallace Pub

The scene opens with Ivan at a corner table in the Edgar Wallace pub with a coffee, going over his notes and looking a little worried. While he is at the table, his two mates Andy and Rob come strolling in.

AW   Ivan, howzit going my man and where's my fucking coffee – hah hah hah.

IH   Heh, good you guys could make it – thanks for helping out.

RW   Well matey – as you said, it's not your problem, it's our problem.

AW   What do you mean? It's his kid we're trying to save.

RW   Jesus man – because if he loses his case then all dwarfs will be aborted before they're born – including your kids. So short-arse, it's your problem too.

AW   Oh yeah, that's right I remember. We discussed this didn't we?

IH   [Ignores AW's last comment] Anyway guys, what can I get you – a tall latte?

AW   Just because I'm short doesn't mean I don't want a decent size coffee – I'll have a grande latte.

RW   I'll have a tall cappuccino.

IH   Sure [he walks off and goes to the bar for service – but finds it difficult to get served as the bar is so high and the barman doesn't notice him waiting].

AW   [From the table, shouts out loudly at the barman] I'm desperate for a coffee – so can you serve the midget at the counter?

The barman, together with Ivan, all look embarrassed and he starts to serve Ivan.

The camera fades out – then fades back in when they are all at the table with their coffees.

IH   [His voice fades in as he is describing the legal process to them using a series of checklist notes that he compiled in the GPA's library.] So the first step is to put an injunction on Sandra to stop her from having an abortion until the GPA's Ethics Ruling Committee hears my case.

Once the injunction is served, we need to apply to the Ethics Ruling Committee to have our case heard – so that they can make a ruling as to whether or not a foetus with achondroplasia falls outside of the three standard deviation threshold. If they rule in our favour – that the embryo doesn't have a genetic disease – then it establishes that I do have paternal rights and I can therefore attempt to stop the abortion by appealing to the courts using my existing statute and common law rights.

AW   And if we lose?

IH   Well, then. I suppose we'll have to appeal to the High Court.

RW   Nice, just a walk in the park then?

IH   No, I never said it was going to be easy. In fact it is going to be a long hard slog. But, fuck it, if I don't do all I can, then I'll never be able to have kids – nor will either of you, nor any other dwarf in this fucked up country.

RW   Not a problem, mate – we'll be with you the whole way. By the way, it looks like we're going to get a big turnout at the special meeting of the Little Peoples Association. I haven't told them what's up – but I let them know it is a massive issue that's going to affect them all. So, if nothing else they'll be there for the curiosity value.

IH   Excellent, hopefully they will be jolted into action for a change – and provide us with a little support. However, we have more pressing issues at hand. Let's go across the road and place a High Court injunction on Sandra. This should be fun.

AW   Just a minute, I haven't finished my coffee.

The other two ignore Andy, get up and start walking out of the pub – then the camera shows Andy getting up out of his seat in disgust as he has to leave his half-drunk coffee behind. The camera fades out as he runs to catch up to them.

The three dwarfs are crossing the Strand (from the Edgar Wallace pub to the High Court).

RW   Ivan, once Sandra is notified that you've placed an injunction on her, I think she is going to be pretty pissed. I'm not sure sleeping on a couch in the same apartment is going to be viable – unless of course, you're suicidal.

IH   Yes, I have thought about this – and you're right. I don't think it is tenable for me to stay in the apartment.

RW   Well, as I said before, you are welcome to sleep in my spare bedroom for a while.

IH   Rob, thanks. Yes, I'd really appreciate it if I could stay with you for a while – as I can't stay at my apartment and I really can't afford another rent.

RW   Well, I've taken today off – so, if you like I could give you a hand to move later today.

IH   Thanks, that would be brilliant. Let's get this injunction organised – then I'll take you up on your offer.

Scene 39 – Placing the injunction at the High Court

10:00am, Wednesday, 22 May 2013

Setting: High Court

The scene opens with the three dwarfs struggling to see over the reception desk at the High Court, explaining their intention and asking for guidance where to go to place an injunction. The receptionist at the information desk is an attractive, well-groomed lady in her sixties. She is very well composed, makeup tastefully applied and has an aura of confidence and authority.

IH   [Speaking to the receptionist] Yes, that's right, I wish to place an injunction on someone, and I'd like directions as to where I should go – or who I should see in order to place an injunction.

Recp   [In a patronising manner] You should go to your local magistrate's court to place an injunction, the High Court only deals with very specific and very important issues. Hardly any injunctions are taken out in the High Court. Can I ask whereabouts you live, and I could direct you to the nearest magistrate's court?

IH   Thank you, but I'm aware of the cases that the High Court hears and what types of injunctions can be taken out here – that's why I'm here and not at my local magistrate's court. So, can you please direct me to the place where I can place an injunction?

Recp   Maybe you could tell me what you are intending to do, then I could direct you to the right area – or the right court.

AW   [In an aggressive tone] He's here to stop the extinction of dwarfs okay? Now just tell us where we have to go to stop it.

Recp   Oh, I see [in a tone of 'we got some loonies here'] Well, I'm not sure that this is the right court for you. I think you really should see a lawyer first and tell him about this, and he could file the right sort of thing in the proper court. I can suggest some excellent lawy …

RW   What my friends are saying is that his [pointing at Ivan] wife is going to terminate her pregnancy on the grounds that the baby will be a dwarf, okay? Now, if this is allowed, then all dwarfs will be aborted. If this happens, then there won't be any more Snow White and the Seven Dwarf plays, no more Fellini movies full of dwarf journalists, no more sicko midget porn videos.

The world will be a worse place without us. Now, all that my friend wants to do is to have a fair trial on this issue okay?

Recp   Hmmmm. I see. Well, these recommended lawyers I have here, well they would be able to help you with your … your quest. So I strongly urge you to consult a lawyer on this issue.

IH   I have, and the bastard sided with my wife and the GPA and wanted to kill us all. I am not going to another lawyer on this.

Now, please, all I want to do is to exercise my legal right to place an injunction on my wife to stop her aborting my child – until such time as the GPA's Ethics Ruling Committee delivers a ruling as to whether or not I have the right to propagate.

So – can I ask you to please direct me to the appropriate counter in order to file the injunction?

Recp   [In a very sultry manner, looking down at the counter she mumbles] Follow the signs to 'Court Administration' [and nods to a corridor which has such a sign].

IH   [Sarcastically] Thank you. You have been most obliging.

The three dwarfs walk off following the signs – with the camera fading out as they walk around the corner of the corridor.

The camera fades back in with the three of them sitting around a 'meeting room' table together with an administrator. The administrator has a 'just barely' detectable sense of amusement on his face, otherwise acting and speaking in a manner that is dignified and non-patronising to the dwarfs.

Admin This is an unusual situation – as very nearly always, injunctions are applied for by lawyers who know the system and the boundaries of the case, as injunctions cannot just be taken out on anyone for anything. The court needs to gain *prima facie* assurance that there is a defensible reason for an injunction to be served on someone. Injunctions can, and do, create severe difficulties for those that have to comply with one.

In this case, you are asking for the court to impose a restriction on a woman, which effectively removes her right of 'choice' as to whether or not she wishes to go the full term with a pregnancy or not. This is a very, very sensitive area. Therefore, the court needs to understand in which way you believe that you have some sort of claim over her, or her actions, so that on balance the court can determine that your claim is greater than her right to exercise her own free will. If the court were to agree with you, and serve Ms Small [a smile becomes just detectable] an injunction, it would be a significant impediment on her life and her right to exercise her free will.

So, tell me why you think your right over her or her actions is greater than her right to exercise her free will on this matter.

IH   She is carrying my child. The reason she wants to terminate the child is due to it being diagnosed with achondroplasia – meaning it will be a dwarf.

In order to justify the termination she is using the GPA definition of genetic abnormalities – which is basically any trait that is in excess of three standard deviations from the human norm. Should achondroplasia meet this profane condition, then I would have all my paternal rights over the child extinguished. I'm trying to place an injunction, in order to prevent an abortion until the GPA's Ethics Ruling Committee hears my case and makes a ruling as to whether or not achondroplasia is a genetic defect that warrants such draconian measures to be taken.

Look, all I want to do is to challenge the basis of this justification and the GPA definition of 'the human norm'. If dwarfs were to be judged that they fall into this category – it would be a travesty of justice. The law then would effectively eradicate us folk in a generation or two purely on the ground that we are short.

Just because we are short doesn't and shouldn't mean that we don't have a right to live, to love, to have families. And, if we were to be eradicated, who is next? Will the GPA go after all NBA players and stop them having families because they are too tall?

This is why I want to stop my wife from terminating my child until I have had the opportunity to argue my case at a GPA's Ethics Ruling Committee.

Admin Okay, but you do realise, even if you win the case, it doesn't overrule her common law rights to terminate the pregnancy – so you may win the case and still lose the child.

IH Yes, I'm aware of that – but I suppose one step at a time.

Admin Okay, I understand your position and agree with you that it is a significant legal issue that you are raising that should be given due consideration by the GPA's Ethics Ruling Committee and the courts if necessary. As such, I'll approve your application to serve an injunction on Ms Small [slight smile again appears on his face].

Now, to apply for an injunction, I do need to get a lot of details from you and go through a lot of administration. Is this okay?

The three dwarfs all jump up on their chairs, then dance and chant as though they have made a significant victory (as they have) – all dancing joyously on their chairs.

As they start to settle down the camera fades out.

Insert Scene – 27

He is a self-taught working man, and we all know how distressing they are, how egotistical, insistent, raw, striking and ultimately nauseating, I'm reminded all the time of some callow board school boy.

A Moment's Liberty *by Virginia Woolf.*

Scene 40 – Sandra is served an injunction

3:00pm, Wednesday, 22 May 2013

Setting: Sandra's work desk and BDW's reception

Sandra is at the offices of Bradbury, Dywer & Waldron, at a Wednesday afternoon staff meeting in a conference room. The room has many glass windows (or glass walls) and is located centrally within the working environment of the law firm. There are 40 odd staff sitting in the conference room – including all five genhances. Pat Rushworth is at the front giving a presentation on the emerging market of defective baby insurance derivatives – both pre and post birth – and the associated complexities of the cross boarder legal framework for such derivatives.

As Pat is presenting, through the glass door, a secretary indicates to Sandra that there is someone at reception to see her. Sandra silently excuses herself, which hardly distracts from Pat's presentation. Sandra makes her way to reception with a wee bit of a puzzled look on her face.

She enters the foyer of the law firm, which is vast, opulent and very impressive, complete with holographic artwork, both stills and moving images.

She approaches reception, where the receptionist nods to a suited, short, balding guy in his mid-fifties.

Recep Mr Matthew Brown is here to see you.

Sandra looks at him, turns back to the receptionist and asks:

SS   Did he say where he is from?

The receptionist shakes her head.

Recep No, he wouldn't say.

Sandra slowly approaches Mr Brown and, when she is standing quite close, says in a timid voice:

SS   Mr Brown, I'm Sandra Small, I understand you wanted to see me.

Mr Brown slowly looks up from the newspaper that he is reading, briefly surveys Sandra, then looks back down to finish the article he was reading. Once finished reading, he folds the newspaper, secures it under his arm, then slowly rises from his chair. Once standing, due to his 5'5" height, he looks up and slowly and deliberately addresses Sandra:

MB   Yes. Indeed I wish to see you [as he says this, he drops his gazes from Sandra's face to her stomach].

SS   What about, do you need some legal advice?

MB   No, not exactly – but I suspect you might, but hey, you are in the right place for it aren't you?

SS   Sorry, why would I need legal advice?

MB   It's your husband … [He deliberately drags out the pause to get Sandra to feel as uncomfortable as possible].

SS   My husband? Is Ivan in trouble?

MB   Not exactly – but he did want this to be given to you.

SS   What?

MB   Yes – can I ask you to sign for it?

Sandra takes out her mobile phone, places her thumb on the thumb print reader, points her phone at the 'electronic acknowledgement and recording' (EAR) device that Mr Brown is holding up to her, and presses the 'sign and acknowledge' button on her phone. Both Sandra's phone and Mr Brown's contraption engage in an 'acknowledgment sent and received' beeping session.

MB   Thank you, I'll be off now, but if I were you I'd go to your office and sit down before you open that little package.

He then walks out of the reception, smiling farewell to the receptionist in a sleazy manner.

Sandra starts to open the envelope – then notices the receptionist and a client waiting in the reception area are both looking at her. With this, she walks out of the reception area. The camera follows her to her cubicle, which is across the room from where Pat is still giving his presentation in the glass walled conference room.

She sits down and opens and reads the enclosed letter.

As she reads the document, we hear her voiceover, which starts off softly and mumbled so that the audience can only hear bits and pieces between the mumbles.

SS   … Her Majesty's Royal courts hereby … subject to the following … alleged pregnancy.

At this point Sandra stops and sits up and looks up – then says out loud:

SS   Alleged pregnancy – what the fuck is this?

While she is reading, Pat is visible in the background presenting to the senior staff in the glass walled conference room, none of whom are paying any attention to her. Sandra looks down again and continues reading.

SS   [Voiceover] Your husband, being the alleged father of the alleged child, hereby has placed an injunction on you prohibiting the forced termination of the pregnancy – until such time as the Genetic Protection Authority's Ethics Ruling Committee makes a ruling as to whether the unborn child meets the 'three standard deviation from the human norm' criteria, as defined by the Genetic Protection Act of 2004, as amended in 2012.

After she finishes reading the injunction, she slams the document on her desk, leans back in her chair, then stares motionlessly at the ceiling in total dismay and total disbelief. Her antics catch the attention of several attendees of Pat's presentation and, with the odd glance and gesture, progressively more attendees glance towards Sandra to satisfy their curiosity.

All of a sudden Sandra jumps up, kicks her wastepaper bin ten metres or so down the cubical walkway and shouts:

SS   The little prick!

Sandra storms out the office. By this time the whole conference room – including Pat, who has stopped speaking – all stare at her in disbelief as she gaits out along the corridor.

Bill puts his hands up over his face and murmurs to himself:

BH   Oh shit, it's started.

Scene 41 – Lunch and distraught conversation: Valentina and Sandra

12:30pm, Thursday, 23 May 2013

Setting: Alfresco café outside the Tate Modern

It is a beautiful day, with spectacular views of the Thames. The camera's view starts from the north bank of the river [near St Paul's Cathedral], travels over the Millennium Bridge, bringing Sandra and Valentina into view, who are having an alfresco lunch at the Tate Modern. They are sitting at a very elegantly set table, with two wine glasses filled from the bottle of Leeuwin Estate Art Series Chardonnay 1996 that is placed at the side of the table. Their luncheon plates are still full, indicating that they have not been there that long, just long enough to have ordered and have their meals delivered.

SS   Valentina, I am so sorry that I cancelled the theatre last Saturday. I have been under just so much stress recently, and my workload at work hasn't abated at all. Then on top of it all, I had to prepare for my Oxford interview – all at a time when, as you are aware, I have a few personal issues going on.

VH   It's okay, I understand.

SS   Were you able to find someone else to go with you?

VH   No, really, I wasn't feeling particularly wonderful either, so it gave me the opportunity to have a great night in.

SS   I am so sorry.

VH   No need to mention it. Now, tell me, how did your interview at Oxford go on Tuesday? Have they given you any feedback?

SS   Well, it went as well as I could reasonably expect it to go. I was as prepared as I could have been – at least given my circumstances. And, they didn't ask me anything that I couldn't give an informed answer to. So, yes, I think it went okay.

198

VH	You've never told me which college you're applying for – which college is it?
SS	Corpus Christi. It's the same college Bill, Pat and Laurie from work went through. I'm not sure whether there is any nepotism involved in my application – but, at the moment, I'll take any advantage I can muster. And if this involves corporate nepotism, well, so be it!
VH	I totally agree with you. I must say, I was wondering why Oxford was considering you – now it all makes sense.
SS	[Sarcastically] Thanks for your vote of confidence – much appreciated.
VH	Anyway, the key point is that, hopefully, you had a successful interview. So, that is good news. I'm so pleased for you. Fancy that – having a lawyer in the family. I can't wait to tell all my Russian friends. They will be so jealous. Sandra, on another subject, have you given any more thought to the conversation we had last Tuesday?
SS	Yes, I'm very appreciative of your advice on the matter, particularly your thoughts on how difficult it is to raise a child with achondroplasia and the difficulties that the child experiences. Ivan has never discussed these issues with me. However, my thoughts on the matter have been put on hold for the time being.
VH	Sandra, this is hardly the time to put the situation on hold. If you are to have a termination, then it must be done within 24 weeks. So, think about your circumstances and make a decision!
SS	Yes, well I did intend to make a decision well before 24 weeks.
VH	[Nods for her to continue] … And?
SS	Well, this is a wee bit tricky – discussing it with you, as you are Ivan's mother.
VH	Why, what has Ivan done?

SS   [Long pause] Well, firstly, Ivan placed an injunction on me. Then, secondly, he left me!

VH   An injunction. An injunction for what? And, what is this about him leaving you – when?

SS   Yesterday. First, while I am at work a guy walks in and serves me an injunction preventing me from terminating my own pregnancy. Then, when I get home to have it out with Ivan, all I find is a note saying he's moved in with his mate Rob.

VH   [Taken aback by the revelations]. He's moved out? And living with Rob? Did he say anything or leave you a note or something?

SS   No. All I got was this post-it note [she opens her diary and removes a post-it note and passes it to Valentina].

Close up of the post-it note – which has written across it 'I've moved in with Rob. See you in court. Ivan'.

VH   I'm so sorry, Sandra. This is not good news.

SS   That's putting it mildly.

VH   So, what's all this about an injunction on your pregnancy and Ivan's note saying he will see you in court?

Sandra reaches into her bag and brings out the brown envelope that contains the injunction. She then holds up the envelope to Valentina.

SS   Ivan has placed this injunction on me which stops me from terminating my pregnancy.

VH   [Long pause – with a confused look on Valentina's face] I'm sorry, Sandra, I don't understand this. Ivan has placed an injunction on you which prevents you from terminating your own pregnancy. That's your choice, that's your right. How can he possibly serve an injunction that takes away your fundamental rights as a woman?

SS   Well, the little prick managed it – the proof is in this envelope.

VH   Let me see this [She reaches over and grabs the envelope, with Sandra 'just' cooperating in passing it to her. Valentina takes the injunction out and reads it.] Well I never have heard of anything like this, never mind seen such a ridiculous document. What a disgrace – that the High Court issued an injunction that so blatantly violates your human rights.

SS   I'm totally at a loss. I don't know what his problem is, honestly I don't. Wouldn't he be happier if he was normal heighted? So why is he doing this, to give his child a handicap, to give my child a handicap. What's the point? The technology available is here to help us, to help our children – not to disadvantage them.

VH   Dear, this is unbelievably distressing for you. I myself cannot understand his motives. Even though his father, Igor, was a celebrated clown in the Soviet Union, given the chance he would have given all his fame and fortune away just to be normal heighted. And, Ivan is not even rich or famous – so I really don't understand where he is coming from.

      Can I inquire as to what has happened between you since I was at your place two weeks ago?

SS   [Deep sigh] Well, I had DNA analysis done on the embryo – which determined that it does have achondroplasia – so, it will be a dwarf. When I found out, I was very upset, and stormed out of our apartment without really discussing the situation with Ivan. I mean, we haven't really been on speaking terms since you came for dinner. A few days later, Ivan brought up the subject and was quite adamant that he wanted us – meaning me – to go ahead and have the baby. At this stage I hadn't made up my mind one way or the other about the pregnancy – in fact I still haven't. But, because Ivan was being so fucking obstinate about the matter and refusing to listen to anything I had to say, totally dismissing any of my views, feeling or rights, well …

Long pause.

VH   Yes, Sandra, what happened then?

SS   Well, you see, my work specialises in genetic law.

VH   Yes?

SS   So, I told Ivan that, as the embryo is a dwarf, it will meet the 'three standard deviation from the human norm' rule.

VH   It does what? And what does that mean?

SS   Well, there is a piece of legislation that states that if an embryo has certain measurable genetic characteristics, meaning that as an adult they will be significantly different from what is a normal human, then the law negates all of the father's rights over the unborn child.

      This means the mother can make a decision on her own, without any legal requirement to consult with the father regarding the termination or otherwise of the pregnancy.

VH   What exactly did you tell Ivan?

SS   I told him, as the embryo has the Ivan's dwarfism gene, it would meet the 'three standard deviations from the human norm' rule. As the embryo satisfies this rule, Ivan has no paternal rights over the child or over my pregnancy. I told him, I didn't need his permission or consent to terminate the pregnancy. As he's made no attempt to understand or sympathise with my position – rather he's done the exact opposite by trying to impose his will on me – I told him that I wouldn't even let him know if and when I did have an abortion.

VH   Well, I see you are having some tense conversations at home at the moment.

SS   Yes. Well, not surprisingly, we haven't really spoken to each other since then.

VH   And, rather than trying to understand your position and talk to you, he goes and takes out an injunction on you?

SS   Yes, I can't believe it. I have just been given a once in a lifetime opportunity – to go to Oxford and study law – and not only do I accidently fall pregnant, Ivan is bullying me to surrender my right to choose. It is just so awful.

VH   Darling, I had no idea it had come to this. You poor girl. Just when you were starting to take some small steps up the corporate ladder, the rungs are taken from under your feet.

SS You know I'm the only person in my family ever to go to university, I'm the only person ever to leave Ripon. The rest of my family haven't even travelled outside Yorkshire, doubtless lived in London. For them, a big day out is their annual Christmas shopping trip to Leeds.

I've grown up thinking, believing, acting as though I'm born to merely serve the toffs, to look up to them, that I'm unworthy to enter the same room as them – unless of course, I'm their maid, their cleaner, their shoe shiner, or their pet. I've fought, I've fought, I've fought all that to get ahead, to get where I am now. The shit I had to put up with from my family:

Oh look who's going to university, she thinks she's too good for us, we're just low down shit that she wants to walk over, she's a fucking traitor to her class.

You know, now when I go home to Ripon if I dare mention a single word about uni, work, London anything I do, anything I do – they all immediately gang up on me:

Oh look who's talking – little miss queenie. Oh yes everything in her life is better than ours, isn't it? Hey Queenie, isn't everything in your life so much fucking better than our little shit hole – hey isn't it? Well, if it's so much fucking better – why don't you go home to London and eat at your fancy restaurants and leave us to eat our tripe and onions. I bet that's what you think we eat don't you – we're so poor and uncultured, that we still eat tripe and onions. Anything else you want to say? Any other insults for us?

I've had to fight all that, year after year after year. They just cannot be happy for me, they cannot accept that there is a world outside of Yorkshire, that we can, they can, all do what we want, we can all be ambitious, we can all achieve. They won't have any of it. They just ridicule me.

And, now, despite all the hang ups that I drag around with me, despite the emotional blackmail I'm subjected to, despite all the guilt and betrayal I feel, I have an opportunity to study law at Oxford. This could change my life. I'll become part of the English establishment. Can you believe it? Me, being part of the establishment! I'll be a lawyer, for God's sake. Then later, who knows, I may become a partner!

I just want it so bad. Then I get pregnant. Then I have this fucking injunction served against me. Jesus, what next?

VH   Oh, dear, dear, dear – I didn't realise the full gravitas of the situation. I'm sorry, darling, that all this has fallen on you just as you were about to … about to … well, about to 'shine', to take your rightful place in our society. You know darling, if I can help in anyway, I am only too willing to do whatever I can.

SS   Valentina, thank you for your offer, but I must say that I feel a bit awkward asking you, as, well I think its fine if – if – if you're helping me which is help to both Ivan and me as a unit. But, if you are helping me – which may be – well, contrary to Ivan's thoughts and interests, then I feel awkward, as I feel you should have a natural tendency to side and support your son.

VH   Sandra, you're right of course. But this is no different. I see my son as making a mistake over this issue. And since he is with you, and you're potentially the mother of my grandchildren, whenever that may be, then I think I need to look objectively at the situation and act in a manner that is best for the family unit. In this case, well I think it's obvious that you're in the right. My role may be to try and get my son to … to, well I suppose twofold, first to try and get him to come to his senses.

There is a prolonged pause.

SS   And secondly …?

VH   Well, this also may be awkward for you – but you will need some help – legally speaking. I have a contact who knows the law on this subject inside out.

SS   I work for a very respected law firm – who specialises in this field. I think I should be able to find my own in-house help. Anyway, thank you for the offer.

VH   True. But, if for whatever reason you can't or don't want to turn to your colleagues for help – then you may want to give 'Jon Raney' a call.

Valentina takes her phone out of her handbag and looks up the number – presses the 'print button' and out pops a personal card for Jon (not a business card – which would have the GPA logo on it). She hands Sandra the personal card.

204

VH   Anyway, darling, if you do get stuck, Jon should be able to help you.

SS   Well, thanks. Who knows, maybe I will need it.

VH   Now, darling, I know this incident, Ivan serving an injunction on you, is extremely hurtful, spiteful and … shall I venture, ridiculous. But, you must try to understand the way in which it is meant – not how it appears.

SS   Like what? The little prick is trying to fuck up my life …

VH   That's how it appears. Obviously that's how it appears.

SS   It's the way it is …

VH   Sandra, this is, shall we say, Ivan's inarticulate way of expressing his desire to have a family, to have you as the mother of his children, for him to be a proud father with a beautiful wife and child. As unimaginable as it may appear, as unreasonable as it may seem, as totally undeserved as it is – after all this mess is over you have to find it within your heart to forgive Ivan. If you don't forgive Ivan you will have missed his message, and the ill will, the bitterness and your hate and disappointment will slowly but surely consume you and cripple you.

SS   What – are you mad?

VH   Sandra, I'm not saying let go now and pretend it's all okay – because at the moment it isn't. But, one day, this mess will be behind us, behind you. Then, you will have to have the strength to forgive – if not for Ivan's sake, for your own sake. If you don't forgive him, you will die with him, bitter and twisted. So now, keep your rage, but start at least thinking how you can start to plan to forgive.

SS   Ivan is on the verge of ruining my life, that is if he hasn't already. So, apologies for appearing a little unforgiving at the moment, but that little shit can rot in hell for all I care.

       Anyway, if you will excuse me, I have to attend a legal briefing.

Sandra gets up, throws €40 on the table and walks off without a further word.

VH   Good luck, darling.

Scene 42 – Bill refuses to represent Sandra

4:00pm, Thursday, 23 May 2013

Setting: Bradbury, Dywer & Waldron Law Offices

Sandra is sitting at her desk with a melamine folder in front of her reading it diligently, with a note pad beside the file, taking the odd note and referring to a checklist, which she puts the odd tick in. After a while of doing this, she pauses and looks up in both boredom and agitation that 'she has bigger things to worry about than reading the stupid file'.

She deliberates for a second, then gets a key out of her purse, reaches down, unlocks her desk drawer, pulls open the drawer and retrieves another melamine folder. She brings the folder to her desk and opens it up, which reveals her 'injunction notice'. She picks up the notice and reads though it. After reading it, she sits up and looks towards the direction of Bill Horowitz's office and notes that his secretary, Josephine is not at her desk, and that Bill's office door is open.

She puts the notice back in the folder, picks up the folder, gets up and walks towards Bill's office. As she walks through the corridors and cubicles she passes an office, which now has a 'Bruce Mayne' office-name-plate on the door, Bruce is inside conducting a meeting with three colleagues (all in their 20s and 30s), where he is obviously instructing his much older colleagues what to do.

Sandra arrives outside Bill's office, peers inside, and sees Bill having an animated telephone conversation. She gently knocks on his door. He looks up and signals her to come in and sit down. Bill continues with the conversation for a while, then hangs up.

BH   That was Dave from genetics for Life Corp – great guy. Like us, just so keen to advance our species, obviously with our help. Anyway, Sandra, what can I do for you?

SS   Well, it is a little … ah, well I suppose embarrassing … a little private.

BH   Well you don't have to tell me. This is your choice.

SS   Bill … I'm pregnant.

BH   Well, congratulations to you – assuming congratulations are in order?

SS   Well, not really – no they're not.

BH   Hmmm, I am sorry to hear that. So … are you worried that this may interfere with your study and work?

SS   Well partly that … but there is more, it's become quite complicated.

BH   In which way?

SS   You haven't met my husband [pauses and looks up at Bill, who doesn't give anything away], but, I suppose a generous description would be to say that he is vertically challenged.

BH   Yes, I understand that Ivan – it is Ivan isn't it? [Waits to get nod from Sandra.] – is a dwarf. I mean he was part of the office gossip after his apparent dazzling Cossack dance performance with Kharechka at last year's Christmas party.

      And – this complicates things?

SS   Well, no – not in itself. Look, I didn't plan to have a baby just now, as I've just started studying, and I want to build my career.

BH   Yes – I see

SS   And, I suppose, I have thought that when I eventually do have a baby, I'd like to have a normal baby.

BH   I see.

SS   [Looking sheepish and embarrassed] Well, I had a DNA test, and the results indicated that the baby will be a dwarf. So, for both of these reasons, I was considering the possibility of terminating the pregnancy.

BH   Well, yes that is your choice.

SS   Well, Ivan thinks otherwise. He thinks that the only reason I am considering terminating the pregnancy is because the baby will be a dwarf.

BH   Uh huh.

SS   So – he has served an injunction on me, preventing me from terminating the pregnancy until the GPA's Ethics Ruling Committee rules whether or not the embryo has a genetic abnormality.

       If the Ethics Ruling Committee rule that achondroplasia, the form of dwarfism that Ivan and the baby has, is not a genetic defect, then Ivan wants to exercise his common law paternal rights to stop me terminating the pregnancy.

       Of course, if the ruling goes against him, then he loses all paternal rights – so, he won't legally be able to stop me from terminating the pregnancy. However, at the moment, I still haven't made a decision as to whether or not to terminate the pregnancy. But I do know that I want to be able to make my own choice on the matter.

BH   [Looks genuinely surprised with this development.] Sandra, I'm very sorry that you have been placed in this situation – it must be very distressing for you.

SS   Yes. I'm not allowed to terminate the pregnancy merely because it's a dwarf. Well, not at least until the Ethics Ruling Committee make their decision on the issue. It's absurd.

BH   I'm sorry – I can see this would be very difficult for you. It certainly limits your options as to how you deal with your situation.

SS   Well, I'm due at a hearing at the Ethics Ruling Committee next Wednesday, which, if I win means hopefully I will be allowed to terminate the pregnancy – that is if I choose to do so.

BH   Well, good luck at the hearing. You already know my thoughts on the GPA's Ethics Ruling Committee.

SS   In my current circumstances, I think I need more than good luck. So, to cut to the chase, can I ask you to represent me at the hearing?

BH   Sandra, I'm really sorry, but I can't.

SS   [In disbelief] What? What do you mean you can't?

BH   I'd like to be able to help you, but, I can't. I'm really very, very sorry, that on this occasion I cannot help you.

SS   Jesus Bill, I'm in need of a little support and help here and I need your help … why can't you help me?

BH   I certainly agree with you that you need legal representation, good legal representation. I can refer you to a brilliant lawyer. But unfortunately, Sandra, I cannot represent you in this case. I am really sorry, and I feel terrible about not being able to represent you. But, I can't.

SS   What, why?

BH   Sandra, please, this is difficult for me as well. I can't go into detail, you just have to accept that I cannot represent you. If I could I would. You will just have to trust me on this. Now, you do need a lawyer, I recommend …

SS   Shove it, Bill. I have my own list of 'B' rated lawyers – I'll give one a call.

Sandra then abruptly gets up and storms out, quite enraged, with her cheeks visibly reddened. She walks through the door and slams it behind her.

Bill sinks back into his seat.

BH   Oh shit.

Scene 43 – Sandra calls Jon Raney

4:30pm, Thursday, 23 May 2013

Setting: Bradbury, Dywer & Waldron law offices and a Books Etc. bookshop.

Sandra storms back to her desk, sits down and puts her face in her hands and starts sobbing. After a bit, she starts to regain her composure and sits up with a sense of determination in her face. She reaches down to her handbag and shuffles through it until she eventually retrieves Jon Raney's personal card that Valentina printed from her phone during their luncheon. She looks at the card, murmurs 'Jon Raney'. She thinks for a moment – 'Jon Raney' – she reflects on past conversations with Ivan [There is a flashback as she recalls these conversations]:

> *[First flashback] Ivan, very excitedly, comes into Sandra's university pad and exclaims:*

> > *I've got an interview with Jon Raney at the Genetic Protection Authority.*

> *[The first flashback fades out and the second fades in] Sandra and Ivan are having dinner in their Croydon apartment, and Ivan boasts:*

> > *I've just been given a new project. Jon Raney was impressed with my paper on 'The need for human genetic diversity for the continued evolution of our species', so he's given me the project to write an ethics submission on the acceptability of 'introduced' diversity verses 'hereditary' diversity. Jon's such a great guy to work for.*

> *The flashback fades out, then fades back in on Sandra sitting at her des].*

SS   [Murmuring] Shit.

She looks stunned for a few moments then a voice over cuts in.

SS   [Voice over] Bugger, Bill won't represent me and I can hardly ask Jon Raney.

Sandra thinks for a few moments.

SS   [Sandra's voice over]: Why can't I ask Jon? After all, the GPA is there for the protection of the public gene pool, and this must be a situation where the GPA can help clean up the pool. Fuck it, I'll give him a call.

Nervously, Sandra dials Jon's number. The scene cuts over to Jon Raney, who is browsing in the art section of a Books Etc. bookshop, flicking through a book on religious art, with several other similar books spread out on a counter in front of him. His mobile phone rings, whereupon he retrieves it from his shirt pocket, looks at the screen quizzically, then answers:

JR   Yes.

SS   Hi, is that Mr Jon Raney?

JR   Who's calling?

SS   Ah, um – I can't say at the moment.

JR   Well it doesn't look like we have much to talk about – goodbye.

Jon hangs up his phone. The phone rings almost immediately again.

JR   You have called my private number, which only my family have. So, if you can't tell me who you are – then I don't think we have much to speak about.

SS   Mr Raney, please. Valentina Henry gave me your number and suggested that I give you a call.

JR   Valentina Henry gave you my number – well there's a blast from the past. So, who are you?

SS   Really, I can't say at the moment, but I'm very close to Valentina and she said that you may be able to help me, as I've got a bit of a problem and she said you're the best in the field.

JR   And what field may that be?

SS   Mr Raney, please, can I meet you to discuss the issue that I'm faced with, then we can take it from there?

JR   Okay, if Valentina referred you to me, then it 'must' be serious. But, I'd still like to know who I'm speaking to.

SS   [With a noticeable pause before she continues] Tina Cavendish.

JR   Urrm [Identifies that the answer was a lie]. Okay Tina, I'll be back in my office in about half an hour so you can pop in and see me then. You know where I work, don't you?

SS   [Before she has time to think about the 'trap' question she spouts out] Yes, the GPA.

JR   Good, so you can meet me at my office at, say, 5:00pm.

SS   Well, I'm not sure whether your office would be a great place to meet – too formal. Perhaps I can take you out for a coffee?

JR   What a surprise, you don't want to come into my office. Okay Tina, let's meet at the café at Gabriel's Wharf court, near the National Theatre, at 5:30 this afternoon.

SS   Thank you, Mr Raney. I'll see you at 5:30.

Scene 44 – Sandra meets Jon

5:00pm, Thursday, 23 May 2013

Setting: The café overlooking the Thames at Gabriel's Wharf Court.

On an overcast day, the scene opens on a rundown café overlooking the Thames at Gabriel's Wharf, with Sandra sitting at an outside table, nervously awaiting a rendezvous with her husband's boss, Jon Raney. Jon strolls over to her.

JR   Sandra, I mean Tina, nice to meet you again.

Sandra has a quizzical expression on her face.

JR   Yes, Sandra, we have met before – in a manner at least. You came with Ivan to the GPA's annual dinner and award ceremony last year. Belated apologies, I didn't introduce myself at the time, as I was assisting with the awards. But I did notice what a nice couple you made.

SS   Ahhh – yes that's right, I do remember you. You were on the stage passing the awards to Max … weren't you?

JR   Yes, Max presents the awards, I merely assist.

SS   Well, obviously, I'm a little embarrassed having to call you – that's why I gave my name as Tina. You see, I have a bit of a problem, and I thought maybe that you would be able to provide me with some direction, or possibly some advice.

JR   Before we get into the details – can I get myself a coffee?

SS   Oh, sorry, of course. What would you like?

JR   No, my shout, what are you having?

SS   Tall latte, thanks.

JR   Sure.

Scene fades out as Jon walks to the counter, then fades back in as he returns.

JR   I'm not sure what advice you are seeking from me. But, as you gave me a false name, you are not with Ivan and you didn't want to meet at my office, where Ivan may see you, then there's a fair bet that it has something to do with him. [Sandra gives Jon an awkward acknowledgement]. So, before you start telling me about your problem, or ask me for my advice, I think it prudent that I let you know my position. Then, hopefully by being up front, it will avoid any conflict or embarrassment later on.

          Ivan is one of my staff, and I think highly of him. So, I may have a conflict of interest if I were to provide you with any legal, professional or personal advice which may be contrary to the interest of Ivan. So, all I can suggest is that you tell me what your problem is and, depending upon the nature of the advice you are seeking, I probably will not provide you with any advice today. Rather, I'll disclose the nature of our conversation to Max, who as you know is the CEO of the GPA, and get him to authorise the GPA to provide you with professional advice. If I do not do this, then potentially I could find myself fresh out of a job. Is this okay?

SS   Fuck, what?

JR   Sandra. Depending what advice you are seeking, if it relates to Ivan in any way then we're entering into an ethically questionable area. Even seeing you like this could be seen as a questionable act. So, really, I'm not risking my job on this issue.

          But, assuming it is professional advice you are seeking, then I think it will be just procedural. As long as I let Max know what I'm up to – it should be okay.

SS   And how long will that take?

JR   If I understand what advice you are seeking today, then I should have it cleared by tomorrow afternoon.

SS   Okay, but first, how do you know Valentina?

JR   Ohhh, well I'm a bit of an amateur art enthusiast, with an interest in Byzantine and Russian religious icons, as is Valentina. A few years ago we both got swept up in the mood to establish a permanent exhibition centre for Russian religious icons. This led to the founding of what is now the London annexe of the 'Andrei Rubliov Museum'.

Anyway, quite unexpectedly, I was awarded honorary life membership of the museum for my efforts in helping to establish the annexe – I mean, I was just doing what I enjoy, so I wasn't expecting to be rewarded for it. Likewise, Valentina was also awarded honorary life membership.

SS   So you are both honorary life members of the museum's London annexe?

JR   No, life membership of the Andrei Rubliov Museum in St. Petersburg. The museum's building used to be the 'St Andronicus Monastery of the Saviour'. This is where Andrei Rubliov lived and worked as a monk, who is arguably Russia's greatest ever iconic artist. So it was a great honour for me to be awarded life membership to possibly the world's most prestigious religious iconic art gallery.

SS   Wow, I knew Valentina was into Russian iconic art – but I had no idea that she was so high up in this esoteric art circle. I'm surprised she's never mentioned it.

JR   Well, I suppose she has her reasons.

SS   Hmm … So, I take it you're quite busy at the moment with the exhibition that is about to begin at the London annexe?

JR   Well, no, not really. After the museum was established and up and running my involvement has somewhat waned.

SS   Why's that?

JR   Well, I'm not as involved with the museum as I used to be, so my current role is pretty much limited to an 'art goer'. Anyway, we're not here to discuss Russian icons, monks or even medieval urinals. So, what's the issue that you think I may be able to help you with?

SS   [A little shocked by the reference to medieval urinals] Well, as you obviously know, I'm married to Ivan. [Looks up to get Jon's acknowledgement – then continues.] And now I'm pregnant to Ivan [again looks up – but this time to also gauge whether this takes Jon by surprise – but Jon has his full poker face on and doesn't give anything away].

The embryo in my womb also has Ivan's genetic disorder. So, left unchecked, I will end up with a baby dwarf.

JR   And – where do I come into this?

SS   Well, Ivan has placed an injunction on me preventing me from terminating the pregnancy merely on the grounds that the embryo suffers from achondroplasia – the type of dwarfism that Ivan has.

JR   Hmm interesting. How can you get the injunction lifted?

SS   Well, he's applied to the GPA Ethics Ruling Committee to make a ruling as to whether or not achondroplasia is a genetic disorder. If the Ethics Ruling Committee determines that it isn't a genetic disorder, then Ivan has indicated that he will exercise his paternal rights to try and stop me from terminating the pregnancy.

JR   And if the Ethics Ruling Committee determine that it is a genetic disorder?

SS   In that scenario, Ivan has his paternal rights revoked, so he won't legally be able to stop me from going ahead with the termination – should I choose to do so. Until, then, I have no choice. I have to continue with the pregnancy.

JR   When's GPA's Ethics Ruling Committee's hearing?

SS   Next Wednesday.

JR   Well, that is very soon!

SS   Yes, it is. Too soon to adequately prepare my case.

JR   And where do you see me fitting into all of this?

SS   [A little surprised by the questions – as she thought it was obvious.] Where do I see you fitting in? Well, for either you or the GPA to represent me at the GPA's Ethics Ruling Committee's hearing.

        After all, aren't you guys meant to be protecting the human gene pool? Isn't this what you're there for?

JR   Good question. But, a counter argument is, if we think a dwarf is competent and productive enough to hire as a social research scientist, wouldn't we be just a little hypocritical if we then go to the Ethics Ruling

216

Committee saying that due to his condition, he doesn't have the right to reproduce?

SS   Jesus, there are about 100 indistinguishable, unintelligible, unconscious and unsentient cells in my womb that cannot be employed at all, doubtless as a research scientist. If they are terminated now, there is no loss of consciousness, no loss of life, no loss of anything – as a human, a life does not exist. But, if left unchecked, they will turn into a baby dwarf. Why not let me have a non-defective child, who then can be employed as a social scientist while sparing me all this grief?

JR   Look, you have every right to get angry, but believe me, come the hearing – you will get far worse than what I've just put to you. So if you want to defend your position – you better start taking an immediate course on skin thickening. Now, I must ask you – how serious are you about … well, about going ahead with a termination?

SS   That is not the point. I may very well choose to have a termination. However, more importantly, I want to defend my right to choose whether or not I terminate. Basically, I haven't really made up my mind – but I want it to be my decision, not somebody else's decision that is imposed on me.

JR   Okay, I'll warn you now, this could end up as a very messy legal case, which will have very personal ramifications for yourself. So, you need to be very sure that you want to defend yourself against this injunction.

SS   Yes, I'm very sure that I want to defend my right as a woman to be able to decide what I do with my pregnancy.

JR   Sure you do. In that case, do you really want the GPA to defend you – as, it may have its own agenda and objectives?

SS   Jon, if the GPA helps me defend my rights to choose whether or not I have an abortion – then, yes, I want the GPA to defend me.

JR   Okay, but between now and when we next meet, please think very seriously on this point – because once you get the GPA involved, they will take over the case and work to their own agenda, which may not always be perfectly correlated to your agenda!

SS   Providing the GPA's agenda supports mine – then that's fine with me.

JR   Okay, I've heard all I need to know for now. I don't need to, or want to, discuss the situation any further, for now at least. I'll see Max either today or tomorrow, and once I clear it with him I'll come back to you. Do you have a contact number or business card?

SS   Yes – sure! [She prints one from her phone and passes it over to Jon.]

JR   [Takes the card and studies it.] You work for Bradbury, Dywer & Waldron. Why don't you get Dr Horowitz to represent you, isn't this his specialty?

SS   [Looks away to hide her inability to answer.] I have my reasons.

JR   [Looking dumbfounded] Okay whatever you say.

Scene 45 – Jon discusses Sandra's request with Max

9:30am, Friday, 24 May 2013

Setting: Max Lyford's executive office at the GPA

Max's Office – a very large and very well appointed office, with an abundance of very high quality antique furniture. One wall is filled with law books and journals. There is not a computer in his office and not a scrap of paper to be seen, and nothing is out of place.

Max sits laid back in a large chair behind his desk with Jon sitting perched upright on his chair (at the other side of the desk).

The scene opens with a pan around the office as the camera slowly fades in with Max and Jon's conversation muffled and just discernible (Jon speaking to Max). The camera sharpens up as Jon finishes his talk, then waits for Max's reply. The camera then focuses on Max – who, obviously has heard Jon, but still isn't saying anything as he deliberates over the information that Jon just conveyed to him.

ML   So, young Ivan has filed an injunction. Well that demonstrates to us that he's got a bit of spunk. Who's his lawyer?

JR   Sorry, I don't know. I didn't ask.

ML   Pity. Never mind though. When's the hearing?

JR   It's next week, Wednesday.

ML   Yes, of course, that's the next time the GPA Ethics Ruling Committee convenes.

Max, looks down with a 'thinking' expression, and fiddles with his Forzieri Visconti white gold fountain pen. There is a long silent pause while he does this. The camera swaps over to Jon, who after a while starts to show signs of discomfort over this prolonged pause. The camera swaps back to Max, who still has the same expression and still playing with his pen, with no evidence that he is feeling any anxiety or discomfort.

JR   [Eventually] Well, Max, what's our position on this?

ML   [Hardly looking up] Sorry, Jon, I thought it was obvious

Another silence ensues. Jon looks a bit startled by Max's comment – but plays the waiting game and doesn't reply.

ML   [Eventually] Jon, we cannot deviate or be side tracked from the mission that was put to us, the very reason why the GPA was established, our raison d'être.

        We're here to protect and advance the human genome. [Another long pause.]

        While this Ivan lad may be a capable worker and may even do some fine work, it can't be denied that he has a genetic disorder. Nor can it be denied that, given the opportunity, he will pass this disorder onto future generations – as will his dwarf kin folk. How you manage your relationship with Ivan is your business. But, this cannot interfere with your duties to the GPA, and more importantly to the human genome and to all the future generations of homo sapiens.

        [Another long pause.]

        This will prove to be an important test case, as it will be the first time the three standard deviation clause has been put to the test. It will set a very important precedent.

        [Another long pause.]

        Get whatever internal or external counsel you require to help you support … Sandra, wasn't it?

JR   [Again looks a wee bit shocked by Max's direction]. Okay I'll start working on it at once.

ML   Jon, make sure that all the paper work is in place. [Waits for Jon's acknowledgement.] I want the new QA process to be followed in its entirety on this case – as I don't want any slip ups anywhere. Understand? [Again waits for Jon's acknowledgement.]

If there were to be an appeal against the GPA's Ethics Ruling Committee's ruling, I do not want us looking poorly on the grounds that we didn't dot the i's and cross the t's – okay? [Looks up and peers over his glasses at Jon – waiting for an acknowledgement.]

So, put your most anally retentive person on the case to be the QA manager – the person who is so pedantic that, if the QA standard says A4 paper is to be used, then they'll physically measure the dimension of each and every page in the file to ensure it is exactly 210mm by 297mm and insists the page to be retyped if it is a single mm outside of the stated dimensions – okay?

JR   Certainly, Max, I have just the person in mind to make sure it's all squeaky clean.

ML   Good. Thank you [with a slight movement of his head signals Jon to leave].

JR   Always a pleasure [gets up and leaves].

Insert Scene – 28

The mass of mankind is soulless,
Most people are dead, and scurrying and talking in the sleep of death.
' Kangaroo' by DH Lawrence.

Scene 46 – Max convenes a Club meeting

9:45am, Friday, 24 May 2013

Setting: Max's office at the GPA

As soon as Jon leaves the room, Max presses his intercom to his PA.

ML   Doris, can you convene a meeting of 'The Club'.

DK   When for?

ML   As soon as humanly possible.

DK   If it's really urgent, then I should be able to get a meeting scheduled within two weeks. If it isn't urgent, then it will probably be a month before you can meet. Is that okay?

ML   Tell them to meet at Claydon House tomorrow at 10am.

DK   Max, that is very short notice. I doubt whether all the members will be able to make it on such short notice.

ML   Just tell them 'We have our case'.

DK   Okay, whatever you say. [She says in the knowing tone 'there's no way']

ML   Thank you.

Max then finishes his intercom conversation with Doris, gets off his seat and retrieves a volume from his library, The letters of DH Lawrence. He flicks through the pages, which show that the volume has been well read with many notes and highlights, until he reaches page 81, when he stops flicking and focuses and mumbles to himself a highlighted passage.

ML   Well, my friend, Mr Lawrence, you knew all along what was good, decent and proper – and now, we'll deliver it.

The scene fades out as Max replaces the volume and retrieves another volume, The Art of Being Ruled by Wyndham Lewis.

ML   You too, my friend, I'll do justice to your dream yet.

Insert Scene – 29

We, by birth the natural leaders of the White European are people of not political or public consequences any more. We, the natural leaders of the World we live in, are not private citizens in the fullest sense, and that World is, as far as the administration or its traditional law of life is concerned, leaderless. Under these circumstances, its soul in a generation or so will be extinct.

The Art of Being Ruled *by Wyndham Lewis.*

Scene 47 – Jon tells Ivan, then Sandra

10:00am, Friday, 24 May 2013

Setting: GPA offices and Jon's office at the GPA

Jon leaves Max's office and is walking through the corridors. He comes into the section that he's in charge of. He walks up to his office, starts to open it, then thinks for a second, turns around and walks into the cube farm – to Ivan's desk.

JR   Ivan.

IH   [Ivan looks up, shocked – as he didn't see him coming] Yes, Jon?

JR   Can I have a quick word with you?

IH   Sure, what's up?

JR   No, I mean in my office.

IH   [He frowns.] Oh, sure.

They both walk back to Jon's office. Ivan jumps up onto the chair opposite Jon.

IH   Yes?

JR   I have some distressing news for you.

IH   Considering my current circumstances, I don't think anything you've got to say about my work is going to give me that much grief.

JR   I didn't say it was anything to do with your work.

IH   [Looks shocked] What?

JR   Look, something has come up which I have no control over. But it's not good news for you.

IH   Meaning?

JR   Sandra. She's requested the GPA to represent her in the forthcoming GPA Ethics Ruling Committee hearing next Wednesday – to help her get the injunction you placed on her lifted.

Ivan gives a blank dumbfounded expression, lost for words, totally still.

JR   [After a prolonged pause] Ivan – did you hear me?

With an expression of total disbelief, Ivan slides down the chair in silence and walks out of the room.

JR   Ivan, please come back and talk about this – really, I had no say in the matter. Max made the call.

Ivan just keeps walking. Once he leaves Jon's office – Jon picks up a paper weight off his desk and chucks it at one of the replica 'Russian Iconic' art works hanging in his office. The glass protecting the art smashes and falls to the floor.

JR   Fuck you, Valentina, you've caused me nothing but grief since the day I met you.

He goes to his bottom desk drawer, pulls out a bottle of Russian Kubanskaya vodka, and takes several swigs. Places the bottle back, puts his head in his hands remorsefully.

JR   Fuck, I hate this job – and the predicament that bitch has put me in.

He then sits back for a moment and regains his composure. His 'distraught' face is replaced by his 'authoritative in control' face.

JR   Well, here goes.

He dials Sandra.

JR   Sandra …

       Yes, it's Jon …

       Yes, I do have some news. But, before I say anything on that front, I just want to be really clear on a couple of points … Firstly, are you sure that you want to go through with this? …

Okay I hear you ... Now secondly, are you really sure you want the GPA to represent you? ... Okay if you are absolutely convinced that you are taking the right course of action and you are equally convinced that you want us to represent you, then, yes, absolutely, the GPA would be very happy to represent you ... Yes, that's right the GPA will represent you at the hearing ... Sandra, it's okay, remember, I'm just doing my job ... Now, you'll need to come into the office, well actually my office may not be the best place ... Yes, for this case, I think it best we use our other offices at the Gherkin. How about 8:00 Monday morning? ... Good, see you then ... You're welcome ... Sandra, before you hang up, there is just one more thing. At the risk of labouring a point, you have from now until Monday morning to think about your position and the extent to which you wish to involve the GPA. Once you sign all the forms on Monday morning there will be no turning back. If between now and Monday, you change your mind – that's perfectly okay, you're allowed to. However, after the papers are signed on Monday morning, then, well there will be no turning back ... I mean after you sign the papers on Monday morning, you will not be able to sack the GPA later on ... Yes, that's right, the GPA will see the case through to its conclusion – with or without you ... No, Sandra, I am not trying to persuade you to change your mind. I just want you to consider all your options and to give due thought as to the consequences of any decision you make in this regard. If you want the GPA to help you then we will definitely help you. But, as I mentioned to you before, the GPA's agenda may not always be perfectly aligned with your objectives ... Okay sure, think about it over the weekend – then we can discuss on Monday morning ... Sure, see you Monday morning.

Jon hangs up, leans back in his chair with a very sorry expression on his face, then speaks to himself:

JR   Poor little bastard, he doesn't deserve this.

Scene 48 – Ivan discusses situation with his mates

11:00am, Friday, 24 May 2013

Setting: The western 'Golden Jubilee' pedestrian bridge, adjacent to the Hungerford Bridge, used by passenger trains to cross the Thames and enter Charing Cross Station.

Ivan is with Andy and Rob, all leaning on the railing of western Golden Jubilee bridge, where they are overlooking the London eye.

IH   Guys, is the meeting still on for tonight

AW   What meeting?

RW   The Small Person's Association special meeting we scheduled for tonight.

IH   You mean 'the Dwarfs Association'.

AW   Oh, yeah that's right, we did schedule something didn't we? IH   So – it's still going ahead tonight?

RW   Sure is.

IH   What sort of numbers are we looking at?

RW   Fifty-two have confirmed. Unfortunately Greg said he is working tonight, so he can't make it.

IH   Fifty-two – that's excellent. And, personally, I don't mind if Greg can't make it. He scares me!

RW   I must say I feel the same. He's a violent bastard – have you ever seen any of the S&M porn he does? I guess by 'work' he's making another porno.

AW   I've watch a lot of porn in my day, but I tell you, the shit he does … it's too much for me to watch. And that's saying something, as I'm a seasoned porn connoisseur.

IH   I went to his porn site once – and never again. Jesus, that was some nasty shit he was doing. Sure wasn't anything you'd want to toss yourself over. Fuck that! Anyway, the 52 that are coming, they can be given the same wakeup call that I've just been given.

AW   Jesus, you're a slack bastard, it's 11:00am and you've only just got your wakeup call?

RW   [Ignoring Andy's comment] What wakeup call?

IH   [With a croak in his voice] The GPA … they're supporting Sandra. RW [In disbelief] What?

IH   Yes. Jon Raney – my boss, would you believe it – just advised me that Sandra requested representational support from the GPA at the hearing. And the GPA has granted her request.

AW   Ivan, even I can figure out that. This is not good news.

IH   Well, I suppose Jon is just getting back at me for calling him a Nazi bastard – by proving that he is.

RW   Ivan, I'm really sorry. Just remember you can count on us to do whatever you need us to do – whenever you need us to do it.

IH   Thanks Rob, putting me up in your spare room is massive support in itself.

RW   That's fine – I was only using it to watch porn via cable broadband. I can make do with the laptop and WiFi in my room. So, it's no trouble at all.

IH   Well, I was wondering why the carpet was so sticky – now I know.

All three dwarfs laugh lightly at this joke.

IH   Your offer of support means a lot to me at the moment. I mean, my mother, my wife, my work and the courts all seem hell bent on conspiring against me – so, to know I have trusted friends means everything to me.

         Just make sure every short bastard you know turns up for tonight's meeting okay? Call everyone – and remind them to be there – and those who haven't confirmed, antagonise them until they concede.

AW   You got it, man. If nothing else I'm good at antagonising.

RW   Sure, I'll start calling now.

IH   Thanks, guys. I gotta finish off my presentation for tonight – so see you at the Institute of Directors at, say, 6:30.

AW   But it doesn't start until 7:30.

RW   Maybe to help setup and greet the guests.

AW   Oh yea – I suppose.

IH   Okay thanks – I'll see you there.

AW&RW Sure, see you then – bye.

Scene 49 – Ivan addresses the dwarfs

7:30pm, Friday, 24 May 2013

Setting: Institute of Directors

Ivan steps up to the lectern, but his head is below the top of the lectern. He opens with 'I hope you can all see me'. To which he receives tremendous laughter.

Ivan then steps off the lectern and puts the box that he had sourced earlier at the lectern's base and steps up. This time he is appropriately positioned to give a speech.

IH   Friends, small people, dwarfs, midgets, short-asses and useless little shits – welcome here tonight.

This results in a degree of nervous laughter and shock, dismay and offence.

IH   You know the only reason I came here to speak tonight – my appointment with a normal-heighted person cancelled on me. I mean, fuck it, I'd rather spend my time with normal people rather than the bunch of freaks assembled in front of me. Damn it, why did they cancel? I could now be bathing in the warm glow of 'normality' rather than being drenched in the stench oozing from a bunch of short-asses.

The forum is now completely silent, stunned, shocked. It is now at the point that if another insult were passed there would be mass exodus.

IH   I trust that I have suitably offended each and every one of you now. I trust you are upset by my language. I trust you are livid by my insults, I trust you are on the verge of throwing your chair at me. I trust you can't wait to meet me outside so you can physically return the hurt you feel.

BUT YOU'RE NOT. YOU'RE NOT FUCKING INSULTED ENOUGH!

You are still sitting there, still not saying anything, still not throwing anything at me, still not coming forward to make me shut the fuck up. Why? Why do you just sit there, why do you put up with me standing up here insulting you little shit midgets down there? Why? It's because you always do, we always do. Each and every one of us is a professional shit eater. We eat shit every day, every night, day in, night out, year in, year out, century in, century out.

You, me, we all know our place in society: unless we're in a circus or a freak show we have no place. Society is now so PC that you: can't call a gay man a fag; can't call a Black man a nigger; can't call a fat bastard fatso; can't call your girlfriend your bitch; can't call a Pakistani a Paki; can't call a gypsy a pikey; can't call people with Parkinson's shaky; can't call anyone anything except a gentleman or a lady – unless they are a dwarf. We're free game. Call us gnomes, call us elves, call us leprechauns, call us doormats, call us midgets, call us short-asses, call us whatever anyone fucking likes – and we say nothing.

[Long pause].

If only it stopped at words. If only the discrimination stopped at the degrading language we are subject to it'd be okay. But it doesn't. We are systematically discriminated against. We are routinely discriminated against. We are blatantly and totally discriminated against. Let me cite just a few examples, but you all know many, many more like these:

New lifts have to have braille on the buttons so blind folk can read the floors, and there have to be audio announcements when the lift arrives at each floor so the blind know when to get off. But the buttons don't have to be placed at a height that we can reach – so we can never get to the top floors because we can't reach the fucking buttons.

If we ever leave a stick or box in the lift so that we can reach the buttons, each day they are cleaned out regardless of the number of pleas and protests we make.

Every public place has to have toilet facilities to accommodate wheelchairs. But, urinals are never placed low enough for dwarfs to reach.

Banks place both their cash machines and their internal counters too high for us to be able to use them – yet they have wheelchair access.

Even though we are adults, theme parks refuse to allow us to enjoy the rides, as we don't meet the children's height test.

Buses have wheelchair access, together with support ruts to prevent chairs from rolling around, but they don't have support handles low enough for dwarfs to reach.

And if we are ever at a bar or in a queue – aren't we always the last to be served?

And who gives a shit, who says anything, who does anything? None of us – that's who.

The average IQ of British dwarfs is 102 – which is pretty much the same as the overall British average.

However, the average earnings of full-time employees in the UK is €27,250. But, for a full- time working dwarf it is only €22,950 – which is very nearly 25% below the British average –a full quarter less than the average British worker gets. And remember, we have the same average IQ as the rest of Britain. So, why are our earnings 25% less than normal-heighted people?

The unemployment level in Britain is 5.5% – but for dwarfs the unemployment rate is at 28%. And, I must emphasis, this figure only includes dwarfs who want to and are capable of working. Why are more of us out of work than our normal-heighted cousins? Remember, most people in Britain are now white-collar workers, so height is no disadvantage. We can use a computer as well as anyone else.

About 7% of the British workforce manages at least one person, but amongst full-time working dwarfs less than 1% are in a managerial role where they actually manage other people. And it doesn't require height to manage – it requires managerial skills. So, why don't we get promoted to managerial positions?

Why? Because we're only dwarfs, we're a fucking joke. We belong in the circus, the pantomimes, porno movies – not the workplace, not the 'real' workplace. Let's face it, we're a joke, and everyone is laughing except us.

This level of discrimination is totally unacceptable to the feminist movement, the Black movement, the gay movement, the blind society, the deaf society, the amputee society, the reformed criminal society and the national racist society. The discrimination we receive is totally unacceptable to everyone else in our society, every bloody association and every fucking movement in the country – except the 'Little People's Association'. Why?

Well, in the unlikely scenario that I've actually excited or moved any of you to do anything about this blatant derogatory discrimination of dwarf folk – then don't worry. You needn't bother.

Help is at hand to solve this discrimination problem. It won't be with us for much longer. I've taken measures into my own hands that will resolve this problem once and for all.

Ivan now pauses and takes a slow drink of water.

IH   Well folks, I think that's about all I came to say, so thanks for coming tonight – and hopefully see you next time.

He jumps down from his box and starts to walk out.

A number of dwarfs from the audience stand up and start shouting:

AUD   Ivan, what do you mean you've sorted it, don't walk off now, tell us what you've done.

IH   [From the side of the hall] What? What do you care? None of you ever do anything about our plight, none of you ever have written a single letter to a politician, a newspaper, the equal opportunity commission. Not one of you has complained openly to your employer, when year after year after fucking year you get passed over for promotion. Each one of you just sees it as your role to be trodden on to be kept down to play your role as a freak and nothing more.

Now that I'm doing something about my lot, about our lot, about your lot, why now ask me to explain – as though you give a shit.

AUD   Who the fuck do you think you are, you're no better than us – you have no right to insult us like this.

IH   That's right isn't it? I have no right to insult you. But you let every normal-heighted person insult you, you let the press, you let society insult you every day. I insult you once at this meeting and you're up in arms saying 'Who is he? He's only a fucking midget, he can't insult us!'

233

But you let everyone else insult, degrade and humiliate you. Well, fuck you!

Let me ask, how many dwarf jokes are out there? How many times have you heard 'dopey fucked a penguin'? How many times have you heard the one about Snow White … How many times have you received offensive pornographic emails from your normal-heighted 'friends' featuring dwarfs? How many times have you been reminded of the dwarf throwing competitions in Queensland Australia? How many times have your normal-heighted colleagues suggested that they set up a similar competition at your local 'All-Bar-One'? How many times have you heard the expression 'an intellectual dwarf'?

But it doesn't stop there – even our normal-heighted partners are open to the jibes, insults and foul jokes. How many times has you girlfriend been called 'Snow White'? Really, how many of you have split up from your normal-heighted partners merely because your partner couldn't take the barrage of insults that goes with being a partner of a dwarf?

So, if you're angry with me for insulting you tonight, if you won't tolerate me insulting you, why do you allow everyone else in society to insult you all day, every day?

AUD   Ivan, you've made your point that we should be angry – and we are. Now, what are you doing to stop the discrimination against us?

IH   Does anyone else want to hear – or should I just leave?

AUD   No – please tell us what you're doing.

Ivan goes back to the lectern.

IH   Well, it's like this. Now that I've been coming to these meetings for several years, both here in London and earlier in Leeds – I've realised that, aside from being short, there is only one other thing that we all have in common. And that one thing, well really it's more of a theme, runs like this: low self-esteem; lack of self-respect; self-pity; bitterness of being born short; and adoration of normal-heighted people!

Essentially, any of us would sell our grandmother to become normal heighted. Let's face it, we don't like ourselves, we don't like each other. All of us here would prefer to be at another function right now, with normal-heighted people, if only we felt as though we were their equal – or more correctly if we felt as though they would treat us as their equal. That ain't going to happen – so we came here instead – as a very poor consolation prize. Given this sorry state of affairs – I've started something that will solve all our sorry plights – once and for all. I've started an action at the Genetic Protection Authority's Ethics Ruling Committee. By action, I mean the committee is scheduled to hear my case next Wednesday. Once they have heard the arguments being put forward – they'll make a ruling.

The ruling, most probably, will be that none of you sorry bastards will be allowed to have children, at least not dwarf children. Therefore, in a mere generation all our miserable worries and frustrations will be solved – as no more dwarfs will be born, so no more dwarfs to worry about. No more miserable dwarfs complaining. No more dwarfs wallowing in their own self-pity.

So, I would like you all to thank me for coming to the rescue of the dwarf self-pity movement.

AUD   [From the audience a dwarf stands on his chair and shouts] What? Speak for yourself. I happen to have a family, and I'm very proud of them. There isn't anything wrong with them, they're bright, beautiful, loving and a joy to be with. I'm immensely proud of them. Being dwarfs has not proved to be any handicap to them whatsoever – they're simply wonderful.

So what right have you got to stop us having children – how dare you?

AUD   [Another dwarf from the crowd] My Rosy is pregnant now with our first child. We are thrilled to bits over our good fortune. We don't care that it's a dwarf – just to have a baby is such a wonderful thing. You have no right to try and take this away from us.

IH   [Eventually – after the level of abuse has started to approach physical hostilities.] Well my friends, I'm so very glad you feel like this. I'm so very glad that you want the ability and the right to have a family. I'm so very glad that you were on the verge of lynching me.

Why? Because – it's not me who is trying to stop us from having families. The state is trying to stop me from having my unborn child. If the state wins this hearing it will set a precedent, which will then prevent all of you from having families.

Think about it. My wife is pregnant – and the state is trying to terminate the pregnancy merely on the grounds that my baby will be a dwarf. The state is saying that you, me, all of us do not have the right to a life – merely because we're short. I mean, as far as I know there are no plans to round us up and send us to the gas chambers, but basically they're saying if they could have killed us all off prior to us being born – then they would have.

They may have missed out on terminating us when we were mere embryos in our mothers' womb, but sure as hell they aren't going to miss terminating our kids.

So, now I let the reason for my earlier insults be known. I want all of you to get off your short-asses and to become active in the defence of our rights. If we don't act now, you, me, all of us, it will be too late. The state will win, which will then require all unborn children to be checked for dwarfism, and if the test proves positive, out they come.

If dwarfs were a race rather then a common physical or genetic condition, this would be called genocide. But as we come from all races it's called 'genetic purification'. Hitler used to call this practice 'eugenics'! And I think we all know how the eugenics programme expanded into 'the Final Solution'. You all know your history. You should all realise that you, personally, are in the midst of an historical act that will both affect – and be remembered – by generations to come.

So, you have to support me at the GPA's Ethics Ruling Committee next Wednesday – there are leaflets at the back with the date, time, place etc., together with a summary of the case and history.

Before then, act now to stop being walked over – like we all have for the past God knows how many centuries. Now is the time to make a stand. Write to your paper, write to your MP. Take your employer to court over discrimination. Demand a promotion. Whatever you do – act now. If you don't, very soon it will be too late, and our heritage will die with us.

Thank you, and see you at the hearing.

Scene fades out on Ivan looking triumphant at the lectern.

Scene 50 – The Club meeting

10:00am, Saturday, 25 May 2013

Setting: Claydon Manor

Max Lyford, in his Range Rover Sports, drives up to Claydon Manor, which has a gravel driveway through its superb gardens. He pulls into the car park immediately outside the house, which is distinguished by the range of high value cars parked there – say fifteen or so.

He gets out of his car and, demonstrating his familiarity with Claydon Manor, rather than going through the main entrance, proceeds to a side entrance and knocks on the door. Max hardly finishes knocking when the door is opened and he is greeted by Chris Braithwaite. Chris and Max exchange pleasantries before Max follows Chris into the house. They walk down a short passageway until they come to a large reading room. It is full of sunlight coming from the window that immediately overlooks the car park in which Max had just parked, which explains why Chris was at the door waiting for Max – as it is evident that Chris saw Max arrive. As Max enters, he is greeted by seven gentlemen already present in the reading room.

The room is superbly appointed with wood panelling, art, books, ornaments and antiques, but still very inviting, comfortable and homely. The piece of art that is placed most prominently and 'overlooks' the room is Wyndham Lewis's 1949 portrait of TS Eliot.

Max and Chris take their seats, resulting in a circle of nine seated gentlemen, some of whom are engaged in casual chatter. Their attire and accents reek of the old English aristocracy, complimented by the manor itself and the interior furnishings.

Upon Max and Chris taking their seats, the ring is composed of the following:

Sir John Poo Beresford

Lord Thomas Denman   *Sir Ronald Lawe-Davies*

Oscar Williamson   *Frederick Rogers*

Sebastian McKibben   *Chris Braithwaite (Owner of Mansion)*

Max Lyford   *Angus Le Bon*

There is a coffee table in the centre of the room, complete with an 'Astbury Black' Wedgwood tea set. Aside from Max, the others have already availed themselves to the tea and cake, which they have placed on the side tables next to each of their chairs.

ML   Well gentlemen, this is an exciting day – a great day for us all. But, you must excuse me, I really can't discuss any of the details of the case until I pour myself a cup of tea and serve myself a piece of that beautiful cake.

Max, with a great deal of aplomb, slowly pours himself a cup of tea and takes a piece of cake – then proceeds to take several sips.

While Max is doing this, the others continue with their light chatter. At one end, Lord Denman discusses with Oscar his recent hawking trip in Scotland, on which he took his eldest son for the first time. On the other side of the circle, Angus is discussing with Chris his recent read of George Gissing's 'New Grub Street' – describing the work as a semi-autobiographical account of Gissing.

While they are speaking and waiting for Max, there is no sign whatsoever that they are anxious or impatient to hear his news – it is relaxed and as cordial as it could be.

ML   [Picking up a serviette wiping his mouth and returning the serviette to the table]. Thank you all for coming at such short notice. But I'm sure after you hear my news you will all agree that it was worth cancelling your other engagements.

LTD   It had better be! I gave up my box at Lords for the second Ashes test just to be here today.

ML   Yes, well hopefully we will even the score to make it one all. Mind you, we do not have much luck against the Aussies at Lords. Anyway, Lord Denman, I don't think you will feel robbed after you hear my news.

       This, I think, will mark an historic occasion. Sir Francis Galton, as we all know, was the father of the eugenics movement in Britain and, for that matter, the world – as eugenics originated in this great country of ours. It was in 1885 that he first coined the term 'eugenic', followed by his battle cry that rings as true today as it did 128 years ago, that being:

       'Let us improve the stock of our own species as we have improved that of others. Let us breed from the best and not from the worst specimens of humanity.'

       We have Karl Pearson to thank for popularising Galton's ideas of eugenics – to the point it became an accepted political and social creed. But, unfortunately, try as we may, Britain failed to pass any eugenic laws – thanks mostly to Josiah Wedgwood. It was his speeches and campaigns, both in and out of Parliament first in 1913 and again in 1934 that stopped the passage of the two eugenics bills from being passed by Parliament.

Max then stops and looks at his cup and saucer.

ML   You know, for a family that made such superb English fine bone china, it's hard to imagine they had a son who so irresponsibly derailed Britain's eugenic programme. Terrible! If it was not for the misconceived ideology and philosophy of Josiah Wedgwood, the great work may well have already been completed by now.

The others join in at this point – concurring that this was a terrible missed opportunity.

ML   I find it nauseating that we were the country that gave birth to the eugenics movement – and yet we were one of the few industrialised countries not to benefit from it. Our competitor nations embraced and benefited enormously from the adoption of a eugenics programme:

       Charles Davenport persuaded the US to pass no fewer than 30 state and federal eugenic laws – which led at least 100,000 feebleminded people to be sterilised. Virginia, being the most bold, continued its sterilisation programme well into the 1970s.

Sweden proved to be a great exponent of eugenics and sterilised at least 63,000 inferiors. Canada managed 2,845, while Finland achieved success with the sterilisation of 11,000 unfit. Denmark, Norway, Estonia and Iceland all had their own legislative eugenic sterilisation programme – but the numbers are not available as to the success they achieved. As far as sheer determination goes, all hats off to France and Switzerland, which continued their eugenics programme right up to the close of the twentieth century.

It is, of course, Germany who benefited, and for that matter continues to benefit, from the sterilisation of at least 400,000 imbeciles, criminals, drunkards and other inferiors. While Germany may have stopped their eugenics programme at the close of the Second World War, by preventing 400,000 plus unfits from further polluting their gene pool it has given them a massive advantage by alleviating them of the need to deal with their inferior offspring.

At the start of the twentieth century, we missed our chance to start taking measures to clean up our population – cleanse it of idiots, the insane, criminals and the handicapped.

Then, of course, in the second half of the twentieth century, the social mood changed – so that every dim-witted creature, every criminal, every psychopath, every dysfunctional family was to be respected, protected and exalted. The whole state went loopy. Britain was doing far more to look after the worst in our society than trying to advance and improve the best. A simply horrid situation. It was, and remains, so socially and culturally damaging. All this without even taking into account the inferior races!

As we missed our opportunity at the beginning of the twentieth century, now, several generations later, we are stuck with this scum in our gene pool. If that is not bad enough, we have to care and provide for these delinquents, criminals and handicaps that are no more than parasites on the rest of our decent society. Worse, we can't even stop this filth from breeding a new generation of parasites that will weaken our gene pool and end up sponging off the rest of us just like their inferior parents did.

Anyway, with the case we have before us – we may, in fact I'll go as far as to say we should, be able to introduce the necessary laws and regulations in order to bring a little balance back into our society again. To start taking measures to rid ourselves of the scum we find not only sharing our gene pool – but taking the pool over. Gentlemen, between us, we can finish the work that Francis Galton and Karl Pearson started but were never able to complete. This truly is a great occasion for all of us and for all true Britons.

Naturally, we can't call it eugenics – as it's a word dirtied by common misconception and political usage. The Nazi's liberal use of the word certainly has forever cast it onto the 'politically incorrect' scrap heap. While we can no longer use the 'eugenics' term coined by Sir Francis Galton, we can still pursue the same noble philosophy, which he rightly saw as an extension of his cousin, Charles Darwin's, scientific discoveries on evolution.

SRLD   Max, this is starting to sound as though it was worthwhile missing my round at Bearwood Lakes. So exactly what is the case before us – and how can we be sure that … that … the media or politicians won't jump in there and wreck this opportunity to start advancing the human race.

ML   Very good question, Sir Ronald. I do have, I believe, the right answer, which is of course why we are all here today – to hear about 'the case'.

        [At this point Max finishes his piece of cake.] Superb. You must excuse me, that really was exceptional – and I simply must have another piece.

There is another pause while Max helps himself to another piece of cake – but again there is no sense of tension among those present. They merely continue with their chitchat. Max finishes getting his second piece of cake, then pours himself another cup of tea.

ML   You will all remember that over the last decade we have laid the foundations for the establishment of the eugenics program, or as we now prefer to call it 'the genome advancement programme', by: defining the definitive human 'genome' via the 'Human Genome Project'; enacting the Genetic Protection Act, which established the Genetic Protection Authority, tasked with the advancement and protection of the human genome; appointing the Genetic Protection Authority's Ethics Ruling Committee; introduced legislation to prevent the transmission of specific inherited or genetic disease to future generations; amending the GPA Act last year to bring in the three standard deviation from the human norm criteria.

These measures came in discrete phases, and none of them were, in themselves, that radical to cause any public alarm. On the contrary, each phase received wide public and media support.

The legislation to protect future generations of specific genetic disorders, for example, Parkinson's disease and cystic fibrosis, could have proved a difficult public relations exercise had it not been for the media empathising with poor parents worrying about their genetically diseased offspring.

As it transpired, with the pressure on families now to have perfect kids and a perfect life – well, in essence mothers and families generally were more than happy to have a state-encouraged position that they should terminate their pregnancies where tests proved that their unborn child was a carrier of a debilitating genetic disease. It removed the sense of guilt they may have felt if they had to make the decision by themselves.

While this has been a huge step forward in starting to cleanse our gene pool, the legislation was quite restrictive. The state had had a position only for specific gazetted genetic disorders. The process to conclusively identify a genetic disorder that can be tested for by pre-birth genetic DNA sampling is excruciatingly slow. For this reason, we only have 62 disorders gazetted at the moment.

So, for the thousands of non-gazetted genetic disorders that are present in embryos up and down the country, we did not have an effective manner to stop the embryos from developing and being born – complete with their genetic defects.

July last year, that changed.

[Max pauses and takes a sip of his tea and a bite of his cake – looks out the window where he see a group of children playing.]

LTD   Max, I assume you are referring to the three standard deviation rule that was introduced last year?

Max nods his head as he takes a bite of his cake.

LTD   Sorry Max, I thought that all the hopes we had for this legislation, well, have essentially fallen flat. Not one case has even been discussed, doubtless taken through the courts. Not one genetic defect has been prevented from coming into this world by the exercise of this legislation.

ML   [Wipes his mouth with serviette] Lord Denman, you are quite right and you are quite wrong.

LTD   Really, Max, how is that?

ML   Well, you are right in as much as this legislation has not prevented a single genetically defective child from being born.

LTD   Ah ah – and why am I wrong?

ML   Lord Denman, because we still have high hopes for this piece of legislation. And, now with the case before us, our hopes may soon be realised.

SM   Max, you've mentioned 'The Case' a few times now – so perhaps you should reveal to us the details.

ML   Certainly. First, the reason it hasn't produced any results to date is that we've had to be extremely careful as to how the provisions of the act are activated, i.e. what we use as the first test case.

       If we took a position that an embryo satisfied the three standard deviation rule – and then the parents and subsequently the media took the contrary view – we would have a major PR problem on our hands. We could be viewed as an overly aggressive hand of the state with Nazi-like ambitions. To avoid such a PR nightmare, we've had to sit and wait for the 'right' case to come along, where we can be seen by the populous as their mere servants, trying to help mothers and families come to a sensible decision on their, and their child's, future. I can't stress how sensitive this matter is – if we pick the wrong case and we find we have a media backlash it could very well mean the end of this aspect of the legislation, which could sink our hopes for the programme.

       So, we've been waiting, waiting, waiting to find the right case to act on. [Picks up his cup again and has another sip and bite of his cake.]

SRLD   And the case is?

ML   Yes, Sir Ronald. We've been so nervous about picking the right case – agonising over so many potential cases and always backing out at the last minute due to the high risk involved. In short, we have one shot at defining the common law on the interpretation and guidance of the three standard deviation rule – as such we are only prepared to back a 100% sure test case.

SRLD And now you've found your case?

ML   No. [Takes another sip]

As Max takes his time sipping/eating, the silence starts to become tense as the others become less willing to play Max's game of 'I'll pause and wait for one of you to ask me a question before continuing'. But this doesn't faze Max. He keeps taking his time – the others refuse to be drawn into the 'tenseness' of the pause, so they too sip their tea, have a bite of their cake or look out the window.

ML   You see, Sir Ronald, we didn't find a case – the case found us!

The others look a little surprised and intrigued. Max notes their expression before continuing.

ML   Yes, something we didn't anticipate, doubtless even hope for, has happened.

SM   Max, this does sound intriguing – what exactly do you mean 'the case found us'.

ML   Sebastian, a man with a non-gazetted genetic disorder has got his wife pregnant – natural enough I suppose. It's arguable whether or not his genetic condition falls within the three standard deviation threshold – well, as this law has never been tested, its arguable whether any condition does or does not fall outside the threshold.

      Anyway, the wife may or may not have decided on a course of action to terminate the child – that's unclear – but it is clear that she is at least thinking about it. Further, it's unclear whether her considerations on this subject were based on personal lifestyle reasons or due to the fact that the unborn child has the father's genetic disorder.

SM   Max, this hardly sounds like the 'decisive' case that we've been looking for. I mean the wife isn't sure whether she even wants the child – and if she does not want the child then it may be for lifestyle reasons.

      So, exactly how is this 'The Case'?

ML   Yes, strictly on the basis you've just described, I think you're correct, Sebastian. But, then something incredible happened that changed everything. The father was afraid that the mother might terminate the pregnancy due to it having the same genetic disorder that he suffers from. As it happens, the father refuses to acknowledge that his condition is a defect. So, he was outraged over the possibility that his wife might terminate the pregnancy, merely because the child will grow up to have the same physical attributes that he has.

SJPB Max, where are we going with this – it still doesn't sound like the case we've been waiting for – so what if the father's a little worked up over his wife's possible actions?

ML   So what indeed, Sir John Poo!

      Well, he took matters into his own hands and went to the High Court and placed an injunction on his wife preventing her from terminating the pregnancy due to its genetic condition – until the case is heard by the GPA's Ethics Ruling Committee, where, effectively, the father has charged it to make a ruling as to whether his wife is within her rights to terminate the pregnancy on the grounds that the unborn child will satisfy the three standard deviation rule.

Max pauses and again sips his tea, while the others all look astonished, as though all their Christmases have come at once.

CB   Max, this really is extraordinary news – what an absolute gift to our cause.

ML   Yes. Now, if the GPA's Ethics Ruling Committee were to find in favour of the wife, then it would be seen as humane and compassionate, merely helping the plight of the would-be mother.

      Assuming we can manage the media on this case, the GPA would not be seen as a Big Brother enforcing a eugenics programme, it would be seen as kind and caring to the mother of the unborn defective embryo.

      In essence, we should be able to influence the media so that it is reported that the GPA's Ethics Ruling Committee is merely holding up the right of the mother to 'choose' without any attention being paid to the more fundamental change in the law, which will revoke all fathers' paternal rights where the state determines an embryo satisfies the three standard deviation rule.

Henceforth, we will only need to persuade mothers to terminate their defective unborn without any threat of legal retaliation from the father.

CB   Max, so just how good is his legal counsel – I mean, is the committee going to be bound up for days on spurious arguments put forward by money hungry KC's?

ML   Chris, there's even better news on this front – he is representing himself, and he is not legally trained.

The group all look delighted and murmur words along the lines of 'unbelievable', 'marvellous', etc.

LTD   Well, Max, after some initial misgivings – you are absolutely right, this news is better than watching the second test at Lords [he looks down on his iPhone], especially as we're down 176 for 5.

ML   I think so. Now, gentlemen – while we have been passed a gift, it doesn't mean that there aren't any risks associated with the gift. The media, academics, politicians or even the courts could still side with, or rule in favour of, the father. Therefore, we need to be extra vigilant in managing this case so that we gain public support and a favourable ruling from the GPA ERC.

      So, I will be calling on all of you to be doing your part to gently persuade your peers and colleagues as to the social benefits that would be achieved should the GPA ERC rule in our favour.

      Remember, just one slip up, one unfavourable media report, or one stupid comment from a politician could blow the whole programme off course. We have to be diligent and show great strength and solidarity as the case progresses.

All   [All of them together] Hear, hear. Of course we will.

FR   Max, can I ask what the father's genetic disorder is?

ML   [A bit bluntly] He's a dwarf, suffering from achondroplasia.

ALB   Achondroplasia?

ML   Yes, achondroplasia is the most common form of dwarfism, you would recognise it – it's the short guys with big heads, big asses, and stumpy little legs and arms.

ALB   Oh, them, okay. What a test case!

FR   Is that really a genetic condition that falls within the three standard deviation rule – I mean, essentially all that's wrong with the poor chap is that he's short.

ML   Well, how do you measure three standard deviations from the human norm? Is it against the 'mapped human genome' or the population average? According to Galton's pioneering work in this area, the average male height in the United Kingdom is five foot eight inches with a standard deviation of one and three quarter inches. Therefore, any man shorter than five foot two and three quarter inches tall, arguably, falls outside the three standard deviation threshold. If the GPA ERC holds that 'height' can be applied as the basis for applying the rule, then the father and the unborn child would fall outside the three standard deviation threshold.

Off hand, I do not know exactly how tall, or should I say short, this poor chap is – but I do know that he is way shorter than five foot two and three quarter inches. My guess he is somewhere around four foot six.

FR   Sorry, Max, I don't buy this. I don't think that being short should put someone at risk of being genetically filtered. The intention was, and is, to cleanse the gene pool of the violent, habitual criminals, the paedophiles, the chronically ill, the handicapped and the mentally challenged.

Being short does not fall into any of these categories.

ML   Frederick, possibly you're right. But, there are a few aspects associated with this case to consider. One, if we don't run with this case – will another come up that is 'as clean cut' to help the introduction of the programme? Secondly, if you were to ask one hundred people whether or not they would prefer to be their own height or the height of a dwarf – what do you think the response would be?

Essentially, no one wants to be physically abnormal, or certainly not sub-normal. And being a dwarf certainly is definitely sub-normal. Now that we have the means to do so, shouldn't we be trying to save future generations from this sub-normality?

FR   Well, I'm not convinced – what do the rest of you think?

Frederick looks at each member in turn and gets their response – all of whom show that they are in favour of using this as the test case.

FR   Well, I seem to be outvoted on the matter. For the moment I'm prepared to show solidarity, but I still see a lot of danger in using this as a test case – it could open the floodgates to the discrimination against all sorts of conditions that are not really a disadvantage to those carrying the condition.

ML   Okay Frederick your concerns are noted …

FR   Max, I don't want to be just noted. I'm going to monitor this case very carefully, and if there is any inkling that the GPA's Ethics Ruling Committee's ruling is to make a too broader ruling I'll step in and have my say!

ML   Sure, how about we meet once a week as the case progresses, just to make sure you are fully informed of the proceedings?

FR   Make it twice a week – Mondays and Thursdays. Shall we meet in my chambers?

ML   [Looks a little stunned by this imposition] Sure, Frederick, twice a week it is. In your chambers.

CB   Well gentlemen, I don't think there is anyone more qualified to assume the governance role over this case than our own Lord Justice. As such, I'm more than happy for Frederick to oversee and monitor this case on our behalf. But, so that the rest of are kept up to date should we meet here every two weeks – say same time, same place?

There is broad agreement by all those present.

CB   Excellent. Now that we have finished discussing business, should we be a little social and join the others?

All   Excellent idea – and thank you Max, Frederick and Chris for briefing us.

The group get up and slowly walk through the large rooms all chatting about the art and literature that they have recently viewed and read. The scene fades out as they walk through a large door and go out of view.

Scene 51 – Off to work we go

9:00am, Sunday, 26 May 2013

Setting: Rob Walker's Apartment

Ivan's at the kitchen table of Rob's home with a number of law books strewn over the table and totally engrossed in one of them.

The scene cuts over to Andy, who is making his way to Rob's apartment via the District Line underground.

Andy gets off the tube at West Ham and walks out of the station. He then walks down a series of quite drab terrace house streets until he eventually come to Durban Road, another terrace house street, walks up it until he finds no. 15. He ascends the stairs and knocks on the door.

The scene switches back to Ivan, who hears the doorbell ring and gets up to open the door for Andy.

AW Hey dude – howzit going man?

IH Hey Andy, thanks for coming over – come in. I trust you're not missing a rehearsal or anything like that?

AW Well yeah – I am. But, I've played Puck so many time that I know my lines backwards.

IH You won't get in to trouble?

AW They can only try, but Lord, what fools these mortals be!

IH What?

AW Don't worry, what are they going to do, sack me a week before opening night? I don't think so.

IH Okay, as long as you're okay with missing rehearsal – I don't want to get you into any trouble with the RSC.

AW   No, I'm fine – believe me, I know my lines better than most porn web addresses.

IH   Cool, I'll just tell Rob that you're here – he's in his bedroom with his laptop, apparently finishing an audit report.

AW   Finishing an audit report? I've never heard of that porn site before.

Ivan and Andy both smile, then Ivan walks off to knock on Rob's bedroom door.

IH   Rob, Andy has just arrived – can you join us?

RW   [From his bedroom, where he is sitting at his desk typing on his laptop with several open binders scattered over the desk]. Sure, I'll just finish this paragraph and be with you in a minute.

The scene fades out – then fades back in with Ivan and Andy sitting at the kitchen table, with Rob approaching the table.

RW   So, where are we? How are we going to win this case?

AW   We're going to win because we're smart little fuckers – that's how.

IH   Well, I got the GPA legislation and the GPA's Ethics Ruling Committee procedures manual.

RW   Good. So, is that enough to get us past the winning post?

IH   What else is there – this is the material that we're going to present at the hearing.

RW   Okay, let's start.

AW   [Spots a bowl of fruit in the kitchen] Can I have an apple?

IH   Sure, go for it. Well, I've been going through the legislation … and well …

RW   Well?

IH   Well, I think I'm going to need your help – I mean the legislation itself is so unjust, if we have to prove our case within the constraints of the legislation then it may be a little difficult …

RW   Why, what does the legislation say?

IH   Well, it says here:

The GPA is charged with developing an accurate means of determining whether an embryo, which is free of any gazetted genetic disorders, will nevertheless develop into an abnormal child or abnormal adult. Abnormal is defined as in excess of three standard deviations from the accepted human norm.

RW   Great – so what's our defence?

AW   That we're not abnormal – we're super normal – the super midgets.

IH   Well, along the lines of what Andy just said, maybe more modestly put, that just because we're vertically challenged doesn't mean we're not normal.

RW   This definition has never been tested before has it?

IH   No, this is it. This will be the first case to get a ruling on the three standard deviation rule.

RW   So, there's lots riding on it – not just us dwarfs but anyone, any group with some form of identifiable genetic trait. In short – to excuse the pun – if we fuck up this case we fuck it up for, well, for everyone I suppose.

IH   Hummm – I suppose I've really only been thinking of it in the context of dwarfs, but I guess you're right.

RW   So, do you think we should get professional help, to help define and fight the case?

IH   No. They're all Nazi bastards – the GPA, the law firms the lot of them.

RW   Come on, Ivan, I think you are going to have to get over your paranoia and conspiracy theories now.

IH   No. Besides, if we admit that we can't fight the case ourselves, then doesn't this give strength to the assertion that we're inferior – we can't stand up for ourselves?

RW   I just think that so much is riding on this case, not just for you – the dwarf community and anyone else who has an identifiable genetic trait. We should do all we can – and use anyone we can – to ensure we win the case. We shouldn't leave anything to chance.

IH   No, we can do it – we're as good as any bloodsucking Nazi lawyer.

RW   Okay. So, how are you developing our defence, Mr Big Shot?

IH   Well, the legislation doesn't provide any guidance as to what is 'three standard deviations from the accepted human norm'. So all we have to establish is that we are within three standard deviations from the accepted human standard.

RW   Well, earlier today I Googled 'average UK height' and, while there were different stats from different sites, typically the average was given as five foot nine or thereabouts with a standard deviation somewhere around two inches. Given these statistics, I guess the argument against us will be that any male shorter than five foot three would fall foul of the three standard deviation rule. Since your stature is a mere four foot four inches, you fall well outside three deviations from the normal height of UK men.

IH   Yes, I know they will put forward that argument, but our argument has to be based on what is the 'accepted human norm', and that height by itself does not define what it is to be 'human'.

RW   Well, fine, in that case what does?

IH   Well, everything about us – us in totality. Not a single attribute like colour, weight, size of nose, intellect etc., but everything taken together. Take albinos. They're pretty rare. There is only one person in every 17,000 that has some form of albinism – so should they also be wiped out?

      No, because they are normal in every sense of the word – except they don't have the same pigmentation rate as the rest of us.

AW   What about albino dwarfs? Then they would have two abnormalities – would that be reason enough to wipe them out?

IH   No, because humans have thousands of discrete attributes, and by singling out one or two of these, saying, 'Hey these guys are so different

252

from the rest of us', that they should be wiped out – it just doesn't fly.

RW   Doesn't fly with you. But we're not arguing with you, we're arguing with the GPA. Now, if we use your argument, by mapping every one of the thousands of attributes that are uniquely human and then defining a standard encompassing every one of these attributes – nobody would ever breach the three standard deviation rule as there is always the defence 'I've still got five fingers on each hand, I've still got a tongue, I've still got two arms and two legs, I still have an average IQ etc.'

Clearly, the legislators wrote this legislation so that exceptions could be identified, and then have the legislative means to stop them from procreating.

IH   Well, aside from the IQ attribute, every other attribute you mentioned was not uniquely human. The attributes equally apply to each of the 193 species of primate on the planet – which includes us of course.

RW   Good point. So, how do we define what it is to be a human, in either a genetic sense or some other criteria – so that the 'accepted human norm' makes sense and is inclusive of all humans but excludes other primates?

IH   Well, there is a key difference between us and primates. Humans only have 23 pairs of chromosomes, whereas the other 192 species of primates have 24 pairs.

RW   Well, I suppose that's a start, and I assume this is no different for us dwarfs?

IH   Yep, it's true for us – but not for everyone. People suffering from Down's syndrome have an extra chromosome. Rather than a just pair, they have three 21st chromosomes. Very odd. Scientifically speaking, chimpanzees are genetically closer to us than kids with Down's syndrome.

AW   So, what makes us dwarfs genetically different, since we have the right number of chromosomes?

IH   Jesus man, hasn't your doctor gone over this with you a million times?

AW   Nnnuh.

IH On one gene within the fourth pair of chromosomes we have a defect –
well, not a defect, it's just different from normal-heighted people.

AW What sort of defect?

IH It's not a defect, it's just different. Within the fourth pair of chromosomes,
we have a genetic misspelling. The gene in question has the flattering
name of 'FGFR3'. To be more precise, on gene FGFR3 at nucleotide
1138 we have the genetic letter 'A' appearing – whereas in
normal-heighted people they have the genetic letter 'G' appearing.

   So, due to a minor genetic spelling mistake, we're short, and those
without the benefit of this genetic dyslexia – well they're not.

AW Well – freaky. So we're not like the rest.

IH Fuck you, Andy. Due to a fucking spelling mistake we're short. That
doesn't mean we're not human. We're just short humans – so yes we are
just like the fucking rest.

AW Take it easy man. I'm on your side, right?

RW Okay, where does this get us? How is this information going to help us
define us as within the 'normal human standard'?

IH Well, the way I see it, on the human genome there are somewhere in the
order of 30,000 to 40,000 genes that work together to define the homo
sapiens species. If 39,999 of our 40,000 genes are all okay, and a single
gene out of the 40,000 has a single letter spelling mistake, then does that
mean this one spelling mistake chucks us out of the human norm?

   Or to put it another way, there are about a billion genetic words that
define the 40,000 genes, which in turn defines the human genome. Of
these billion words, one is misspelt.

   To me, having 999,999,999 correctly spelt words out of a possible billion
– means we're pretty fucking normal.

RW Excellent analysis. But, I think the conclusion needs strengthening.

IH What, you don't think we're normal?

RW Of course I do – otherwise why would I be here? But, you're missing the point that specific genetic diseases have been identified and gazetted. Using your argument, these sufferers are also normal.

IH I don't get what you're on about.

RW You haven't separated 'cause' from 'consequences'.

IH Meaning?

RW No doubt cystic fibrosis sufferers could make a case based on your argument that they too are normal. But clearly they're not – they're very sick and incapable of leading an independent normal life.

So, based on their disadvantage, their disease has been gazetted. Now, are we fighting for their rights as well – based on the fact that they too have nearly a billion normal genetic words out of a possible billion?

IH Hmmmm, I see your point, but where does that leave us – our defence?

RW I think our defence has to be based on human behaviour and accepted social customs.

IH Sorry, how can that be defined, so it can be used at the hearing?

RW Well, since you've been putting in a little study on genetics let me ask you: does each gene translate into some observable human trait?

IH Well, no – in fact quite the reverse. Most of our DNA is just genetic junk – it doesn't appear to serve any purpose at all.

RW What do you mean genetic junk? And, just how much junk is there?

IH Well, only about 3% of our genes actually serve any purpose. The other 97% of our genes are just junk – they don't have any impact or input into our physical or behavioural development.

RW So is there any variation in between our junk DNA?

IH Yep. Lots of it. In fact, as there is so much variation in our junk genes, it makes it possible for DNA fingerprinting. I mean, we all have such varied junk DNA that each of us can be uniquely identified.

RW Well here is my point – your defence is that just because one of our 40,000 genes is different from the rest of the population this does not make us significantly different from the human norm. But, there is variation in everyone's genes – in their junk genes. And as there is such variation in the junk genes, no two genomes are the same, making it possible to uniquely identify each of us via DNA fingerprinting.

IH I'm not following you?

RW You cannot use the defence that only one of our genes is different – because they will come back and say we're all different.

IH Yes – so they're not planning on killing everyone. So what's your point?

RW The point is that there is variation in 97% of our genes and this variation has no effect, no impact, no nothing on the persons carrying such genetic variation.

The GPA will argue that you cannot define 'the human norm' by consideration solely on the genetic letters of one gene. They will argue that it is the consequence of the lettering that is important – not the lettering itself.

So, while all but one of our billion genetic words are okay, it is the one gene that is misspelt that has a physical manifestation, that is observable and measurable against some … as yet undefined human norm.

IH So what are you saying – that we don't have a defence?

RW No. I'm saying that if you use genetic lettering as a defence you'll get crushed.

IH Well if we use physical measurements we'll also get crushed, so we're running out of options here.

RW   As I said earlier, we have to define the 'human norm' in the context of human behaviour.

IH   What sort of defence is behaviour?

RW   Well, it has to be on the basis of the extent to which we can live productive lives, contribute to society and show all the same behavioural social patterns as any other healthy person.

The point I'm making is this – what's the difference between us, someone with cystic fibrosis and a normal-heighted healthy person? We all have unique genes. In the case of the cystic fibrosis sufferers they have a mutant gene that causes their debilitating disease. We have a mutant gene that prevents us from reaching full height. Normal-heighted people have unique genes, but as this variation is in their junk genes it has no impact on their physical or behavioural development.

IH   Where is this leading?

RW   Simple, it's not the genes that are important – it's the impact it has on the carrier. So the difference between us and a cystic fibrosis sufferer is that we can live a normal productive life and contribute to society equally as much as anyone else. We're short but 'normal'.
Whereas a cystic fibrosis sufferer cannot live an independent and productive life. The question is, essentially, what can a normal-heighted person do that we can't?

AW   We're not good at the hurdles.

RW   Thank's Andy – I was actually thinking more broadly?

AW   There aren't any dwarfs in the NBA.

RW   Okay there are some sports that we're not brilliant at – but aside from sport, what can't we do that normal-heighted people can do?

AW   It's hard for us to get shelf stacking jobs.

RW   Jesus Andy – this isn't the time to do a parody on Monty Python's 'What have the Romans ever done for us'.

IH   Isn't it? I mean, if we go in and claim that we can do anything that a normal-heighted person can, won't they recite a list of all the things we experience difficulties achieving.

RW   Come on, guys, I think we need a more positive outlook here. We should be able to demonstrate that we can and do live full and productive lives. I mean, only freaks of nature get to play in the NBA – and I think it is pertinent to point out that 'normal' people don't play in the NBA either.

Look, Ivan's a social scientist with the GPA. Andy's an actor with the Royal Shakespeare Company. And I'm a chartered accountant

IH   Some comfort. Andy has a job to act as a dwarf – I mean, no one else aside from a dwarf can do it. I'm with an organisation which is actively trying to wipe dwarfs out. And you've got a job that requires a genetic personality bypass.

RW   Fuck you. Why do you have to keep demeaning our accomplishments, our lives? Why don't you just go over to the GPA now and hand them your balls in a glass jar filled with vinegar, and tell them, 'You're right – dwarfs are all fucked up and deserve to be castrated'?

IH   Sorry – yes, you're right. We do have to promote our achievements. I mean, the average salary in this country is €27,250 – I know this as I researched it for my speech to the dwarf society. And, aren't we all doing better than this?

AW   You guys get more than €27K? Wow, and I thought I was doing okay.

RW   Okay – so, is this the line of defence that we are going to take, that we live normal, productive lives, and that we contribute to the welfare of society as much as any other … other … ah 'special interest group'?

IH   Well, I suppose.

AW   [At this stage Andy has edged his way closer to the fruit bowl.] He reaches for another apple and slides it into his jacket pocket. You guys get €27K?

RW   Okay – we have to build our case on this rationale that we are productive and full members of society, and stature, tall or short, is irrelevant to our contributions to society and to the fullness of life we enjoy.

IH   Okay, let's run with this.

RW   Good, because I have to go now, as I have to finish the accounts for one of my clients. Andy, what are your plans – do you want to come with me?

AW   Sure, I don't mind travelling with the rich guy.

The scene cuts to Andy and Rob walking down the same drab street that they walked up before, where the scene fades out.

Insert Scene – 30

> *London's suburbs are a tumorous growth of endless streets of undistinguished houses, shabby families and second-rate shops, with outcrops from the main cancer producing such horrors as ignoble Croydon and tragic West Ham.*
>
> Tono-Bungay *by HG Wells*

Scene 52 – Sandra meets Jon – then Tess

7:45am, Monday, 27 May 2013

Setting: GPA's other offices – at the Gherkin

A camera follows Sandra hurriedly walking down a street with a bit of a distressed look on her face. She periodically comes to a junction, looks at the street signs, then checks her phone for direction, which responds, 'Turn left here into Leadenhall Street'. As Sandra approaches the GPA's offices at the Gherkin, the phone starts a countdown 'Twenty more metres on your left', 'Ten more metres on your left', 'Five more metres on your left' – then as she arrives outside the building – the phone buzzes, with the voiceover 'You have arrived at your destination'.

Sandra looks at the phone, then at the Gherkin building. She goes into the foyer.

SS   Hi, I'm Sandra Small, and I have an appointment with Jo …

G-Recp   With Jon Raney. Yes Sandra, Jon is expecting you. I've printed out your pass [she hands Sandra her security pass] – and Jon has instructed me to send you straight up to the level five meeting rooms as soon as any of you arrive. So, please go through these double doors – turn left …

SS   Sorry, did you say, 'any of us arrive'?

G-Recp   Yes, aside from Jon, there are three of you attending this meeting …

SS   [Concerned] Who are the others?

G-Recp   [Guessing that she may have said something that she shouldn't have] Eh … sorry, yes there are several visitors scheduled today, but, I guess they are different meetings. I mean we do have a number of meeting rooms, used for counselling and external visitors.

SS   [In a voice and expression which indicates that she doesn't believe this explanation] Oh, okay. So, you were saying I go to level five …?

G-Recp Yes, that's right, catch the elevator to level five – then walk straight down the corridor until you come to the 'Francis Crick' meeting room. Jon will be there waiting for you.

SS [Pins the security name tag to her blazer] Thank you ever so much, have a nice day.

Sandra catches the elevator to level five, exits the elevator and finds herself on a floor with a long corridor – with rooms off each side of the corridor. She starts to walk down the corridor – where she passes a number of meeting rooms, including 'Charles Darwin', 'Gregor Mendel', 'Thomas Hunt Morgan', 'Ronald Fisher', 'Herman Joe Muller', 'Archibald Garrod', 'Friedrich Miescher', 'Marshall Nirenberg', 'Johann Matthaei', 'Jacquers Monod, Fran ois Jacob & André Lwoff', 'Jim Collins' 'Len Adleman', 'Francis S. Collins', 'Barbara McClintock', 'James Watson', 'Rosalind Franklin', 'Maurice Wilkins', 'Stephen Gould' and the 'Richard Dawkins' meeting rooms.

Sandra eventually arrives at the Francis Crick meeting room, looks in and sees Jon in the room with a number of legal books and papers spread over the table, with Jon studying one of the texts closely and taking the odd note. Sandra gently knocks on the door. Jon slowly looks up (after finishing the passage he was reading). Jon sees Sandra at the door and gestures her in, and then stands up to greet her.

JR Sandra, good to see you. You obviously found the place okay?

SS Hi Jon, yes I found the place okay – thank God for GPS, otherwise I would have been a little late. I see you are hard at work already, you're keen.

JR Yes, I'm an early riser. I'm normally at work by 7:30am, so I thought I'd start some background research on your case. So, how are you feeling? Are you still okay with the GPA representing you?

SS Yes, that's why I'm here.

JR Good. But just to press the point home, shortly you'll need to fill out and sign a bunch of forms. After you sign – then there will really be no turning back. The GPA will do all it can to defeat the motion put forward to the GPA Ethics Ruling Committee by your husband. I just want you to be fully aware that you're signing up for a one-way ticket with the GPA.

SS   Well, I too want to defeat the motion put forward to the Ethics Ruling Committee by my husband. So, I think we're all on the same page here. Therefore, I have no qualms signing up for the GPA's help in this matter.

Why do you keep on about the perils of soliciting the GPA for assistance to support my case? If I didn't know better, I'd have thought you were trying to talk me out of getting your support... [Long pause.] Well, on reflection, I'm not sure that I do know better. Are you trying to talk me out of asking you for support?

JR   Sandra, no, I'm certainly not trying to talk you out of soliciting the GPA's help – that's why the GPA was established. I just want to be sure that you have made a considered, rational and informed decision in soliciting our help.

SS   Yes, if the GPA and my objective is to defeat the motion put forward by my husband in regards to my body, my life and my choice, then, yes – it is a fully informed and considered decision that I've come to you in order to gain the support of the GPA to defeat this absurd motion that Ivan's conjured up.

JR   Okay then, let's get to work.

SS   Jon, the receptionist let slip that others may be joining us – is this right?

JR   Yes, all in good time. I took the liberty to invite one of our external counsel law firms to join us at 10:00am – as we may have to call upon them to provide some of their legal resources as, frankly, all our internal counsel are already tied up on existing cases. I trust this is okay with you?

SS   Oh, sure – I mean they do have expertise in the field of 'social and genetic manipulation'?

JR   Sandra, you needn't worry – we are getting experts in to help. Anyway, before we start there is some admin we need to get through – which requires about 35,000 forms to be filled in, and around 15,000 these need to be officially witnessed. So, I've done what I can – and put them all in this folder.

Now, what I suggest we do is for you to take this lovely bureaucratic folder and sit in the 'Richard Dawkins' room [he points to the room immediate across the corridor]. I've arranged for a justice of the peace to be on call so that he can officially witness all of your signatures. I've programmed the room's phone so that the JP is number one on the speed-dial – so please call him every time you need a signature witnessed.

I reckon it will take about one and a half hours for you to complete all the forms. There are some questions that may require a little research – so I've set up a laptop in the room with internet access. Hopefully this will help.

Also, there are a series of questions about the support you are to receive and the involvement of the GPA – when you come across these just knock on my door, or dial me on the no. 2 speed-dial and I'll come and help. Apologies for not engaging in normal social light chitchat, but we do have to get through a lot before the hearing – so I want our time to be as productive as possible. Is this okay?

SS   [A little taken aback with the speed at which Jon wants to progress] Yes, Jon, this is fine. I mean, I too am very busy at the moment. So, yes – let's get cracking.

JR   Excellent. Now, we – I mean the GPA – needs all the bureaucracy etc. to be strictly complied with. And believe me, I really can't overemphasise this. So, just to make sure all our i's are dotted and our t's are crossed – I've assigned Tess Coleman to be the quality assurance manager for this case.

Now, the first thing you will notice about Tess is that she is unbelievably pedantic and totally fails to see the big picture, getting unbelievably caught up in mindless detail, arguing over the size of the font you use, etc.

And that's why I've asked her to assist us on this case. There may be too many of us looking at the big picture and the social consequences of this case with no one paying attention to the detail. And it is the detail, or the lack of it, that can create an opportunity for appeals due to technicalities. Are you okay with this?

SS   I suppose. So why are you telling me this – what are the quality assurance processes that she will be managing?

JR   Sandra, each and every form in this folder Tess is going to go over with a fine-tooth comb. If she doesn't understand something she's going to pester you until she does. And believe me, there is going to be a lot that she doesn't understand.

        I suggest you fill in one form first then get Tess to review it. Then you can get an appreciation of her style – which should help with the remainder of the forms.

SS   Okay, but I do work with a law firm – so I think I can handle form filling.

JR   Of course. But, just get Tess to check your first one to make sure we're all singing from the same hymn sheet.

SS   Sure. So, it's the room immediately opposite – I'll start straight away.

JR   Good – and Tess's number is three on the speed dialler.

Sandra gets up and walks out the door. The camera follows her across the corridor and into the Richard Dawkins room opposite. She opens the folder, pulls out the top form and quickly sails through the completion of the form.

She then dials the speed-dial no. 3 (which has liquid crystal display on the speed dialler – with the name next to each of the discussed three buttons, 'Justice of the Peace', 'Jon', 'Tess'.) and gets Tess.

SS   Hi – is that Tess? Yes, that's right it's Sandra here … Yes, that's right, Jon asked me to phone you … Yes – that would be great if you could come and give me a hand … Yes – to check my forms … Yes, I've only completed one so far … Yes – yes – yes I understand it is a quality assurance procedure … Yes, of course I understand it's importance … Good see you soon. I'm in the Richard Dawkins meeting room … You know, excellent – see you in a minute.

The scene fades out and fades back in with Tess entering the room and introducing herself to Sandra. The scene fades back out – then back in – with Tess going over the form with Sandra.

SS   Yes, Sandra is my first name.

TC   Are you sure – have you ever checked your birth certificate? It's surprising how many people think their name is something other than it actually is. Just last week there was a guy in here who thought his name was Bill, when it really was William. [With this Sandra has a look of complete frustration and despair.]

SS   So – do I have to prove to you that my name is Sandra?

TC   No, this is just a quality assurance check – you don't have to prove anything.

SS   Okay, then you accept that my name is Sandra?

TC   Yes, once you – say – show me your birth certificate or passport.

SS   Okay. If we go online to the Registrar of Births and Deaths and I show you my birth certificate online, will that do?

TC   Yes – but how will I know whether it's the real Births and Deaths Registrar or another site that you've hosted to spoof the births and deaths register?

SS   Well, if I bring in my birth certificate, how will you know whether it's the real thing or if I've just printed it off myself?

TC   Birth certificates have the registrar's seal on it.

SS   Couldn't I forge that?

TC   Hmmm good point – well, how about we go to the online Births and Deaths Register now, and then tomorrow you bring in your birth certificate. If I've got both – and they reconcile – then I think that should do the trick.

SS   Good, so let me just make a note to bring in my birth certificate tomorrow and to be sure to be sure I'll also bring in my passport – to prove my first name is Sandra. Now, shall we go online to the Births and Deaths Register?

TC   It's up to you – this is your form. I'm just assisting with the quality assurance process. The form is yours.

SS   Sure, okay, just for my benefit let's go to the registrar's website and look me up – is that okay?

TC   [Give a pathetic dopy expression of self-importance] Let's.

The camera fades out then fades back in on them fifteen minutes later.

TC   Now, Small, how do you know this is your maiden name?

SS   It's not only my maiden name – it is still my surname. I have not changed it to 'Henry', which is my husband's surname.

TC   This is a little confusing. So you're married but have a different name than your husband – how does that work?

SS   [Totally bewildered expression comes across her face – then says sarcastically] Tess, look, let me bring in my birth certificate, my passport, my parents' birth certificates, my parents' marriage certificate and my own marriage certificate and my husband's birth certificate. I'll also bring in five utility bills addressed to my home address, five bank statements from five different banks and the last six months' worth of salary advice slips.

TC   I think that would help a lot. But just to be sure, I think your rent agreement with your landlord and, say, your Inland Revenue P60 form would just about get us through the name and address part of this form.

The camera fades out on Sandra's face as a look of complete dismay and horror crosses Sandra's face as she concedes to these bizarre requests.

The camera fades back in, where Sandra looks even more distressed and frustrated. There is a knock on the door and Sandra and Tess both look up to see Jon.

JR   Hi. How are you doing – have you finished your first form yet?

TC   Jon, we're getting there, but I just don't think Sandra realises the importance of filling in these forms correctly so that the answers on the form can be properly scrutinised and verified.

SS   [On hearing Tess's comments, Sandra clutches her hair in sheer frustration – doing all she can to stop herself from screaming at her, as to what a complete idiot and waste of time she is. Sandra then tries to compose herself.] Yes, Tess has been educating me in the importance of form filling. It has proved an area of law that I have obviously underestimated up until now.

JR   [Smile comes across his face – then says half sarcastically] Excellent, it's always satisfying to know that we civil servants can still teach a thing or two to the big law firms. Now, Tess, you've had the opportunity to teach Sandra the correct way to fill in forms – do you think you've trained her sufficiently so that she can complete the rest by herself?

TC   [In a serious self-important tone] Jon, I really think that Sandra has made great improvements in properly reading and answering the form questions, but the GPA does require all the t's to be crossed and the i's to be dotted. And if you just look at her answer on Question 45A(3)(b)(ii) – she has spelt 'university' as 'universety', as she hasn't dotted the i.

JR   Sandra, do you think you've learned sufficiently from Tess to complete the rest of the forms yourself without further instruction?

SS   [An expression of 'I have a window of opportunity to get out of this torture' flashes across Sandra's face] Ah, yes, definitely yes – Tess's been a huge [finds herself lost for words] … instructor.

TC   I beg your pardon – I'm only size 16.

SS   No, No, sorry Tess – I meant that you were a huge help as an instructor.

TC   [Looks snarly at Sandra] Thank you for the clarification.

JR   [Enjoying the moment] So, Sandra – do you think you could benefit from any more instruction?

SS   No, no – I mean, Tess certainly has a lot to teach – and she has. I think she has taught me all I need to know about form filling – even to the point where I'll make sure that I spell university correctly by making sure I dot the 'i'.

TC   I was just using university as an example – any 'i' that is not dotted is an incorrect spelling.

SS   Yes, exactly – and I've certainly learned about my i's and t's today.

JR   Okay Sandra, sounds like you can complete the rest yourself – but if any discrepancies or ambiguities are found on the forms, we may require you to have further instruction from Tess.

SS   NO – no, believe me – the rest of my forms will be perfect.

JR   Good. Anyway, the reason I interrupted you two is that we have visitors – our external counsellors – and we all need to convene to discuss the case. So, if you're ready, let's go.

Both Tess and Sandra get up to join Jon.

JR   Tess, thank you very much for your help and for giving up your time to instruct Sandra, but, I think we're fine to proceed by ourselves now.

A smile comes over Sandra's face.

TC   I think I should join the meeting – just to ensure that proper minutes are taken and that our QA process is properly applied.

JR   Thanks Tess, but really this is not necessary.

TC   Yes, it is – in our quality procedure – 'QP 19 – Meeting with external counsel' it clearly states that the assigned quality manager for the assignment is to be present at all external counsel meetings and to ensure proper minutes are taken, written up and filed.

JR   That's correct – but on this occasion, I think we should proceed without the QM present.

TC   Sorry Jon, but Max – after hearing that I was the QM – phoned me this morning and he told me to make sure that each and every one of our quality procedures is fully and totally complied with – and that if anyone refuses to comply with any of the procedures that I am to phone him directly.

JR   [Taken aback by this revelation – after he recovers he says indignantly] Okay Tess, you're right – the QA procedures do have to be complied with – that's why we have them.

       So, shall we go and meet our guests. And Tess, can you take the minutes of the meeting – there isn't anything preventing the quality manager from also taking minutes is there?

TC   [Scours] I suppose not, but I don't think it is the role of the QM to take minutes.

JR   But they can – so could you?

TC   [Snidely] Okay.

Insert Scene – 31

You may regard a throng of people as containing a certain small minority who have sensitive souls; these, and the aspects of these, being what is worth observing. So you divide them into the mentally unquickened, mechanical, soulless; and the living, throbbing, suffering, vital, in other words into souls and machines, ether and clay.

Thomas Hardy

Scene 53 – Pat and Laurie arrive to help on the case

9:00am, Monday, 27 May 2013

Setting: GPA's Gherkin offices

Jon, Sandra and Tess leave the Richard Dawkins meeting room and exit the meeting room and enter the corridor.

JR   I just need to grab a couple of files and my notes

Jon walks into the Francis Crick meeting room and grabs his files.

JR   Well then, shall we go and meet our external counsel?

SS   [With a degree of apprehension] Sure.

They walk down to the end of the corridor and come to a reception area. In the reception area, there is a set of large double doors signed 'The Aristotle Boardroom'. On a brass plate next to the doors is a quote from Aristotle:

> *The form of an oak tree is defined within the code of the acorn.*

Jon nods in the direction of the board room, whereupon the three walk up to and into the boardroom.

When they walk into the boardroom, Sandra is startled to find that Pat Rushworth and Laurie Coulson are there to greet them.

Sandra is in a state of shock at seeing Pat and Laurie from her work and a sense of near-rage engulfs her. The overall feeling encompasses a number of emotions including extreme embarrassment that her personal affairs are now 'the property of her firm', betrayal that Jon didn't tell her or consult her on who the external counsel was to be, puzzlement – as, if her law firm is willing to represent her (via the GPA), then why wouldn't Bill? – guilt that she accepted such good concessions/training from her firm, and now it is obvious that at the time she accepted them she would have known of her condition and failed to tell her firm, which now they've found out via other means.

SS   [Blushing bright red.] Pat, Laurie – what are you doing here? [Before she allows anyone the opportunity to reply she turns to Jon] Jon, what's going on here? I thought you said you had external counsel – Pat and Laurie are not external. To me they're internal counsel. Oh Jesus, what the hell is going on here Jon? What the hell are you trying to do? Have you no respect for my situation, for my feelings?

       Tell you what, Jon, you can shove your external counsel, together with your 35,000 forms where they will never see the light of day again – and I don't mean Tess.

TC   Sandra, there are only 28 forms – not 35,000!

JR   [Everyone completely ignores Tess] Sandra, I apologise. I did foresee that this would cause you some difficulty. However, as this is such an important case, I wanted to ensure that you were provided with the best legal counsel available. This is to ensure you have the greatest chance of protecting and exercising your rights.

SS   Really – if you wanted the best for me – then where's Bill?

PR   Sandra, well …

JR   Pat, can I deal with this please? Sandra is still my client. Sandra, tell you what, let me take you for a coffee, just to give me an opportunity to explain and to apologise, and to go through all the options that are available to you?

TC   Actually, if you count your application for your security pass, then there are 29 forms.

JR   Sandra, please. One coffee, then if you wish to leave, fine, that's your decision. But, please at least be gracious enough to allow me to explain and apologise over a coffee.

SS   Just one coffee, just fifteen minutes, just you, without external counsel and without your size 18 QA manager.

TC   I'm size 16. Now, if Pat and Laurie go, then as the quality manager for this case I will have to go as well. In fact, even if just one of them went for coffee then I also would have to go – it says this right here in 'QP 19 – Meeting with external counsel'.

JR   Okay – agreed. Let's go. Pat, Laurie, please bear with me for the next quarter of an hour or so. Tess, can you please ensure Pat and Laurie are looked after and could you please see to it that they have tea, coffee or water or whatever? Please now excuse me – I'll be back soon.

TC   Who should I ask to ask Laurie and Pat what they would like as refreshments?

JR   Tess – just see to it will you!

The camera fades out as Sandra and Jon walk back down the corridor. As the camera fades out, Tess is advising the guests:

TC   There is a coffee point on the third floor which has tea, coffee, hot chocolate and water. To get to it, you walk down the corridor … [Voice fades out as scene closes.]

Insert Scene – 32

The useless and cumbersome and mischievous have to die, they ought to die. All those damn little clerks, cautious, law abiding with no proud dreams and no proud lusts, just railway season tickets, life-insurance policies and small, safe investments. They will all be wiped out. Life is real again

The War of the Worlds *by HG Wells*

Scene 54 – Bill starts researching

9:15am, Monday, 27 May 2013

Setting: Bill's home study

The scene opens with Bill working from his home office, with his phone ringing. Bill picks up the phone.

BH   Hi Josephine – what's up?

JC   [His PA] Will you be coming into the office today?

BH   Hmmmm. What's in my calendar?

JC   The bulk of your meetings are internal – but I think these may be cancelled anyway.

BH   Which meetings?

JC   Well, you have a meeting with Pat at 11:30am and a meeting with Laurie at 2:00pm. But they both went out together this morning and indicated that they will be out for the rest of the day. The other internal meetings are conference calls with Joel Lawrence and Larry Stockton in the States.

BH   Sorry – what did you say about Pat and Laurie?

JC   They went out this morning together – and said that they're not expecting to be back in the office today.

BH   They're not working on any cases together, certainly nothing that requires an all-day client visit. Can you go into their calendars and see who they're seeing?

JC   Sure – just wait a minute while I get their calendars up on my screen. Hmmm – it's blocked out as confidential, so I can't see the detail of who or where they're visiting.

BH   Okay thanks, but, no, in that case I won't be coming into the office. Can you phone Joel and Larry, and give then some excuse why I won't be able to phone in. And ask them to re- schedule, at least in two weeks' time or longer.

JC Sure. Do you still want me to screen your calls, or do you want them to be redirected straight through to you.

BH No, please screen. And, pending a disaster, please don't put any through.

JC Is that a blanket screen – or is there any I should put through?

BH Oh yes, my wife, my rabbi, the crèche ... and Ivan Henry.

JC What, Sandra's husband?

BH Yes – but like before this is to be kept quiet!

JC You got it.

Bill then hangs up and resumes his study of a variety of books/text/legislation scattered over his desk. The material includes the Genetic Protection Authority Act, the Consolidated GPA Gazette of Genetic Diseases, the GPA Ethics Ruling Committee Mandate and Hearing Procedures, Tribunal Hearings and Associated Appeal Processes and The Law of Judicial Review.

Bill concentrates on the Genetic Protection Authority Act, and reads out a passage:

> *The GPA is charged with the isolation of disabling genetic diseases and a means to identify such diseases in embryos. Once the GPA has both isolated and developed a means to identify a disabling genetic disease in embryos, the GPA shall gazette the disease.*
>
> *The GPA is charged with developing an accurate means of determining whether an embryo, which is free of any gazetted genetic disorders, will nevertheless develop into an abnormal child or abnormal adult. Abnormal is defined as in excess of three standard deviations from the accepted human norm.*
>
> *The GPA is charged with establishing a screening process in order to identify embryos that suffer from either a gazetted genetic disease or where the embryo will develop into an abnormal child or abnormal*

adult. Where such embryos are identified, the carrier shall be encouraged to have the pregnancy terminated.

BH   [Bill reads the above, and shakes his head] This isn't right, this just isn't right. This is way too open to abuse.

As he says this aloud he looks at the photo of his son, Samuel, on his desk.

BH   Samuel, maybe the short guy is right after all, don't you think you've got a better life with us than being dead? And, you know what – I think your new diet is making a difference. I don't care what your mum says. After all, what would a psychologist know?

As Bill contemplates the legislation while gazing at the photo of his son, an expression rolls down his face indicating that he's just thought of something incredibly important. With this, Bill gets out of his chair and meanders through his impressively large collection of books within his study. He eventually pulls out a book.

BH   This is it, the 'The Annotated Universal Declaration of Human Rights'. He walks back to his desk and starts flicking through it.

The camera slowly fades out on Bill as he is getting excited.

BH   Bingo. Article 16.

Scene 55 – Jon and Sandra have a chat and a walk

9:30am, Monday, 27 May 2013

Setting: On the banks of the Thames.

Jon and Sandra are strolling along the banks of the Thames between London Bridge and the Tate Modern on the south bank of the river. It is a beautiful day with lively spring colours everywhere.

JR   Well, I think your idea of going for a walk rather than a coffee was a simply splendid idea – this is truly a spectacular day.

Anyway – why? You asked why I didn't give you advanced warning that we had approached Bradbury, Dywer & Waldron to provide external counsel support on this case. The reason, I didn't ask or forewarn you is that I knew that if I had asked you whether it was okay– you would have flatly rejected the notion. I was quite sure that nothing would have changed your mind on this subject. From the GPA's perspective we want you to win this case, and we want to give you the best possible chance of winning.

SS   Jon, you may very well have wrecked my career. Pat is putting me through Oxford and allowing me time off work to attend classes and mid-semester work-ins. One of the reasons I've been toiling with the idea of terminating the pregnancy is to allow me to keep my end of the bargain, to complete my Oxford law degree and work towards becoming a partner at Bradbury, Dywer & Waldron. This is going to prove difficult enough – even without a baby. Now that Pat's found out about my predicament there is a good chance he will withdraw his offer of supporting me through Oxford.

JR   The bet is still on. As much as it may not look like it, i did use considerable discretion in sounding Pat out prior to asking him to take on this case.

Pat and I go back a long way. I know that his personal integrity is beyond reproach. He will still keep his side of your bargain.

SS   [Looking and sounding rather shocked.] It makes no difference – this is my life, my pregnancy, my husband and my fucking injunction. This is my case, for which I asked for your assistance. This is NOT your case, with me being an insignificant bystander. You should have asked me! [There is a long pause.] By the way, is there anyone in my life that you don't know? I mean, you know my husband, my mother-in-law, my boss, Bill, his boss, Pat, and my role model Laurie.

JR   Well, I think I can pretty much name all the partners at your law firm, but aside from them, I think the only two people I know in common with yourself are your husband and mother-in-law. Mind you, there may be countless others about which we just have not made the connection that we both know them – but I doubt there is anyone in this category that is close to you.

      But, back to the point, if I had raised the issue of Pat with you, you would have forbade me from approaching him. I want the best legal assistance possible to support you on this case, as I think it is a terrible invasion of your free will to have such punitive measures being taken out against you. So I found myself caught between a rock and hard place – I wanted the best for you, but you would have prevented me from obtaining it.

      So, my only way of reconciling these two opposing positions was to engineer a big bang, so that everything was all out in the open so that there weren't any more secrets or fears of deals being broken. Now, we do need to keep focused on the main issues, not the distractions. The main issue is to get your personal rights back, to have this terrible violation lifted. And to do this we need the best legal minds in the country. So, are you okay to return to the office and start preparing for your hearing?

SS   Oh fuck, well as you said, it's all in the open now, so what have I got to lose? Okay let's go. But let me tell you now, it will be a long time, if ever, that I will feel as though I can trust you.

JR   Well, providing we win this case for you, then I can live with that. But, in my defence, when I approached Pat I did exercise a degree of discretion and diplomacy, from which I was able to extract an absolute assurance from him that this case, and your predicament, will not impact Bradbury, Dywer & Waldron's commitment to you, nor their continued support of your legal studies at Oxford.

SS   [Looking a little shocked] I'm sure. I'll believe that when I see it.

There is a pause in the conversation as they turn and start walking back towards London Bridge.

SS   Tell me, Jon, why aren't you as involved in the Russian museum anymore? Sounds a little odd, I mean being awarded a lifetime honouree membership to the world's most eminent Russian iconic museums, then withdrawing your involvement with the annex that you helped to create.

JR   It's a long story.

SS   Well, just give me the abridged version, we've got ten minutes before we get back to the office.

JR   Well, some of the exhibits we were purchasing – I didn't think we were necessarily always getting value for money, and in some cases I wasn't comfortable that the sellers of the icons had obtained permission from the churches that they were bought, or taken, from. I raised my concerns with the management of the annex, then to the museum itself. But, nothing happened. So, as I couldn't change the museum's acquisition and purchasing policy – I resigned from the management committee and have since withdrawn totally from the running and activities of the museum.

SS   I see. It sounds like it could have been a little painful for you at the time.

JR   Well, I guess so. But, at least London now has the best Russian iconic museum outside of Russia. So, I'm still proud of my role in that achievement.

The scene fades out as they continue walking back along the river.

Scene 56 – Bill calls Ivan

11:55am, Tuesday, 28 May 2013

Setting: Bill's Home Study and Ivan's work desk.

Ivan is sitting at his desk at the GPA looking quite grumpy and still studying legal textbooks etc., obviously still working on his case. He hears Elaine, Mark and Gough approaching but doesn't bother to look up. Gough thinks there was a chance Ivan didn't hear them approaching, so takes advantage of this possibility and tries to scare him by sneaking up behind him.

GR   [Shouts as he grabs Ivan by the shoulders] Boo!

IH   Fuck off Gough – I'm not in the mood – and besides I heard you coming a mile off.

GR   Well, I was just trying to cheer you up. Anyway, we're going to the pub in half an hour. It will be good, as Elaine has agreed to tell us all about the wonderful time she had at the Mosque during Shavu'ot. Do you want to join us, so we can play tag as to who has the 'I'm still interested expression'?

EK   Gough, really, you will take a step too far one day – it's a Synagogue – and really, I didn't think I'd ever say it, but I'd rather watch a strip show than to tell you about Shavu'ot.

GR   No, no, please, I'm really, really interested, please tell me all about your time in the Mosque?

EK   Gough – fuck off. So, Ivan, are you coming?

IH   No, I've got work to do.

MH   Ivan, don't bullshit me, you aren't doing any work. Since when have your assignments needed analysis of legal proceedings?

IH   Whatever, I still gotta study this shit.

EK   Okay but if you change your mind – well you know we'll be at the pub. [Elaine then drops down into a whisper and puts her hand over her mouth.] Time's up guys, Jeff's approaching at two o'clock.

The others glance in the direction motioned by Elaine – and see Jeff Portwood approaching with the aim of joining their conversation. Gough and Elaine turn and walk away, but Mark remains behind. Just as the others walk away Jeff arrives.

JP   Hey guys, howzit going over here? Wow, Ivan you must be getting some seriously good assignments – I was here twelve years before I was assigned any legal work.

IH   Well, it's just a little thing that Jon asked me to do for him. Nothing much.

JP   Cool. Has anyone seen Tess? She hasn't been in all day, and she wasn't in yesterday either.

MH   No, no idea. I didn't even know she wasn't here until you just mentioned it. Hang on a minute, yes I did notice – as a cloud of glum hasn't darkened my spirit for the last couple of days.

JP   Ivan, do you know?

IH   Sorry Jeff, not a clue.

JP   So guys, doing anything for lunch?

IH   No, I got to get this finished for Jon.

MH   No, I got to buy a birthday card for my mum.

JP   Really – where are you thinking of going?

MH   What?

JP   Well, just last week I discovered this great card and gift shop only about twenty minutes' walk from here. Had the best selection of mothers' birthday cards. If you like I could come with you and show you where it is.

MH   [A wee bit stunned by the offer.] Thanks Jeff, but no, I was just thinking of going to Tesco's – their cards are fine with me.

JP   Mark, believe me, Tesco cards are not in the same league. Come with me and I'll show you – and I guarantee you won't regret it.

MH   It's not called the Blue Oyster card shop is it?

JP   No, it's 'Fritz's Cards and Small Gifts Shop'. Why?

MH   Just asking – but thanks Jeff, maybe next year.

JP   I really think you're making a mistake with a Tesco's card …

MH   Jeff – sorry, but I'm buying the fucking birthday card and Tesco's is fine with me – even if it is for my mother. But, thank you for your offer.

JP   [Looking very offended] Well I don't think that sort of language was called for – I was just trying to help.

MH   Thank you, Jeff. Your offer is very much appreciated, but on this occasion I'm pretty set on the Tesco finest range of birthday cards. In fact, at the moment, I'd even settle for their six pack of 'Cards for Your Mother' – which includes cards for her birthday, Easter, Mother's Day, Christmas, New Year and a thinking of you card!

JP   Ok, but now, even if you do change your mind, I don't know if I could be bothered showing you where Fritz's card shop is now.

IH   Jesus Jeff, give it a rest. You're talking about a fucking birthday card. Who gives a shit where you buy it from? [He then stumbles a moment to try and recover] … After all, it's the thought that counts.

JP   Well, I still like to take time to choose just the right card for the right person. Anyway, I too have an assignment which I'd better get back to.

Jeff walks off.

MH   Christ, what the fuck was that all about – I didn't think he was gay.

IH   Scary isn't it. No, he's not gay – just very strange. It's reassuring to know that it's guys like him that are protecting our genetic heritage.

MH   Anyway, Ivan, as it happens, I do know where Tess is.

IH   Yeah, so?

MH   Well, haven't you noticed that Jon also hasn't been in the office?

IH   Uhuh. [Nodding his head – and starting to feel awkward.]

MH   Ivan, I don't know what's going on … and I don't know what's happening with you. I suspect something, as when you're at work, which isn't often anymore, you've been very quiet and all you do is study those legal text books. As there are not any approved legal assignments on the 'Staff Resource Calendar' at the moment, I'm guessing you're working on your own case.

IH   Could be. What's it got to do with you?

MH   Ivan, it's got nothing to do with me …

IH   Good – is there anything else?

MH   Ivan, I don't know what it means, and it's none of my business, and I'm probably about to breach GPA Policy – but Tess has been working as the QA officer with Jon on 'The Sandra Small Case'.

IH   [Pricks up his eyes with interest – but attempts to maintain a disinterested posture]. Uhuh.

MH   For what it's worth, they've called in external counsel to assist on the case.

IH   [Now, incapable of maintaining his disinterested pose] What?

MH   Yes, I thought you may want to know. The legal firm is Bradbury, Dywer & Waldron. Everything has been approved, the funding, the clearance forms everything, and they started yesterday at our offices at the Gherkin, presumably so interested parties that may be in this building wouldn't see them – whoever those interested parties may be.

IH   Approved already – including the funding. That bastard! That's unbelievable. It normally takes at least a month for GPA external counsel representation to be approved.

MH   Ivan, look, I don't know what's going on – but if you need any help just ask okay?

IH   [Genuinely moved by Mark's offer] Mark, thanks. I really appreciate your offer. Since everyone I know is lining up to knife me in the back – including my wife, my mother and my employer – it's good to know not everyone is out to get me.

MH   Well, look, I'm not going to delve into your private life, but I guess a lot of shit is going on.

But, remember, if I can help in any way, then please don't hesitate to ask and I'll do whatever I can to assist.

IH   Thanks, Mark, that means a lot to me.

Mark walks away from Ivan's desk – and Ivan looks down at his desk with a sense of despondency.

IH   [Speaking to himself] That fucking Nazi lawyer bastard is now going to lead the case against me – what an arsehole.

Ivan leans forward to rest his elbow on the desk and places his face in his hands in a further sign of despondency. As he contemplates for a few moments, his phone rings. Ivan doesn't immediately pick it up. He lets it ring seven times, then eventually slowly reaches across and lifts the hand piece to his face.

IH   Genetic Protection Authority, Ivan Henry speaking, can I help you?

BH   Ivan, glad I found you at last. It's Bill Horowitz speaking.

Stunned silence.

BH   Ivan, are you there? It's Bill Horowitz … we had lunch together last week …

IH   Why are you calling me – just to taunt me a little prior to your planned humiliation at the GPA's Ethics Ruling Committee's hearing tomorrow?

BH   What? No, I'm phoning to help – not to taunt or humiliate you.

IH   You sure help in strange ways. Well I guess the Nazis thought they were helping the Jews too – so I suppose I shouldn't be surprised to hear that you think you're actually helping me by trying to have my child forcibly terminated. It must be one of the advantages of being a lawyer – you never have to wrestle with your conscience. Thanks for your offer of help. [Ivan then hangs up the phone].

The phone immediately rings again. It rings several times before Ivan picks it up.

BH   Ivan, please don't hang up – I've got to speak to you.

IH   That's terrific, Bill, still trying to help – and if you're wondering, no I don't need a life-insurance policy either.

He hangs up again. The phone rings almost immediately again. After seven rings Ivan reluctantly picks it up.

IH   Is that you, Bill?

BH   Honest, I'm on your side – please give me a little time to explain.

IH   Bill, what was that quote you read me from Ashleigh Brilliant? 'The task I've been given seems absurd – to wait here on Earth until I no longer exist'. I take it you're just helping me, and my offspring, to achieve this task?

BH   [A little stumped for words] Well, in retrospect, that was an unfortunate quote I recited.

IH   Unfortunately – but let's say ruthlessly to the point.

Again, Ivan hangs up. Again the phone rings almost immediately.

IH   [Picks up the phone and shouts] No. [Then hangs up].

Mark Hardwick, on hearing the exchanges that Ivan was having over the phone, walks back to Ivan's desk

MH   Ivan, is everything alright? [He gestures towards the phone]?

IH   Wanker.

MH   Who?

IH   You know that law firm, Bradbury, Dywer & Waldron, that you said has been brought in as external counsel to the GPA? Well it was one of their lawyers 'offering to help me'. Do you believe that? I'm sure there is a law against lawyers pretending to be on your side, only to take the information they've gleaned back to your adversary and then use it against you.

MH   Unbelievable. I've never heard anything like it. I think you should put in a complaint to the Law Society.

IH   Well, in other circumstances I probably would, but at the moment I've got enough battles going without opening up new ones. So, I think I'll just drop it.

MH   Well, what I said a minute ago still holds – if you need any help just ask.

IH   Thanks. You know what, if you're still going to the pub then if it's okay I will join you.

MH   Sorry mate, I just had a chat with Jeff, and I've decided to go with him to Fritz's Cards and Small Gifts shop.

IH   [An alarmed expression rolls down Ivan's face, as he assumes that this is a disgustingly poor excuse for uninviting him to the pub.] Oh, okay then.

MH   Got ya. Of course you can join us. We're still shooting for 12:30. And we've got to leave one at a time – otherwise Jeff will spot us and follow us. So, meet you down there in half an hour or so.

The scene fades out as a bit of a smile starts to emerge on Ivan's stressed face and Mark walks off.

Insert Scene – 33

> *But the Old World of heroes is over now. The skies above are dark with sentimentalism, nothing remains for us to worship but the Mass, the blind, inchoate, insatiate Mass; fog and fenland before us, we shall founder in putrefying mud, creatures of ooze and rushes about us.*

> Confessions of a Young Man *by George Moore.*

Scene 57 – Max meets Frederick

2:00pm, Tuesday, 28 May 2013

Setting: The High Court and Frederick Rogers judge's chambers

Max Lyford walks into the High Court and, once inside, it becomes apparent that he is very familiar with the layout of the building. As he walks straight through to the restricted area turnstile he swipes his card to activate the turnstile. The attending security guards nod in their recognition of him. He walks to the staff lifts – but as he approaches them he see a 'closed for service' sign hanging on them with lift maintenance staff working on them.

Max walks back through the turnstile, the security guards again politely nod to him, and he walks up to the lifts in the public foyer. He presses the call button and waits.

The lift arrives, he gets in the lift and presses the button for level five – which has written beside it 'Restricted – Judges' Chambers'. As it is restricted, the light on the button fails to illuminate.

Noticing this, Max inserts his swipe card into the swipe reader, presses the level five button again, and this time it illuminates. As the doors are starting to close, a hand waves through the closing gap and sets the lift senses to open the doors. A young student couple of Asian descent enter the lift.

Max, in his expensive and impeccably fitted suit, retreats to the back corner of the lift and looks at the couple in the lift in quiet indignation that commoners, immigrants at that, have managed to get this close to him.

The man (Amerjit Ghuman) presses the button to floor three, the public gallery. He then inquisitively points to the 'Schindler Lift' badge and comments to his girlfriend (Sambhi Khangura):

AG   Hey, look at that, I just watched the DVD last night and here it is again 'Schindler's Lift', or is it Schindler's List?

SK   Really, you watched it last night? You know why it's called Schindler's Lift?

AG   I suppose because a company called Schindler made the lift. I mean, they wouldn't call it an Otis or an O&K lift would they? As those lift names are already taken.

SK   [Giggles] Sorry, I mean do you know why Thomas Keneally called the book 'Schindler's List'?

AG   Who's Thomas Keneally?

SK   He's the author of the book that Spielberg turned into the movie.

AG   I guess the name is to emphasise the arbitrary and unjust nature of the situation the Jews were in – those that were on Schindler's List were saved, and those that weren't – well they weren't.

SK   Not only that, but also because the name is a play on the German word 'list' which means 'trick'. So it was Schindler's trick that saved the Jews – that were on his list.

AG   Interesting. I didn't know you knew German?

SK   I don't. [Gets a look from her boyfriend asking 'well how do you know that'.] I know from an old episode of University Challenge that I've watched a few times.

AG   [Mockingly] You are the saddest person I know. You watch old episodes of University Challenge, and you watch them multiple times. Boy oh boy. I'm going to have to reconsider this relationship.

SK   It's an old episode – a final. The year we won.

AG   Give me a break. Birkbeck has never won University Challenge.

SK   We have! Back in 2003, we beat Cranfield in the final to become the champions. Believe me, I know. Every first year student is forced to sit down and watch it, over and over again – it's forced hero worship.

AG   [In a joking, sarcastic tone] Well, as long as you're having fun – that's the main thing isn't it?

      But really, you Birkbeck students really do need to get a life.

The lift arrives at level three.

The two students both giggle as they get out.

Max continues his journey and exits at the fifth floor. The lift opens to an opulently appointed reception room with deep red carpet, oak panels and plenty of polished brass. As he gets out he is greeted by security guards who politely but firmly request to see his pass and why he is there. Max takes out his security pass from his pocket and passes it over for inspection.

Guard And your business sir?

ML   I have an appointment to see Judge Rogers.

Guard Very well sir, please proceed to reception.

ML   [Walks over to the reception desk.] It's Max Lyford. I'm here to see Judge Rogers at two.

CD   Very well Mr Lyford, would you please have a seat while I call the judge.

Clarissa speaks to the judge via the intercom, advising of Max's arrival.

FR   [Via the intercom] Thank you, Clarissa. Please send Mr Lyford through to my chambers.

CD   Very well, Judge Rogers. I'll send him through right away. Would you like tea to be served for your meeting?

FR   Yes, Clarissa, tea would be very much appreciated.

CD   Very good, I'll get some going straight away.

FR   Thank you.

CD   Mr Lyford would you like to go through to the Judge Rogers' chambers – it's just down …

ML   Thank you for your directions, but yes, I do know the way.

CD   Very good then.

Max walks past the reception desk through a door, and then navigates his way through a corridor until he comes to an open door – and walks straight in without knocking.

Max enters into Judge Frederick Rogers' opulently appointed chambers, which has three Chesterfield sofas and four single matching leather sofas surrounding a large coffee table. There is a sideboard housing the Lismore range of Waterford decanters, scotch and wine glasses together with an assortment of expensive photo frames housing various portrait photos.

FR   Max, good of you to come – please come in and have a seat.

ML   Thanks, Frederick. Good of you to make the time to see me.

FR   Well, we all have a keen interest in the development of this case – so it's only right that we should get together and discuss its progress.

ML   Yes, indeed.

FR   So, I take it that you've left nothing to chance in avoiding any future judicial reviews – every single form, process, and procedure completely and fully complied with?

ML   Frederick, believe me, the form filling and adherence to bureaucratic rules is absolutely watertight. I've got my thickest, dumbest but most tenacious quality manager on the job. She was made for this job – and for no other.

FR   That's what I like to hear. Where would we be without tenacious idiots to enforce the filling out of all those pointless forms, ensuring compliance with our own mind-boggling, senseless bureaucracy? Funding?

ML   Yes, we had it signed off by the minister – can't be too cautious on these matters.

FR   Excellent, and who did you get for your external counsel?

ML   Bradbury, Dywer & Waldron.

FR   Excellent, so Bill is your king's counsellor?

ML   No, there is something strange going on with Bill. He refused to act on the case – claiming that he was overcommitted. So, Pat agreed to head the case.

FR   That's rather odd of Bill. I thought this was the type of case he lives for. But I'm sure Pat can handle the case equally as well as Bill. However, perhaps not with quite the same level of enthusiasm that Bill brings to bear on cases like this.

ML   Indeed, in that sense it may turn out to be a plus – as Bill does have a habit of creating a little strain within a team due to his constant changing demands.

FR   Yes, we've all seen that. Now, are you sure [stops and looks down at some papers in his lap] that Henry is representing himself? I mean, Bill's not going to pop out of the woodwork to defend Henry is he?

ML   Yes, Ivan Henry is still representing himself. Bill can't defend him – after all it is his assistant that Henry has taken the injunction out on, and it is his firm that is representing her. So, he can't represent Henry, as it would be a professional conflict of interest.

FR   Excellent. But hasn't the GPA also taken a few steps along the conflict of interest path? I mean, Henry works for the GPA and yet the GPA is providing assistance and financial support to the other party involved in the case.

ML   No. Henry has been advised that the GPA will be providing assistance to his estranged wife. And Henry is not an 'assistant' to anyone at GPA – he is merely an employee and governed by the same laws as the public at large is. So, the GPA has not taken a step down the conflict of interest footpath.

FR   Well, I just hope all your paperwork on this matter is squeaky clean, as it could be argued that there is a conflict, which could form the basis for a judicial review, which I think all of us would like to avoid.

ML   Frederick, believe me, this is well in hand.

FR   Now, for the aspect of the case I have the most concern about. What is the basis of your legal argument – that being a dwarf makes him three standard deviations from the accepted human norm? I must admit I'm far from convinced of the social benefit to be derived from creating common law determining 'the human norm'. Unless you can convince me that this law isn't open to abuse, then I'm afraid I'm not sure whether I can support it.

ML   Well, Frederick, we all share in your concern, of course we do. And we've spent a considerable amount of time defining the legal boundaries within which the law is to operate – to ensure that the law cannot be abused.

FR   Good. I have an hour before I'm due back in court. So, in this hour, I'd like to go over with you both the case against Henry and, should the GPA be successful, how the ruling will not be open to abuse in later cases.

ML   Sure, well let's start with the GPA's legal position. After reviewing the legislation and associated GPA regulations, the GPA has the power under section … [As Max continues to talk the camera slowly fades out on him.]

Insert Scene – 34

It has become apparent that whole masses of human population are, as a whole, inferior in their claim upon the future, to other masses, that they cannot be given opportunities or trusted with power as the superior peoples are trusted, that their characteristic weaknesses are contagious and detrimental in the civilising fabric, and that their range of incapacity tempts and demoralises the strong. To give them equality is to sink to their level, to protect and cherish them is to be swamped in their fecundity.

Anticipations *by HG Wells*

Scene 58 – Jon and Valentina exchange comments at the museum

6:30pm, Tuesday, 28 May 2013

Setting: Covent gardens and the London Andrei Rubliov Museum of Early Russian Art

There is a large crowd being entertained by a 'Sad Clown' professional street entertainer at Covent Gardens and, as the clown entertains, his minders solicit donations from the watching crowd. After a moment, one of the spectators turns around to leave, at which point the camera can see his face [Jon Raney] before he exits the crowd and again turn his back on the camera as he walks off towards a building. The camera follows him from his back as he climbs some stairs, and as he does so the camera falls back so that more of the building can be seen.

The building is the 'London Annex of the Andrei Rubliov Museum of Early Russian Art', with a big banner advertising the 'Russian Iconic Art Exhibition' dates from Monday, 27 May 2013 to Sunday, 21 July 2013.

Jon climbs the stairs and goes through the main entrance. The camera follows him in. He bypasses the queues buying tickets and heads for the gallery entrance, where he is stopped by a junior attendant (Jane Kemp) requesting him to show his ticket.

JR   Sorry, I'm a life member of the museum – I don't need a ticket.

JK   Very good sir, do you have your life membership card with you?

JR   Actually, no I don't.

As he starts to explain his position, a more senior attendant (Elizaveta Alekseev) walks over to where Jon is being challenged by Jane.

EA   Jane, it's okay. Jon is a life member, he can go through.

JR   Thanks, Elizaveta, nice to see you again. And Jane, it is good to see that you are doing your job so diligently – keep up the good work.

EA   Why are you coming now? Why didn't you come to the private viewing last Sunday?

JR   I was busy.

EA   You know you can come anytime out of hours, so why are you coming now when you have to fight the crowds?

JR   [Leans across to her and whispers] Coming now may not be as enjoyable, I'll grant you that, but when I am with the crowds I am anonymous, which does have its advantages.

EA   I guess you're right. But you're not anonymous with me, and it is good to see you again. It has been a while. You really should come more often – the place just isn't the same without you.

JR   Elizaveta, that's nice of you to say, but I'm sure the museum is managing fine without me.

EA   Maybe, but it's not as much fun.

JR   Thank you, I do miss the place. Anyway Elizaveta, I'll let you get on with dealing with the public – and I'll try and briefly quench my Russian cultural thirst. Did all the exhibits go up, including the 32 Rubliov works?

EA   Jon, they're all there – fully restored to their golden glory.

JR   Fantastic, last time I saw them they were still covered in candle silt and I could hardly make out any of the finer details or the colours that Rubliov distinguished himself with.

EA   Enjoy the exhibition, Jon – and here's a complimentary programme.

JR   Thanks, Elizaveta. [He looks to the first attendant that spoke to him.] Thanks Jane.

Jon walks on through the foyer of the exhibition centre, stops and starts flicking through the programme. As he's figuring out what gallery to go to, Elizaveta walks up to him and tells him.

EA   Jon, they're in Gallery 5.

JR   [Jon, shows her a big genuine smile] There are some things I don't miss about this place, but you're certainly not one of them – thanks.

Jon walks off in the direction of the galleries with the camera fading out. The camera fades back in with a close up of Jon's totally motionless face filled with the very picture of 'study' and yet a satisfied expression. Slowly the camera pans back – which brings into view the icons on the opposite wall that Jon's facing. The camera slowly pans around the room so that eventually it is focused on the same icon as Jon is studying, with the back of Jon's head in the left hand side of the frame.

A voice close to him speaks.

VH   It is truly magnificent isn't it? It took Rubliov nine months to paint it.

With this comment, Jon does not move at all. After a few seconds Jon eventually responds.

JR   [In a civil, but hardly a warm tone] Nine months. Time well spent in creating such beauty.
[Now with a sense of dismissive tone] And, how are you, Valentina?

VH   [In a warmer tone] I'm very well, thank you. Can you remember the last time we saw this? How dark it was – and now look at it. Doesn't it look fantastic? It sure was worth every rouble it cost to restore it.

JR   Yes, it is really remarkable. It has changed the feel entirely, from a dark hellish Bosch scene to a symbol of hope, light and redemption. Now, it is truly inspirational.

VH   Can I join you for the viewing?

JR   I feel as though you already have – which is surprising as I thought you would have already seen the exhibits at the private viewings.

VH   Of course I did. But I was here discussing our next exhibition with the curator when I overheard Elizaveta mentioning your name. I had an intuitive hunch which gallery you would be in, so I came up to say hi.

Anyway, the private viewings are not much fun anymore. Nobody understands the passion of the icons like you do, so I get very bored with the superficial comments the other private guests make, and I find it difficult not to be rude to them, however unintentional my comments may be.

JR   [In a sarcastic tone] You? Your comments offending people? Never!

VH   Jon, even through your vile sarcasm, I still hear your gentle, moving, inspiring and yet tortured voice. [A long pause follows.] It's been too long, Jon. The war is over. It's time to stop hurting, to stop hating. [A long pause.] Jon if you cannot forgive me, then you should at least start trying to forgive yourself for not forgiving me. Your sense of guilt and hurt – it is gradually corroding your spirit. You're not as proud and spirited as you once were. It shows in your eyes, in your walk, and most of all in your voice.

JR   Valentina, thank you for your concern over my pride and spirit. I must admit I do have much to learn from you – to do what you've done, clearly you had conscience bypass surgery. And yes, look at you, you still have the gall to act as though you have some sense of pride. Then you have the audacity to lecture me on pride and spirit. My pride and spirit may be corroded – but that is only because I have some to corrode.

VH   Jon, please don't be angry now. We've said too many angry words to each other – we need to stop now and reach the peace that resides within us.

        [A long pause]

        Remember how we used to talk all night on Russian and Byzantine art. How we went to Venice just to view all those Byzantine treasures that the Venetian navy brought back from the fourth crusade that pillaged Constantinople.

        [A long pause]

        Those were good times, Jon, they still exist. No matter what you say to me now or later, I shared those times with you and we still share those memories. Who else know or cares as much as we do? We only have each other to share in the admiration of such beauty.

JR   You don't ever give up do you? You get me to help establish the museum. Then I find that 40 percent of the art is to be purchased off some unknown Swiss company. You had the independent valuations of the art that I had commissioned overturned by the board on the grounds that the Swiss company was not prepared to sell at the valuation price. The board then ups its offer by 25% to secure the acquisition before some other alleged unnamed museum bought the collection.

Once we've secured the icons, and published our collection on the web, we start getting sued by Russian churches on the grounds that they never sold or gave permission for the art to be removed from their churches. After lengthy legal battles, we lost 31 of the most treasured icons and it costs us a fortune in compensation and litigation fees to keep the rest.

After all the litigation was eventually resolved, I find out that it was your Swiss company we bought the art from. Then you're surprised that I leave you, merely on the grounds of unethical behaviour.

VH   Jon, we've discussed all this before and, really, you are being a little harsh.

JR   Yes, I suppose – but even if I discount all the above there's all the rest you've done since, isn't there?

VH   Like what? What have I done now?

JR   You always spoke to me about your son, but never introduced me to him. The lengths you went to ensure that we never met. You even sent him off to Leeds Metropolitan University for three years just to get him out of the way. He gets married; I wasn't even informed of his wedding, doubtless invited to it.

After years of hiding Ivan from me, the invisible boy graduates and can't find a job. So, all of a sudden, you want me to meet him. Not as a friend, not as a potential family member, none of that – but as a potential employer interviewing him. It goes on. Per your dictate, I never even hinted that I knew you, just so that I don't arouse Ivan's suspicion that nepotism may have been an influence in him getting a job at the GPA.

What's worse is now that I've gotten to know Ivan, I like him. While at times he can prove a little difficult, he is basically a nice guy. And, despite your low opinion of him, he shows all the signs and aptitude to suggest that he has a promising career as a social scientist.

Probably for the first time in his life, things are starting to look up for Ivan. Naturally, you bring this to a crashing end by sending his wife to me, to help her stop him from having a child. Not just this child, not just the children she conceives of him, but all his children from any mother, ever.

Naturally, whatever the decision of the GPA tribunal hearing it will be nigh on impossible for Ivan to remain with the GPA. I mean, nobody with any pride can stay on with an organisation that is making a case that they are too unfit to breed. And yet, you knew that I would have no option but to support his wife – because I've told you enough about the legislative objectives for you to know that we support all cases that attempt to eradicate genetic abnormalities.

[Long pause.]

So, yes, you are right – my pride and spirit is gradually corroding and eroding away. One day none of it will be left. Then, once again, I'll be your equal. At that future low point in my life when I have no soul left, I will return to you – where once again we can talk long into the night on the finer points of dead artists whose pride, like ours, is dead.

But, while there is there still is the smallest smouldering flicker of pride within me, then I'm morally prevented from talking to you beyond mere social conviviality.

VH   Jon, one day you will get over all of this silliness and see all the other events that were going on. You paint a black and white picture – there is no such thing. Only those who never mature beyond adolescence still believe in absolutes, still believe in right and wrong. Jon, we're older now and appreciate the world is painted in shades of grey. The events were never that black and white and, for the most part, you have taken them out of context. I may not be a saint, but I'm certainly not the fallen angel that you paint me to be.

JR   A world painted in shades of grey. [He pauses for a few seconds.] Look at this Rubliov. It doesn't convey a world of confused morality. It is strong – portraying the saviour as the redeemer. It portrays the triumph of good over evil, and in doing so holds out hope for all humanity that we too can achieve immortality and live in eternal light. There isn't a single brush stroke of grey in any of his works, he paints a world of absolutes – where there is right and there is wrong, where there is good and there is evil.

Forgive me for thinking that this adds not only something to his art but also to his character. Now, if you would excuse me, I have to exercise a little private dead artist appreciation – before I challenge your son's right to reproduce tomorrow morning.

VH   Jon, that was unnecessary.

JR   Goodbye, Valentina.

VH   Goodbye, Jon. When you get over your anger and learn to love yourself again, give me a call.

Valentina then walks off, leaving Jon in the gallery to admire the icons, together with a few other members of the public.

Insert Scene – 35

Democratic art! Art is the direct antithesis to democracy … Athens! A few thousand citizens who owned many thousand slaves, call that democracy! No! what I am speaking of is modern democracy – the mass. The mass can only appreciate simple and naïve emotions, puerile prettiness, above all conventionalities.

Confessions of a Young Man *by George Moore.*

Scene 59 – The hearing of the GPA Ethics Ruling Committee

10:00am, Wednesday, 29 May 2013

Setting: The hearing room of the GPA's Ethics Ruling Committee

The three members of the GPA Ethics Ruling Committee are all sitting at the hearing room bench of the GPA Ethics Ruling Committee. The three members of the ruling committee presiding over this hearing being Sir John Poo Beresford (sitting at the left) distinguished by his proud nose, the chairman, Lord Thomas Denman (sitting in the middle) and Sir David Griffiths (sitting at the right).

The three are sitting at a superbly made long bench made out of beech wood. The bench is at the front of the hearing room, the three members have their backs to the front wall so that they are facing the rest of the room – and the camera.

The camera slowly moves back, revealing that the room is similar to a university lecture theatre. It has an aisle down the middle, with long benches stretching out from each side of the aisle which face towards the front. As the camera keeps moving back, it reveals that the room is also built like an auditorium, with each successive row from the front being a little higher than the bench in front of it.

The first two benches are larger where the two legal parties are seated – the GPA legal team to the left and the dwarfs to the right. On the two front benches numerous legal texts, acts and other reference material are scattered.

The left legal team is comprised of Max Lyford, Jon Raney, Pat Rushworth, Laurie Coulson, Tess Coleman and Sandra Small. The right legal team is comprised of Ivan Henry, Andy Watts and Rob Walker.

The public and witnesses sit on the smaller benches behind the front two legal parties.

As the camera continues to draw back to reveal more of the 'public' rows, it shows that there are a number of dwarfs sitting on the right-hand side of the public benches. The public rows on the left hand side are mostly empty, with the exception of Angus Le Bon, only the odd unrecognisable person sitting here and there.

As the camera continues to withdraw from the front – around halfway the backs of Mark, Elaine and Gough slowly come into view – all sitting together on the dwarf side of the hearing room.

There is some muttering coming from the GPA legal team at the front. As they mutter they take turns to look back at Mark, Elaine and Gough – demonstrably not impressed that members of the GPA are sitting and showing their support to the GPA's legal adversaries.

The camera cuts over to the dwarf legal team [so that the camera is capturing their front/faces].

RW   Okay, Ivan, what do we do now? I mean, presumably the GPA Ethics Ruling Committee will commence proceedings soon – then what do we do?

IH   You're the chartered accountant – I thought you knew this stuff.

RW   Yes, that's right I am a chartered accountant – not a barrister, not a solicitor and not a lawyer. If you want me to produce a trial balance, make an accrual for pre-paid insurance expenses or make a provision for bad debts – then I'm your man. But, to conduct a legal tribunal hearing, this has remarkably little to with the double-entry accounting system.

IH   The double-entry what?

RW   The double-entry accounting system

IH   What's that?

RW   Well, in 1494, the Franciscan monk Luca Pacioli published his work 'Summa de Arithmetica, Geometria, Proportioni et Proportionalita', which, translated, means 'Everything about Arithmetic, Geometry and Proportion'. In it he defined the accounting equation: assets minus liabilities equals owner's equity.

       Therefore, you cannot change the value of one of these entities without changing another by the same amount so that the equation remains true. Anyway, to ensure the equation remains true, Pacioli developed the double-entry accounting system …

IH   What the fuck are you talking about? We've got a trial that's about to start, which, if we lose, will be the starting gun for the genocide of our kinfolk. But rather than trying to stop the genocide, you're bragging about how much you know about an Italian monk who died over five hundred years ago.

RW   He died in 1514.

IH   What?

RW   He died in 1514.

IH   So?

RW   Well that's only 499 years ago – not 500

IH   Who gives a shit when he died? And what the hell has all this got to do with the hearing?

RW   Well, you asked what the double-entry accounting system was.

AW   I thought it was just a joke that accountants have personality bypasses – but it's obviously true.

RW   Well, fuck you too. The point is I'm a chartered accountant – not a lawyer. I don't know how to conduct formal legal proceedings.

IH   Why didn't you tell me earlier?

RW   What? What makes you think an accountant should know about legal proceedings?

AW   It's all the same isn't it, lawyers and accountants? No matter which you go to for help they end up with all your money – and you end up with no help.

RW   This is not the time we should be having this conversation. Ivan, I thought you were studying the legal proceeding, wasn't that why you had all those legal books scattered over your table, together with all those great notes you produced when we met for coffee prior to placing the injunction?

IH   Yes, but after that you became involved and, well, I thought you would run it from there – especially after we worked out our legal case last Sunday.

AW   Look, I've played the court jester in enough Shakespeare plays with court proceedings to know how courts are run. So, just leave it to me.

Rob and Ivan look at Andy to ascertain whether or not he was joking – and quickly determine that he was serious. They then both look at each other.

RW   Okay Ivan, just how much work have you done to understand the legal proceedings of this hearing?

IH   A little.

RW   A little – how much is a little?

IH   Well, let's just see how we get on.

RW   Jesus, Ivan, you do realise my right to reproduce is also on trial here as well? Just how solid is our case?

IH   Well, we went through our legal position on Sunday – so it's as solid as we discussed. It's just that we're not so strong on the proceedings. But that should be okay, as this is not a court, it's a hearing of the GPA's Ethics Ruling Committee. So, they should help us – to understand what we have to do next.

AW   Well, this case looks set to permanently mitigate my fear of having illegitimate kids.

IH   Look, providing our legal position is solid, who gives a fuck about the proceedings? The Ethics Ruling Committee members, or whatever they are, will tell or ask us what to do.

RW   Well, here's hoping.

As the dwarfs keep nervously discussing their case the camera slowly pans back to take into view the full hearing room – as viewed from the position of the three GPA Ethics Ruling Committee members at the front of the room. As the fuller picture of the room slowly comes into view, it reveals the presence of permanently fixed audio/visual equipment, obviously installed to record and broadcast the hearing sessions.

The muttering of the dwarfs is interrupted by three loud knocks, as the chairman of the GPA ERC hearing hits his gavel on a wooden block.

LTD   Okay I think all parties are present to start this, the 28th GPA Ethics Ruling Committee hearing.

Prior to formally starting the hearing, I think it best if I describe the nature, purpose, procedures and legality of this hearing – as I'm aware that at least one of the parties may not be fully familiar with these concepts.

Firstly, this is not a court. It is a hearing of the Genetic Protection Authority's Ethics Ruling Committee.

Under the GPA Act of 2004, as revised in 2012, Parliament has invested the GPA the necessary powers to develop regulations governing the legal and ethical use of genetic technology in relation to humans. Such regulation becomes enforceable once it has been approved and gazetted by this Genetic Protection Authorities Ethics Ruling Committee.

Additionally, this committee has the authority to interpret and make rulings on the meaning of the GPA Act itself. Therefore, once this committee makes a ruling, the decision effectively becomes law.

Appeals against a GPA Ethics Ruling Committee hearing can be made to the High Court. However, the appeal can only be on the grounds that 'due process was not followed' in arriving at a decision. As such, an appeal against the decision, per se, cannot be made.

At this point another parallel scene is flipped over to, which is Bill in his office watching the proceeding on his computer via the internet. Bill mutters, 'Bullshit'.

The scene cuts back to the hearing.

LTD   [Continues after a long pause] Now, do both parties understand what I've just said – or are there any questions?

AW   Does this have anything to do with the double-entry accounting system?

As Andy asks this question, Ivan and Rob shrink with embarrassment.

LTD No, the accounting profession does have a number of doctrines, accounting principles and rules. Collectively, these are legally binding via the regulations passed by the Companies Act 1985 and the International Accounting Standards and Other Accounting Amendments Regulations 2004.

But really, this hearing has as much to do with accounting as it does with the Easter Bunny. Does this answer your question?

AW So, this hasn't got anything to do with Luca Pacioli [mispronounced] and the accounting equation?

LTD Absolutely nothing.

AW [Andy turns to Ivan.] Not only is he boring, but he's useless. Why did you bring him along?

IH [Highly embarrassed.] Andy, just shut it will you?

LTD Mr Henry, this does bring me to the next point I wish to raise. It has not gone without notice that you do not have legal counsel representing you. Given that the decisions of this hearing are effectively law, with limited recourse to appeal against the decisions, I think it is very unwise to represent yourself.

IH Thank you, Your Honour, but I did seek legal assistance, but those I sought tended to side with the GPA's position, which made it untenable for me to ask them to represent me.

At this point the camera cuts over to Bill. 'Jesus Ivan, I did apologise, and offered to represent you – what more do you want?'

LTD There are many fine lawyers in the City – I'm sure they do not all share the same attitude.
Exactly how many did you approach?

IH Enough to know that I don't trust them – and that I should represent myself with the help of my colleagues here.

LTD   Mr Henry, we are dealing with a very serious legal issue at this hearing. I would no more recommend you conduct your own brain surgery than represent yourself at this hearing.

IH   Thank you, Your Honour. But excuse me if I'm the last person on Earth to believe in justice. I don't believe justice can be purchased from either a box of Corn Flakes or in the form of an overpaid king's counsellor. I expect that this tribunal will come to its own just and fair decision – without allowing itself to be unduly persuaded or influenced by the presence of a bank of toffee lawyers.

LTD   Your trust in the legal system is admirable. But we, as the members of this hearing, must reflect on all arguments, positions and counter arguments put to us. If a KC is able to provide more convincing arguments or argue his or her points more strongly by citing legal precedence, then this undoubtedly gives that party an advantage – as it is not up to this hearing to submit arguments on either party's behalf. Our role is to reflect and decide on the merits of the arguments that have been put forward.

       Now, I urge you once again to reconsider your decision to represent yourself at this hearing. If you do agree to reconsider your position, I will adjourn this hearing for two weeks to allow you sufficient time to identify, secure and brief legal counsel.

The scene cuts over to Bill who quickly phones Ivan's mobile.

IH   [At this point Ivan's mobile goes off. Ivan apologises to the hearing for the mobile.] Sorry, I forgot to switch it off. [He grabs his mobile and turns it off without answering the call].

The scene cuts back to Bill. 'Damn'.

IH   Thank you for your advice and being prepared to adjourn the hearing for two weeks. But, as much as I would like to take the offer up for the extra time, I think it could cause complications for my wife in coming to a decision on her pregnancy.

LTD   Indeed it could. So, are you absolutely convinced that you wish the hearing to go ahead now? You are under absolutely no pressure from the members of this hearing to do so – in fact the reverse is true.

IH   Yes, Your Honour, I am convinced and I wish to proceed with the hearing now.

LTD   Okay then, the hearing shall proceed.

Scene cuts over to Bill, who brings his hands to cover his face, shouting 'No.'

LTD   Now, notwithstanding that hearings of the GPA Ethics Ruling Committee make decisions that effectively become law, the hearings are not overly formal – not like in the courts. The modus operandi of the hearing is akin to a group of friends having a passionate debate.

        So, I'll ask both sides to present their positions to the GPA Ethics Ruling Committee members presiding over this hearing – upon which the members can, and will, ask both parties questions to clarify their positions, or to highlight inconsistencies in their arguments – should any inconsistencies exist.

        Further, we will invite both parties to cross-examine each other's line of argument. Is that clear to everyone?

The camera shows the faces of both parties, at which all agree that they understand. Then Andy surprises all by asking a question.

AW   So, where is the GPA Ethics Ruling Committee that you're referring to?

LTD   [Pointing to the three of them on the bench.] We are the three appointed representatives, or members, of the twelve members who constitute the full Genetic Protection Authority's Ethics Ruling Committee. The GPA Act allows such appointment, and as such we speak and act with the full authority of the GPA Ethics Ruling Committee.

AW   So where are the others, have they got the day off?

LTD   Their whereabouts is irrelevant to this hearing. So, can I please ask you to confine your questions to issues that are germane to the case?

AW   Ivan, you were right, he's saying we have to stick to the German case – was that the Nazi thingy you were talking about?

The camera cuts over to Bill, who is shocked, and then starts shaking his head as he mutters 'goodbye little folk everywhere.'

The camera then cuts back to the hearing room.

IH   Andy, shut it – he said germane not German.

AW   Yeah?

IH   He is asking you to only ask questions relevant to the case.

AW   What relevance have the Nazis got to do with this case?

LTD   Mr Henry, let me rephrase my request to Mr …?

IH   Mr Andrew Watts, Your Honour. And this is Mr Robert Walker.

LTD   Mr Watts, you appear to have the word German confused with the word germane. Germane has a similar meaning to relevant. Thus, I was asking you to please keep your questions relevant to the case at hand.

AW   Sure, all you had to do was ask.

LTD   Unless there are any other questions or objections – can we proceed?

      Ms Small? [Sandra nods and says 'yes'] Mr Raney? [ditto]

      Mr Rushworth? [ditto] Ms Coulson? [ditto] Ms Coleman?

Tess looks back at him with a very long and meaningful look, slowly nodding her head – Lord Thomas Denman looks back at her to confirm – but she fails to pick up the hint that he is seeking a verbal confirmation to his question.

LTD   Ms Coleman, do you have any questions before we start the hearing?

Tess thinks for a while longer – as she does the camera cuts over to Bill, who is almost going frantic with frustration, muttering 'What is this? The new goon show?'.

TC   [Slowly and deliberately] No, Your Honour, I do not have any further questions for you.

LTD   I'm glad you gave yourself sufficient time to think about that question.

Mr Watts? [No, Your Honour, no more questions at the moment.]
Mr Walker? [No more questions, Your Honour.]
Mr Henry? [No, I'm ready for the hearing to commence.]

Good. Given that Mr Henry placed an injunction on Ms Small, I will ask Mr Henry to explain the reason and rationale behind placing the injunction, what he hopes the outcome of this hearing will be, and what he believes will be the social benefits, should his objectives be realised.

Mr Henry, would you like to come to the front and, firstly, just explain your reason for placing the injunction?

IH   What, now?

LTD   Yes, I'm sure we all just agreed that we should proceed with this hearing – so now would be a good time to start. And since you placed the injunction, you get to go first.

IH   [Ivan takes a big breath and blows out to psyche himself up]. Okay then.

As he says this, there is loud cheering from the dwarfs in the gallery. The camera then cuts over to Bill, who puts his head in his hands in expected embarrassment for Ivan. The camera cuts back to the hearing room – where Ivan gathers some of his papers and a few books off the table, then slowly gets ups and starts to make his way to the front of the hearing room – with both Andy and Rob patting his shoulders as he does so. He slowly gets to the front.

IH   [Very nervously] Sorry, what did you want to know again?

LTD   [Somewhat more sternly] Mr Henry, your wife is pregnant with your child. You have placed an injunction on her which prohibits her from terminating her pregnancy until this GPA Ethics Ruling Committee makes a ruling as to whether she is within her rights without the need to consult or get your agreement for the termination.

If this hearing rules that the embryo she is carrying is three standard deviations from the human norm, she will be within her rights to make a unilateral decision as to the course of her pregnancy, or not, as the case may be.

So, please explain why you believe that your wife should be prevented from terminating her pregnancy without your prior consent.

IH   Well, we are now expecting our first child. This came as somewhat of a surprise for both of us. I think it is fair to say that it was a pleasant surprise for me and an unpleasant surprise for Sandra. We discussed the situation and it became apparent that Sandra had not ruled out the possibility of terminating the pregnancy. I objected to the prospect of termination. The discussion ended unresolved and with a degree of acrimony between us.

The camera cuts over to Bill, who is glued to his screen – then the camera cuts back to the hearing.

There is a long pause while Ivan struggles to continue with his recollection of the events and the associated legal argument.

SJPB   Mr Henry, then what happened?

IH   Well, we didn't discuss it for several days. Then one evening Sandra came home a little earlier than usual and performed an online 3- in-1 test.

SDG   Excuse me, Mr Henry, exactly what is a 3-in-1 test?

IH   Well, I have the empty box here …

Ivan goes to his bench and retrieves the 3-in-1 box, showing it to the judge.

IH   Sandra conducted the test without telling me – and without any intention of telling me that she was conducting the test.

LC   That is quite a presumptive statement. How do you know she wasn't going to tell you?

IH   Well, for the paternity test it requires a blood sample from the 'assumed father'.

        Rather, than involving me in the test, or even asking me for a blood sample, Sandra caused me to cut myself – then used a bloodied tissue to provide the blood sample for the 'assumed father'. Not only did she hide the fact that she was performing the test from me – she deliberately hurt me just to conceal the testing.

SDG   Interesting. So, how did you find out that she had conducted the tests?

IH   Well, the test results were displayed on the computer monitor. Sandra, saw the results, which disclosed that our child has achondroplasia, the same condition that makes me short. On seeing this, Sandra stormed out of our study and flew into a rage. She said that having a baby with achondroplasia was not reversible – unless it wasn't born in the first place. In this she strongly hinted that she was considering terminating the pregnancy.

SDG   So, what prompted you to place an injunction on Sandra, pending a ruling of by the GPA Ethics Ruling Committee?

IH   A few days later I tried to talk to Sandra about the issue, to put forward my views that there was nothing wrong with being a dwarf and we should go ahead and have the baby. Sandra replied that as the DNA tests indicated the embryo has achondroplasia, the decision as to whether or not to terminate the pregnancy was no longer up for discussion. I asked how she arrived at this conclusion.

SJPB   Yes, and how did she?

IH   She said that since the embryo proved to have a defective gene, she was not legally obliged to consult, or even inform me of a planned or actual termination.

SJPB   And did she indicate how she arrived at this understanding?

IH   Yes. Sandra works for a law firm that specialises in genetic and reproductive law. Upon learning that the embryo was afflicted with achondroplasia, she consulted the GPA Act and the GPA Gazettes.

SJPB   Yes – go on.

IH   Well, as I'm sure everyone at the front of this hearing is fully aware, the GPA Act identified two broad categories of genetic abnormalities.

        The first is for those genetic conditions that are both severe enough and can be identified via DNA testing to warrant the condition being gazetted.

        The second category is an ill-defined catch-all definition – that, if the child or adult will be three standard deviations outside the accepted 'human norm' then it can be considered as genetically defective.

SDG   Mr Henry, where is all this leading?

IH   Achondroplasia is not a gazetted disease. Therefore, Sandra has wrongly concluded that it falls within the second definition, the catch-all definition of being genetic defective, merely on the grounds that those with the condition, well, their physical height is three standard deviations from the human norm.

SDG   Can you brief this hearing as to the consequences, should your wife be correct in her conclusion?

IH   She is not right, she has drawn a false conclusion.

SDG   This hearing will make the eventual ruling as to whether or not achondroplasia satisfies the three standard deviation rule – that is why you have brought this case before us. However, we are some way off making such a ruling. At the moment we are seeking from you an explanation as to what the consequences would be, should your wife have correctly concluded that achondroplasia falls within the second definition you cited.

IH   I'm sorry, but here I have a problem. The definition of the second category is … is … is … just appalling. It's written in a manner that gives you guys sitting at the other side of the bench the right to decide my fate as a father, and my child's right to life. What and who puts you in a position to decide what is best for me, for my child, [turns around and points to the dwarfs in the gallery] or for their fate. Who the hell are you?

LTD   Mr Henry, The members of the GPA Ethics Ruling Committee presiding over this hearing may, or may not, agree with your sentiments. Regardless of our personal opinions, this is not the forum to discuss the merits and obligation of this hearing or the legitimacy of the GPA or the GPA's Ethics Ruling Committee. The time for discussion and debate was during the act's passage through Parliament in 2004 – then later in 2012 when the act was amended.

    Parliament has now passed the act and the amendment, which vests this hearing with the authority of the state. Therefore, the time to discuss the legitimacy of this hearing has now passed. Now, could I ask you to confine your arguments to the case at hand? Please inform this hearing, in your own words, the likely consequences should your wife's assertions prove to be correct – that achondroplasia falls within the second category.

IH   Okay. My wife is asserting that I, and my child – and all these good people in the gallery [points to the dwarfs in the gallery] – are three standard deviations or more from the accepted human norm. Therefore, she is saying we are too short.

She is saying that because we are short, we don't have the right to have kids. She is saying, that because we are short, we do not have the right to life. She is saying that because we are short – society should do whatever it can to rid itself of us. My wife is saying she wished I'd never been born.

LTD   Mr Henry, again, for the benefit of this hearing, can you explain the causal relationship from an embryo being diagnosed with achondroplasia to your wife's assertion that you no longer have a say in the decision concerning the termination of the pregnancy.

IH   Yes. If this hearing's ruling concurs with my wife's position, then the state too will be saying that dwarfs should be eradicated from this sorry society that we've been born into.

LTD   Mr Henry, please just explain why, if your wife's position is correct, you will no longer have a say in the decision to terminate the pregnancy.

IH   It's hideously simple. If you guys sitting on that side of the bench decide that we folk sitting on this side of bench fall outside the human norm, then the state revokes my paternal rights to the unborn child, meaning, I will not have any right or say as to whether the pregnancy is to go full term – or is aborted and killed prior to birth.

SDG   And how does that work?

IH   Again, horrendously simple. The GPA Act states quite clearly, and I quote [as he says this he picks up a copy of the act from his bench] and reads from it:

> *The GPA is charged with developing an accurate means of determining whether an embryo, which is free of any gazetted genetic disorders, will nevertheless develop into an abnormal child or abnormal adult. Abnormal is defined as in excess of three standard deviations from the accepted human norm.*

The GPA is charged with establishing a screening process in order to identify embryos that suffer from either a gazetted genetic disease or where the embryo will develop into an abnormal child or abnormal adult. Where such embryos are identified, the carrier shall be encouraged to have the pregnancy terminated.

Should the parents not agree to terminate the pregnancy, the following penalties shall be levied on the parents and the subsequent child. Firstly, the paternal rights of the embryo's father will be extinguished – preventing the father from exercising any statute or common law rights over the embryo and/or pregnancy.

Secondly, the State will removal all support and aid for the entire life of unborn and born child from the moment of diagnosis through to the death of the child; including: pre-natal care; birth; post-natal care; medical support; education and training; social welfare and benefits; State-funded housing for both parents and the child; funeral and burial costs of the child.

With the imposition of such draconian penalties, no parent could possibly afford to have a child deemed to be outside the three standard deviation threshold. Therefore, rather than 'encouraged', in reality parents will be 'forced' to terminate such pregnancies.

So my kinfolks' lives are in your hands. Just say the word that we are abnormal adults – or that our kids will be – and bingo, you pretty much rid the Earth of dwarfs for eternity.

SDG   Mr Henry, had you availed yourself to quality legal advice, then no doubt that your counsel would have understood the construct of the first phrase that you have just read out:

The GPA is charged with establishing a screening process in order to identify embryos that suffer from either a gazetted genetic disease or where the embryo will develop into an abnormal child or abnormal adult. Where such embryos are identified, the carrier shall be encouraged to have the pregnancy terminated.

This passage makes it very clear that the onus of proof is on the GPA to prove a particular genetic abnormality falls outside the three standard deviation threshold.

Therefore, up to this point, you have had your full statute and common law paternal rights over your unborn child – and will continue to do so – unless and until the GPA Ethics Ruling Committee rules that your particular genetic abnormality falls outside the three standard deviation threshold.

So, if you had not brought this case before the GPA Ethics Ruling Committee, you would have continued to enjoy your paternal rights over your unborn child through to birth. That is, unless the GPA was to bring the case before us. However, while I cannot speak for the GPA, as far as I am aware it had no plans to bring your particular case to the Ethics Ruling Committee to rule on.

In short, every father to be has full statute and common law paternal rights over his unborn child – until and unless – they are specifically revoked by this Ethics Ruling Committee.

Therefore, you would have been far better served by exercising your paternal rights and taking your case to the family law court.

However, you have brought this case to this Ethics Ruling Committee, the direct consequence of which is that this committee is now forced to make a ruling on this issue – in which the possibility that the ruling will go against you cannot be entirely dismissed.

So, by your very own action, you have created a situation which has put your … to use your term … 'kin' at risk. Be that as it may, this hearing has now officially commenced, as such your action is now non-reversible. I shall take this opportunity to remind you that we did strongly encourage you to seek legal advice and to get legal counsel to represent you at this hearing. However, you steadfastly refused and now you and your kin must live with the consequences of the action that you have set in motion. The action you set in motion will directly lead to this committee making a ruling as to whether or not those with achondroplasia fall outside the three standard deviation rule.

Had you not brought this action against your wife, this committee would never have been placed in a position of having to make such a ruling – in which case your paternal rights over your unborn child would never had been put at risk or open to question.

There is a long pause. Ivan slowly retreats to his bench and gets in a huddle with Rob and Andy, where he is admonished by the others. The dwarfs in the gallery shout at Ivan in very disparaging terms.

LTD   Quiet please – please be quiet. I shall hold anyone making any further unsolicited comments in contempt of court, in which they will be fined and, if necessary, forcibly removed from this hearing room.

Eventually, the hearing room settles down.

LTD   Mr Henry, as yet you have not explicitly said so, but, I'm assuming you disagree with the assertion that those afflicted with achondroplasia fall into the second category of genetic disorders.

IH   Good call. I can see why you sit on that side of the bench.

LTD   [With a touch of sarcasm] Thank you. Now, since you called this hearing, I'm assuming you have a reasoned argument as to why those suffering from this affliction do not fall into the definition of [reading from his copy of the act]: 'Being in excess of three standard deviations from the accepted human norm'.

IH   Yes.

LTD   I'm glad. Would you like to share it with this hearing?

IH   Yes. [Long pause.]

LTD   Tell me, before you start to relay your argument, does this affliction carry with it any detectible attitudinal traits?

IH   No, that is, aside from giving the carrier a piercing insight into the injustice of the state and society.

Camera cuts over to Bill who cringes at the antics being used by Ivan.

LTD   Very good, please continue with your position.

IH   At the heart of this issue is an incredibly complex question, which paradoxically has a very simple answer. The question is to define what is the 'accepted human norm' – so that exceptions to the norm can then be identified. Using the definition and guidance in the act, I can assert that I am human. Therefore, I fully fall within the criteria of 'the accepted human norm'.

SJPB   I see. However, there is an observable physical phenotypical effect of your genetic affliction – from which a position could be mounted that such a phenotype falls outside the 'human bell- curve', so to speak.

IH   Sorry, are you calling me short?

SJPB   I'm saying that the phenotypical expression of your genetic affliction is physically observable. Further, the physical expression of your condition, comparatively speaking, may put you outside the three standard deviation threshold – or outside the 'human norm' for this particular human physical attribute.

IH   Excuse me, sir, but your line of inquiry betrays the fact that you have come into this hearing with pre-conceived ideas as to what it is to be human. I was under the impression that this was a fair and open hearing. This hearing, I believed, was to listen to both parties' definitions, arguments and counter arguments of 'what is the accepted human norm', and then the GPA Ethics Ruling Committee would come to a reasoned determination and make a ruling on this case, based on the merits and social good of such arguments.

I wasn't quite expecting an updated Wild West justice system where a judge would say of an outlaw, 'We'll give him a fair trial and then hang him in the morning'.

SJPB   Mr Henry, you are quite correct in asserting that we will come to a reasoned ruling based on the strength of the arguments put before this hearing. Rest assured of that.

However, in order to tease out the full depth or the positions being put before us, to give consideration to the nuances of each case, to analyse the consequence of any ruling we may make, we do feel obliged to challenge both parties' arguments and positions.

If you make any further accusations against the members of the GPA's Ethics Ruling Committee presiding over this hearing, including innuendo or implying that we are unethical, biased, unprofessional, incompetent or aren't disinterested – then you will be charged with contempt of court. Do you understand?

IH   [Long pause.] Then what happens?

SJPB   When?

IH   If you charge me with contempt of court – what happens then, what happens to this hearing? What ruling will you decide on?

SJPB   It will effectively collapse, and by default, the injunction will be lifted.

IH   What power you have – you can eradicate dwarfs from Earth merely because you feel a little insulted. Where were you when Snow White's stepmum needed you?

LTD   That last comment brings you perilously close to being charged with contempt of court. As you have rightly pointed out, such an action would have implications beyond your particular circumstances – it may indeed have an impact on your supporters sitting in the gallery.

        There is a way to avoid the situation where your behaviour has such an impact on your friends – control you behaviour and don't insult the members presiding over this hearing. Now Mr Henry, can I ask you to press on with your position?

IH   Thank you for the lecture on court etiquette. Okay, coming back to the point of defining what being human is. What is it about me, or indeed any of my colleagues sitting at the bench or in the gallery that isn't human?

        We all have jobs; we all contribute to the fabric of London work, social and political life. We are all sentient beings. We all have a rich appreciation of the arts, sports and other cultural events. We provide a rich element to the diversity and uniqueness of the species known as homo sapiens. To pull out a single attribute, whether emotional, behavioural or physical and make a judgment on the humanity of a person merely on this single attribute is, quite frankly, bullshit.

        It is because we are diverse, because we are all unique, because we come in all shapes and sizes, because we differ in our attitudes and intellectual abilities that has brought humans to where we are today – to this hearing, discussing this very issue. Is any other species on Earth as diverse as we are? No. Is any other species as socially, intellectually and physically advanced as we are? No. This is no coincidence. The greater the diversity within our society that we accept and respect, the fuller the social culture of society becomes.

If we, as a society, start removing diversity from within our ranks, we shall also, with the same blow, start to inhibit human growth and advancement. I am, we all are, human and we are normal humans – because being human is an inclusive concept. Literally, if you think you're human, you are human. Non-humans do not have the intellectual power to grasp the concept 'I am Human'. So, to paraphrase Rene Descartes, I think I'm human therefore I am human. And as I'm human, I'm a normal human. There is no other type of human.

With this there is loud applause from the dwarfs in the gallery and from Mark, Gough and Elaine.

The camera swaps over to Bill – whose expression gives limited credit to the argument, but betrays that it's far from a done deal.

LTD   Now, before the members of this Ethics Ruling Committee ask for clarifications on the position you put forward – we would like to afford Ms Small and her counsellors the opportunity to ask any questions they may have. Is this okay with you, Mr Henry?

IH   Do I have any choice?

LTD   Ultimately it is up to you to decide whether or not you respond to a question. However, I don't think it would do much to advance your position if you refused to answer questions put forward to you on behalf of your wife – who I'm sure you need no reminding is pregnant with your child.

IH   Sure, fire away.

LTD   I understand that it is Ms Coulson who will be the primary representative of Ms Small. So, Ms Coulson, please seek clarification on any question you may have on Mr Henry's position.

However, before you start, can I remind you that (a) this is <u>not</u> a court and (b) Mr Henry does *not* have professional legal counsel representing him. Therefore, please refrain from asking legalese questions and refrain from intimidating tactics. Is this clear Ms Coulson?

LC   Yes, Your Honour.

LTD   Good, now please proceed.

LC   Mr Henry … at the start of this hearing, we were told that this hearing is
       more informal than a court, so, in that spirit I would prefer it if I was
       merely referred to as Laurie – not just by you Mr Henry, but everyone in
       the hearing. Is this okay with everyone [she first looks at Ivan]?

IH   Whatever you like Laurie.

She then turns to the bench – who nod their agreement.

LC   Good to get that sorted. Now, Ivan – it is okay if I call you Ivan, isn't it?

IH   Actually, I'm getting used to Mr Henry.

LC   So …

IH   Sorry Laurie, I'm aware that it takes a while for a lawyer to pick up on
       some of the subtleties of the English language. So, to clarify, I would
       prefer you refer to me as Mr Henry.

LC   [Somewhat taken aback] Okay Mr Henry, let me start off with
       commending you for putting forward such a utopian view of our society –
       and reminding us all of the uniqueness and obligations associated with
       being human.

IH   Thank you.

*Camera cuts over to Bill – who draws in a deep breath, predicting the arrival of
the 'storm after the calm'.*

LC   Rene Descartes. What an inspired man, what an inspired human. I think
       therefore I am. Tell me Mr Henry, was Descartes just referring to humans
       when he articulated this revelation?

IH   Yes. Descartes was explicitly referring to humans. He totally rejected the
       notion that animals, or brutes as he referred to them, could think.

LC   So, we could merge yours and Descartes revelations and merely say 'I
       think therefore I am human'?

IH   [A little worried where this is leading to] I really haven't given it much thought – but, prima facie, it sounds like a logical extension of the two propositions.

LC   Mr Henry, can animals think?

IH   I don't believe they discuss philosophy?

LC   Mr Henry, can animals think?

IH   Not the way we do.

LC   Mr Henry, can animals think?

IH   My knowledge does not extend far enough to be able to conclusively answer your question.

LC   Mr Henry, you are a social scientist. You have studied the cognitive abilities of the animal kingdom. You have, in your first year at university, read texts on Pavlov's dogs and how they learn. You have studied the learning and social skills of non-human primates. You would have seen film footage of chimpanzees not only making tools, but also improving the design of their tools. You would have studied the great apes and how they prepare and wash their food prior to eating it. Mr Henry, can animals think?

IH   [Somewhat nervously] Current theory suggest that animals do think – as defined by their sentinel, cognitive and learning abilities.

LC   Mr Henry, aside from thinking, what would you define as a central human trait – say, an attribute that defines us as species? Can you name, say three such defining traits?

IH   We're bipedal, we communicate more than any other species and we tend to live in families and societies.

LC   Good. What other species live in close family units?

IH   Gorillas, chimpanzees, lions, wolfs to name a few.

LC   Isn't one of the reasons that dogs and human families get on so well that the wolf pack family structure is similar to the human family structure –

inasmuch as wolves have the alpha male and alpha female. All the rest of the family members respect this, at least while they are a part of that family. If they don't respect it they either have to move off and create their own pack or challenge the alpha male.

Isn't this similar to the human family, where there is the mother and father as the head of the family and essentially the same social laws apply?

IH   Zoology is not my field of expertise.

LC   Mr Henry, you are a social scientist. Are you telling me that in your degree you didn't study ethology and learn about behavioural patterns of other species in comparison to human behaviour?

IH   Yes, we did.

LC   Then, I'm asking you as a social scientist that has studied ethology, in regards to behavioural patterns, are there similarities between a human family and a wolf pack?

IH   Yes, a comparison of ethograms between wolves and humans, in regards to family life, show many similarities.

LC   Mr Henry, isn't there growing support for the thesis that the reason dogs can be adopted into human families so readily is that dogs don't actually feel adopted by the family, they actually feel they are a member of the family?

IH   There is growing support for this thesis.

LC   Do some dogs think they're human?

IH   That's just speculation.

LC   Mr Henry, allow me to read the abstract from a paper published in the prestigious Journal of Progress in Neuro-psychopharmacology and Biological Psychiatry, by K.L Overall.

> *Dogs exhibit pathological behavioural conditions that may be equivalent to certain human psychiatric conditions. These canine conditions appear spontaneously or endogenously in the absence of genetic or neurochemcial manipulation, and as such, may be homologous to the human condition.*

If canine conditions approach homology with human conditions they should have excellent face, predictive, and construct validity.

The canine conditions of separation anxiety, obsessive-compulsive disorder, cognitive dysfunction, dominance aggression, and panic disorder have good to excellent validity at all explored levels for human generalized anxiety disorder, obsessive-compulsive disorder, Alzheimer's disease, impulse control disorders, and panic disorder.

These natural canine models can aid our understanding of human psychiatric conditions.

LC   In many, many ways, dogs think like humans – to the point they share the same psychiatric conditions as humans. When they live with a family of humans, they believe they are a member of that family and they think they are the same as that family. They believe they are human. In your ethology units at university, you undoubtedly would have covered this phenomena – is this correct?

IH   Yes, I did study this phenomena at university.

LC   So, as utopian an ideal is that 'I think therefore I'm human' or 'I think I'm human therefore I am human' – like so many other utopian ideals, when questioned and scrutinised, we find it full of contradictions – and in the current case, clearly false. Mr Henry, would you concede that these two propositions, these two ideals that we've discussed are wrong?

IH   I wouldn't say wrong – just that they just require a little refinement.

LC   Well, we know other animals think. And we know other animals think that they're human.

        What parts of your propositions need refinement to make them correct? So, unless you are saying that dogs that think they are human are in fact human, your proposition is wrong.

IH   Okay, they need to be rewritten.

LC   They need to be rewritten? Well, what is the extent of the rewrite you are thinking of? Will it take into account the psychiatric condition referred to as 'lycanthropy delusion'?

IH	Laurie, thank you for the compliment of crediting me with a full working knowledge of all psychiatric conditions, but unfortunately my knowledge does not encompass this entire medical field. And, if you're asking, no I did not study psychiatry as part of my sociology degree.
LC	Let me explain, someone suffering a lycanthropy delusion, is where they believe they are an animal. Usually, the delusion in reference to a large dog – but it is certainly not limited as such. Using your first definition of being a human, namely, 'I think I'm human therefore I am human', will your new definition hold the same, that if someone thinks they are a dog, then they are a dog?
	I must say, I am very keen to hear your rewritten definition of a human that correctly caters for all these … shall we call them 'variations'.
IH	Laurie, you have made your point. I don't think I can refine my definition to cater for all these variations.
LC	So the two propositions we discussed – are you withdrawing them from this hearing as part of your argument?
IH	[Long silence, then eventually concedes.] Yes Laurie, I'll withdraw them. Are there any other questions you wish to ask?
LC	Just a clarification. In putting forward your position, you mentioned that you all [pointing to Ivan, Rob, Andy and the dwarfs in the gallery] have jobs, contribute to life, and appreciate sport, the arts and cultural events.
IH	Uh huh – that's right.
LC	So, what are you saying here, that if you don't like the arts, sport and culture and, say, you happen to be unemployed – what then?
IH	Laurie, sorry, I don't understand your question.
LC	Mr Henry – given that you've withdrawn your argument based on the failed logic of Descartes, your remaining argument is that you and your unborn children should be treated the same as the rest of society – because you contribute to society. Which I think is worthy of debate. So, I'm asking you what should we do with the unemployed who don't contribute or appreciate the offerings and cultural events that our society has to offer?

IH   I'm not here to argue the merits and rights of the unemployed – I'm here to argue the merits and rights of dwarfs.

LC   I see – so you're better than the unemployed.

IH   What? Look Laurie, the unemployed really do not come into this argument.

LC   They do – because you have compared yourselves with them. You are saying because you contribute socially and culturally then you should be treated exactly like others who do likewise. So I'm asking since you have made a distinction between those who work and those who don't, those who appreciate the arts and those that don't, what are you suggesting should happen to those social parasites that you've identified – that neither work nor appreciate the arts?

IH   Laurie, you've really taken my comments way out of context. What I was saying is that as we, like other members of the community, both contribute to our society and appreciate cultural events – then why should we be singled out and denied our rights for having families?

LC   I see. [Long pause]. So, it's okay with you to prevent unemployed dwarfs from having families?

IH   No, I'm not saying that at all.

LC   Yes you are – you are saying that as you contribute to our society, the genetic abnormalities that you have should be overlooked. But those unemployed with the same genetic abnormality – well, bad luck boys, you can't have a family.

IH   No. I'm saying that our genetic makeup does not prevent us from becoming full contributing members of society. Therefore our genetic condition alone should not determine our rights in regards to reproduction.

LC   Now the truth has been revealed. Before, you were claiming that just by being human – or by thinking you're human – we all should be treated the same. But, now your real agenda has been revealed. Isn't this the case, Mr Henry?

IH   What do you mean, 'reveal my real agenda'?

LC   Isn't it clear? Any genetic disorder that inhibits the carriers from contributing to society as much as dwarfs – then you want the state to recognise that they are the ones who should be prevented from reproducing.

IH   Laurie, I give you credit for your tenacity in constantly twisting the words I've said into some other meaning – but, the context of my statements is that, as our genetic disposition does not inhibit our contribution to society, therefore society should not discriminate against us.

LC   Exactly – therefore you agree that for those with a genetic disorder that does prevent them from being fully paid-up social contributors, society should discriminate against them to stop their genetic condition being passed to future generations.

IH   That is not what I said.

LC   It is a valid consequence of what you are saying isn't it?

IH   I haven't thought about it in that context.

LC   Think now – is this a valid comment on the consequences of your argument?

IH   I guess so.

LC   Good. To sum up – we agree that not everything that thinks it is human is human, and you agree that some genetic disorders should be prevented from being passed to the next generation.

IH   Yes, but, to quote Robert Burns, 'Those who change their opinion against their will are of the same opinion still'.

LC   Mr Henry, if you have a different opinion, this is the place and this is certainly the time to state it and make it clear. You may not get another chance. Now, have I correctly summarised your arguments – or at least correctly identified the consequences of your arguments?

IH   [After a long tortured pause] Yes.

LC   Good. Now, all we have to do is agree 'what' genetic disorder should be prevented from being passed on to future generations – as we've agreed that some should be prevented from taking this passage. Your Honours, I have no further questions.

The camera cuts over to Bill which shows him shaking his head muttering, 'Oh boy'.

LTD   Well, neither do I have any further questions. Do any of the other members of the Ethics Ruling Committee have any further questions?

SJPB   Yes, Mr Henry, I feel that you were cornered into making an admission that you didn't necessarily agree with, that is, when you agreed that some genetic disorders should be prevented from being passed to further generations. Can I ask you to explain your views on this issue?

IH   The definition provided by the GPA Act of being in excess of three standard deviations from the human norm – if this definition focuses exclusively on a comparison of a gene, a chromosome or even the genome, in total isolation of all other social, cultural, economic and ethological factors – the definition is unjust.

SJPB   In which way?

IH   Well, it has not gone without my notice that you have an abnormally large nose. No doubt the reason for this lay in your genetic heritage rather than environmental factors. But, your big nose has not inhibited your obvious success in life – demonstrated, if by no other means, your membership of this, the GPA Ethics Ruling Committee.

          Even if the gene responsible for big noses could be isolated and measured – I would argue that this should not inhibit your rights to sire children. Now contrast your condition with the following hypothetical condition. If a man, say something like the Elephant Man, had a nose so big that the weight of it prevented him from holding his head up straight, forcing him to be feed intravenously as he couldn't get food in his mouth, and the sheer size of his nose prevented him from walking through standard sized doors. Due to all the consequences associated with this massive nose, he could not gain or stay in employment, nor drive a car or catch public transport. Due to the limitations forced on him by his unique anatomy, he requires others to shop, cook and care for him and – due to his inability to fit into a standard size toilet – assist him in his daily movements.

In this hypothetical case, the consequence of the genetic disorder has a direct impact on his ability to live a normal life and to contribute to and appreciate social and cultural events. So to put this in context, I would argue against introducing laws to prevent you [pointing to SJPB] from reproducing due to the size of your nose – even if it is three standard deviations bigger than normal. However, I would not object to laws being passed to prevent this hypothetical elephant nose guy from reproducing – as his genetic condition mires his ability to contribute to our society and to appreciate the cultural events it has to offer.

What I'm saying is, I may be short – but this does not interfere with my ability to contribute to and enjoy the social and culture events that London has to offer. What have I done that is so wrong that I should be punished by having my paternal rights revoked?

SJPB   Thank you, Mr Henry, for helping me come to terms with my success. Do you wish to elucidate further on your position before we ask Ms Small's team to present their position?

IH   No, Your Honour – I think I've made my case.

LTD   Okay, before we ask Ms Small's team to present their case, there shall be an adjournment for one hour. Are there any questions?

The camera scans past both legal teams and all indicate that they have no further questions prior to the adjournment.

Insert Scene – 36

Sooner or later we must limit the families of the unintelligent classes. Since about 1900 the better stocks have not been replacing their numbers, while the stupider and less healthy have been more than replacing theirs.

On the Boiler *by WB Yeats, 1939*

Scene 60 – Bill gets through to Ivan

11:30am, Wednesday, 29 May 2013

Setting: The Ethics Ruling Committee's hearing rooms

The scene fades in with the three dwarfs huddled together outside the GPA's Ethics Ruling Committee hearing rooms talking about the case. Their posture indicates that they have been there for several minutes, as Andy and Rob are both casually leaning against the building.

IH   Well guys, how do you think we're going?

AW   That Laurie's a bit of a babe, isn't she? I think she may have been giving me the eye.

RW   Andy, I think this is the time to show a little solidarity. Please don't pursue your interest in the opposition.

AW   Why, Ivan's married to one of them?

IH   Andy, that was a little tactless – it is because she is my wife, who is pregnant with my child, that we have this dispute. Anyway, how are we going?

AW   I think the question is, where are we going? Let's go across to the pub and have a pint before the next session.

RW   No, not the pub – maybe a Starbucks.

AW   Look, I'm having a pint. If you want a coffee, then the pub serves hot coffee. So, let's go.

RW   No, really, I don't think a pint is a good idea.

AW   Suit yourself, but, I've made up my mind where I'm going and you are welcome to join me if you so desire.

IH   Oh, okay, I'll have one of their over-brewed stale coffees.

AW   Have your stale coffee if you want, but I'm having a pint.

The three set off to the 12 Bar Club just around the corner from the hearing rooms.

There is an awkward moment when the dwarfs enter the bar – only to be faced with the GPA legal team, with the exception of Laurie, already there standing around the small bar. The GPA legal team stop their chatter and drinking and turn and stare at the three dwarfs – with unspoken communication of 'this is our pub, go find your own'.

The three dwarfs stop, stare back and get the unspoken message to 'go find another place'. Andy turns to Ivan with a questioning eye and, in response, Ivan gives a barely detectable nod of approval. With this, Andy walks forward into the pub and secures a table – with the other two dwarfs quickly following. Andy surveys the pub, and realises that, aside from the two teams, there is no one else in the pub.

AW   [Talks to his colleagues – but in a voice deliberately loud enough to carry to the other team]

        They're a bit busy today. Some of the crowd may have to leave just to ease the overcrowding.

PR   [Speaking to the dwarfs generally, but Andy specifically]. Gentlemen, you are correct in your implied assumption that the defendant's and plaintiff's legal teams should not interact informally during the course of a legal hearing. However, I'm obliged to point out that the defendant's legal team was the first to occupy this public house – and, further, if it was to be put to a vote, the defence has more hands than the plaintiff.

AW   Has more hands – are you threatening me?

        Because I am so dwarfish and so low?
        How low am I, thou painted maypole? speak; How low am I? I am not yet so low
        But that my nails can reach unto thine eyes.

PR   Very good, you read Shakespeare. However, we were here first.

AW   Well, suit yourselves, we're staying.

With this the dwarfs move to a table, pull out the chairs and sit down.

The GPA legal team appear quite dismayed by this obvious and intentional breach of protocol and give each other a defeatist look, knowing that regardless of their 'Pub Rights', they cannot possibly stay in the same pub as the dwarfs.

They gesture to each other to finish their drinks and then leave – muttering about having to first wait for Laurie to return.

Soon after, Laurie exits the 'Ladies' and is stunned to see the tribe of dwarfs. She looks at the dwarfs, then looks at her colleagues for an explanation. In response they give her a gesture of 'Don't know how this happened but it did – so we have to leave'.

With this, she walks up to her colleagues, picks up her briefcase, as do the others, and they all exit the pub.

The camera pans back to the dwarfs, who all have gloating expressions due to their small victory.

RW   Ataboy Andy, the winner of the great pub standoff.

IH   Hmm, yes, you did manage to kick some ass there – well done.

AW   Well, with that, I think you guys should shout me.

RW   Just for the joy of witnessing your antics – I'll gladly shout.

IH   Excellent. In that case, I'll go and take a piss.

Ivan gets up and heads to the gents. He walks in and immediately sees that the three urinals are too high for him. He then turns his attention to the cubical, which has a big sign across it 'Out of Order'.

IH   Fuck this, why does it always happen?

He walks out of the gents – then crosses the small corridor to the 'Ladies' on the other side. He swings open the door, enters, looks around to make sure it is vacant, then makes his way into one of the cubicles.

Once in the cubical and sitting on the loo (to relieve himself sitting down), he notices a prescription medical box placed on top of the sanitary disposal bin. He curiously picks the box up and reads the label – then from his facial expression the label obviously contains something that is of high interest. After he ponders on the significance of the label, he then places the box in his shirt pocket.

The camera pans out and shows Ivan exiting the cubical, washing hands awkwardly at the basin, leaving the 'Ladies' and sitting back down at the table with the others.

AW   So, is there something you are not telling us Ivan?

IH   Hmm, like what?

AW   A little thing gone missing – your dick. Did you have it chopped off?

IH   Yes, yes, yes – because I used the ladies, then obviously I've had a sex change. It wouldn't have anything to do with public lavatories habitually placing their urinals too high for dwarfs – and then closing all the fucking cubicles would it? Like, you guys have never been caught out?

RW   We all get caught out – but the trick is not to let your mates see you pissing in the ladies.

IH   Guys, enough of these 'midget moments'. How do you think we're going in the trial?

RW   Well, I think Laurie pretty much whipped you in round one. And, I'm not sure that highlighting the fact that one of the committee members had a big nose helped much.

IH   But it was a good analogy wasn't it?

AW   I agree with Ivan, he did have a big nose.

RW   Well, I think that since it is these guys who will be determining our fate, we should be trying to get on the right side of them rather than antagonising them. Admittedly it was a good analogy – but couldn't you have discussed an alternative analogy that didn't insult one or all of the committee members?

IH   Well, I had to think fast – and that's the example that immediately came to mind.

At this point Ivan's mobile rings. Ivan pulls out his mobile and answers it.

IH   Ivan Henry speaking.

BH   Ivan, it's Bill Horowitz – I've been watching the hearing on the internet. You certainly put in an impressive performance.

IH   Sorry Bill, why are you calling?

BH   Well, I suppose first of all to congratulate you on your performance – you really took Laurie and those Ethics Ruling Committee members to task.

IH   [A barely detectable smile starts to appear on his face] Do you think so?

BH   Absolutely, you put forward your case articulately, forcefully and intelligently.

IH   [Still with a hint of the grin on his face] Thanks. [The grin disappears] Now, why are you calling?

BH   Well, I just want to check with you that you have thought through all contingencies – and put in place all the defensive measures that you can.

IH   Like what?

BH   Well – even though you are doing a great job defending your paternal rights, like all legal cases, there is always the risk that you will lose this case …

IH   What, you don't think I'm doing a good enough job?

BH   Ivan, you're doing an excellent job, but with all cases there is always a risk that you may lose the hearing – and then what?

IH   What do you mean by 'then what'? You must have heard the chairman say that their decisions are essentially final.

BH   Well that is not strictly true – there are provisions within our judiciary system to make an appeal that is above the GPA legislation and the Ethics Ruling Committee.

IH   So, what are you suggesting?

BH   Ivan, there is a possibility, despite the injustice of the decision, that you will lose this hearing.

       The very moment such an unfavourable decision is made by the hearing – that is, should such a decision be made – Sandra is free to terminate her pregnancy.

IH   [Very slowly] Yes?

BH   So, if you did lose the hearing, by the time you organised an appeal and slapped another injunction on her it probably will be too late, she would have had ample time to casually stroll to a clinic and terminate the pregnancy.

IH   So what should I be doing?

BH   Ivan, you need to place a 'conditional injunction' on Sandra.

IH   A what?

BH   A conditional injunction – which only comes into force if you lose the hearing and stays in force until such time as an appeal can be heard.

IH   Fuck, I'm due back at the hearing in 10 minutes – I don't have time to apply to have another injunction issued.

BH   Ivan, will you allow me to do it on your behalf?

IH   [Long silence.] You have tricked me into this haven't you? What the fuck is your game?

BH   Yes that's right Ivan, it's a trick – to tell you now when you don't have any time so you have to ask me to do it for you. That explanation might work – except for the fact that when I tried to explain this to you before, when you would have had ample time to organise another injunction, you refused to take my calls.

IH   Only because you proved to be such a wanker when I went to you for help.

BH   Okay, I apologise for being a wanker. Now, will you allow me to act on your behalf to place the conditional injunction on Sandra?

IH   What's the cost?

BH   The cost is that I'll only do this for you if you allow me to represent you at any appeal – should there be a need for one.

IH   And the cost?

BH   Ivan, I'd be happy to represent you free of charge.

IH   Well, since I'm quickly running out of options – and you admitted you were, and apologised for, being a wanker – I'll begrudgingly accept your offer.

BH   Excellent. I'll get to work on it straight away. I'll send some forms to your phone in about an hour. Can I ask you to electronically sign them at your earliest chance and then send them back so that I can start the legal process?

IH   [In a voice of that reluctantly concedes to these arrangements.] Sure, Bill – thanks for the call.

BH   You're welcome.

IH   [Terminates the call and looks up to Rob and Andy.] That was Bill Horowitz. He has offered to represent us at the appeal – that is, if we lose this hearing.

RW   So what was the talk of a conditional injunction?

IH   To provide cover – if we lose this hearing, we need to place another injunction on Sandra, until an appeal can be heard.

RW   But, isn't Bill's firm representing Sandra?

IH   Yes it is. That's odd isn't it?

RW   Sure is. Sounds like a conflict of interest.

AW   A conflict of what? Who cares – he's offered to help hasn't he?

RW   Yes, but, I don't think he can … unless …

AW   Unless what?

RW   To represent Ivan, Bill will have to resign from his current firm.

IH   What – you're joking aren't you?

RW   No. I'm pretty sure that the same law firm cannot represent both parties at a legal hearing, as this gives rise to a conflict of interest. So, if Bill is going to help us then he will have to resign.

IH   Shit ah, maybe I shouldn't accept his help after all. Anyway, we better discuss this later, as I think we need to make a move to get back to the hearing.

AW   Sure. Laurie will still be there won't she?

Scene fades out with the others ignoring Andy's comment while they get up from their chairs and leave the coffee house.

Scene 61 – Session two of the hearing

12:30pm, Wednesday, 29 May 2013

Setting: Inside the hearing room

The scene opens with Lord Thomas Denman hitting the gavel against the gavel block and announcing:

LTD   This is the second session of the 28th hearing of the GPA Ethics Ruling Committee in the case of Henry vs the GPA and Ms Small.

       In the last session we heard Mr Henry present his case as to why the affliction affecting his unborn child should not be determined to be outside the three standard deviation threshold, which legally defines the human norm. We also heard challenges to the rationale and logic of the case put forward by Mr Henry.

       In this session we will be asking Ms Small and the GPA to present their case as to why the affliction should be determined to be outside the three standard deviation threshold – which would result in Mr Henry having his paternal legal rights over his unborn child revoked. It would also require the state to encourage the termination of the pregnancy, principally via withdrawing all financial and social support from the child. As such, we are dealing with a very serious issue.

       So, can I ask the Small/GPA team to ponder the consequences of their stance as they deliver their rationale as to why an embryo or foetus afflicted with the genetic condition of achondroplasia should be subjected to this degree of state intrusion?

       Ms Coulson, can I ask you now to present your case?

LC   Thank you, Your Honour. Indeed as you have highlighted, the consequence of this hearing is not isolated to the case we have before us. Whatever the ruling, it will have an impact on our society for generations to come.

       Due to the gravitas of this case and the complexities associated with the outcome, it is necessary to take a step back and view this case from the perspective of thousands of couples, across all communities, across all backgrounds, across hundreds of generations – all tormented over the same issue, the same choice, the same dilemma.

In each of these thousands of cases, the couples will make their decisions – not on what is right and best for the child, but on what is best for them as the parents. The couple's decision ultimately will be a selfish choice, whether it be not wanting the stigma associated with having an abnormal child, whether it be based on the ability of the child to meet the parents' career hopes, whether it be the avoidance of guilt imposed by a religious institution or whether it be a desire to have a child in one's own image.

Whatever the decision, the parents will choose a course of action that is right for them – not what is necessarily right for the child, not what is right for the future generations that are seeded by us, now.

It is for this very reason the GPA was established. To protect and improve the genetic heritage of this and future generations of our species. And, it is why the GPA Ethics Ruling Committee was established. It is here to provide a mechanism for complex issues – like the one before us – to be properly discussed, constructively challenged so that a reasoned ruling can be made. A reasoned ruling based upon considered reflection of all the arguments put forward and assessing the social good or otherwise of any decision made.

SDG   Ms Coulson, thank you for reminding us what our job is – now can I ask you to get to the point?

LC   Certainly. The point is that every mother, every father, every family that is faced with this sort of predicament will all arrive at a decision as to how to treat their unborn child based on their own personal circumstances. Their decision will be based on what they believe is right for them.

I'm sure that everyone in this room is very sympathetic to this decision-making process – and if anyone of us was put in the same unfortunate situation it is exactly how each one of us would arrive at our own decision.

Unfortunately, such personal decisions fail to take into account the long-term consequences. The decision focuses on, at best, two generations – the parents' and child's, but more usually on a single generation, namely the parents'. However, genes have a habit of passing from generation to generation to generation. In fact, some of the genetic sequences that were first formed some four billion years ago are still found in the genomes of every person at this hearing.

We as humans have an incredibly short life – even if we live to 100, it still only represents a mere 0.0000025% of the time life has been on Earth. Yet, those original life-forming genes are still with us 4 billion years later.

So, how can we say that what is right for me and possibly what is right for my child is right for future generations – for generations that will span potentially billions of years.

In essence, planting a defective gene in the next generation is not so much planting and creating a problem for us – but planting and creating a problem for countless thousands of generations that will follow us. It is the parents and children of future generations, who have no way to have their future thoughts, anxieties and problems taken into account in the decisions we make today – but are forced to live with the consequences of our decisions.

Therefore, it is the GPA and the GPA's Ethics Ruling Committee who are charged with representing those future generations – as they cannot be with us today to present their case. The decision that Sandra and Ivan make now will affect thousands of generations to come. It is up to this hearing to anticipate the views of the thousands of future generations to come, and consider their anxieties, their heartache, their quality of life – and bring to bear such consideration into the decision being made now.

It is totally unjust when we know in all certainty that the decision Sandra and Ivan make will have a massive impact on the health and welfare of thousands of future children, that we as a society fail to bring their welfare into consideration when this decision is being made.

It is a well-established legal doctrine that 'we owe a duty of care to our neighbours'. In this context, future generations are our neighbouring generations and we certainly owe them a duty of care. Therefore, we cannot allow a selfish decision to be made now, which will decrease the quality of life of so many in our future neighbouring generations.

Thank you, your Honour.

LTD   Thank you, Ms Coulson. Before I open the proceeding to the members of the bench, I will offer Mr Henry the opportunity to question and challenge your position.

        Mr Henry, do you have any questions for Ms Coulson?

IH   Thank you, Your Honour.

        [He gets up from his seat and moves towards the centre of the court.]

        Surprising as it is, in such a sensitive case and with the emotional and legal tensions I've been subject to recently, no I do not have any questions.

SJPB   Sorry, Mr Henry, did you say that you do not have any questions for Ms Coulson?

IH   You heard me correctly.

        [There is a stunned pause throughout the hearing room].

        You see, Ms Coulson's argument is infallible – how can any of us in all seriousness raise an objection to her foresight and the soundness of her arguments and concern for future generations?

There is a prolonged pause as Ivan looks thoughtfully at the floor – avoiding any gaze.

LTD   Mr Henry, are you withdrawing your injunction on Ms Small's pregnancy?

IH   Why would I do that?

LTD   Well, you are now in agreement with Ms Coulson's position.

IH   Yes, indeed I am.

LTD   Sorry Mr Henry, how can you reconcile these two contrary positions?

IH   There are not any contrary positions. Ms Coulson correctly articulated that we need to take into account the rights and welfare of future generations – for any action we take now in regards to genetically defective embryos. I fully agree with this. If a child is born which can pass debilitating genetic defects into future generations then we do need to balance the rights of the 'parents' against the welfare of future generations.

However, being short does not constitute a genetic defect of any kind – no more than being tall, ugly or having a big nose is a genetic defect. So, while I fully commend Ms Coulson's insight into the dilemma facing some parents – this is not a dilemma that Sandra and I are faced with.

The issue we need to clarify before we proceed in this hearing is making a distinction between genetic conditions that have a 'cosmetic' impact on a person as opposed to genetic conditions that are 'debilitating'. The genetic condition we are discussing in this hearing is not a debilitating condition.

This hearing is half-filled with very capable people [pointing to the dwarfs in the gallery] and very productive people who all live independent lives and all contribute to the community.

Because they are short does not in any way make them less of a person than any one of you sitting on the other side of that bench [gesturing towards the bench that the three Ethics Ruling Committee members are seated at] or those overpaid weasels opposite [gesturing towards the GPA's legal team].

To say to any of us short-statured people present at this hearing:

You are short. If the state knew you were going to be short, it would have killed you before you were born. This would have been for your own good, as it would have spared you living your life as a midget.

Such an argument is not only ignorant, but also total nonsense. Each and every one of us is glad we were born – as no doubt you guys sitting on the other side of bench are glad you were born and not killed prior to birth. Now, to tell me that you are going to kill my unborn son on the grounds that he is short – and this is for his own good and the good of future generations – is a pathetic argument. The argument is not based on ability, health, mental agility, cognitive prowess, love or the ability to live full, rich and loved lives.

You are pursuing a ridiculous line of reasoning, maintaining you are doing something for the good of someone without asking that someone what they think of the proposed good – or asking their peers to assess 'what is right' for the person in question.

Australia did just what you're proposing. From the 1920s to the mid-1960s Aboriginal mothers had their babies forcibly removed from them by the state. Many of these poor babies were then brought up in churches or white foster homes. Many were subject to abuse by their carers and many were never able to find their natural parents again. This whole period crushed the strong proud traditions of the Aboriginal culture, as the parents could not pass on their knowledge, their traditions and their values to their children.

The reasons the Australian state put forward to justify this horrific racist programme was 'to breed out the colour', and that the Aboriginal mothers 'would want' to give their babies up to strangers so that their child could get a 'white education'.

Unfortunately, the white Australians never actually asked the Aborigines what they wanted. They just made the decision for them, which had horrific consequences for all concerned. This whole tragic event could have been avoided simply by asking the Aborigines what they wanted, rather than assuming what was right for them.

You, now, are trying to do the same to us. Trying to make a decision on our welfare – thinking you know what is best for us without actually asking us – just like the white Australians did for, or more correctly 'did to', the Aboriginal Australians.

So, I'll help you out here – I'll ask a representative sample of short people whether they wished they were terminated during pregnancy, just because they were going to be short adults.

Ivan turns to the gallery and speaks to it.

Okay, all those in this hearing room who are less than four foot six inches tall – can you please get up and stand on the bench in front of you?

There is a lot of clamouring as all the dwarfs climb up onto the benches.

Okay Now please put your hand up if you wished you were never born?

Nobody puts their hand up.

Good.

Now, please raise your hand if you are happy that you were born.

All the dwarfs raise their hands.

Good. Thank you. You can now sit down.

So, Your Honours, we are all happy that we were born – albeit we are short. Don't be like the Australians and assume you know what is best for us – especially when it is exactly the opposite of what we think is right for ourselves.

SDG   Mr Henry, you have put forward a very compelling argument, and you have correctly identified the key issue in this hearing ascertaining the difference between 'cosmetic' and 'debilitating' condition arising from a person's genetic makeup.

I agree with you that Ms Coulson's argument is only valid, if, and I stress 'if', the condition we are discussing is determined to be, shall we call it, 'non-cosmetic'.

And, you have already agreed to the course of action that Ms Coulson is proposing for non- cosmetic genetic conditions, namely to prevent the condition from being passed to future generations.

Now Ms Coulson, between Mr Henry and yourself, you have managed to define exactly what this hearing is about – the extent to which the three standard deviation rule is to apply and the exactness of this measure to correctly distinguish cosmetic from non-cosmetic genetic conditions.

Do you wish to respond to Mr Henry's challenge?

LC   Cosmetics and genetics, what a mixture to be discussing in such an important hearing. Mr Henry indicated that genetics conditions that make someone ugly should be distinguished from genetic conditions that make someone debilitated.

I suppose from this argument, he would welcome the genes of the Elephant Man to be passed on from one generation to the next and to the next again. Mr Henry no doubt would argue the only condition the Elephant Man had was that of being ugly – but seriously, would any of us want our children to have such a condition?

But, let's return to the condition in question – dwarfism caused by achondroplasia. Is this 'just' a cosmetic condition? I would certainly agree that the condition has a cosmetic element. But I wouldn't agree that it is 'only' a cosmetic condition. But rather than me try to define and build an argument as to why achondroplasia has a non-cosmetic element to it, I will leave this task to Mr Henry himself.

A confused mumble comes over the hearing room in response to Laurie's last statement – with Ivan looking particularly perplexed.

SJPB   Ms Coulson, what exactly do you mean by this?

LC   I had the privilege of reading this month's online edition of *Life's Short* – a journal targeted at the short statured. I was particularly impressed with a transcript of a speech made by Mr Henry himself at last week's meeting of the 'Small Person's Association'. Mr Henry showed great insight as to how achondroplasia impacts its sufferers in a very deep and profound way – far, far beyond mere cosmetics. I quote Mr Henry:

> *You know the only reason I came here to speak tonight – is that my appointment with a normal-heighted person cancelled on me. I mean, fuck it, I'd rather spend my time with normal people rather than the bunch of freaks assembled in front of me. Damn it, why did they cancel – I could now be bathing in the warm glow of 'normality' rather than being drenched in the stench oozing from a bunch of short-asses.*

This reveals that Mr Henry himself thinks being a dwarf is much more than cosmetics – but he continues:

> *You, me, we all know our place in society – unless we're in a circus or a freak show we have no place.*

What exactly does Mr Henry mean, 'we all know our place in society'? Being ugly doesn't solicit this level of social exclusion that Mr Henry indicates dwarfs feel they get. But what he said up to now, admittedly, is just opinions and perceptions. But he goes on, brilliantly I might add, to give empirical backing to his assertion that being a dwarf has a major impact on one's passage through life. To do so, he compiled the following statistics:

> the average earnings of full-time employees in the UK is €27,250. But, for a full- time working dwarf it is only €22,950 – which is very nearly 25% below the British average –a full quarter less than the average British worker gets. And remember, we have the same average IQ as the rest of Britain. So, why are our earnings 25% less than normal-heighted people?

> The unemployment level in Britain is 5.5% – but for dwarfs the unemployment rate is at 28%. And, I must emphasis, this figure only includes dwarfs who want to and are capable of working. Why are more of us out of work than our normal-heighted cousins? Remember, most people in Britain are now white-collar workers, so height is no disadvantage. We can use a computer as well as anyone else.

> About 7% of the British workforce manages at least one person, but amongst full-time working dwarfs less than 1% are in a managerial role where they actually manage other people. And it doesn't require height to manage – it requires managerial skills. So, why don't we get promoted to managerial positions?

> Why? Because we're only dwarfs, we're a fucking joke. We belong in the circus, the pantomimes, porno movies – not the workplace, not the 'real' workplace. Let's face it, we're a joke, and everyone is laughing except us.

And it's not just the work environment in which dwarfs fail to perform, is it Mr Henry? No, the condition comes complete with profound psychological conditions doesn't it? As you bitterly pointed out as follows:

> Aside from being short, there is only one other thing that we all have in common. And that one thing, well really it's more of a theme, and the theme runs like this: low self-esteem, lack of self-respect, self-pity, bitterness of being born short and adoration of normal-heighted people.

If being a dwarf is only a cosmetic condition, how can you explain the depth of your desperation, when you summed up the feeling of those suffering from the condition with the following:

Essentially, any of us would sell our grandmother to become normal heighted.

I pity your grandmothers, and for that matter I pity your mothers, your fathers, your wives and husbands – but most of all, I pity your children. But your most telling, your most insightful observation of those with your condition was saved to last, when you delivered your final betrayal of the frustration and agony sufferers of achondroplasia must live with, that is if you can call it living, and again I quote:

> *Let's face it, we don't like ourselves, we don't like each other. All of us here would prefer to be at another function right now, with normal-heighted people, if only we felt as though we were their equal.*

What a revealing admission. 'If only we felt as though we were their equal.' Unbelievable – and you have the audacity, less than a week after delivering that speech, to stand before this hearing and argue that achondroplasia is only a cosmetic condition – no different from having a big nose. I'm sure His Honour [gesturing towards Sir John Poo Beresford] would not want to kill his grandmother just to get a smaller nose.

[Long pause.]

Mr Henry, you agreed with me earlier that genetic abnormalities that cause non-cosmetic diseases or conditions should not be passed into future generations. Mr Henry, just last week you very forcefully argued that being a dwarf is much, much more than merely a cosmetic condition.

Your Honour, therefore, I think there is only one conclusion that this hearing can make – dwarfism is a genetic condition and its impact is non-cosmetic. Therefore, the condition should not be passed on to future generations.

Thank you.

LTD   Mr Henry, do you have anything to add to Ms Coulson's … position – or shall we say, counter challenge?

IH   If I may, Your Honour, yes I would like the opportunity to respond.

LTD   Very well, the hearing is yours.

IH   I suppose a few points of clarification are required. Firstly, I did not make the distinction between cosmetic and non-cosmetic genetic conditions – it was Big Nose on the bench who coined that distinction.

I made the point that cosmetic conditions have to be distinguished from debilitating conditions. I'm sure each of us could immediately think of several genetic conditions that go beyond mere cosmetics but nevertheless are not debilitating. So, with all due respect to the members of the Ethics Ruling Committee who are presiding over this hearing – I would prefer to stick to my original definition, as I'm sure you can all appreciate the modified distinction has created a little confusion with Ms Coulson.

Secondly, you have taken my speech completely out of context. That speech was delivered as part of a reverse psychology strategy to get my genetic kin folk off their short-asses and start standing up for their rights – like other minority groups do. To quote back my speech to me as though it is the way I actually feel is, frankly, missing the joke. However, we must bear in mind that Ms Coulson is a lawyer, so we should give her a little latitude when it comes to understanding humour.

If I really felt so strongly that we should all die in our own self-pity – would I really care about the welfare of my unborn child that has the very affliction I was supposedly ridiculing?

Thirdly, you failed to quote me completely where you quote me as saying:

All of us here would prefer to be at another function right now, with normal-heighted people, if only we felt as though we were their equal.

The actual quote was:

All of us here would prefer to be at another function right now, with normal-heighted people, if only we felt as though we were their equal

346

– or more correctly if we felt as though they would treat us as their equal.

This is what this whole hearing is about isn't it? The right to be 'treated as an equal'. We can, and we do, feel that we are your equal, but you do not oblige us with reciprocal respect. We are human, we're capable, we work, we live, we love, we fully participate in this world and life of ours. But, you want it all for yourselves. You don't want to share it with anyone who is remotely different from yourselves – it makes you feel uncomfortable doesn't it?

So, rather than admitting that you feel uncomfortable with dwarfs around, and rather than having short-asses around, you place the blame on us for being dwarfs and say 'to hell with it, let's kill the little buggers off.' [Long pause as Ivan has a drink of water]. Ms Coulson, can I ask you a few questions?

LC   Actually, I'm not on the register of witnesses – so I don't think you can.

IH   You kicked off these proceedings saying let's keep all this very informal, now you're hiding behind the skirt of court proceedings – don't you have any balls?

Your Honours, would you object if I asked Ms Coulson some questions?

SDG   Providing it is okay with Ms Coulson and her client.

IH   Well?

The GPA and Sandra huddle to discuss – and then Laurie steps out and turns to the bench.

LC   Your Honours, yes I agree to being questioned.

LTD   Very well, Mr Henry, fire away.

IH   Ms Coulson, are you a partner in your firm?

LC   I'm not sure of the relevance of the question.

IH   Well, you just quoted from my speech – from which you implied that it was just dwarfs who are discriminated against in the work place. My guess: there are other forms of discrimination in the work place. So, are you a partner?

LC   No, I'm not.

IH   How many partners are in your firm?

LC   I believe it's around 35.

IH   How many female partners are there?

LC   I think it's five.

IH   How many Black partners?

LC   I think we have only three Black partners

IH   I see. And how many Black female partners?

LC   None.

IH   Earlier, you quoted the statistics in my speech – which you attempted to use in a negative manner – that dwarfs are less capable than normal-heighted people. But, in your own firm, there is clearly discrimination against some sectors of the community, unless you're saying that women or people of colour are less capable than white men.

Are you saying this, Ms Coulson – that people of colour or women are less capable than white men?

LC   No.

IH   Then how do you explain the disproportionate number of white male partners in your firm?

LC   Well, there are a whole host of reasons, let's start …

IH   I'm sure you can start to explain – the point is, whatever the reason, at your firm as in just about every other firm in the country, women and people of colour are under-represented in the senior management positions. Whatever the reason, there is discrimination against women and people of colour. And God help you if you're both.

The statistics you quoted back to me merely highlight dwarf discrimination, but it is far from the only form of discrimination that exists in the work place. However, you have an advantage. There are equal opportunity laws to protect women and people of colour from workplace discrimination. There are no such laws for short people.

[Another long pause while Ivan gathers his thoughts.]

Ms Coulson, during the 60s and 70s the Black Panther movement was quite strong in the US. When I see footage of them and their plight, as with footage of Malcolm X and for that matter Martin Luther King Jr, they always seemed, well, a little angry, always trying to make a point of something. Ms Coulson, do you think they were justified in being a little angry and trying to prove their point?

LC   What a question – how do you expect me to give justice to an answer in the time we have available to this hearing, which, unless I've missed something, is about Ms Small's right to terminate her pregnancy, not about Malcolm X.

IH   Really? The reason they were angry and trying to make a point is that they, Black Americans, were institutionally discriminated against. They couldn't go to the same university as whites. They had to sit in the back section of buses – and then had to stand if a white person wanted their seat. Most couldn't get a job. State Governors refused point blank to take white men to court who openly admitted murdering blacks, even murdering black sympathisers.

With this level of institutionalised discrimination against them – I can understand why they were angry and why they were trying to make a point. Now, you have the audacity to quote to me my own speech citing the fact that we're angry – and that this is 'bad', and using it as one of your arguments as to why you should kill us all off.

We're angry because we too are discriminated against – as were the feminists in the 70s. However, unlike people of colour or the feminists, rather than giving us the same rights as the rest of the population, your strategy to keep us quiet by killing us all off within one short generation.

Ms Coulson, you quoting me was a wee bit flattering for me, and I admit it added a degree of dramatics to the hearing – but that's all it was – dramatics. You demonstrably failed to establish or further your case to terminate my child.

Thank you, Your Honour.

LTD   Well, this is turning out to be quite a lively and intelligent debate, and I must say that I am very impressed with the level of research both parties have obviously undertaken to advance their respective positions.

Ms Coulson, earlier when you addressed this hearing, you quoted Mr Henry's own speech to build a case as to why achondroplasia should be … well, either non-cosmetic or debilitating, depending upon what definition we adopt. In either case, you were still attempting to build a case as to why achondroplasia falls outside the three standard deviation threshold.

Do you have any other material that you would like to present to this hearing to support the GPA's and Ms Small's position?

LC   Thank you, Your Honour, yes I do have additional material that I would like to present to this hearing.

Your Honour, I would like to read a passage from the prestigious British Medical Journal, that describes the nature of achondroplasia:

Achondroplasia is a genetic disorder also called Chondrodystrophia Fetalis, which is visually evident at birth. However, with embryonic genetic testing, it can be detected at the embryonic stage of development. It affects about one in every 20,000 births and it occurs in all races and in both sexes. Its depiction in ancient Egyptian art makes it one of the oldest recorded birth defects.

It is a genetic disorder characterised by a lack of cartilage cells during the development of the foetus and the growing phase of the sufferer's life.

The gene, or genetic mutation, responsible for this disorder has been conclusively identified. It is one of a family of genes that make proteins called fibroblast growth factor receptors.

The fibroblast growth factor receptor gene dictates the production of a protein that is located on the surface of cells of different tissue types, including cartilage. The protein normally responds to signals from chemicals called growth factors, which stimulate cell growth and maturation.

During normal foetal development and childhood, cartilage develops into bone, except in a few places, such as the nose and the ears. However, for sufferers of achondroplasia, something goes wrong during this process, especially in the long bones, such as those of the upper arms and thighs. The rate at which cartilage cells in the growth plates of the long bones turn into bone is slow, leading to short bones and reduced height.

Those afflicted with the disorder have limbs that are very short, for example their fingers reach only to their hips. However, their trunk is almost normal in size.

Sufferers of achondroplasia usually have relatively straight upper backs with markedly curved lower spines, referred to as 'lordosis' or 'sway-back'. Their poor muscle tone may lead to development of a small hump, referred to as 'kyphosis' during infancy. Their small vertebral canals can lead to spinal cord compression in adolescence. The lower legs may become bowed, and feet are generally short, broad and flat. Hands are short with stubby fingers. There is a separation between the middle and ring fingers, which is referred to as 'trident hand'. Their heads are enlarged due to the overgrowth of the vault bones following premature closure of sutures at the base of the skull. There is usually a bulging forehead, saddle nose, protruding full-sized jaw, deeply incurved lower back with prominent buttocks, and a narrow chest. Their teeth are usually over crowded and upper and lower teeth are usually poorly aligned. Women with the condition usually have narrow pelvises, which generally causes complications during childbirth.

Because of their large heads, short arms and legs, poor muscle tone and loose joints, babies with achondroplasia are slow to sit, stand and walk alone. Lower back and leg pains are common, especially in adults, partly because there is pressure on the spinal cord from their small spinal canal. This pressure on the spinal cord can also cause paralysis of their legs.

Sufferers also are prone to frequent middle ear infections, which often leads to major hearing loss.

Further, those afflicted with the condition frequently develop psychological problems due to the difficulties of adjusting to a world geared for taller people.

Children with achondroplasia occasionally die suddenly in infancy or early childhood. These deaths often occur during sleep and are thought to result from compression of the upper end of the spinal cord, which can interfere with breathing. The compression is caused by abnormalities in the size and structure of the opening in the base of the skull, referred to as 'foramen magnum', and vertebrae in the neck through which the spinal cord descends. Breathing problems also may develop as a result of small chest size, large tonsils and small facial structure.

Infants and children with achondroplasia need to be thoroughly evaluated for skeletal abnormalities by a specialist. Other conditions that the specialist needs to check infants, children and adults for is bone abnormalities that may cause spinal cord compression, breathing difficulty, leg pain and loss of function. If kyphosis, the hump in the middle back, does not go away after a child begins walking, it may have to be corrected by surgery. Early surgical correction of leg bone abnormalities is often needed to lessen the severity of bowleg deformity. Additionally, surgery is often needed to relieve nerve or spinal cord pressure from surrounding bones.

The achondroplasia condition is caused by an abnormal gene located on the fourth chromosome. A child can inherit achondroplasia from a parent who has the condition. If one parent has the condition and the other does not, with each pregnancy there is a 25 percent chance that each child will be affected. If both parents have achondroplasia, there is a 50 percent chance that the child will inherit the condition, a 25 percent chance that the child will not have it, and a 25 percent chance that the child will inherit two copies of the abnormal gene, i.e. one from each parent, and have severe skeletal abnormalities that will lead to early death.

So, Your Honours, however you cut it or define it, achondroplasia is certainly not just a cosmetic condition. The medical problems resulting from the condition are numerous, complex and complicated – including infant death. Given our agreed 'duty of care' to our neighbouring generations, is this really a condition that we should be passing down to future generations?

Are we really going to give the okay to a condition that comes with a high risk of infant death? That comes with a high risk of deafness? That comes with a high risk of leg paralysis? If this hearing agrees that achondroplasia is okay to pass onto our neighbouring generation – then I challenge you all, what genetic condition wouldn't we pass on?

SJPB   Ms Coulson, you certainly have established your case that achondroplasia is more than a mere cosmetic condition. However, before we digest you medical depiction of the disorder, I'm sure that Mr Henry would like to say a few words. Mr Henry, do you have anything to add to, or subtract from, Ms Coulson's medical analysis of the condition in question?

IH   Sorry, Your Honour, I must have misheard you, I thought I heard you say that Ms Coulson established a case that achondroplasia is more than a mere cosmetic condition. What did you say, in fact?

SJPB   Well, Mr Henry, assuming factual accuracy in Ms Coulson's medical summary and associated conditions of achondroplasia – in my mind, she established that achondroplasia is more than merely a cosmetic condition.

IH   Interesting, I'm a dwarf but my hearing isn't going after all. I did in fact hear you correctly – which is a little perplexing.

SJPB   What is so perplexing?

IH   Well, if Ms Coulson's objective was to establish that achondroplasia is more than a cosmetic condition – why the focus on the cosmetic elements associated with the condition?

SJPB   Meaning?

IH   She rightly pointed out that the condition lends itself to 'prominent buttocks'. If this is more than a cosmetic condition, then I'm not sure Ms Coulson should really be the one highlighting this as a medical or genetic defect – as one look at her big bum would mean that she too should be prevented from having kids.

        And if I'm going to be penalised for having a 'saddle nose', then I think His Honour with the big nose should also be penalised. Let's face it she quoted a series of cosmetic conditions.

        Does it really matter if I have an incurved lower back, a narrow chest and over crowded teeth? Let's get real, are you really going to prevent me from having a family because I have crowded teeth, which incidentally, like millions of others in this country, I've had fixed with braces?

LTD   Yes, we do hear you, Mr Henry, and we do agree that Ms Coulson did cite a number of cosmetic conditions – but, she did not restrict herself to purely cosmetic conditions. Therefore your reply should really redress the medical conditions that she did cite.

IH   Sure, I'll address the medical conditions she cited. Laurie cited, if I remember correctly, just three medical condition, namely: risk of infant death; risk of deafness; and risk of leg paralysis.

First, I'd like you to all look around the gallery. Do you see any wheel chairs, any deaf dwarfs or any dead infants? No. Because the conditions mentioned are medical 'risks'. The conditions do not always materialise – in fact they rarely materialise. It is just that with dwarfs, there is a higher 'risk' that these conditions will materialise than in non-dwarfs. However, with today's modern medicine, the risks associated with achondroplasia are now very low.

But, let's hypothesise for just a moment. Laurie, say rather than deafness, leg paralysis and infant death the risks associated with achondroplasia were instead: the risk was just dying young – say having a life span of only 70% of the UK average. And rather than having a risk or deafness, the risk was blindness. And rather than leg paralysis, the risk was kidney failure.

Would you still say dwarfs were unfit to pass their genes onto the next generation?

LC   [Taken completely by surprise with the question – and it takes her a while to gain her composure.] Sorry, I fail to see the relevance of your question.

IH   Well, I suppose I'm still probing to find where this magical distinction is, which separates normal and non-normal humans. In your thorough summary of our condition, you only managed to cite three medical conditions which dwarfs have a higher risk of contracting than the population as a whole. Since you cited them, I'm just trying to get a fix on how important you think these three conditions are, as opposed to other common medical disorders.

So, if we were at risk of early death, blindness and kidney failure – rather than the three conditions you cited – would you still be trying to stop me from having a family – trying to stop all of us here from having a family [gesturing to the gallery of dwarfs]?

LC   [Blushing and getting quite agitated.] Your question is irrelevant – because achondroplasia does not expose you to those conditions.

IH   But what if it did, what then?

LC   Sorry Mr Henry, I will not be drawn into hypothetical discussions. Achondroplasia increases the risk of infant death, deafness and paralysis.

IH   Laurie, why don't you tell the hearing the real reason you are refusing to answer my question?

LC   [Very aggressively] There is no reason why I won't answer the question – aside from its total irrelevance to this case.

IH   Well, say if this hearing decided in your favour on the issue of achondroplasia – but there was another genetic condition that increased the risk of blindness, early death and kidney failure. Would you also represent the GPA to have that genetic condition outlawed – to prevent those carriers from having a family of their own?

LC   [A look of fury in her face as she speaks slowly and deliberately.] This hearing is about achondroplasia. We do not have the time to discuss every other real or hypothetical genetic abnormality at this hearing. So, can you please limit your questions to the case at hand and the facts associated with the condition in question?

IH   It's okay, Laurie, remember we're all friends just having a passionate debate, so you can tell us your little secret.

LC   I do not have any secrets that are remotely relevant to this case or to this hearing.

IH   [Turning to the bench.] Your Honours, not only does Laurie have a big bum, which makes her our equivalent on the cosmetic front, but she too carries a genetic disorder that increases her risk, and others carrying the same genetic disorder, of suffering similar medical disorders to dwarfs. For example:

Dwarfs have heightened risk of infant death – she has a heightened risk of premature death. Dwarfs have a heightened risk of deafness – she has a heightened risk of blindness. Dwarfs have a heightened risk of leg paralysis – she has a heightened risk of kidney failure.
You see, Your Honours [As he says this he reaches into his pocket and retrieves the same pharmaceutical prescription box that he pocketed when he was in the ladies lavatory at the '12 Bar Club' and holds it up to the ERC members, then to Laurie] Laurie is a diabetic
– this box contained her prescribed insulin.

The court goes quiet and all look at Laurie, no one knowing what to say or do, but awaiting her response.

Laurie stands up and looks directly at Ivan with an expression that is trying to control the obvious rage she is feeling. She slowly raises her arm and extents her index finger so that it is pointing directly at Ivan. Then with a voice that is 'controlled aggression'.

Mr Henry, I am not the one who got your wife pregnant, I am not the one who has put an injunction on your wife, I am not the one who submitted an application to have this hearing make a ruling on your situation, I am not the one suffering achondroplasia, I am not the one who is carrying a medical condition that this hearing has been convened to debate.

If you include or reveal my private life at this hearing again, I will sue you for invasion of privacy. Do you understand?

IH   Sure, I understand.

LC   So you will cease your comparison of achondroplasia with diabetics?

IH   No – Laurie, I concede I had no right to bring your personal life into this hearing – and for doing so, I unreservedly apologise. But, regardless, the comparison is still valid. If the argument is that dwarfs are to be prevented from having families due to the medical conditions you cited that we're at risk of contracting – then this hearing does need to consider the logical implications of its ruling. If dwarfs are outlawed – then who is next? Those suffering from diabeties must come soon after us.

Laurie Starts to walk towards Ivan, arms by her side with her face leaning forward making her look quite awesome.

LC   This hearing is about dwarfs and the disadvantages those suffering from the disease have to live with. The hearing is not about any other disease [by this stage she is only a few metres away from Ivan] so you have no right to cite other medical conditions and conjecture what the GPA and the Ethics Ruling Committee may have to say in relation to these conditions. [At this point she is only a metre away from Ivan, leaning towards him, still carrying an expression of fury on her face].

LTD   [Verbally stepping in to stop what appears to be imminent physical exchanges between Laurie and Ivan.] Well, this discussion and exchange of views has brought us to a natural break.

LC   [Ignoring Lord Thomas Denman.] Dwarfs are a genetic spoonerism – close to human DNA but not quite. Both have a couple of letters transposed, making them an object of amusement – rather than respected as the 'real thing'. In short, dwarfs, or if you like achondroplasia, is not what nature intended.

IH   [Taken aback by Laurie's emotional outburst and her personal slurs.] Not what nature intended? What sort of pathetic, silly and unscientific argument is that?

        Just what did nature intend? Well mother nature has been speaking to philosophers for centuries now, so let's ask a few of them what she has told them shall we?

        Nature told Spinoza that she was a logical system, but to Leibniz that she was a congeries of souls. She said to Diderot that the world was a machine with cords, pulleys and springs, whereas to Herder she said that it was an organic living whole. To Montesquieu she talked about the infinite value of variety; to Helvetius of unalterable uniformity. To Rousseau she declared that she had been perverted by civilisations, sciences and the arts; whereas to d'Alembert she promised to reveal their secrets. Condorcet and Paine perceived that she implants inalienable rights in man; to Bentham she says this is mere 'bawling upon paper' – 'nonsense upon stilts'. To Berkeley she reveals herself as the language of God to man. To Holbach she said there was no God and churches were conspiracies. Pope, Shaftesbury, Rousseau see nature as a marvellous harmony. Hegel sees her as a glorious field in which great armies clash by night. Maistre sees her as an agony of blood and fear and self-immolation.

So Laurie, just what do you mean when you say dwarfs are not what nature intended. What exactly did nature intend? And what makes you so gifted that you understand nature's intention better than the world's greatest philosophers?

LC   [Taken aback from Ivan's overpowering rebuff – and takes a while to build her confidence back up.] Left to their own, those suffering from genetic abnormalities that lessen the carrier's level of fitness would not survive in nature's 'survival of the fittest' competition.

The reason dwarfs have survived is due to charity – the rest of society carrying and caring for them. Let's face the facts, dwarfs, or runts as they are usually referred to, do not survive in other species. It is just within human society where, due to the grace and charity of the rest of society, dwarfs survive.

Let's return to nature's survival of the fittest – in which only the strongest and fittest survive and go on to procreate.

IH   I couldn't agree with you more Laurie. Let's just let nature take its merciless toll and allow only the fit to survive. However, this is not what you are proposing! You, or the GPA, are actively trying to kill us off. This is not letting nature take its natural course. This is not leaving it up an individual's level of fitness to define their reproductive success.

You are saying the reason why the dodo became extinct was that they, as a species, collectively became unfit – and that it had nothing at all to do with the sailors that arrived at Mauritius and, for a bit of sport, mercilessly clubbed them all to death.

If what you mean by nature is the survival of the fittest – I fully agree with you. Let each one of us play our hand as nature dealt it to us and let us and nature determine our success. If survival of the fittest is what you are advocating – then you have no right to intervene and kill off our reproductive successes.

There is a long pause as Laurie, again, is taken by surprise by the lucidity of Ivan's rebuff.

LTD   We three members of the Ethics Ruling Committee have been very impressed by the quality of the debate and the reasoned arguments put forward during this hearing. We are rarely privileged to witness the depth of constructive reasoning that the two sides have put forward today.

I would think that we have reached the point of exhausting all the for and against arguments. Everyone at this hearing should now have a very clear picture of the issues at stake and the consequences of the ruling that the members of the Ethics Ruling Committee will make.

So, when we reconvene we should be able to provide you with a summary of our ruling, with the written ruling to be published by 12 June.

That being said, I now declare this hearing adjourned until 4:30pm today. Could I ask you all to have already reconvened and be ready to proceed at 4:30pm sharp?

AW   Sir, when we next meet, you will have already made up your mind as to what the ruling will be – assuming you haven't already. Before, we leave, can I just paraphrase a quote from Roland Barthes on his commentary of the trial of Gaston Dominici in 1952:

> *We are all potential Ivans, not as inferiors but accused as such, deprived of our right to be human, or worse, rigged out that of our accusers, humiliated and condemned by it. To rob a man of his humanity in the very name of humanity: this is the first step in all legal genocides.*

If you deprive us of our right to be human it will lead to genocide – as everyone has a defect that could be defined and genetically measured and eventually outlawed. So, be very, very careful in arriving at your decision.

LTD   [Visibly moved by Andy's quote] Thank you Mr Watts … we will indeed exercise great care in arriving at our ruling.

The camera fades out on the three Ethics Committee members closing their folders and getting up to leave the hearing room.

Scene 62 – Discussing Ivan's team's performance at Starbucks

2:00pm, Wednesday, 29 May 2013

Setting: Starbucks on the Strand

The three dwarfs are sitting in silence at the Starbucks table, each staring into space.

The camera goes around the table picking up each of the three dwarfs in turn. The camera picks up the exhausted expression on each of them, with their emotional thoughts visible via their tormented expressions – 'Did we do the best we could?', 'Did we miss something?', 'What else could have we said that just may have made a difference to the deliberations now taking place between the three members of the Ethics Ruling Committee?' The unspoken collective thought raging around the table being:

> *Were we worthy to defend our kin?*
> *Were we worthy to stop the impending genocide of dwarfs?*
> *Were we worthy to stop the genocide of every other genetically identifiable minority?*
>
> *The silence is broken with the familiar Nokia ring tone. Ivan reaches into his pocket and retrieves his phone and looks at it.*

IH   Hi Bill. I'll put you on speaker phone – so that my former Legal Counsels can hear the conversation.

Ivan presses the speaker button on his phone then places it in the middle of the table.

IH   Okay, Bill, you're on speaker phone, and I have Andrew Watts and Robert Walker on the line with me, these two gentlemen being my former legal counsel.

BH   Hi guys – I'm glad to be on board. I hope I am not causing any offence with Ivan appointing me the team's legal counsel.

RW   Hi Bill, this is Rob. Welcome aboard. And, definitely not, you are very welcome in replacing us as Ivan's legal counsel.

AW   Hi Bill, it's Andy here. Sure I'm okay with you being Ivan's lawyer – but, Ivan, I'm still going to get paid for services rendered aren't I?

IH   Yes, the three of you can take an equal share in the moneys I pay out in legal counsel fees.

        Now, remember, don't spend it all at once.

AW   Cool!

RW   Andy, he's being sarcastic – he means you will be paid 33% of fuck all!

AW   Well, that's better than 0% of fuck all.

BH   Hey Ivan, that was an impressive performance, well done.

IH   Thanks, but save your compliments until after the ruling is made, then we'll know if it was good enough or not.

BH   Take credit where deserved. Regardless of the outcome, you put in a very impressive performance, particularly your rebuff to Laurie's statement that 'dwarfs are not what nature intended'. How were you able to quote those philosophical positions?

IH   I guess I got lucky. When I was in the debating society at university one of the subjects was 'does nature still have a voice?' So, I learned that Isaiah Berlin passage verbatim so that I could drop it into the debate. It worked then – and I pray it works now.

BH   Well, I certainly hope so, as it was pretty impressive.

IH   Thanks. Anyway, did you manage to get the conditional injunction placed?

BH   Yes, it becomes effective the second the ruling is handed down – but it should be presented to Sandra before then.

IH   When? The ruling will be read out in two or so hours.

BH   Well, I guess when the hearing reconvenes, you can walk over and give it to her.

IH   [Sarcastically] Nice, you don't think she's been through enough already?

BH   Well yes, but we're a little short of options at the moment – what do you suggest?

IH   You're right – I have to give her the injunction when the hearing reconvenes. Unless of course you know where Sandra and the GPA team are currently huddled, in which case we could put a downer on their caffeine high.

BH   Let's just wait for the resumption of the hearing.

IH   Bill.

BH   Yes, Ivan?

IH   After I agreed for you to represent us at the next hearing, assuming there is one, well after discussing the matter amongst ourselves – we were wondering whether you can actually represent me. As we didn't think the same law firm could represent both parties at a trial.

BH   Yes, I can represent you.

IH   How?

BH   The minute you gave me the okay to represent you – I tendered my resignation, effective immediately.

IH   Shit, I wasn't expecting you to do that – thank you. Do Pat and Laurie know that you've resigned?

BH   I guess they would do by now.

IH   It will be a nice surprise for them – another injunction and forewarning that you will be representing me going forward.

BH   Look guys, on a great day like this, let's try and clear our heads and take a stroll. We spend far too much time indoors – and it's just inexcusable on a day like this.

I'm in the foyer of the High Court. Where are you, and I will come and join you – or if you're up for it, let's go for a stroll along the Thames.

The three dwarfs all look at one another and agree.

AW   Sure, we got the takeaway cups – so we won't be wasting any coffee. Let's go. If you're at the High Court, we can meet you on the corner of Embankment and Middle Temple Lane – say in fifteen minutes?

BH   Sounds good – see you in fifteen minutes or so. And, by the way, was that you, Andy, who quoted Bathes?

AW   Yes, why?

BH   Well, where on Earth did you find that quote? It was unbelievable. It really brought home exactly what this case is all about!

AW   Thanks Bill. But, I'm not a total ignoramus – I do actually know how to read.

BH   Well, you're obviously reading good literature. Well done.

Scene fades out with the three of them leaving the coffee shop.

Insert Scene – 37

Let the schools be closed at once, the great mass of humanity should never learn to read and write – never.

Fantasia of the Unconscious and Psychoanalysis and the Unconscious, *by DH Lawrence.*

Scene 63 – Discussing GPA's performance with the lawyers

2:00pm, Wednesday, 29 May 2013

Setting: Pat Rushworth's office at Bradbury, Dywer & Waldron.

The scene fades in with Laurie, Sandra, Jon Raney, Tess and Pat all sitting around Pat's opulently appointed office with near full cups of tea in front of them, the china tea set being a selection of 1930's Schumann Betsy Ross Figural Cup and Saucer, each present with a different coloured cup and saucer (i.e. dark pink, blue, green and yellow, light pink) complete with complementing biscuit plates, milk jug etc.

Pat looks up as though he is about to break the tense silence. As he fills his lungs, and adjusts his body language to assert his authority as the most senior person at the table, he is trumped unknowingly by Tess, who pulls out her note pad and pen, looks up at him with her unnerving, unchanging glum expression. Pat becomes aware of Tess's glum, piecing stare and becomes momentarily unsettled. She is not hanging off every word he says due to his expertise, authority and seniority within the legal profession; she is hanging off every word because she is blindly following a QA procedure which requires her to write everything down that legal counsel says. Pat recomposes himself and starts:

PR   Laurie put in an impressive performance today. She certainly hit all the necessary buttons to get the members of the Ethics Ruling Committee excited in the right way. I think we can all look forward to a favourable ruling in two hours or so.

JR   Pat, at the risk of being a party pooper, my thoughts are that you underestimated the strength of Ivan's arguments in support of his position – and, frankly, Laurie was not nearly researched enough to be able to forcefully refute his arguments before they gathered momentum and started to make sense. In fact the opposite was almost true – Ivan was for the most part able to take the wind out of Laurie's arguments more effectively than she did his.

LC   Jon, I think you're being overly critical. The position we went in with is that dwarfism is an undesirable disposition, it has its origin in an identifiable genetic defect, and its physical manifestation is clearly beyond three standard deviations from the human norm. This is exactly what we established during the hearing. All the other arguments Henry raised were, for the most part, irrelevant to the issue at hand.

SS   Irrelevant to the issue at hand – sorry Laurie, what exactly do you mean by that statement?

LC   Sorry Sandra – what are you asking?

SS   Why did you say that Ivan's arguments were irrelevant?

LC   Sandra, I said they were irrelevant to the case at hand, mainly due to the fact that the feminism and Black rights argument was a diversion that went nowhere, and I believe the members of the Ethics Ruling Committee saw it as such.

SS   So, even though dwarfs work, pay taxes, vote, are good upstanding members of society – this counts for nought does it? Ivan doesn't have a redeeming quality in him – is this what you are saying to me?

PR   Sandra, we are on your side – we are here to support you and represent you in this case, to protect your rights to choose your future. You are okay with this aren't you?

SS   You went way further than to try and protect my rights as a woman and as a potential mother. You were out to destroy Ivan, to destroy dwarfs. All I wanted was to preserve my rights to choose what happens to me, my life and my pregnancy.

You, on the other hand have a far wider agenda – what happens to me is incidental to the social agenda you're trying to engineer. Essentially you don't give a fuck about the pro-life pro-choice social debate that I thought I was fighting – you were there to get your foot in the door to re-introduce a broad-based eugenics programme. Get rid of the feeble minded, the feeble bodied, and you dare to use my unplanned pregnancy as the battering ram to introduce this horrid social agenda – merely because my husband is a dwarf.

PR   Sandra – I think now is an …

JR   Pat – please [in a tone and facial expression that demands he shuts up]. Sandra, can I suggest we take a stroll along the river? It was such a beautiful day last time we walked along the Thames – and it looks as though it is another lovely day, so it would be a pity to waste the opportunity for a nice walk.

SS   Jon, I'm really not in the mood to be patronised at the moment – so with all due respect, why don't you take a short walk by yourself?

JR   Sandra, please. I understand you're pretty pissed at the moment – and yes, you have every right to get up and leave, that's your prerogative. But, by leaving, by not discussing the issues, the issues won't walk away. So, please, join me for a stroll along the river.

SS   Okay let's go – but leave your weasels here.

TC   Jon, to complete the QA forms, I think I should come on the walk so that I can minute the meeting.

JR   Thanks Tess, but external counsel will not be present – therefore, the QA manager is not required.

TC   Still, I think it is in the spirit of the QA system that I should be present to minute any discussion you may have.

SS   Tess, shut the fuck up. You're not coming – do you understand?

TC   I was just offering.

JR   Thanks Tess, but on this occasion, I don't think our conversation is meant for the public record. So thank you – but no thank you.

Sandra and Jon get up and leave the others a little startled in the office – all staring in silence as they walk out the room.

Scene 64 – The Club discusses the case

2:00pm, Wednesday, 29 May 2013

Setting: Judge Frederick Rogers Law Chambers

*The gentlemen of the Country Club are convened in Judge Frederick Rogers'
chambers, the same room as where he and Max previously met. The meeting
consists of two of the three Ethics Ruling Committee members that presided
over the hearing (namely Sir John Poo Beresford and Lord Thomas Denman),
Max Lyford, Sebastian McKibben, Angus Le Bon (who was in the public gallery
during the hearing), Chris Braithwaite and Frederick Rogers.*

*The scene fades in with several of the members describing England's victory
over Australia in the second test at Lords.*

ML   You know England is in such good form now, beating the Aussies by 2
      wickets and 70 runs, I think we'll go on and win the Ashes back.

CB   I still wouldn't write off the Aussies – they're still smarting after losing the
      World Cup to us in India and they're pretty determined to prove a point
      and retain the Ashes.

FR   Nevertheless, Chris, it is always good to savour a victory over the Aussies.

      Now, we only have an hour or so to discuss the hearing – so, Sir John
      Poo can I ask you to brief us as to how the hearing has gone thus far,
      and how 'safe' our ruling would be if we were to make the ruling in favour
      of the GPA?

SJPB Well, I think it's fair to say that we underestimated the dwarf. He has
      mounted an impressive and credible argument that dwarfs should not be
      considered any different from the rest of the 'normal' healthy population.

      Unfortunately, the GPA's position was not helped by the fact that
      Bradbury, Dywer & Waldron appear to have also underestimated the
      strength of the arguments that the dwarf would put forward – and, let us
      say, Laurie wasn't brilliant at thinking on her feet to rebut some of the
      arguments that he put forward.

p   Lord Denman, what did you think of the proceedings?

367

LTD   Yes, I agree, the midget certainly developed a strong case as to why dwarfs should not be defined as being outside of the three standard deviation threshold. Further, as you have suggested, Bradbury, Dywer & Waldron did get somewhat sidetracked and lost their focus. For God sake, she even engaged in a discussion over feminism and Black rights – a no-win argument.

But, the undeniable truth is still there – dwarfs do have an identifiable genetic condition, that condition has a physical manifestation, and the physical manifestation is widely regarded as detrimental to the carrier of the condition.

At the end of the day this is what the hearing is about – nothing more, nothing less. Dwarfs have a genetic mutation that physically manifests in a manner that nobody – including dwarfs themselves – would voluntary choose to have. The condition is measurable both on the genome itself and in its physical manifestation – and pretty much regardless of the measurement used the carriers of the condition are clearly outside the three standard deviation threshold.

The case is that clear cut. We do not need to delve down into all the distractions that he put forward, about being compared to Black people and feminists. Black people and feminists are not Black or female due to a genetic mutation, but he is a dwarf due to a mutation.

If we were given the option at birth, not everyone would reject being either Black or a woman. But given the option at birth, everyone would avoid being a dwarf. There's not a dwarf out there who didn't wish they were a normal-heighted person.

Angus, you were there as an observer, what are your thoughts on the proceedings?

ALB   Lord Denman, I mostly agree with you, but I do think you have taken an extreme position. Let's face it – would you be Black, female or a dwarf, given the option? I guess most would choose to be a normal-heighted white man. I know I would. But, we're not saying we want to stop these other groups from procreating are we?

ML   Heh, heh, heh – well not yet anyway.

FR   Max, that was a little uncalled for.

ML   Sorry Frederick, I didn't realise you were so sensitive about this subject.

ALB   However, there is an aspect of the proceedings that does trouble me.

FR   What would that be, Angus?

ALB   Well, the little guy at the end – he quoted Roland Barthes for God's sake.

ML   Meaning?

ALB   Aren't we, of all people, trying to restore the intelligentsia to its rightful place in society? We come across a guy, admittedly a short guy, but nevertheless obviously a student of the classics, and we are passing judgment on him as an inferior? This was not rote learning – as he was able to paraphrase Bathes in the absolutely right context. He is not a middleclass twat. There is something special about that little guy – and if he's special, then it is possible there is something special about the others.

ML   Angus, I think you're losing the plot a little bit here. We're attempting to bring back the natural order of society, with the emphasis on 'order'. Since the masses with their pathetic democracy have taken over – just consider for a moment their achievements in bringing our once proud and tall nation to its knees.

      They've put a drug dealer on every other street corner. They've appointed judges who espouse that burglary isn't a serious crime – allowing burglars to rob and mug old decent people without so much as a threat of incarceration. They've created an education system that manages to turn out university graduates who can hardly string a sentence together – doubtless being acquainted with the classics. They've created a legal system so steeped in the interest of civil rights and minority groups that the rights of suspects and even criminals take precedent over their victims. They've created a social value system that exults the virtues of the petty middle class over the salt of the Earth values of its tradesmen and farm folk, a value system that actively scorns high culture and the upper ruling class.

      The swill they eat isn't fit for pigs. Who would have ever believed that they would create and propagate McDonalds across the globe – such disgusting food that it even makes canned food seem nutritious?

They've created a society whose cultural values are directed at the lowest common denominator. A mere 70 odd years ago we had such a depth of literature genius among us – Shaw, Pound, Lawrence, Forster, Woolf, Moore, Wells, Huxley, Lewis, Eliot, Joyce, Yeats just to name a few. Now that the masses have taken over the cultural direction of our society – name a single living author who even approaches the intellectual stature of the authors from yesteryear!

Literature these days is nothing more than pornography. Theatre is worse, overtaken by tasteless musicals. Cinema is firmly directed at the lowest common denominator of the mass – leading to one banal film followed by another. And have you ever tried reading one of their newspapers? I tried once and failed. The only chance of understanding that ... that excuse for a newspaper, is to get a full frontal lobotomy.

So Angus, before you get sentimental about the short guy, just reflect a little on the damage that this mass culture and mass rule has done to our society, and what we need to do to cleanse our society of what George Moore referred to as, 'the blind, insatiate, putrefying mass, the creatures of ooze that rush all about us.'

If we do not take this opportunity to start the process – God only knows when we will get another chance. And, can we really afford to wait any longer?

CB   Max, just listen to you. Complaining that there are no more intellectual authors and that the university graduates of today are not versed in the classics. And, here we have one of the few intellectual authors of our time being read by a student of the classics who understands the very sentiments and frustrations that Barthes felt, and yet you're willing to condemn him and his kin?

ML   Chris, we are talking about a dwarf!

CB   Max, please bring a degree of perspective to this debate. We're talking about an intelligent guy here – I don't think the fact that he's short should influence our views here. Our objective is to restore the ruling class, restore order and clean up the dregs within our society. Where does wiping out short intellects fit within this framework?

SJPB Chris, I agree that perspective is the key to this issue. But, let's get the perspective right. Firstly, to realise our objectives we need to set a precedent within the GPA from which we can start culling out the inferiors. A clear-cut case like this will take probably years, if not decades, to come up again – and if we don't take this case the legal precedent will be against us, which will make it difficult to actually win the next test case.

And secondly, as Max said, we are talking about a dwarf.

ALB [Looking around the room to the others for support] Aside from Chris, does any of you share my view about the little guy?

SM I admit, it does sadden me. We quite possibly have come across genuine intellect versed in the classics. And, due to a higher calling of duty, we are preventing this intellect from having his own family.

But, I do sympathise with Max and Sir John Poo's position, that if we don't take this case it could prove to be the derailment of all the work we've done so far to realise our objective, and quite frankly I think it could very well take another generation to get the process back to where we are today.

I have sympathy for the little guy, but it is a question of priority, i.e. should we allow him to have a family at the expense of restoring our society to its natural order? This truly is a clash of principles and moral judgments. My view is that the restoration of the ruling class is a higher order of priority than allowing a dwarf parental rights.

ALB Anyone else?

FR As I indicated last time we met, I'm sceptical about this case. If we win the case now – then later lose control of the GPA and the Ethics Ruling Committee – it is possible that whoever ends up controlling the GPA and the ERC could use this precedent for other objectives. In a worst case scenario, they could turn the process against us as a means to get rid of the intelligentsia or the remaining aristocracy.

Further, I am somewhat sceptical about the return of the ruling class. I can quite quickly name several recent countries and societies that have had the supposed ruling class return, complete with benign dictator, only to find that the dictator wasn't so benign after all.

I agree, mass rule via democracy has demonstrably failed, but, I'm far from convinced that the restoration of the ruling class will solve all our societal ills.

ML   Frederick, you may be right that a restoration to the natural ruling class may not do a better job than what the masses have achieved. But I put it to you we would be hard pressed to do a worse job.

FR   [Looks down at his watch.] The tribunal is due to reconvene in less than two hours' time, so we do need to reach agreement on this issue reasonably quickly. I'll put it to the vote. As chairman, I'll abstain – unless there is a tie, in which case I will cast a vote against using Ivan Henry as our test case. So, please think very carefully before you cast your vote.

Okay, all those in favour of using Mr Ivan Henry as our test case – and thereby decide in favour of the GPA and Ms Small in the case before us?

SJPB I vote we go ahead and use him as our test case – that will teach him for making snide remarks about my nose.

ALB   I vote against using him as our test case.

SM   I say we go ahead with our plan – and use him as our test case.

ML   You know my views – I vote we go ahead with the plan.

CB   I'm against it – he put up a far too strong and credible defence to be so easily dismissed due to other objectives that we may have.

ML   Well, Lord Denman, it's now effectively up to you to decide – as if we tie, due to Frederick's position, all the work we've done to get to this point will be for nothing, and it will be at least another generation before we are in a similar position to implement these much needed societal reforms.

LTD   Yes I do see that. Wasn't it silly for me not to vote earlier so I could have avoided being in this position where, based on my next words, the course of history will change? Hardly an honour I was seeking.

To be quite frank, I see and appreciate both sides of the argument and both bear strong moral questions and judgments, and I'm not convinced that one is a stronger moral position than the other. Therefore, I am going to abstain from voting, which I realise effectively brings a victory to the

'Yes' vote. But, the yes vote was won on aggregate – not due solely to my abstaining.

FR   As you are aware, my preference is not in accord with the outcome of this vote, but now that we've voted and reached a decision, all of us are to support it and demonstrate solidarity when and if discussing the issue with any of the other members of the Club – or in any other forum. Do you all agree?

All those present affirm their agreement to solidarity of the group decision.

ML   Thank you, gentlemen. Let's get to work!

ALB   Lord Denman, is there any chance that you could get me a ticket for the third test? It's been some time since I last saw a game at Headingley and I think it is high time I went to show my support for the team.

LTD   Of course, my dear chap. I'm taking a few chums up next Saturday, so you are very welcome to join us in my box.

As ALB and Max discuss logistical aspects of getting to the game the camera slowly fades out on the scene – with all the Country Club members slowly getting up, chatting and leaving the room.

Insert Scene – 38

There is no doubt that in our headlong rush to educate everybody, we are lowering our standards … destroying our ancient edifices to make ready the ground upon which the barbarian nomads of the future will encamp in their mechanised caravans

Christianity and Culture *by TS Eliot.*

Scene 65 – An impromptu meeting on the Thames

2:30pm, Wednesday, 29 May 2013

Setting: On the banks of the Thames

The scene opens with the Mayflower pub coming into view – situated on the South Bank of the Thames (but being shot from the north bank) with river cruise ferry passing and momentarily breaking the line of sight. The ferry has a vaccination advertisement/announcement on its side:

> *Avian Flu vaccination – it is compulsory.*
> *Get vaccinated – or be fined or die – whatever comes first.*
> *UK death toll remains lowest in Europe. Keep it that way.*

JR   The 'whys' of the world are never obvious. Do you know there is no private enterprise outside of the USA that is supplied with stamps by the US Postal Service for resale? That is, no place anywhere in the world ... except that pub over there.

Why is that? Why is there a total exclusion on all foreign agencies selling US stamps – with the sole exception of that insignificant pub on the Thames? Any ideas?

SS   Jon, I've actually got a few other things on my mind that are probably going to prevent me from taking up a keen interest in the US Postal Service at the moment. So what's your point?

JR   Without history, there is nothing particularly special about that pub. Without its historical context, it's just a pub – like all the other undistinguished pubs scattered throughout London.

What distinguishes that pub is its connection with the past, its history. See that jetty, just in front of it, that's where Captain Christopher Jones used to moor his ship. Funnily enough that ship was also called the *Mayflower*. It is from that very jetty, in 1620 that 102 pilgrims set off to the new world, calling first at Southampton and then Plymouth before heading across the Atlantic to settle in America.

As we all now know, those poor pilgrims suffered terribly once they arrived in New England. Within four months of arriving, over half of them had died from scurvy, pneumonia or tuberculosis. But, in 1621, Captain Jones returned to England and he again moored his ship at that very jetty. Despite their terrible hardships, none of the pilgrims returned with him. That took strength, courage and commitment. If the pilgrims didn't have those special qualities, America as we know it today wouldn't exist.

So, due to it special historical connection with America, that pub has been granted special dispensation by the US Postal Service to sell US stamps.

SS   Thank you for the history lesson – but knowing you, I feel that an analogy is to follow, so let's have it so we can get it out of the way.

JR   If it wasn't for its history there would be nothing special about that pub. But, because of its history, it occupies a very unique position in the world – you could call it a trivial position, but unique and special nevertheless.

Like that pub, without history, we are nothing, or at least nothing particularly special. But unlike that pub, which is only 500 or so years old, our personal history is much, much older. Our history started four billion years ago. Going back all those billions of years, a single inorganic molecule did an extraordinary thing – it split in two, making a replica of itself. The replication was so perfect it meant that each of the two new molecules could also split and replicate themselves again – and again, and again.

That act, the molecule splitting itself was not, of course, life. But without that extraordinary act, without that molecule splitting in two, neither you, me nor that pub would exist. Since that initial act of molecular self-replication four billion years ago, it has taken an unbroken chain of billions of generations of parent, child, parent, child for that simple molecule to slowly evolve, generation after generation, to allow you and me to come into existence. Your history can be directly traced back to that first self-replicating molecule – as indeed all of our personal histories can be.

SS   And your point is?

JR   The point is, we only came into existence due to the pressure of natural selection. In every species, in every generation, only the 'fit' survived.

The fit paired with the fit to have even fitter children. The two drivers of evolution were born – firstly, having to be fit to survive the environment and predators; and secondly, appearing sufficiently fit and attractive to attract a partner to have offspring. These two evolutionary drivers are what got us here today.

It is these same two drivers that allowed the fittest of the pilgrims to survive the harshness of New England and to found and populate America.

SS   Meaning [in a somewhat sour voice].

JR   We're ceasing to evolve.

SS   Sorry?

JR   The environment in which the process of natural selection occurs has been replaced by an artificial manmade environment – in which the same survival values are not tested.

SS   So?

JR   Humanity's continued existence depends on becoming stronger, smarter and most of all, more adaptive to the changing environment. The applauded advances we, as a society have made, to protect and help the disadvantaged, has not come without a cost to humanity.

One of the more notable costs, not to just humanity, but to the world as a whole, has been the population explosion with all the human hallmarks it brings with it – deforestation, water pollution, land pollution, the hole in the ozone layer, the speeding up of the greenhouse effect, the rise in the sea level, the accelerating rate of species extinction, the creation of new super bugs and diseases.

However, notwithstanding the damage we've done to our mother Earth, there is still hope that we can resolve these problems. The hope lies in human ingenuity, human intelligence, human technology and intelligent global agreements. But, there is a catch.

SS   [Looking despairingly – like just get to the point] Since you want me to ask – what is the catch?

JR   Due to the egalitarian culture and policies we've adopted, both here in the UK and the world at large, the average IQ of our species is declining.

SS   What?

JR   We've created a society, a culture … a situation if you will, where in the human world it is no longer the fittest, the strongest, the smartest that reproduce the most – which would advance our species. The opposite is true. The fertility rates of the dumbest and weakest within our society are by far and away higher than the strongest and smartest. This has led to a situation where the average level of fitness and intelligence in our species, far from evolving and advancing, is actually going into reverse.

SS   That's a pretty righteous, right wing view of the world. Exactly what options are you proposing?

JR   Let's take those poor 102 pilgrims as an example. If they had the ability to do so, I'm sure the fit pilgrims would have cared for and supported the weaker pilgrims, so that they all would have survived.

It's estimated that possibly as much as 15% of Americans can trace their ancestry back to the Mayflower pilgrims. To put this in context, if all the pilgrims were nursed and supported and all managed to have families, then the genetic weaknesses of those weaker pilgrims would be widespread throughout the American population. But, as only the fitter pilgrims survived, those weaker genes are not as widely dispersed through the American population, as otherwise would have been the case. This may indeed account for why Americans were so strong and adventurous in the early years of colonisation.

But now, like here in the UK, America has re-engineered its society so the survival of the fittest rule no longer applies. Instead, dysgenesis has taken root, meaning the least fit, the least intelligent, have the highest survival rate – or at least the highest reproduction rates.

SS   So, you consider Ivan and me inferiors do you? Dumb, unfit and overly fertile.

JR   On the contrary. You and Ivan are both very competent, fit and intelligent people. Society should rejoice that a couple like you are fertile – and at such a young age. You two are the stock that could help to reverse the trend that has set in over the past century – so that once again, our species advances with each generation.

SS   You've confused me now – after your thinly veiled attacks on Ivan – you are now praising him – but your position is still to kill off any of his children.

JR   Yes, it is unfortunate.

SS   What do you mean by unfortunate?

JR   Sandra, you were a little slow in realising that the GPA has its own agenda, which unfortunately is not perfectly aligned with yours. However, I'll give you credit, you've finally realised there is a difference between the GPA's and your own agenda.

      If you wish to terminate your pregnancy, the GPA's agenda will assist you in realising your wish. If you change your mind and wish to see the pregnancy to full term – then you will have to fight the GPA, as they do want to succeed in realising their own agenda.

SS   What, the GPA's agenda is to terminate my pregnancy?

JR   No, not really.

SS   But you just said …

JR   Come on, Sandra, in the office back there you blurted it out – the GPA is following its own agenda, which, while you wish to terminate your pregnancy, will support yours.

      But their agenda is to introduce the necessary legal framework so that it can reverse the downward trend of human intelligence and the general level of unfitness, or survival value of our human race.

SS   But, you just said that Ivan and I were fit and …

JR   That's my opinion, and I guess it is the position of everyone else who personally know you and Ivan – particularly after Ivan's impressive performance at the hearing earlier today.

      But, to those who do not know you, and more specifically Ivan, then this makes a perfect test case. A wife wishes to terminate her unwanted pregnancy as the foetus is deformed. But the bastard deformed husband wants her to have the deformed child, presumably just to keep him company or to spite his estranged wife. With such a stark case, the GPA could reasonably expect to get widespread media support, as journalists would be unlikely to delve into the long-term implications of such a ruling.

By assisting you in winning this case, the GPA succeeds in establishing the necessary common law to revoke the paternal rights of fathers and to encourage the termination of any pregnancy where the unborn child is determined to fall outside the three standard deviation threshold. This pretty much covers anyone the GPA desires to get rid of, as in one way or another, each and every one of us falls outside the three standard deviation threshold. As Ivan correctly observed, one of the tribunal judges has a big nose; that may well be enough to invoke the rule and have all his unborn kids that exhibit signs of rhinocerical aborted.

SS   So, what are you saying?

JR   When we first met, and again when we first met at our offices at the Gherkin, I repeatedly asked you if you were absolutely sure you wanted to go ahead and ask the GPA to support you in this hearing. Because it was always going to be a one-way trip. Once asked, the GPA was not going to stop helping you to realise your original objective, even if you have a change of heart and decided to keep the child.

SS   That's absurd. I can terminate my legal counsel any time I like.

JR   Indeed you can. But, the course of action you set in place by asking the GPA to assist you in your defence will not stop simply by changing your counsel. Ivan brought this case to the Ethics Ruling Committee to make a ruling as to whether or not achondroplasia falls outside the three standard deviation threshold. Regardless of your intent in regards to your pregnancy, the Ethics Ruling Committee has to proceed with the hearing and must make a ruling on achondroplasia.

Therefore, regardless of whether you were to sack us or change your mind on the issue of termination, the GPA is within its rights to initiate parallel legal proceedings and make representations in its own right to the Ethics Ruling Committee that achondroplasia falls outside the threshold.

Unfortunately for you, this case is far too important for the GPA to drop. If you cease your defence, or agree to Ivan's demands, or sack the GPA as your counsel, the GPA will take up the case independently of yourself and make its own representations to the Ethics Ruling Committee.

SS   Sorry, what are you saying?

JR   Sandra, yes, the GPA will keep fighting your case – regardless of whether or not you want them to.

SS   So, if I now decide to have my child, but the GPA wins the case in its own right, what happens then?

JR   That's why I kept asking you whether you were really, really sure you wanted to go ahead with this line of action, and whether anything would change your mind. And you kept assuring me that your decision was final and nothing on Earth would stop you from fighting for your rights to choose. On this basis you insisted that you wanted the GPA's support in fighting your case.

SS   You mean you would force me to abort my pregnancy against my wish?

JR   No, we would not force you, we would merely encourage you to terminate the pregnancy …

What a coincidence, there's Ivan and his legal team. And, oh my, it looks like his legal team has expanded to pick up Bill. This is a new twist in the case, isn't it?

The camera picks up Ivan and his team walking in a close-knit group, with Bill towering above them in the middle – and as always being the centre of attention, with him telling some riveting amusing story, oblivious to the presence of Sandra and Jon.

The camera pans back to Sandra, who is now looking at Ivan and his team. She realises that at any second Ivan and Bill will look up and see her. A deep sense of anguish and anxiety rolls down her face. Her recent questioning and self-doubt pierces a hole through the dyke holding back her suppressed emotions. Through this small hole, Sandra's concealed feelings for Ivan start to seep through into her consciousness. The seepage turns to a trickle as the sense of betrayal engulfs her, not just by Jon, not just by the GPA, but by the whole judicial system. The sense of betrayal and her feelings mix together to form a toxic cocktail of emotional guilt – as she now senses that it was she who betrayed Ivan, and it was she who betrayed herself. As the guilt floods her from within, the futility of the position that she now finds she is unable to stop the events that she put in motion, starting to crush her from without. The overwhelming tide of negative emotions strips her of any sense of demeanour – her shoulders slump, her head sinks, her face crumbles as her upper lip starts to quiver, her body sulks. She turns away, so that when Ivan looks up he will be spared the sight of her tortured face. She sinks her head into her hands and starts to sob, but after a moment, her arms drop down to hold her stomach as the emotional weight she's carrying bends her over double.

Bill looks up and sees Jon – then Sandra. He's taken aback with the incongruence of the body language between Jon and Sandra. There is Jon, [who is unaware that Sandra has just had an emotional collapse] giving a half-friendly wave, and yet a few paces behind him … is someone, that must be Sandra. But it can't be – as Sandra is a proud upright woman, whereas the woman in view, is a debilitated wreck. But, if it's not Sandra, then who is it?

Bill gives a not-so-convincing wave back to Jon as he is still perplexed whether or not it is Sandra behind him. And if it is her, what has Jon done to her?

BH   [In a low voice.] Ivan, there's Jon and I think it may be Sandra with him [pointing towards them].

IH   What? Where?

Ivan turns to the direction that Bill is pointing. Ivan, too, looks for a moment, then a disturbed frown protrudes from his forehead as his eyes retreat deep into their sockets.

IH   What's going on, what's he done to her?

BH   I've no idea – but it doesn't look a pretty sight!

IH   Sandra, are you okay?

As Ivan shouts, he starts to first walk, then run towards Sandra. Sandra hears Ivan, and then hears his running towards her. The crushing emotions she's experiencing intensifies with hearing Ivan's endearing words, and his rush to help her. Her emotional stress presses itself against her stomach, forcing bile up her throat into her month. The acidic bile burns her throat and brings with it a putrid acerbic taste to her mouth. She tries to swallow, but the vileness of the bile can't be overcome. She tries again and swallows the bile. She immediately realises her mistake, as her stomach rejects the bile and forces it back up to her mouth – but this time it includes the full garrison of her digestive fluids, complete with the partially digested. She opens her mouth and vomits violently over the paving – the vomit splatters and bounces off the payment and covers her shoes, ankles and calves.

The sound of vomiting catches Jon by surprise. He turns around to see Sandra bent over double, still vomiting her heart out with the spew going everywhere. He calls to her:

JR   Sandra, are you okay? [He starts walking towards her.]

Ivan, now runs to Sandra to offer her comfort and support. As he approaches, Sandra heaves up again and as she does so, she hears Ivan's footsteps and turns her head in his direction. A new bout of projectile spew gushes out of her mouth and runs down the pavement towards Ivan.

Ivan, seeing Sandra's distress – keeps his focus firmly on her tormented eyes and as he rushes towards her, he fails to fully appreciate the circumstances he is rapidly approaching. Three metres before he reaches Sandra, the torrent of vomit reaches Ivan. His eyes follows her as she pauses from her disgorging, and with her eyes shut, she stands up right to fill her lungs with much needed air. He steps into the oncoming stream, his leather-soled shoe fails to make adequate traction on the paving beneath the stream, his foot gives way. He falls over backwards and slides upstream through the deluge of vomit, slowly coming to a rest just in front of Sandra. Sandra, unaware of Ivan's recent horizontal arrival, feels the onset of another contraction, bends over and spews over his head.

As the spew ejects, Sandra opens her eyes to witness the horrified look of Ivan as he gets dosed with her spew.

IH   Fuck!

The camera pans back to Bill, Jon, Andy and Rob, who have all just witnessed the horror of the events and are standing motionless, save the shaking of their heads from side to side in disbelief. Rob and Andy are standing behind Bill, with their eyes and mouths open in a reflex reaction to their revulsion of the scene.

Sandra drops down on her knees next to Ivan, without a word, slowly and, with immense composure, moves her face slowly towards Ivan's soiled and very anxious face. The two sets of eyes lock. Sandra, now in total emotional charge of the encounter, ever so slowly moves closer and closer to Ivan's ever increasingly startled face. There could not be a more unattractive and repulsive couple than these two, both soiled, anxious, weary and exhausted, but somehow emotionally charged. Yet, paradoxically, this is the most beautiful and moving scene ever encountered. As Sandra steadily moves closer to Ivan, inner strength starts warming Sandra from the core, her strength brings with it 'her'. Her real feelings, her real beliefs, her real love returns to her in force. Her assuredness transforms her in to a figure of strength – which scares Ivan further, making him cower away in fear. However, as Sandra steadily moves closer and closer to Ivan, her strength is revealed in compassion, respect and love. She moves closer until she rests her forehead on his and caresses his forehead with hers in a way that reveals the tenderest of feelings. She reaches and embraces his shoulders, she then whispers with utter conviction.

SS Ivan, we're going to have a baby.

Ivan reaches up and embraces her as a child embraces a mother, he rests his head on her shoulder and slowly starts to weep.

Insert Scene – 39

The modern world has not room for sexual heroines, woman must stop flaunting her sexuality, and if she does not, men must remember that genetic engineering allows them to determine the sex of children. If woman is too much for us, we'll reduce her to a minority.

The World Set Free *by HG Wells*

Scene 66 – Poor hygiene at the hearing

4:30pm, Wednesday, 29 May 2013

Setting: The GPA Ethics Ruling Committee hearing room

The scene opens on the Chairman of the Ethics Ruling Committee (Lord Thomas Denman), sitting at the bench, where he is in light conversation with Sir John Poo Beresford sitting to his right. He breaks the conversation, looks up at the court room (towards the camera) and does a brief scan, assuring himself that all the key players are in attendance.

He suddenly stops his scan and a quizzical expression erupts from within his face as he stares at something in the courtroom (out of view of the camera). His expression changes from quizzical to disbelief, as it changes, the horror of what he's seen becomes apparent through his body language as he leans back into his chair and crosses his arms in front of him.

The camera slowly zooms closer to his face, where it becomes visible that he has started to smell something unpleasant – as he keeps slightly lifting his head and makes just audible sniffs, resulting in an expression of revulsion.

LTD   Mr Henry, there is a dress and hygiene code that apply to persons attending this hearing, are you familiar with them?

IH   No, Your Honour, I cannot say that I have read the dress and hygiene code for Ethics Ruling Committee hearings.

LTD   Well, without going into detail – the dress and hygiene code, essentially, requires persons to attire themselves to, say, the same standards, as you would observe when you attend church or, say, a Michelin-star restaurant.

IH   Yes, Your Honour, I guessed it would have been similar standards to restaurants.

LTD   Then what, may I ask, happened? And why have you chosen to attend this hearing in the state you are in?

IH   Well, Your Honour, I …

AW   His wife hurled all over him! It was an awesome sight.

IH   No, no, it was just a wee accident …

LTD   Ms Small, did you vomit over Mr Henry?

IH   No, Your Honour, it was my pet dog, I had to go home to feed him, and he was sick …

LTD   Mr Henry, that is an unlikely story, as if this had happened at your home, then I believe you would have taken the trouble to change your clothes. Now, Ms Small, did you vomit over Mr Henry?

SS   Yes, Your Honour, I did vomit over him.

LTD   Well, in that case, I do not believe it to be fair to ban Mr Henry from these proceedings, when it is probable that his basic hygiene violation was, at least in part, caused by the other party to the hearing. I therefore adjourn this hearing until 9:00 tomorrow morning.

      And could I ask all parties and members of the gallery to observe the hearing's dress and hygiene code and please refrain from any acts that could place others in jeopardy of violating these codes.

IH   But, Your Honour we do not have time to wait another day, this is an urgent case.

LTD   Indeed, it is, and it is also a very important case. Therefore, we all need a clear head to consider the many ramifications of the ruling – and quite frankly, the stench currently in this room muddles rather than clears the head.

      I hereby declare this hearing adjourned until 9:00 tomorrow morning. Goodbye.

Scene 67 – The embrace of Ivan and Sandra

6:00pm, Wednesday, 29 May 2013

Setting: Ivan and Sandra's apartment

The scene opens in Ivan's/Sandra's apartment, with Ivan walking out of the bathroom with a bath towel wrapped around his waist, with another in his hands vigorously drying his hair.

Throughout the scene the noise of trains can be heard approaching and passing.

IH   If it takes being vomited on, humiliated in front of my friends and counsel, then being kicked out of court just to speak to you – then I'd do it any day all day.

SS   Henry, I'm so sorry.

IH   It's okay, after a quick shower, I don't smell that bad.

SS   I'm not referring to the vomit …

IH   What, so you're not sorry you spewed all over me?

SS   If it takes me spewing over you just so that we can talk, then no I'm not sorry.

IH   Huh?

SS   I'm sorry that things got so bad and that it took such a drastic chain of events for us to start talking again.

IH   Sandra, I know I have a bit of the 'little man' syndrome and I can be uncompromising – just to prove that I'm not a push over. I know I have not acted, behaved – dealt with the situation we're both in – at all well. Rather than trying to speak to you, to try and understand you, to help you in your time of need, I have been a monster, a bully. I have done all I can, all the law can, to try and enforce my feelings, my views, my opinions, my rights, my will on you.

I now realise, that while I do have rights – they're not absolute. There are two of us in this marriage, and I should have, I need to, learn to think and act in a manner that is right and true for both of us – not just what I think is right for either me or what I think is right for us.

I don't know where or how to start to apologise.

SS   Henry, you do not have to apologise for doing what you believed in, for doing what you believed what was right. That is one of the most enduring and respected traits of your character.

What you can apologise about, is the way you treated me in the process of pursuing what you believed was right. And, after you apologise for the way you treated me, then I will apologise for the horrendous manner in which I treated you – and the way I completely ignored your feelings and your rights in regards to both our relationship, and to our unborn son.

IH   [A long pause passes as Ivan composes himself and then looks up to Sandra.] Sandra, please forgive me – I've been such an arsehole, such a fucking arsehole.

SS   Ivan, only God can forgive, all I want is an apology.

IH   Sandra, I am truly very, very sorry. Please take me back.

SS   I accept your apology. Now, please accept my apology for being such a bitch?

IH   Sandra, apology fully accepted.

SS   Will you have me back?

IH   [Ivan looks up to Sandra and opens his arms] Who loves you, babe?

Sandra falls to her knees and embraces Ivan. Ivan starts to weep as he rests his head on her shoulders and embraces her. Sandra holds firm for a few seconds – then the tears start to trickle down her face, which then turns into sobbing. The scene fades out with both of them crying in each other's arms.

As they embrace, the lights of a mainline train appear through their lounge room window – with the sound of the train following.

Insert Scene – 40

Vicious, helpless and pauper masses have appeared, spreading as the railway systems have spread, and representing an integral part of the process of industrialisation, like the waste product of a healthy organism. These great useless masses of people are the People of the Abyss.

The nation that most resolutely picks over, educates, sterilises, exports, or poisons its People of the Abyss will be the most prosperous of nations.

Anticipations *by HG Wells*

Scene 68 – The ruling of the ruling committee

9:00am, Thursday, 30 May 2013

Setting: The GPA Ethics Ruling Committee hearing room

This is a close repeat of the last hearing room scene. The scene opens on the Chairman of the Ethics Ruling Committee (Lord Thomas Denman) sitting at the bench, where he is in light conversation with the committee member to his left (Sir David Griffiths). He breaks the conversation, looks up at the hearing room (towards the camera) and does a brief scan to assure himself that all the key players are in attendance.

As he scans, he suddenly stops and a quizzical expression erupts from within his face as he stares at something in the hearing room (out of view of the camera). His expression changes from quizzical to disbelief. As it changes, the absurdness of what he's seen becomes apparent through his body language as he leans forward, raises his glasses, and stares at something in the hearing room.

The camera slowly zooms closer to his face, where it becomes visible that he is both confused and anxious. He briefly looks down and just visibly shakes his head before lifting his head again in preparation to speak.

LTD   Ms Small, it is not only customary, but the protocol has been enshrined in UK court proceedings, which this hearing follows, for the defendant to sit on the left side of the courtroom with their counsel, while the plaintiff sits on the right side of the courtroom with their counsel.

       Thus, could I ask you to observe this protocol and join your counsel on the left side of this tribunal hearing?

SS   I'd prefer not to.

LTD   And, may I inquire as to reason for your conscious breach of protocol?

SS   I am not familiar enough with the hearing's protocol to know when I'm meant to inform you that I have changed my mind – and I am now siding with my husband. And, as my own counsel chose not to instruct me on such matters, I guess this is the time to inform you of my decision.

LTD   Can I ask you what you mean by 'I am now siding with my husband', and never mind with the hearing's protocol just for the moment?

SS   I no longer wish to terminate my pregnancy, so now both the plaintiff and defendant agree to go full term and have the child. As we both have agreed to go ahead and have the baby, then, I wish – we both wish – for this legal action to cease and for everyone to go home and just let us get on with our lives.

Thomas leans forward in his chair, looks down at the bench and shakes his head in recognition of the unbelievable legal minefield that Sandra has just thrown the hearing into.

LTD   Mrs Small, as I'm sure you are fully aware, this hearing of the GPA's Ethics Ruling Committee was effectively summonsed by your husband to make a ruling as to whether or not your unborn child falls outside the three standard deviation threshold. For better or worse, whether fair or unfair, the hearing procedures dictate that once the Ethics Ruling Committee has commenced a hearing, it shall continue until such time as a ruling is made.

       Therefore, regardless of your current or future state of mind and irrespective of whether or not you and your husband have reconciled your differences, this hearing will continue and will make a ruling on the case put before it.

SS   What? Both my husband and I have decided to have our child, and you are telling me that it is up to this hearing to rule whether we can or can't have our child?

LTD   Your husband placed an injunction on you which prohibits you from terminating your pregnancy until this committee makes a ruling as to whether your unborn child's genetic makeup falls outside the three standard deviation threshold.

       Your husband argues that the genetic condition of your unborn child is not outside of the three standard deviation threshold – and therefore, he has his full statute and common law paternal rights over the unborn child.

       However, if this hearing rules that the genetic condition will result in the child falling outside the threshold, then the GPA will then be within its rights to revoke the paternal rights of the father and to encourage you, the mother, to terminate your pregnancy.

SS   You cannot make me terminate my pregnancy.

LTD   Ms Small, you are absolutely correct. This hearing will only make a ruling as to whether or not the embryo falls outside the defined limits of the 'human norm'. Should this hearing rule that the embryo falls outside of the three standard deviation threshold, it will be up to the GPA to revoke your husband's paternity rights and encourage you to terminate your pregnancy. It should be borne in mind that the GPA has very little discretion over such decisions – as much of the process and rules are embodied in legislative mandates.

SS   They can encourage me all they like, but I am still having my baby. I mean, what can they do to stop me from having my baby?

LTD   Well, the legislation is quite clear on this matter. Encouragement involves:

> *The removal of all state support and aid for the entire life of the unborn and born child from the moment of diagnosis through to the death of the child, including: pre-natal care; birth; post-natal care; medical support; education and training; social benefits and social welfare; state-funded housing for both parents and the child and funeral and burial costs of the child*

> *Notwithstanding that the father had his paternal rights revoked, the father and mother of the child shall be jointly responsible for all costs associated with the child for the full life of the child, including but not limited to any costs cited above.*

> *For the full duration of the life of the child, should the state incur any costs whatsoever in relation to the child, the state shall take action against either or both parents to fully recover these costs. The recovery of costs shall include the sale or liquidation of any asset, including: bank accounts, shares, cars, houses (both primary and secondary), chattels, pension or any other current or future asset whatsoever.*

IH   That's outrageous.

LTD   Mr Henry, please bear in mind that it was you who petitioned this hearing into making a ruling over your unborn child. And, considering that you are a research officer with the GPA itself, you should be in a better position than most to understand the legislative framework that defines and directs the GPA's actions and remit.

Now, the situation in this hearing has become considerably more awkward for all concerned.

However, notwithstanding the awkwardness that we now find ourselves in, the Ethics Ruling Committee are nevertheless compelled to make a ruling on this case.

SS   [Sandra stands up.] Sorry, I object to this. Before I reconsidered my position, the GPA repeatedly assured me that they were supporting my decision on this issue, that they were there to defend my rights as an independent woman, to support my right to choose the course of action that was right for me.

Now that I've taken the liberty to change my mind on this matter, they no longer wish to support 'my right to choose'. In fact, they, more so than Ivan ever did, wish to remove my right to make that decision, and for the GPA to assume the right to make such a decision for me.

This case was never about me, about Ivan, nor about our unborn child. The case was and is about the government taking rights away from prospective parents, so that the government can decide who is worthy of life and who isn't.

If the GPA is successful at this hearing, then both the 'pro-choice' and 'right to life' camps will lose – as parents will not have a choice and there will be no fundamental right to life.

LTD   I understand that you are upset with the position that you now find yourself in. Given the juncture of the proceeding we have arrived at, I'll take this opportunity to point out that this is almost entirely of your husband's and your own making.

Mr Henry brought the case to the Ethics Ruling Committee to make a ruling and you sought the GPA's assistance in defending yourself against the injunction placed on you by your husband. You work for a reputable law firm that specialises in reproductive, genetic and embryonic law and your husband works for the GPA itself. As such you two were in a far better position than nearly anyone else in society to have foreseen the consequences of your actions. Now, notwithstanding your change of heart, the hearing must proceed in accordance with the original position put forward by your husband. [Long pause.] Have I made myself clear – that this committee hearing will proceed and make a ruling as to whether your unborn child falls outside the three standard deviation threshold?

Lord Thomas Denman looks sternly at Sandra for a response.

SS   I don't have any choice or say in the matter, do I?

LTD   If your statement is directed at this hearing's proceedings, then no. The hearing's proceeding have been defined by statute and, as such, neither you, Mr Henry, the GPA nor I for that matter, can change the proceedings. This committee shall make a ruling.

        [Lord Thomas Denman now looks at Ivan] Mr Henry, do you have any further questions over this hearing's proceedings?

IH   No, I fully understand that you've got me over a barrel.

LTD   Well, Mr Henry, you were the one that placed the barrel that you now find yourself over. I'll conclude from your response that you do not have any further questions in regards to the proceedings.

        Now that we have the discussion of proceedings behind us, let us turn to the matter for which this committee was convened. We, the Ethics Ruling Committee, have now heard all arguments from both the plaintiff and co-defendants – and no more have been submitted for this hearing to consider.

        As such, the proceedings are now at a stage where the members of the GPA Ethics Ruling Committee presiding over this hearing will read out the ruling.

BH   [Steps up] Your Honour, given the changed dynamics of this case, I impress upon you to re- open the hearing to arguments by both parties on the merits of their respective positions.

        Certainly, this hearing has not previously heard the case alluded to by Ms Small on 'remove the right of choice' from parents, which you must agree has considerable social consequences.

LTD   My learned King's Counsellor, of course the ruling will have significant social consequences. But we are not here to consider the social consequences, as such matters are embedded in other acts of Parliament and common law, and are therefore outside the jurisdiction of this hearing.

This hearing is here to make a ruling as to whether or not those carrying the achondroplasia genetic condition fall outside the three standard deviation threshold from the human norm. This hearing does not have the power or remit to dictate to any other person, party or agency as to what happens once an embryo or foetus has been ruled as falling outside of the three standard deviation threshold. That is the preserve of the GPA and its enabling legislations and associated regulations.

Therefore, I do not see how discussing the social consequence of this hearing's ruling will bring to light any discourse relevant to the ruling to be made. King's Counsellor Horowitz, do you have anything else to add?

BH   No, Your Honour.

LTD   Thank you.

Now, can I ask you to please oblige me by stating under what authority you are at this hearing – and who gave you permission to address the bench?

BH   My apologies for my lapse in protocol. I am Mr Henry's appointed legal counsel.

LTD   Hmmmm. Mr Henry, what is the meaning of this – and why have you not had the sense or courtesy to inform the committee members of your change in legal counsel?

IH   Your Honour, I reflected on your advice, that you would no more recommend that I conduct my own brain surgery than represent myself at this hearing. Upon consideration, I asked King's Counsellor Horowitz to represent me.

I would have informed you a little earlier this morning – but before I had the opportunity, you started asking questions of my wife. Since then, there was never a 'right moment' to halt the proceeding in order to duly inform you that I had changed my legal counsel.

LTD   This is highly unconventional and is a clear breach of the Ethics Ruling Committee hearing protocol. However, in order to expedite this case, I am prepared to overlook this breach of protocol and continue unabated.

Now, unless I hear an objection from any of the parties, I shall proceed and read the Ruling. [Long pause]

So, are there any objections?

Looks at each party in turn, and they all shake their head and mutter 'No your Honour'.

LTD   Very well then – the ruling.

There is a long pause while the chairman consults with the other two members, Sir John Poo Beresford and Sir David Griffiths, and shuffles his papers about.

LTD   This is the first case to come to the GPA Ethics Ruling Committee which tests the 'three standard deviation from the human norm' regulatory definition. The consequence of the ruling made by this hearing will be far reaching for many, many people, not only in our generation but for generations to come. This ruling will set a precedent, not only for those suffering from the effects of the achondroplasia genetic condition, but all forms of dwarfism, and all forms of genetic disease that manifest with an abnormality that can be objectively measured and the genes responsible conclusively identified.

IH   [The camera crosses to Ivan's face – he looks in horror.] You fucking Nazi bastard, you've ruled against me! You fucking pricks.

SDG   Mr Henry, please keep you composure, or you will charged with contempt of court, then barred from this hearing.

IH   No need to make any such fucking order, I'm not going to stay around and listen to Hitler pass a ruling on the Jews. Do you have any idea what you've done – why? I hope you all rot in hell, I'm out of here.

SJPB   Sirs, the ruling is yet to be read out – so I implore you to sit, be quiet and listen. Then, you can form an opinion on the outcome of the hearing.

IH   I don't have to hear the words to know that you have ruled against me, against my wife and against our son. You're just like the Spanish, they didn't consider the Aztecs and Mayan human – so, they wiped every last one out during the 30 year conquest of South America. Not one exists today, because like you, the Spanish didn't consider them human, so they committed total genocide.

Your actions, your words, your ruling here today puts you in good company with the likes of Torquemada, Prince Vlad Dracula, Francisco Pizarro and Josef Stalin – not to mention Hitler. Tonight I will sleep with a clear conscience. You will not, not tonight, not tomorrow night, not any night, not ever.

I hope you're all proud of yourselves.

With this Ivan gets up and storms out and, with the exception of Bill Horowitz, all his entourage join him and leave the hearing room.

LTD   Irrespective of whether or not all parties involved in this hearing are present to hear the ruling, the ruling will nevertheless be read and it will be binding on all parties – present or not. Now, the ruling. Irrespective of the consequences of the ruling, irrespective of those that may be impacted by the ruling, both in our generation and in generations to come, this hearing's remit is solely to hear the evidence for and against why those suffering from the physical manifestation of the genetic disorder achondroplasia, are, or are not, three standard deviations from the human norm – and to make a ruling accordingly.

Clearly, in making the ruling, the members of the GPA Ethics Ruling Committee took into account the position put forward by Mr Henry that being 'human' cannot be measured merely by its physical attributes, but rather the value and contribution that each of us makes to society.

However, the argument put forward by Mr Henry is counterintuitive to the tenet of the legislation. By writing the legislation in such a way as defining a means to 'measure', the legislators obvious intent was for the Ethics Ruling Committee to determine 'what needs to be measured'. If this hearing accepts Mr Henry's argument, then it means the legislative passage is a nonsense, i.e. trying to measure the unmeasurable.

Therefore, this hearing accepts that the legislator's intent was for making rulings based on the objective measurement of human attributes. In the current hearing, we have been asked to make a ruling on physical attributes, and deviations from, the normal human. Future hearings hold the possibility of making rulings based on non-physical conditions, which can still be objectively measured.

In the current case, we also took into consideration the possibility of a condition being corrected through medical means, whether drugs, surgery or gene therapy. Such considerations rule out the intuitively absurd instances, like the one Mr Henry cited, that those with big noses could be ruled as being three standard deviations from the human norm. Such conditions could, if so desired, be easily corrected through surgical measures. Therefore this hearing sees no need to include such conditions as being included in the current ruling.

This leaves us with the genetic condition in question, namely achondroplasia. In arriving at the ruling of this condition, the following aspects of the condition were considered:

- the physical manifestation of this condition are clearly and undeniably visible and measurable;
- by and large those with the condition would rather not have the condition;
- the vast majority of people without the condition would not voluntarily contract the condition, if such a choice were available;
- the vast majority of the population view the condition as a significant disadvantage to those who have it, and would, if they could, take steps to prevent their children contracting the condition;
- the condition, aside from a narrow range of theatrical parts, bestows no advantage to the carriers of the condition – on the contrary, the condition can be concluded as being disadvantageous, given the high rate of unemployment of those with the condition;
- the condition increases this risk of medical and health complications to the carriers of the condition;
- however, not all ailments associated with the condition can be medically corrected;
- the genetic cause of the condition can be precisely, accurately and conclusively identified;
- physical manifestation of the condition can be accurately predicted by embryonic genetic tests;
- the physical manifestation of the condition can be accurately and objectively measured;
- the physical manifestation of the condition results in the carriers being shorter than the normal human, as defined by the average height of the population, by a magnitude in excess of three standard deviations.

Given the above attributes of the achondroplasia genetic disorder, this hearing hereby makes the ruling in favour of the defendant, namely in favour of, at least originally, Ms Small.

Therefore, given the GPA Act, the impact of this ruling is as follows:

- Mr Henry's paternal rights, to prevent the termination of the pregnancy, are revoked;
- Ms Small has the right to terminate the pregnancy;
- the state, via the GPA, will encourage Ms Small to terminate the pregnancy, which includes the withdrawal of all state aid and funding relating to the life and upbringing of the child – up to and including the death and burial of any such child.

BH [The camera pans onto Bill who sits silently in his chair, slowly shaking his head and muttering] No, no – do you know what you have done?

He slowly adjusts his papers, gets up from his chair, composes himself – and then walks over to the defence counsellors.

BH Pat, Jon, Laurie – that was a good win for you, fully undeserved, but nevertheless a good win for the state. However, before you get too excited, and try to encourage the termination of the pregnancy, I've already placed an injunction on you and Ms Small to refrain from any such action until an appeal is heard at the High Court.

JR Bill, thanks for your congratulations – given so generously. But, if the grounds of the appeal are based on due process, then I'm afraid your team is in for another defeat, as I've had Tess on the case, and believe me, every 'i' has been dotted and every 't' has been crossed.

BH No, it's nothing petty like that. The hearing just announced is in violation of Article 16 of the Universal Declaration of Human Rights – which grants the right to found a family to all citizens. And, Article 6 – which states that everyone has the right to recognition everywhere as a person before the law.

So, you are not treating either Ivan or his unborn child as a person, and you are violating his right to found a family. So, I'll be seeing you in the High Court next Thursday – the sixth of June

He hands Max the injunction papers, then turns and walks away without further comment. The scene fades out on Bill's back leaving the hearing room – with the out-of-focus faces of the defence counsel looking at each other, with an expression of 'Well, I guess we could have expected that'.

Insert Scene – 41

> *Nothing but a eugenic religion can save our civilization.*
> *George Bernard Shaw*

Scene 69 – Bill at home with the dwarfs

11:00am, Sunday, 2 June 2013

Setting: Bill and Cynthia Horowitz's home

The scene opens with the sound of a front doorbell ringing. The visual fades in on Bill carrying Samuel, who is wearing a protective helmet, as he walks to his front door.

BH   Samuel, these are some of my friends. They have come here to talk to Daddy. Is that okay?

SH   Daddy, Daddy, Daddy.

BH   Samuel, Samuel, Samuel – you are a good boy aren't you eh?

SH   I beat Daddy, I beat Daddy, I beat Daddy.

BH   Yes you can, you are a champion table tennis player.

SH   I beat Daddy now, I beat Daddy now.

BH   Soon, I have to talk to my friends – who are just at the door.

SH   [Progressively louder.] I beat Daddy now, I beat Daddy now.

BH   Not now Samuel, I have to speak to my friends.

SH   [Louder still.] I beat Daddy now, I beat Daddy now.

At this point, Bill reached the front door and opens it, letting in Sandra, Ivan, Andy and Rob.

BH   Hi guys, please come in. This is Samuel. And Samuel, these are my friends Sandra, Ivan, Rob and Andy.

SH   [A look of sheer delight explodes on Samuel's face as he looks at the three dwarfs, and starts shouting.] Snow White and her dwarfs, Snow White and her dwarfs.

BH   Now, now Samuel be a good boy and don't call my friends names – they are Sandra, Ivan, Rob and Andy.

SH   [Studies the three dwarfs for a few moments, points to Ivan.] He Grumpy, [then points to Andy] he Dopey, [then points to Rob] he Doc.

BH   Sorry guys, I'll just take Samuel to his play room, then we can start. Please make yourselves at home – there are some drinks and nibbles on the sideboard, so please help yourselves.

Dwarfs [Looking all embarrassed and pissed – but unable to say anything or grumble.] Thanks

Without any more exchange, they sluggishly walk through to the lounge.

BH   [Bill carries Samuel up the corridor.] Samuel, you can play table tennis with Nanny and beat Nanny, is that okay?

SH   I beat Daddy, I beat Daddy.

BH   No, I have to speak to my friends, you beat Nanny – okay?

SH   [As Samuel says this, the scene/voice fade out] I beat Daddy, I beat Daddy.

The scene fades back in with Bill entering the opulently appointed lounge room.

BH   Guys, I am so very sorry for … well, for Samuel's remarks. I wasn't expecting that.

RW   Well, at least he got me right – the intellectual one.

AW   Yes, he got Grumpy here right too [pointing to Ivan].

IH   Well, then he got all three of us all right then, didn't he?

With this, Ivan and Rob break into laughter as Andy takes a second to figure out he's just been insulted. Sandra and Bill both look on awkwardly.

BH   Okay, in that case, it's 'off to work we go'.

On hearing BH's attempt at humour, the three dwarfs all immediately stop laughing, turn and scowl at Bill. This makes Bill incredibly uncomfortable, which is very evident in his body language and facial expression. Upon making Bill so visibly uncomfortable, Rob bursts out 'We got you', and the three dwarfs all burst out laughing. With this, Bill relaxes and gets over his awkward moment.

BH   Okay guys, yes you got me. Now, we do have to get to work.

Bill then walks over to a flip chart, opens it up, where his previous handwritten text is displayed on a flip chart page.

BH   Do any of you know anything about the [he then turns and points to, and reads from, the flip chart]:

- Universal Declaration of Human Rights
- United Nations Resolution 96(I) 'The Crime of Genocide'
- The Nuremberg Trials judgments
- International Covenant on Civil and Political Rights
- European Convention on Human Rights
- International Covenant on Economic, Social and Cultural Rights

RW   Only that at the Nuremberg trials the Nazis were tried for war crimes.

BH   Anything else?

The three dwarfs look at each other – then look at Sandra, then back to Bill.

RW   No, not really.

BH   Sandra?

SS   Well, if I'm picking up your line of reasoning correctly, all six are recognised instruments of international law, of which the UK is a signatory to each of them. Therefore, these international conventions are binding on UK courts.

All six have provisions to either protect the rights of individuals or minority groups from persecution.

BH   Very good, Sandra.I have obviously trained you well. Yes, it is these six international conventions that we are going to use to overturn the hearing's ruling. You three [gesturing towards the three dwarfs] are going to have to learn quickly – as these conventions are going to save you and your families.

Now, I have copies of each here, together with relevant case law. I suggest that you take two each, learn it backwards, then present the relevant legal framework to the rest of us, specifically citing how we can use the international law to win our case. Now, any volunteers or preferences?

RW   I'll take the Universal Declaration of Human Rights and the European Convention on Human Rights.

IH   Okay, I'll take the UN Crime of Genocide and the International Covenant on Civil and Political Rights.

AW   [Talking to Bill.] What are you taking?

BH   Well, I'm going to co-ordinate the case – where I'll get you to brief me on your findings, then I'll direct you towards further research. Also, I have to come up to speed on the High Court legal proceedings to avoid the risk of our case being ruled invalid due to a procedural irregularity. I'd like Sandra to help me in this line of research.

AW   Okay. That's fine with me!

RW   Well, thank God for that. Now Andy, how about volunteering to take on the Nuremberg Trial judgments together with the International Covenant on Economic, Social and Cultural Rights?

AW   And what were they again?

BH   Well, Andy, it looks like you've got a lot of reading to do – here is the reading material that you have to wade through. [At this point Bill picks up a pile of books, journals and photocopies from a coffee table and passes it to Andy.] Your friends tell me that you're an avid reader – so, this will put your skill to the test.

AW   My gracious counsel, though I must confess myself far inferior to the report men have published, and nothing answerable to the honour of our cabal, yet, for that love and duty binds me thereunto, I am content to do whatsoever our counsel shall command me.

BH   Marlowe?

AW   Dr Faustus, act four, scene one.

BH   Great quote. Now here's your reading material so, get cracking. Ivan, this is your material. [Passing Ivan a similar pile of documents.] Rob – and this is your material.

IH   So, what do we do now, I mean what is the game plan?

BH   Good question, and I think it is such an important question that it needs answering over lunch. I don't think anyone can research properly on an empty stomach.

AW   I totally agree – I don't do anything without a decent meal first. I mean, how can you go onto stage and take on the persona of a court jester if your mind is on food? It just doesn't work – even if the court jester is meant to be hungry!

BH   Looks like we got agreement then, so let's go and have lunch. I'll just call the caterers to let them know we're coming.

Ivan and Rob look at each other and say together, 'Caterers?'

Insert Scene – 42

Society has no business to permit degenerates to reproduce their kind … Some day, we will realise that the prime duty, the inescapable duty, of the good citizen of the right type, is to leave his or her blood behind him in the world; and that we have no business to permit the perpetuation of citizens of the wrong type.

President Theodore Roosevelt, 3 Jan 1913

Scene 70 – The Club's sinister strategy

3:00pm, Sunday, 2 June 2013

Setting: Claydon House

The scene fades in with the same gentlemen that last met at Chris Braithwaite's Mansion, all standing in a circle with a glass of white, chilled sherry (evident by the condensation on the Waterford sherry glasses). They are engaged in small chatter regarding the third Ashes test that started the previous day.

LTD   It was certainly a magnificent 154 opening partnership. While the Aussie pace bowlers kept a good length, they were severely punished anytime they were wide. Dennett, in particular, was unforgiving with any loose ball.

ALB   Yes, for an opener, Dennett showed surprising aggressing – 31 boundaries in his 152 stand.

OW   Well gentlemen, I just hope we can keep up that form and win a second Test. Then, we should be able to force a draw for the final two Tests and bring the Ashes back home.

FR   Yes, it is time the Ashes came back home. Unfortunately, gentlemen, we do have important business to discuss, so shall we get seated and agree a course of action?

CB   Indeed, there is much to discuss.

The room quietens while they all move over to the circle of chairs and take their places, being the exact positions they were seated in during the last scene in this house.

ML   Well, as you are all aware, we've had some ups and downs over the last week or so, in our quest to bring some order back into the chaotic society that we now find ourselves living in.

        The obvious good news is that we won our case at the GPA Ethics Ruling Committee's hearing – thank you, gentlemen (nods to Lord Thomas Denman and Sir John Poo Beresford).

Unfortunately, there are three pieces of bad news. Firstly, Small swapped sides, which will make it a little more difficult to gain a PR advantage from the case before us. However, if well managed, I'm sure we still will gain some advantage. Secondly, Henry is appealing the ruling of the Ethic committee based on the Universal Declaration of Human Rights. Thirdly, Dr Horowitz is now representing Henry and Small. Given that Bill is the leading KC in genetic related law, this has indeed thrown a bug into the ointment.

Now, we have to wait until the outcome of the High Court appeal before the necessary legal precedence is established to allow the GPA to 'encourage' the terminations of genetically defective foetuses. So, any suggestions on tactics?

ALB   Yes, I have been giving this a lot of thought over the last day or so and even dusted off my copy of the Universal Declaration of Human Rights and read through it.

         Long pause while ALB sips on his sherry.

ML   Good – and did your thoughts and reading result in anything worth articulating?

ALB   Patience, dear boy. The ruling handed down by the GPA's Ethics Ruling Committee is in flagrant breach of the rights established by the UDHR. The ruling breaches Sandra's and Ivan rights, as defined in just about each and every one of the 30 articles within the UDHR.

         I have not been able to conjure up a single argument as to how and why we are not systematically breaching their defined rights.

ML   Sorry, Angus, I trust you are not suggesting that we drop the case?

ALB   No, not at all. But we could endanger our whole programme if the press became suspicious of us due to winning the case without mounting a credible argument as to why we're not breaching his rights.

ML   Well, I guess that is why we're here today, to establish a credible argument – so that when the appeal is heard in the High Court, the presiding judge will be able to find in favour of us, without giving any impression of bias.

FR   Who said there is going to be any bias?

SM   You all seem to be missing the point on this whole issue. You are speaking as though the ERC's ruling is unrelated to the human rights challenge.

FR   And in which way are they legally related?

SM   The UDHR, by definition, only applies to humans. The UDHR does not attempt to define humanity. Therefore, it is under the state's legal jurisdiction to define what is 'human'. And my friends, is that not what we, or shall I say the ERC, has just done?

FR   Must I state the obvious, that there is a world of difference between identifying a genetic disorder and taking legislative action to stop the condition passing from one generation to the next, and defining what it is that constitutes being human.

SM   What is human? Jesus Christ, we share in excess of 98% of our genes with chimpanzees – so should our law be inclusive of chimpanzees? I suggest not. Let's face it, those with Down syndrome, who have three copies of chromosome 21 rather than the standard 2 copies, are at greater genetic variance to us than chimpanzees. So, should they be protected by human law?

        It is our genes that define us as human, therefore I suggest that our law should not extend to those with Down syndrome. Or at least our law should offer them no more protection than is currently afforded to, say, other protected species like the chimpanzee.

        If we accept the position that it is our genes that defines us as human, then we are within our right as a state to quantitatively define the boundaries of humanity. We have now done this. We have appropriate legislation and a duly appointed body and forum to make such decisions – and it has just made such a ruling.

        As defined by English law, our friend Mr Henry is not human. Therefore he is not entitled to the protection offered under the Universal Declaration of Human Rights.

ML   Sebastian, excellently put. This is exactly the argument that we need to promote with the legal profession and the media at large. We can cite examples of bad cases of Down syndrome, and having the media ask the rhetorical question – should this being have the unreserved right to 'found a family'? We can swing it so that we get media support on this – no one wants to see babies neglected due to having feebleminded parents.

We can mount the case that in these circumstances, the UDHR simply does not apply, as they do not possess all the necessary human attributes to bring up a family. This message can be reinforced by pointing out that it would neither be in the interest of the children nor society to allow such beings to have children unchecked.

Oscar, why don't you have a chat with your chums at Pearson – and see if they can't exert a little influence over the FT. Sir Ronald, I'm sure you can have a chat to the Editor – and get a favourable editorial special in the *Telegraph*. Sebastian, I'm sure you can catch up with your contacts at *The Times*.

FR I'm going to have to give a lot of thought to this position. I must say that I'm not totally convinced, and without a lot of safeguards such a High Court precedent would open the decision to wide scale abuse and human rights infringement.

LTD Frederick, we did not seek this test case. But, since we have been challenged on the grounds of the UDHM, then this possibly will be our only chance, ever, to found the correct legal basis and correct moral basis to proceed with our forefather's work. Now, if you do not see the clear rationale of this argument, then quite frankly, I don't know why you bother to be associated with this gathering!

FR Well, there could, certainly there should, be a more subtle approach to the re-introduction of eugenics, with more safeguards and more within the power and decision of family and friends, as opposed to the state stepping into this arena and making such decisions that might be against the wishes of both the person concerned as well as their family and friends.

ML Frederick, families left to themselves can never entirely be trusted to do the right thing for society as a whole. They may be aware of the genetic deformities within an embryo that they are carrying, but for reasons best known to themselves, decide to carry on and have the child – which creates the very real potential of the genetic deformity being transferred to yet another generation, creating more misery within our sorry world.

LTD   Frederick, what I think we require, in the circumstances we find ourselves in, is to provide the necessary common law provisions to allow state intervention to terminate a pregnancy on the grounds of genetic deformity. However, the state does not have to immediately exercise this right.

FR   Meaning what?

LTD   Well, I think we all recognise the sensitivity of the current case where the actions of the state may be diametrically opposed to the desires of both parents. I think forcing the issue in this case would create a wave of bad publicity.

However, if the state wins the right to intervene, but does not exercise the right in this case, then the risk of bad publicity will be substantially reduced – well at least nowhere near as much as if we were to exercise the right.

CB   Exactly. Then once we have secured our right to intervene and encourage the termination of pregnancies, we can take our time to cherry pick the most media friendly case – where the public would back our decision to intervene due to the nature of the deformity.

Then, of course, over time, once precedence has been set, and we secure public support for extreme cases of deformities – we can gradually tighten the threshold on the cases or conditions in which we intervene. The way to get public support is through gradualism. Gradualism allows the exploitation of the public's ability to remain apathetic about anything that does not directly affect them today.

FR   I understand the case and the circumstances. However, the trial will be in the High Court. Therefore, not only will every lawyer and academic in the UK be pouring over the *obiter dictum*, the *rationale* and the judgment of this case – but so too will every lawyer and academic in every other civilised state in the world. In short, to withstand the worldwide academic and legal scrutiny that this case is going to receive, the GPA is going to have to mount a very convincing, substantive and legally plausible case.

The High Court is not going to find in favour of the GPA just because the presiding judge has a degree of sympathy to their case. To find in favour of the GPA, they are going to have to win the case on the merit of the legal argument being put forward.

Now gentlemen, if you will excuse me, I have to return to my chambers to write up last week's judgment on the rights of the forcibly dispossessed.

CB   Frederick, thank you for joining us – and I absolutely agree with you, the case must be judged on the strength of the legal arguments put forward by both parties. I would be the first to say, and I'm sure everyone here would agree with me, that we are not asking anything more of you other than a fair trial. Am I correct, gentlemen?

All   [In unison.] Hear, hear – just a fair trial.

FR   Gentlemen – you can be assured that it will be a fair trial. Good day.

All   [Along the theme.] Thank you, Frederick, and thank you for joining.

There is a prolonged silence until Frederick leaves the room, until eventually Max breaks the silence.

ML   Well, Frederick is starting to prove a little difficult, isn't he?

CB   Yes, somewhat. But, I think his roar is louder than his bite.

SM   Meaning?

CB   Well, in his position, he wants the strongest possible case presented by the GPA – so that it makes his job easier when he has to make a judgment. If he indicated to us he was going to find in favour of us regardless of the strength of the legal argument we put forward, I guess he is afraid that we may become complacent, which may make him look foolish by finding in favour of us when we didn't present a strong enough argument to win the case.

SM   Possibly, but I'm not so sure. We may have a small advantage that Frederick is sympathetic to our case, but I don't think we can rely on him to find in favour of the GPA. Therefore, we really do need to deliver a compelling legal argument to ensure we win the case.

ML   Well, let's get to work.

CB   Yes, let's get cracking. [Pause.] Anyone for more sherry?

With this the camera fades out on the group as they engage in legal debate as to the strength of the legal argument of declaring someone not entitled to protection under the UDHR after the state deems them not human.

Insert Scene – 43

> *Whiteness, in a pigmentary sense, is aristocratic, and the proper colour for a gentleman. Blackness is irretrievably proletarian, which is an absolute law established in our senses.*

> Paleface: The Philosophy of the Melting-Pot *by Wyndham Lewis.*

Scene 71 – The dwarfs present their research

6:00pm, Sunday, 2 June 2013

Setting: Bill and Cynthia Horowitz's house

Scene opens on Ivan just finishing a call on his mobile

IH: Mark, thank you for phoning, I really appreciate your support – it means a lot to me … And yes, I may keep you to your offer and ask you to retrieve reference material for me … Thanks … Bye.

The camera pans back from the close up of Ivan to show that he is in Bill's study, with the rest of his group all looking at him with questioning eyes as to who was that, and what was it all about?

IH   [Looks up to the rest of the group and notices their questioning eyes.] What?

BH   Was that your friend from the GPA?

IH   Yes, why?

BH   They're not trying to seek intelligence for use by the GPA?

IH   No, no – they're my workmates. They were concerned about me, and even offered to help if I need any reference work etc. They said that could try and obtain them for me.

BH   Very good. But be careful – it could just be a sneaky ploy to find out what our game plan is!

IH   No, I'm sure it isn't.

BH   Okay then – let's get on with the first briefing. Rob – what are the salient points of the Universal Declaration of Human Rights?

RW   Well, if the Universal Declaration of Human Rights is binding on the government and UK citizens – then I can't see that the GPA has a leg to stand on. The UDHR prescribes everyone with the following rights:

- All human beings are born free and equal in dignity and rights.
- Everyone is entitled to all the rights and freedoms set forth in the declaration – without 'distinction of any kind'.
- Everyone has the right to life, liberty and security.
- Everyone has the right to recognition everywhere as a person before the law.
- All are equal before the law and are entitled without any discrimination to equal protection of the law.
- All are entitled to equal protection against any discrimination in violation of the Declaration.
- Everyone has the right to an effective remedy by the competent national tribunals for acts violating their rights.
- Everyone has the right freely to participate in the cultural life of the community, to enjoy the arts and to share in scientific advancements and its benefits.
- No one shall be subjected to arbitrary interference with his privacy, family, home or correspondence.
- Everyone shall have the protection of the law against such interference.
- Men and women of full age, without any limitation, have the right to marry and found a family.
- States cannot engage in any activity which reduces any of the above rights.

So, unless I'm missing something, then, Ivan and Sandra have every right to have a family – and the state has no right to interfere with them or their family.

They all look towards Bill.

BH   Well, that is the way I read it. But, there must be another angle, as the GPA knows that we intend to use this defence and are still prepared to meet us in court. So, we have to figure out how they intend to demonstrate why these rights do not apply to Sandra and Ivan.

Rob, you can work with Sandra on this. Remember to think imaginatively and go through every case that has been brought before The Hague that has used the UDHR as a basis of legal argument. I've got the website address here so you can start pulling these cases out.

Okay who's next – Andy, the Nuremberg Trials:

AW   After World War II, a meeting was held in London in August 1945, with representatives from United States, the United Kingdom, France and the Soviet Union, which concluded in an agreement to provide for the establishment of an International Military Tribunal ('IMT') in Nuremberg to try the leading Nazi for war crimes.

In article 6 of the charter it lists the acts which constitute crimes for which individuals are responsible, as opposed to the state. In this context, war criminals can't just say they were following orders. The type of crimes included in the IMT include: crimes against peace, war crimes and crimes against humanity.

Crimes against humanity, includes the following:

- Murder.
- Extermination.
- Enslavement.
- Deportation.
- Other inhuman acts committed against any civilian population.
- Persecutions on political, racial or religious grounds.

So, individuals could be charged by the IMT for any of the above, even if it was not a crime in their own country – or where they were merely following orders.

The IMT also allows, pretty much, for a country to be tried, whether it is treating its own civilians poorly or civilians in other states. Therefore, state sovereignty is no longer a defence.

BH   Very good, Andy. So, this raises the prospect that those involved in making any decision regarding the intervention of Sandra and Ivan's right to have a child could be held personally responsible at an international court though I think this is on the very extreme of the practicalities of the current case. However, more importantly, it defines a number of crimes which arguably would be committed if the state or persons were to proceed and forcibly terminate Sandra's pregnancy.

Okay Ivan, tell us about the crime of genocide.

IH   Well, it appears to reinforce the same law as what Rob and Andy have presented on.

BH   Sure, tell us how.

IH   Okay, well the Convention on the Prevention and Punishment of the crime of genocide – or as it is more commonly referred to, 'the Genocide Convention' – was approved on 9 December 1948, before the UDHR was approved, in a unanimous vote of 56 states of the United Nations.

It entered into force on 12 January 1951. It was the first post-war human rights convention. The Genocide Convention makes genocide a matter of universal criminal jurisdiction. The definition of genocide requires the intent to destroy, in whole or in part, a national, ethnical, racial or religious group and lists acts such as killing members of a group, imposing measures to prevent births within the group and transferring children of the group to another group.

Interestingly, if we as dwarfs can be defined as a national, ethnical, racial or religious group – then it is an act of genocide if the state attempts to impose measures to prevent births. For my part, I'd certainly say we can be defined as an ethnical group, so, the GPA has no grounds to try and prevent us from having kids.

The crime of genocide has had relatively recent confirmation as an enforceable piece of international law, as it is one of the crimes within the jurisdiction of the permanent International Criminal Court that was established in Rome in 1998.

So, under the Genocide Convention – we seem to have a very solid case that the GPA's intended act is illegal under international law.

What may be more influential in arguing the merits of the Genocide Convention is that those responsible for any act of genocide can be held personally responsible for their participation in the genocide. Therefore, presumably Big Nose and his friends could be tried for their participation in dwarf genocide – as could the judges who preside over our appeal at the High Court.

BH   Excellent, again, I have the links to all the case studies involving the Genocide Convention so you can research this material and check each case so that we can cite precedence.

Now, who is doing the 'International Covenant on Civil and Political Rights'?

IH   That would me – again.

BH   Well Ivan, while you are on a roll – go for it and tell us all about it.

IH   The ICCPR came into force on 23 March 1976, and incorporated almost all of those proclaimed in the Universal Declaration of Human Rights, including the right of non-discrimination.

However, the ICCPR designates a number of additional rights that were not listed in the Universal Declaration of Human Rights, among them the right of all peoples to self- determination and the right of ethnic, religious, or linguistic minorities to enjoy their own culture, to profess and practice their own religion and to use their own language.

Each signatory state undertakes to respect and to ensure all individuals within its territory and subject to its jurisdiction the rights recognised in the ICCPR: without distinction of any kind, such as race, colour, sex, language, religion, political or other opinion, national or social origin, property, birth or other status.

Just to pause for a moment, let's consider what 'other status' might mean. I'll come back to this in a minute.

Specifically, the ICCPR provides the following rights:

- Every human being has the inherent right to life. This right shall be protected by law. No one shall be arbitrarily deprived of his life.
- Everyone shall have the right to recognition everywhere as a person before the law.
- No one shall be subjected to arbitrary or unlawful interference with his privacy, family, home or correspondence, nor to unlawful attacks on his honour and reputation.
- Everyone has the right to the protection of the law against such interference or attacks.
- The family is the natural and fundamental group unit of society and is entitled to protection by society and the state.
- The right of men and women of marriageable age to marry and to found a family shall be recognised.
- No marriage shall be entered into without the free and full consent of the intending spouses.

- There is equality of rights of both parties within a marriage and when it is dissolved. In the case of dissolution, provision shall be made for the necessary protection of any children.
- All persons are equal before the law and are entitled without any discrimination to the equal protection of the law. In this respect, the law shall prohibit any discrimination and guarantee to all persons equal and effective protection against discrimination on any ground such as race, colour, sex, language, religion, political or other opinion, national or social origin, property, birth or other status.

Now, if we do not meet the criterion for race, colour, sex, language, religion, political or other opinion, national or social origin, property or birth – then surely we meet the criteria of 'other status'.

BH   Excellent. The international treaties keep reinforcing the same basic rights that we all enjoy – and that no state has the right to interfere with. Now, Rob, the European Convention on Human Rights, tell us all about it.

RW   Well, really, I'm just continuing a theme that's already been established by the other international treaties – but here goes:

- Everyone's right to life shall be protected by law. No one shall be deprived of his life intentionally.
- No one shall be subjected to torture or to inhuman or degrading treatment or punishment.
- Everyone has the right to liberty and security of person.
- No one shall be deprived of his liberty.
- Everyone has the right of respect for his private and family life, his home and his correspondence.
- Men and women of marriageable age have the right to marry and to found a family, according to the national laws governing the exercise of this right.
- The enjoyment of the rights and freedoms set forth in this Convention shall be secured without discrimination on any ground such as sex, race, colour, language, religion, political or other opinion, national or social origin, association with a national minority, property, birth or other status.

BH   Excellent. Again, reinforcement of all of our basic rights – and critically, includes the term 'other status'. Andy – are you okay to tell us all about the International Covenant on Economic, Social and Cultural Rights?

AW   Sure. Well, it pretty much covers the same areas as the other conventions that have been discussed – but this is what I think it's saying:

- The state recognises the inherent dignity and the equal and inalienable rights of all members of the human family and that this is the foundation of freedom, justice and peace in the world.
- All citizens may enjoy economic, social and cultural rights as well as civil and political rights.
- States are to respect and observe all human rights and freedoms.
- All citizens have the right of self-determination – including the right to determine their political status and freely pursue their economic, social and cultural development.
- The state shall observe these rights without discrimination of any kind as to race, colour, sex, language, religion, political or other opinion, national or social origin, property, or other status.
- The state shall not do anything to destroy the rights defined within the Covenant.
- The widest possible protection and assistance should be accorded to the family – particularly for its establishment.
- Everyone is entitled to enjoy the benefits of scientific progress and its applications.
- Everyone is to benefit from the protection of the moral and material interests resulting from any scientific, literary or artistic production of which he is the author.

BH   Again, the ICESCR reinforces our basic rights, and again has the catch-all definition of 'other status'.

A key aspect of the ICESCR is the protection it provides 'the family'. To use its terms: 'The widest possible protection and assistance should be accorded to the family – particularly for its establishment.' I think a husband and wife that are expecting their first child certainly falls within the definition of 'establishing a family'.

So, to wrap up – we have six pieces of international law, namely:

- The Universal Declaration of Human Rights
- The Genocide Convention
- The International Military Tribunal which allowed the Nuremberg Trials to take place

- The International Covenant on Civil and Political Rights; and
- The European Convention on Human Rights
- ICESCR

The United Kingdom is a signatory to each of these six instruments of international law, which provide Ivan and Sandra with fundamental human rights that prevent the state from interfering with their family life – and prevents the state from discriminating against dwarfs or any other section of our society.

These laws are of a higher authority than the GPA, the GPA Ethics Ruling Committee and their associated rulings arising from their hearings.

Therefore, providing we can mount a case that demonstrates how and why Ivan and Sandra are protected by these six instruments of international law, we should be in a strong position to have the GPA Ethics Ruling Committee's ruling overturned.

Okay – any questions?

SS   What do you mean by 'Providing we can mount a case that we're protected by these laws' – why wouldn't we be able to mount a case?

BH   Well, I guess what I mean is that we have to prepare the case so that it can be effectively argued in court. We can't just march into the courtroom and cite the acts and expect the judge to be conversant in the conventions and then immediately overturn the ERC's ruling.

IH   Well, what work do we need to do to prepare for the case. It seems pretty black and white to me?

BH   We need to go through all the case material that has already been heard in any court anywhere in the world, as case material can be influential on our case. So, while it may appear black and white – if a definition or proposition of these acts has been successfully challenged then we need to know about it, so that we can cater for it in our legal position or mount a case that such challenges do not apply in our case.

RW   If it's so black and white, why are the GPA prepared to go to the High Court over it? I mean, what on Earth could be their counter argument?

BH I still cannot figure that out. But, I suspect, that they are using this as a test case and are prepared to take it all the way to the High Court so that it defines the legal framework in which they operate – regardless of the outcome of the High Court's decision.

AW You mean that they don't care who wins?

BH No, I didn't say that – I think they care an awful lot about winning the case – but, in the end, this case will define for them the legal grounds and limits in which they can operate.

   Okay let's get to work and research the case material and prepare our case.

Scene fades out as Bill starts issuing a new round of instructions to each of the team members.

Insert Scene – 44

   Fostering the good-for-nothing at the expense of the good is an extreme cruelty. It is a deliberate storing up of miseries for future generations. There is no greater curse to posterity than that of bequeathing them an increasing population of imbeciles.

   The Pivot of Civilisation *by Margaret Sanger, Pioneering American 'Pro Choice' Campaigner, 1922*

Scene 72 – A pint of discontent

12:30pm, Monday, 3 June 2013

Setting: The Old Thameside Inn (Pub – SE1 9DG).

The scene opens at another riverside pub, the Old Thameside Inn, with Gough, Elaine and Mark sitting at an outside table adjacent to the river, complete with a pint and some pub food. They all look distressed and a degree nervous. There is a large plasma TV in the background tuned into Sky News.

MH   You know, I've worked here for five years now, and it never once occurred to me that this place, well, how shall I put it …

EK   Is a ruthless, murderous, bastard organisation?

MH   Nicely put. I always believed the work we were doing was for the good, not only for society at large, but for all people within our society.

GR   It is shocking that the organisation that we work for and have supported can so callously define someone as outside the human norm, and revoke all their paternal rights.

EK   Has anyone spoken to Ivan – to see how he is?

MH   I called and chatted to him on Sunday evening. Under the circumstances, he appeared to be in good spirits. I offered to help him – if there is any way that I could. I don't want him to think that just because I work here, I support the actions of the GPA. He mentioned that he and his legal team were preparing an appeal to the High Court.

GR   His legal team? You are joking – the three dwarfs. However, I'll give it to Ivan, he did put in an impressive performance. But, in the end, he still lost.

        Now he's going to the High Court with his fellow dwarfs as his legal counsellors. Excuse me if I'm being ungenerous, but this is not a fucking fairy tale where Prince Charming comes along and gives him a little peck on the cheek and that nasty GPA witch disappears and everyone lives happily ever after.

EK   Gough, I think you're forgetting that Dr Bill Horowitz has joined his legal team.

GR   Yes, that's right, Horowitz has joined – but he has had to resign from BDW to do so. So, he has no legal clerks supporting him, no access to BDW's library, no access to all his prior case notes. All he has is Snow White and the three dwarfs. Now, that is what I call the legal awesome foursome.

MH   Horowitz is meant to be the best geneticist legal mind in the world – but, I take your point, he doesn't have a great support team.

EK   Unlike the combined strength of our very own GPA and their external counsel, BDW. I won't comment on the legal merits of the GPA – but, certainly BDW is a strong legal force.

      I must say, I feel really uncomfortable working for an organisation that is actively trying to revoke one of its own staff's paternal rights, with the longer term objective of getting rid of everyone like him – then anyone else they don't like the look of.

GR   Well, you know, I've been thinking about that, I don't know if I want to work for an organisation that has … such a sinister side to it. For fuck's sake, Ivan's a good guy, a productive guy. Truth be known, I'm sure he's more productive at work that any of the rest of us. But, just because he's short they're going to encourage the termination of his child. Now that is just way out of order. I really don't think I can stay here.

EK   Well, what are you going to do?

GR   Well, I have saved a little, I could probably move back in with my mum and go back to university – and study law.

EK   Just like your dad?

GR   I'd say despite my dad, not because of my dad.

MH   You still haven't thought about contacting him?

GR   You know, I might. Last time we talked about it, and reflecting on what Ivan said and how he longed for just one chance to talk to his father – and now he is being prevented from becoming one – I started to think, maybe, just maybe it's time to call him and say hello.

EK   And what then?

GR   Fuck knows. I think I'll just have to play it by ear. Who knows, he may not
       even want to see me.

MH   Unlikely, given that he has never missed sending you a present every
       Christmas and every birthday.

GR   True, but that could be just a guilt thing – it could all change when I make
       contact. Then it becomes real, a real son, not just a conceptual son.

MH   Well, I think you're doing the right thing by trying. And while you may be
       right that there may be a risk of something funny happening when you
       contact him – I think it is only a small risk. Otherwise, why does he
       always write to you asking you to contact him?

EK   Gough – contact him. If you do, there is a small chance that you will end
       up regretting it. But, if you don't you will always regret it – until the day
       you die, particularly the days after he dies.

GR   Well, I'll see. Anyway, what are you guys going to do – are you going to
       stay here?

EK   I don't know. I don't know what else I can do, where I can go?

GR   Come on, Elaine, you're a professional researcher – your skills can be
       used anywhere.

EK   Well, yes I'm none too happy about what has happened recently, and
       none too happy about working here on grounds of principle. But I've got
       a mortgage to pay off, and the bank doesn't give a hoot about my
       principles – only its principal. As long as I make the monthly payment,
       they don't care where the money comes from.

GR   Mark, what about you?

MH   I think I'll leave. I don't know where or when. I'll just keep applying for
       other jobs until I score one – then resign from here. Anyway, all this is a
       little too depressing – so, can I get you another round …

Scene fades out with the Sky News becoming audible – with the plasma screen becoming more in focus. The anchor leads into the special news item:

NA   We now bring you a disturbing report about a growing epidemic that is sweeping the nation. Unfit parents that are having more and more children that are ultimately left to the taxpayer to raise and care for.

Our social welfare correspondent, Susanna Ling, takes up the story.

SL   Thank you Nathan. Sky News has tracked 120 recent cases where mothers have been found unfit to look after their child, which resulted in social welfare agents obtaining a court order to remove the children from their care.

Of these 120 cases, no less than 72 mothers have had another baby within twelve months of having their last baby taken away. On further examination, we found that of these 72 mothers, 54 had had prior babies removed from them.

Talking to the welfare officers, some of these mothers have had up to five children removed from their care. They describe these mothers as chronically unfit to look after themselves, doubtless their children. The welfare officers find it heart breaking and very difficult to understand that a mother who has a child removed due to their poor parenting is allowed to have another baby and mistreat the next baby in the same manner as they did to their other babies.

The cost to the taxpayer for every child taken into care is estimated to be in excess of 1.3 million euros – that is the cost of raising the child to the age of 16. But the cost does not stop at sixteen. Many of these kids end up living lives of crime. Many have kids of their own, which in turn are taken away from them – as they are found to be unfit parents.

The question that society must stop baulking at – is when is enough, enough? If a mother has one, two or three children removed due to them being an unfit parent – should the state take measures into its own hands and have the mother sterilised, to stop this vicious circle of poor parenting and criminal activity.

I now turn to Professor Harry Laughlin, who has recently had a book published on this phenomena, titled *Analysis of the UK's Melting Pot*, which explores the damaging social cost of these unfit parents. Professor Laughlin, can you provide us with an overview of your research?

The TV switches over to Professor Harry Laughlin, a balding middle age professor.

PHL   Thank you, Susanna. This is a very complex subject and it is difficult to provide brief soundbites. However, I can say that different socioeconomic groups have differences in social values, which represent, in turn, real differences in the inborn value of the family stocks from which poor parents have sprung. These degeneracies and hereditary handicaps are inherent in the genes …

The scene fades out on the TV as Professor Harry Laughlin goes on.

Insert Scene – 45

The swart cockney in Britain is a resurgence of the primitive Mediterrranean stock, and probably a faithful replica of his ancestors of Neolithic times. As in all mixed breeds – where the parent stocks are diverse, as in mating between Whites, Negroes and Amerindians, the offspring is a mongrel – a walking chaos, so consumed by his jarring heredities that he is quite worthless.

Lothrop Stoddard, American Eugenic Leader, 1926

Scene 73 – The dwarfs' Schindler

8:30am, Thursday, 6 June 2013

Setting: High Court

The scene opens with Bill, Sandra and the three dwarfs walking into the High Court. Like when Max entered the court House, it is apparent Bill is familiar with the layout of the building, unlike the others who are a little overwhelmed by the grandiosity of the building. By habit, Bill starts to head toward the restricted area protected by the turnstile and guards – then he remembers his companions and without saying a word changes course and heads toward the public lifts.

The five wait, and then enter a lift. They go in and turn around so that they face the interior doors of the lift. Rob looks up and notes the 'Schindler' branding of the lift. He murmurs 'Schindler's lift'.

BH   What was that Rob?

RW   I was just commenting to myself – that it's a Schindler's lift.

AW   So? What the fuck's the make of a lift go to do with anything when our continued existence is under threat?

IH   It's because Jew boy's ethnicity was also under threat from Hitler and the Third Reich – and an engineer called Schindler managed to save a number of Jews from the final solution.

BH   Ivan, thanks for the eloquent manner in which you portrayed the historical facts and, in particular, the touching way in which you presented me and my relationship with Hitler and the Third Reich. But, be that as it may, you too have fates that are historically bound to Schindler.

AW   What are you talking about? I'm not Jewish.

RW   He didn't say you were. [Then looking at Bill] So, your folks were saved by Schindler?

BH   Yes. If it wasn't for Schindler I wouldn't be here today. He saved both my maternal grandparents.

IH   Unbelievable. I've seen the movie – and while I found it really moving, I never thought that what Schindler did would ever personally affect me. I thought his impact on the world was just saving a few Jews. I never thought that through a weird set of coincidences, he would have an impact on me or my unborn son.

BH   Ivan, you do want me to try and win this case for you, don't you?

IH   Yes. [Oblivious to the offence he has given.] Why?

BH   Never mind. But, when you're giving evidence – can you attempt to speak in a manner and tone that doesn't get the court so excited that they feel the need to immediately terminate you there and then?

AW   Bill, do you know why people take an immediate dislike to Ivan?

BH   No, why?

RW   It saves time!

SS   Guys, lay off, I like him.

AW   Come on Sandra, lighten up a little.

The scene fades out and in with the five of them entering the courtroom, and as they walk through the doors they look down to a semi-filled court room – with the GPA team already in place and quietly speaking amongst themselves in a manner so relaxed that it oozes a disconcerting degree of confidence. Bill eyes up the GPA team, and is visibly taken aback by the relaxed demeanour of his opponents.

Jon Raney looks up and sees Bill and his team enter, –signalling a polite 'hello'. The rest of the team merely look up and note their arrival, and look back down and continue with their conversation.

Bill and his team walk down to their bench to the left of the courtroom (as viewed by the judge), and start to compose themselves. Bill makes his way to the front of bench and starts talking to his team, with the three dwarfs standing on their seats and leaning over and resting on the bench listening to Bill – with Sandra in the middle of the dwarfs, also listening intently.

The 'huddle' is disturbed by the sound of a court official bellowing 'All rise for Judge Rogers' (FR). With this announcement, Bill returns to the other side of the bench and stands respectfully with Sandra, Ivan and Rob – whereas Andy, while standing, portrays a stance that projects anything but respect to the judge.

Judge Rogers walks in with an impressive air of understated confidence, stands briefly in front of his chair, surveys the courtroom – then sits, signalling ever so slightly for all others to also take their seats.

The court sergeant then commences to read out the official title of the case, together with all the dates, numbers etc. As the sergeant babbles on in the background, Bill's team huddles together again.

IH   Bill, I, I mean we, really appreciate your efforts to help us in our case, and the very generous amount of time that you have given us – not without considerable cost to yourself. But, the cost to us, if you lose this case, will be far greater, so, if you lose, your efforts and time will amount to false charity. You failing us now will be worse for our decedents than if Schindler failed your folk.

BH   Ivan, thank you for not mincing your words …

IH   I haven't started yet. If you fail us, we're fucked. If the GPA wins today, they will be our Third Reich of tomorrow. And, I'm guessing, if they win this case, unlike Hitler, the GPA will be able to round up every last one of us – and in one way or another prevent all of us from having children.

       There isn't going to be any Allied army charging in to this courtroom to change the law if this case goes against us! If you fail us, then there won't be any more dwarfs anywhere, ever. So we, as a genetically related group of individuals that has existed since man first started walking on two legs, will disappear from the planet in a mere single generation.

       What is between us and state-sponsored genocide – is you.

BH   Anything else?

AW   Yeah – don't fucking fail us.

BH   Thanks for your vote of confidence – it's just what I needed as I contemplate my opening position.

SS   Bill, we're just all tense. We'll do whatever we can to support you. Just go out there and kick ass.

BH   Thanks, I'll do my best. And believe me, you are going to see the world's best arse kicker do his very best arse kicking. That may be all I have to offer, but it's the best you're going to get.

RW   Well, Bill, Schindler saved you by way of saving your grandparents. Now you find yourself in a similar role – you're our Schindler!

As Rob says this, Bill is visibly taken aback with the gravity of the situation and the role he now finds himself in.

Insert Scene – 46

The white race of this land is the foundation upon which rests its civilisation, and is responsible of the leading position which we occupy amongst the nations of the world. It is not, therefore, just and right that this race decides for itself what its composition shall be, and attempt, as Virginia has, to maintain its purity?

Eugenics in Relations to the New Family and the Law on Racial Integrity
Virginia Bureau of Vital Statistics, 1924.

Scene 74 – The High Court appeal

9:00am, Thursday, 6 June 2013

Setting: The High Court

Judge Frederick Rogers seats himself and looks at the papers awaiting him on his bench. As he sits, the court sergeant bellows to the courtroom that they can be seated. Judge Rogers then looks up and carefully surveys the courtroom and notes the seating arrangements and body language on display between the various personalities present – with particular scrutiny being paid to the appellants, namely the interaction between the dwarfs, Sandra and Bill. Once his mental map of the courtroom is sufficiently composed, he hit his gavel on its block and opens the proceedings.

FR   I think all in the court today are very aware of the significance of this hearing. In essence, this court is being asked to make a judgment as to what, in this brave new world, is 'genetically acceptable'. In making such a ruling, the decision of this court will not only impact those present in this court today, but families and individuals for many generations to come.

This court, in effect, is being asked to balance the rights between those who will live in the future against the rights of those who live today. This is a very sensitive area, and any judgment on this issue will have ramifications well beyond these shores and well beyond our lifetimes.

Therefore, I sincerely ask everyone in the court, especially our learned king's counsellors, to act and provide reasoned and reasonable arguments so that the court can rule to achieve the appropriate balance between the rights of the current generation versus the rights of future generations. Without further ado, I now ask the appellant to open the proceedings with their case.

BH   Thank you, My Lord.

I move that the High Court immediately annuls the GPA's Ethics Ruling Committee's Ruling on the basis that they overstepped their authority and therefore pronounced an *ultra vires* ruling.

As the ruling was *ultra vires* to the authority of the GPA, my client does not have a case to defend, he is not bound by the rulings of the GPA's Ethics Ruling Committee and therefore, upon this court's agreement, he can get on with his life and act as any concerned 'father-to- be' should.

FR Thank you, my learned colleague, for opening the discussion with such a forceful argument.

And I'm assuming you are going to continue to outline the basis as to why your client's position is based on the GPA acting in an *ultra vires* manner. If my assumption is correct, then there is no better time than now to outline your client's reasoning for this position.

BH Certainly, My Lord.

The United Kingdom is signatory to six pieces of international law and treaties – each of which protect the rights of individuals, the disadvantaged and minority groups within the signatory states. The six treaties being:
- the Universal Declaration of Human Rights;
- the International Military Tribunal;
- the Genocide Convention;
- the International Covenant on Civil and Political Rights;
- the European Convention on Human Rights; and
- the International Covenant on Economic, Social and Cultural Rights.

Upon the state signing these treaties, the state is governed by the provisions within the treaties. Therefore, nobody, no agency, no court, and no GPA Ethics Ruling Committee can pronounce decisions or rulings that are in violation of the tenets of these treaties.

In the current case, the GPA Ethics Ruling Committee pronounced a ruling that is in flagrant violation of each and every one of these six international treaties.

Other than citing the key tenets that each of the six treaties are based upon, which the Ethics Ruling Committee showed frightening disregard for, I'm not sure of the need to cite each and every article within each of the six treaties.

FR We may well wish to discuss the specific articles of these treaties that you are holding that the Ethics Ruling Committee violated, however, for now I'll allow you to focus the discussion to what you maintain is the key tenet of these treaties. So, please proceed.

BH   Thank you, My Lord.

The basic tenets of each of the six treaties are as follows:

1) Men and women of full age, without any limitation, have the right to marry and found a family.
2) No one shall be subjected to arbitrary or unlawful interference with his privacy, family, home or correspondence, nor to unlawful attacks on his honour and reputation.
3) Everyone has the right to the protection of the law against such interference or attacks.
4) The family is the natural and fundamental group unit of society and is entitled to protection by society and the state.
5) Everyone shall have the right to recognition everywhere as a person before the law.
6) All persons are equal before the law and are entitled without any discrimination to the equal protection of the law. In this respect, the law shall prohibit any discrimination and guarantee to all persons equal and effective protection against discrimination on any ground such as race, colour, sex, language, religion, political or other opinion, national or social origin, property, birth or other status.
7) The state cannot engage in any activity which reduces any of the above rights.

The Ethics Ruling Committee's ruling violates each of the above seven tenets, or rights, that are bestowed on my client by way of the six international treaties.

If, for now, we study the 5th and 6th tenets that I cited, namely that my client, Mr Henry has the right to be recognised as a person before the law and therefore is equal with everyone else before the law. As such, he is not to be discriminated against on any grounds whatsoever.

Quite clearly, the GPA took a contrary position. The GPA either did not recognise Ivan as a person before the law or discriminated against him. In either case, the GPA decision violated all six international treaties on human rights.

As the state has signed each of these treaties, it cannot make decisions that are in violations of them. Therefore, this court has no other option than declaring the Ethics Ruling Committee's ruling null and void.

Thank you, My Lord.

FR   Thank you, a solid unambiguous argument concisely yet robustly presented. Is this the only argument you are putting forward to advance your client's position?

BH   Only! There are six international treaties, which collectively represent 40 articles that have been violated by the GPA ruling. If necessary, we shall fight on any and all of these 40 articles.

FR   Thank you. Could I ask for the GPA and Ms Small's case to be put forward?

LC   Yes, My Lord. My Lord, we do not dispute the provisions of the six international treaties that the appellant has cited. All states that are signatories to these treaties must treat all persons equally and without discrimination.

The camera pans over to Ivan as this is being said, who shows a sense of 'nervous relief', whereas Andy shouts 'Yes' – but Bill has a look of utter dismay and disbelief, knowing therefore that they must be coming out with a very sinister argument.

LC   However, My Lord, it is within the state's right and remit to determine what attributes and what conditions and what developments of a living entity collectively define what it is to be a human, to be a person.

There is ample precedence for states making such distinctions, both here in the United Kingdom, and for that matter just about every other state that is a signatory to the six treaties that have been cited by the appellant.

The ruling made by the Ethics Ruling Committee is merely the application of a state's right, used countless times before in defining, or rather refining, the definition of a person, a human.

The only difference in this case, as opposed to the precedence, is that the Ethics Ruling Committee's ruling was based on quantifiable aspects of the physical attributes of a living entity.

The GPA has, and rightly so, defined a measurable criterion as to what this state recognises as human, as a person. All such living entities that meet this criterion are afforded the full protection and rights of the six treaties that have been cited. However, the provision and protection of these treaties only cover the rights of 'persons' before the law.

Under this criterion, such rights are not extended to Mr Henry. Thank you, My Lord.

FR   Thank you, Counsellor, for stating the case in such stark terms. I only can presume you are armed with details of the precedents that you referred to. As, I'm sure everyone in the court would be fully aware, these precedents may well prove to be critical to the decision of this court.

LC   Yes, My Lord, we have details of numerous precedents of states, including the United Kingdom, making rulings as to what constitutes a person.

FR   Now that both parties have presented their opening positions, let me summarise the legal arguments of this case, which will ultimately define the rationale of the judgment arising from this appeal. It is undisputed that persons are protected by the six international treaties that have been cited. These treaties protect persons from discrimination.

However, the treaties only apply to persons. If Ivan is a person, then the Ethics Ruling Committee acted *ultra vires* in its ruling – and therefore, the ruling will be annulled.

So the key questions for this court to consider in arriving at a judgment are:

a) Does the state have the right to determine what constitutes a human or a person?
b) If it does, then under what circumstances can a state make such a determination?
c) What controls are in place to prevent arbitrary or discriminatory practices in making such a determination?
d) What controls are in place to prevent arbitrary or discriminatory practices. Given the above, were these controls observed when the GPA made its ruling?

If the above four conditions are satisfied, the Ethics Ruling Committee acted within its authority and, therefore, its ruling stands.

This court will not be revisiting the Ethics Ruling Committee's ruling. This court will only be determining whether the ERC had the necessary authority to make such a ruling, and if so, were the correct controls and due process observed in making its ruling.

BH   I object to the whole proposition of the legal framework that you just cited. This hearing is fundamentally flawed. The state cannot go around determining who is human and who isn't. If it could, the government would immediately classify the entire shadow government as inhuman and have them exterminated.

FR   I think that eventuality would be covered under the 'controls and safeguards' to prevent discriminatory practices. The GPA maintains there is precedence for states determining who is a person before the law. So, please let us hear these arguments – and then you can counter-argue, so that this court can come to a considered and just conclusion on this delicate matter.

Now, I am going to call a recess for one hour or so, in order that all parties have time to consider the positions of their counterparts and the construct of the legal framework in which their positions are to be discussed. When we reconvene, all parties are to put their arguments forward in consideration of the above questions – starting with the GPA as to what right and what precedence the state has in determining who or what is a person.

This court will reconvene at 11:00am. Court is now adjourned [knocking his gavel on the sound block].

The scene closes with the camera focused on Ivan and party with an expression of total disbelief and exasperation.

Insert Scene – 47

Permanent improvement of the race can only be brought about by breeding the best. Charles Davenport, Director Cold Springs Harbor Laboratory, 1903.

Scene 75 – The high cost of free legal advice

10:00am, Thursday, 6 June 2013

Setting: Outside Table, St Clements Café & Bar

The scene opens with Ivan and his team sitting at an outside table of St Clements Café, with encompassing views of the Temple Green and the Thames. There are very few other patrons in the café. They are all sitting around the table with a coffee in front of them – with glum expressions, each staring into the heavily overcast 'space'. The poor light and hint of drizzle gives the scene an aura of depression.

IH   What do you mean you didn't anticipate the GPA using this argument to condemn us? For fuck's sake, you're meant to be the country's leading genetic lawyer, and you come totally unprepared to defend us against genocide. Jesus Christ, you may be representing us for free, but the cost to us is still too fucking high.

       What the fuck can you do, can we do, to prepare a defence in one hour to prevent state-perpetrated genocide?

SS   Bill, on every other case I've worked with you, you have always been totally on top of every legal argument, every angle, every nuance of every case that the opponents may have thrown at us. You've never left anything to doubt or chance. In each and every case, you had all bases covered. Why have you chosen this case to be so bloody unprepared, so fucking negligent? Is this why you offered us your services for free – to ensure we lose our case?

BH   I don't know what to say. I don't know how to apologise. But, I can say I'll do everything in my power, everything within my capability, whatever it takes – to win this case.

       If the GPA wins this case, this will be nothing short of the return of the Third Reich – which, remember, declared Jews sub-human. This allowed the political and legal foundation to start the Holocaust, to start the systematic extermination of Jews, Catholics, Freemasons, Gypsies, epileptics, homosexuals, Poles, amongst others.

This hearing is a farce. To raise such an argument, and for the court to accept it as an argument, is nothing short of a crime against humanity. You have to win this case. We have to win this case. I have to win this case!

If we lose, who will be next? To recite a poem by Rev. Martin Niemoller:

> First they came for the Communists, and I didn't speak up,
>   because I wasn't a Communist.
> Then they came for the Jews, and I didn't speak up,
>   because I wasn't a Jew.
> Then they came for the Catholics, and I didn't speak up,
>   because I was a Protestant.
> Then they came for me,
>   and by that time there was no one left to speak up for me.

If I don't defend you now, if I don't win this case for you now, sooner or later they will come for me and my son.

RW   Bill, I'm relieved that you are passionate about this case and passionately want to defend us and win this case. But that doesn't alter the fact that you haven't prepared for it. Let's face it, they've had time to prepare and refine their legal argument to win this case – and the best you can do, with the time that's left, is to wing it.

Let's face it, we're fucked.

BH   NO, we're not fucked. I can win this case. I will win this fucking case – if it's the last thing I ever do.

AW   Well, if you don't, it will be one of the last things you attempt to do.

BH   Thank you, Andy. Making threats against me is really going to help isn't it? Oh, I'm so fucking scared of a pack of midgets coming after me. With that scary threat, now I'm going to work twice as hard to win the case.

Upon Bill uttering these words, without any communication between the three dwarfs, they all leap across the table and attack Bill, forcing Bill's chair to fall over backwards. With Bill winded, lying on his back on the pub floor, the three go into a frenzy, violently punching and kicking him – breaking his glasses, making his nose bleed and breaking one of his teeth.

Sandra starts shouting at them to stop and starts to systematically pull the dwarfs off Bill, throwing them backwards away from Bill. She then starts on the next, only for the last to return and again proceed to assault Bill.

After a while Sandra realises that her tactics for breaking up the attack are not working. She decides on a new tact; she throws off Ivan and watches for his return. As Ivan moves his right leg back to kick Bill, she sizes him up and kicks him fairly and squarely in the groin from behind.

Ivan doubles up in pain and squirms on the floor. Andy hears his agonised moaning and looks up at Sandra – which is the very moment that she kicks Rob from behind, straight between the legs. Rob flies through the air and hits Andy, whereupon the both fall into a heap on the floor.

SS Look you bunch of fucking arseholes – this is the most important legal case since the Nuremberg War Trials. Probably more important. And, all you can do is insult and fight each other. Do you really think you are doing yourself justice? Do you really think you are doing justice to all the decent, honest, hardworking people who are going to be totally stripped of their rights as a human if you lose this case?

  The way you four are insulting and fighting each other – you may as well be members of Hitler's SS – because if you lose this case, each of you will be condemning countless thousands, possibly countless millions to their death.

  Now, get your shit together – and start preparing for this case.

AW Why do you say 'condemns people to their death' – this case is about your unborn child.

SS You stupid fucker midget. If the court holds that you are not human, if someone kills you – it won't be murder will it? It will be the same crime as killing an animal. Your time on this Earth is going to be pretty fucking short if you lose this case. While there may be a ban on fox hunting, there isn't any ban on dwarf hunts.

  Now, stop taking everything so fucking personally, and work together to win this ghastly case.

Insert Scene – 48

Those guilty of outrageous conduct to women or children, or cowardly and brutal assaults, together with the criminally insane, will be humanely put down, on the principle that people who cannot live happily and freely in the world without spoiling the lives of others are better out of it. The death penalty will also be used to prevent the transmission of genetic disorders. People suffering from genetically transmissible diseases will be forbidden to propagate, and will be killed if they do.

Anticipations *by HG Wells.*

Scene 76 – Dishevelled In court

11:00am, Thursday, 6 June 2013

Setting: High Court

The scene opens with Frederick Rogers walking up to his seat, picking up his gavel – with the obvious intent to hit the sound block. However, when he looks up, it becomes evident that something has caught his attention. He winces as his expression transforms first into an expression of 'studying', then to being startled.

FR   Can I ask what happened to Mr Henry and his legal counsellors?

The cameras brings into focus Ivan and his team, all showing a high degree of ruffelledness – with Bill revealing bad bruising all over his face with noticeable cuts, a bloody split lip and a faint trace of blood trickling out of his left nostril – and without glasses.

BH   My Lord, unfortunately during the recess we ran into some hostilities.

FR   Did you inform the police?

BH   With all due respect, My Lord, given the gravitas of this case, we thought our time better spent preparing for our legal arguments than spending time in a police station reporting a minor crime.

FR   [Focussing on Ivan.] Mr Henry seems to be in particular distress. I take it you haven't sought medical assistance either?

BH   No, My Lord, for the same reasons.

FR   My learned King's Counsellor Horowitz, I understand that you don't wear contact lenses – and you do not appear to have any glasses. Are you able to effectively represent your client in the state you are in with your limited ability to even read?

BH   It would be my preference, My Lord, to have the hearing adjourned for 24 hours – so that we had the opportunity to recover from this incident.

FR   Granted. Court adjourned until 9:00am tomorrow morning.

Bill gives a nod of gratitude to the judge as the scene fades out.

Insert Scene – 49

The pauper is the victim of heredity, but neither Nature nor Society recognises that as an excuse for his existence.

David Starr Jordan, President of the University of Indiana and first President of Stanford University.

Scene 77 – What do we do now?

11:30am, Thursday, 6 June 2013

Setting: Outside the High Court

The five members of Ivan's team walk out of the court in total silence. They find themselves on the Strand, in the drizzling rain in a loose fashioned circle, without anyone looking at each other – all avoiding each other's eyes and having to talk.

BH   Let's obey the judge's wishes, and go and report this act of violence to the police.

The other four stop avoiding eye contact and look up at him with furious expressions. At this point, a big warm smile livens up Bill's face – revealing his broken tooth. A second later he bursts out laughing.

BH   Well, I've never been mobbed by a bunch of dwarfs before. I'm going to have to start treating you guys with a serious amount of respect.

Bill's laughter breaks the tension, and proves infectious, as within seconds all five are belly laughing so loudly that they are forced to hold on to each other for support.

BH   [Through laugher.] Anyway, guys and girl, congratulations, you just got us an extra 24 hours.

       If you guys will still have me, I want us all to go back to my place so that we can clean up, eat and prepare for tomorrow Is this okay?

The others all look at each other, nod to each other, then look up to Bill.

All   Let's do it.

Insert Scene – 50

The best minds of today have accepted the fact that if superior people are desired, they must be bred; and if imbeciles, criminals, paupers and the otherwise unfit are undesirable citizens they must not be bred.

The Rapid Multiplication of the Unfit *by Victoria Woodhull, Pioneering American Feminist, 1891.*

Scene 78 – The appeal – a fresh start

9:05am, Friday, 7 June 2013

Setting: High Court

The scene opens in the court, after the 'opening ceremony', with the judge providing direction for the day's hearings.

FR   … precedent of states, including the United Kingdom and Northern Ireland, determining what is a 'person before the law'. Could I ask you now to present your case?

LC   Thank you, My lord.

Just before the court went into recess yesterday, my Lord, you defined the terms of legal argument under which this appeal was to be conducted, namely:

a) Does the state have the right to determine what constitutes a human or a person?
b) If it does, then under what circumstances can a state make such a determination?
c) What controls are in place to prevent arbitrary or discriminatory practices in making such a determination?
d) Given the above, were these controls observed when the GPA made its ruling?

If the above four conditions are satisfied, the Ethics Ruling Committee acted within its authority and, therefore, its ruling stands.

I shall address point A by illustrating examples of how and when the state has already determined what constitutes a person. If the state already determines what constitutes a person, and no legal body, whether domestic or international objects to such rulings, then by definition the state has the right to determine what is a person.

BH   I object, My Lord. Just because there is not a legal challenge to the legality of an activity, does not give it a legal status. Our common law is full of cases where activity has been going on for years, only to be eventually challenged and found to be an illegal activity.

FR   Upheld. The mere exercising of power does not make the 'act' of exercising such power a legal act.

LC   My Lord, let me rephrase my assertion: the state has exercised this power, which when challenged, this very *court has endorsed the right of the state to make such determinations.*

My Lord, I will be presenting a number of examples where the state has determined who is, and who is not, a person before the law. Let us start off with the basics. Of all the international conventions cited by the appellant, none defines what a person is – nor even when someone becomes a person.

Of all the international treaties, of all the UN resolutions, if there was one where we would hope and expect to find a definition, or at least find some guidance, as to when an embryo, or foetus, or unborn child becomes a person, we would expect to find such guidance in the UN Declaration of the Rights of the Child – which the appellant, interestingly, failed to cite in their opening position.

However, I invite you to scour and scrutinise this UN resolution of the Right of the Child for any such guidance and you, like me, will be disappointed, as the only reference or more correctly acknowledgement that a child may have existed before birth is the single phrase:

> '*Special care and protection shall be provided both to him and to his mother, including adequate pre-natal and post-natal care.*'

None of the conventions cited by the appellant, nor for that matter any other international treaty, provides any guidance whatsoever as to whether an embryo is a person, nor whether a fertilised single-cell egg is a person, nor whether an unborn child a day before its full-term birth is a person.

Obviously, this is a very important issue. The normal gestation period of a human child is nine months. As such, arguably, there is nine months of life in which the international conventions are all silent. In the absence of any guidance from these conventions, each state has defined their own criterion as to when an unborn child becomes a 'person before the law'.

Starting with the starkest contrast in the legal rights of the unborn child, abortions are legal in most western countries – but not all. In Ireland, from the point of conception an unborn child pretty much has the same rights as a fully functional, normally born child. Most other western countries do not extend such rights to embryos. Therefore, unequivocally, different states have differently defined 'who is a person before the law'.

However, even for those states that have legalised abortions, the laws governing them vary significantly – and in some cases even within the same country the law varies like in the USA and Australia. What this amounts to is, depending upon the length of the pregnancy, an abortion could be legally conducted in one country, whereas if the same abortion was to be conducted in another country it would be murder.

Each state, including this state, has made determinations as to when an unborn child is 'a person before the law'. Furthermore, there is wide variation between different states as to when they determine an unborn child is a 'person before the law'.

Even within the United Kingdom, at different times we changed the legal definition as to who or what is a person. More pointedly, the state has changed the point in time someone becomes a person. For example:

- In 1861, the 'Offences Against the Person' Act was introduced – which made abortions a crime. At this time, all embryos were given the same rights as someone who was born and alive.
- In 1929, the Infant Life Preservation Act allowed abortions when the life of the mother was at risk. This effectively reduced the rights of an embryo or foetus – but clearly, they still had rights.
- In 1967 the Abortion Act was introduced allowing abortions if there was a risk or injury to the mother or her existing children's physical or mental health. This allowed abortions up to 27 weeks into the pregnancy, which is within the third trimester of the pregnancy. This act further reduced the rights of the embryo and foetus; if they posed a risk to either the mother or the mother's existing children they had no rights.
- In 1990 the law was changed to reduce the latest date for an abortion from 27 to 24 weeks – still later than some surviving premature babies. The 24 week limit was re-ratified by Parliament on 20 May 2008.
- However, the law still allows abortions after 24 weeks if the life of the mother is threatened – or there is substantial risk of foetal abnormality.

This is a little odd isn't it? If a premature baby is born at 22 weeks and is abnormal – killing the infant would be murder. But, if the same child is yet to be born, and even if it were normal, then it is quite okay to kill it. The key difference is not the health or degree of defectiveness of the infant, but only the location of the infant – specifically whether the infant is inside or outside the womb. This is how the UK determines whether a person is equal before the law – based solely on the location of the infant, not on its health or any other attribute.

Inside the womb – no rights. Outside the womb – full rights.

This is not just a theoretical legal debate. In 2001, a woman from Herefordshire was more than 24 weeks pregnant. She found out that her unborn child had a cleft lip so two doctors authorised a late abortion on the foetus solely on the grounds that the child would be born with a cleft lip and palate. Definitely, there was foetal abnormality – but the abnormality was far from debilitating, let alone life threatening. However, when the case went to court – charging the two doctors with murder, the court found in the doctors' favour as they had made their assessment 'in good faith'.

Because the unborn child had a cleft lip it was afforded different rights than a child with no foetal abnormalities. If, however, the child had been born, rather than aborted, at 24 weeks and the same decision was made – i.e. to exterminate the child – the doctors would have been charged with murder.

This state has the right, and has exercised this very right, to determine when and what is human. In doing so, it has determined exactly what is a person and who is to be afforded the protection of the laws of our land and the laws of the international conventions that this state has signed up to.

Such rulings by this very court have survived challenges by the Court of Appeal and the House of Lords. In this context, the state, endorsed by this court and the highest court in the land, has established and enshrined a very fundamental legal concept: if a being is inside the womb, it is not a 'person before the law'. If it is outside the womb, it is a 'person before the law'.

It is entirely possible that at the same time, in two adjoining hospital theatres, there could be two pregnant women – both 26 weeks into their pregnancy. One has an abortion and the other a caesarean section birth. Upon both being forcibly extracted from the womb by the presiding doctors, one has the full legal rights of the state bestowed on it, the other has absolutely no rights.

Different beings within our society have different rights. It is entirely right and proper for the state to be able to make distinctions and bestow different rights accordingly.

In this context, if the state has determined, and the House of Lords affirmed, that a 24 week old foetus with a cleft lip has no rights – and the mother and doctors who terminate the pregnancy were within their rights to do so, then it holds true that the state has the right to make a similar decision as to the rights of a foetus that is, or will be, a dwarf.

Let us for a moment take a broader perspective of this issue – with three exceptions, all Western European countries have legislation allowing abortions. If the conventions that the appellant refers to is applicable to all – then why is there a disparity between Western European countries as to what constitutes a person, and who or what is to be afforded the protection of their legal system?

To stress this point further, the period of gestation in which an abortion is legal varies widely between different states, for example:

In Ireland, abortions are illegal. In France abortions are only allowed within the first 70 days of conception. However, Belgium, Finland and Germany all allow abortions up to 84 days after conception, whereas Italy and Russia allow them up to 90 days, Denmark 112 days, Sweden 126 days, both the Netherlands and the UK allow abortions up to 168 days – however, in the UK, if the foetus shows signs of abnormality then there is no prescribed maximum time limit.

The difference between sovereign states in the manner they treat the unborn demonstrably illustrates that states not only have the right, but also exercise the right, to determine exactly who and what should be afforded the protection of the law. The state decides, and only the state decides, what is a person – what is human.

Thank you, My Lord.

FR   Thank you for illustrating circumstances where states have indeed bestowed different legal rights in regards to who or what is afforded the protection of human law.

Before the court progresses any further, in which other examples may be presented to the court for consideration, I would like to give the appellant the opportunity to respond to the argument thus far that has been put forth.

King's Counsellor Horowitz, would you like to respond to the opening position put forward by the defendant?

AW   [In a hushed voice that can be heard throughout the courtroom] Go get 'em, Billy babe!

BH   [Sort of hushed] Thanks, Andy.

My Lord, thank you for giving me opportunity so early in these proceedings to respond to the shallow and narrow argument put forward by the defendant.

In all the examples cited by the defendant – does one of the states have a different law for those 'born' prematurely from those who are born after a full term of pregnancy? Do any of the states, say, if a child is born before 24 weeks, allow the parents or doctors to look at the newborn baby and if they don't like it simply kill the damn thing?

NO, not one state allows that – as each and every state recognises the rights of a child, a person, of a human, when they are born into this world of ours. Kill a newly born child – and, regardless of what state you live in, you will be on a murder charge. The law is for all. For all those born and living.

We do not have separate laws for different 'classes' of humans. If you were to plan and deliberately kill any of the following: a premature baby, a 105 year old man on a life support system, a dwarf, a giant, a black man, a white man, the criminally insane, a Down syndrome child, a paedophile, a company executive who authorised toxic chemicals to be dumped in a neighbourhood swimming pool, resulting in the death of entire families, or Idi Amin, the law makes no distinction. If you kill a person, you are charged and tried for murder of a person. All of the above have equal rights before the law – the same rights that you and I enjoy, with no exceptions and no bias.

So, My Lord, let us suspend the argument put forward by the defendants and concentrate on the issue at hand, which is Ivan Henry's right, as a born, living person before the law.

FR   Thank you, King's Counsellor Horowitz, for putting forward this clear and succinct perspective to the court.

Before we explore this perspective further, I would like to turn to the defendant, who, in the opening of their position, cited that this court has previously ruled that different people are entitled to different rights. Could I ask the defendant to elaborate on this assertion?

LC   Certainly, My Lord. This is the case of 'Airedale NHS Trust vs Bland', generally referred to as the *Bland Case.* At the age of 17, Tony Bland was a victim of the 1989 Hillsborough Disaster where 95 football fans were crushed to death. Tony survived – well, he survived in as much he did not die from the disaster. However, his lungs were crushed, his breathing stopped, and his brain was damaged due to oxygen deprivation. Tony was in a coma, or what his doctors termed a persistent vegetative state, or PVS for short, for four years.

Whether Tony's condition was permanent or not has been hotly debated. However, the definition of a PVS sufferer is that they can breathe on their own and all their vital organs function normally, they also respond to pain with reflex movements. In the case of Mr Bland, he could open his eyes, but his doctors maintained he was not focussing on anything when he did – and they also maintained that he couldn't communicate or respond to the people around him.

Regardless of whether his doctors were correct in the above assessment, one thing is for sure: they could not say with any certainty whether Mr Bland was aware of the people around him and the things they were saying to and about him. Some of his loved ones were adamant that he was aware of their presence and that when they spoke to him he responded.

Like a baby, Mr Bland could not feed himself. And, like a baby, once fed, he could digest his food normally. In a case of outrageous hypocrisy, his doctors, wouldn't allow his loved ones to feed him – because they claimed it was 'dangerous' to let him swallow his food. So they hydrated and fed him intravenously.

Once the medical establishment had denied his family from feeding Tony orally and had him dependent on a tube for his water and nourishment, this same establishment came to this very court and had the audacity to raise the question as to whether 'tube feeding' was a medical treatment.

As the medical profession prevented his loved ones from feeding him orally, his intravenous feeding should have been regarded merely as 'a tool for daily living'. In this regard it is no different from specially adapted spoons that enable arthritic patients to feed themselves. Yet, we don't – this court included – condone the removal of all special spoons from arthritis patients so that they will starve to death.

Tony was, however, receiving medical treatment for his septicaemia. Common Law allows doctors to withdraw treatment if it is not of any benefit to the patient or has no effect on their condition, or if it is a burden. If his doctors had lawfully withdrawn his septicaemia treatment, he would have died naturally within a week or so.

The legality behind the withdrawal of medical treatment is simple – doctors do not have to do everything in their power to keep someone alive. But, in Tony's case, they did. The reason Tony's case came to 'this' court was not because he was dying. It was because he was NOT dying.

This court ruled in NHS's favour and ruled that the feeding tube was a medical treatment, rather than 'a tool for daily living'. In making this ruling, the Airedale Trust was allowed to remove and withhold this 'medical' treatment. So, despite the fact that the doctors banned Tony's loved ones from feeding him naturally because it was 'dangerous', and that the Airedale Trust could have withdrawn his medication for his septicaemia at any time, allowing him to die naturally, this court sided with the medical establishment – and allowed his doctors to remove his feeding tubes and let him starve to death.

This court endorsed the NHS to kill Tony by starvation. While he was being starved to death, his loved ones were still banned from spoon-feeding him – because it was still 'dangerous'. It was so dangerous it may very well have kept him alive!

This very court was instrumental in granting different members of our society different rights. Tony was expressly kept alive by the NHS, purely to use him as a test case in this court to reduce the rights of the most vulnerable members within our community.

Upon the NHS succeeding in revoking Tony's rights as a living person, it turned his feeding tubes off on 22 February 1993 and he died nine days later on 3 March. The cause of Tony's death was not PVS, or even the Hillsborough Disaster. His death was due to starvation and dehydration – that was allowed and endorsed by this very court, [pointing directly at Judge Rogers] by this very judge.

Laurie turns and looks at Judge Rogers directly.

LC   I hope you are proud for being one of the three judges who not just allowed, but effectively sentenced Tony to death by starvation and dehydration.

Our state, this court, this very judge before us, not only advocates that different people should be treated differently – but is active in the execution of such abuses of human rights.

The 'Airedale NHS Trust vs Bland' ruling is not just a theoretical construct or of abstract relevance to the case currently before the court. The appellant's position has been firmly grounded on the so called universal rights defined within six international treaties that the United Kingdom is a signatory to. However, this court ruled, which was subsequently endorsed by the House of Lords, that in essence each case must be treated upon the merits and circumstances germane to those involved with the case – and what is right and just for those concerned. Therefore, regardless of what international treaties we are signatories to, different people within the United Kingdom and Northern Ireland have different rights.

We are asking the same court, the same judge, no more and no less than what has been previously ruled on, and that is to make a ruling as to what is right and just for the unborn child – and all those with similar conditions – both now and in the future.

I shall finish my reference to the Bland case by drawing out some obvious parallels with the current case. Mr Bland had been in a coma for four years. In this state there was much suffering, hardship and cost – not only to Mr Bland but to his parents, his girlfriend [as she says this she visibly chokes], the medical staff treating him and to those denied access to medical attention due to the medical resource consumed by Tony. However, once food and water was withdrawn, he died nine days later. During these nine days, Tony may have been in more distress than before

– but this is unknown, as his sentient state of being was unknown. However, it is true that during this time his parents and girlfriend were certainly far more distressed. Once he passed away and the mourning and grieving period was over, his friends and family were relieved of the daily stress of witnessing their son, their loved one, suffering. One could say that the sharp but comparatively short increase in stress brought an end to the lesser, but relentless, never-ending daily stress of living with a loved one in a state of PVS.

In the case currently before the court, the same philosophy should apply. To lift the burden and stress of future generations, future children and future families from the unfortunate genetic condition that the appellant suffers from requires a comparatively short increase in stress, a mere single generation, which will save an infinite number of generations to come of this terrible condition.

In this case, it is not just the welfare and wishes of Mr Henry that are at stake. Those involved include the countless generations to come, which Mr Henry has some perverse desire to pass his genetic disease onto. This court not only has the power and authority to prevent Mr Henry from passing his own misfortune on to poor future generations of children – it also has an obligation to do so. This court is the only voice that those future generations of children have to speak up for them – because as sure as hell, Mr Henry is intent in destroying their lives, those lives that haven't even started yet.

Long pause.

FR   Ms Coulson, does that conclude your assessment of the Bland case and how it relates to the case presently before the court?

LC   Yes it does, My Lord

FR   Thank you, Ms Coulson. Mr Horowitz, would you like to present your position on the Bland case?

BH   Yes, My Lord, I would. A foetal abnormality? What does this mean? To paraphrase Christ, according to Saint John at 8:7, – 'Let he that is without genetic abnormality perform the first abortion'.

Each of us, to greater or lesser degrees, has genetic abnormalities. The prominent biologists Eyre-Walker and Keightley estimate that there are, on average, at least 1.6 harmful new mutations in each of us. As such, when each of us was a mere foetus we too had 'harmful foetal abnormalities'. We too were, and are, deviants from the 'human norm'.

If this law had been enacted 70 years ago, then due to the inherent number of genetic harmful mutations in each and every one of us, there would have been a sufficiently strong case to have aborted pretty much everyone in this court room. Haven't you all lived rich fulfilling lives? Do any of you regret being born? Or, would you have rather been aborted and spared living your life with the genetic mutations within you?

The very reason why we humans as a species have been so successful, more successful than any other mammal ever – probably more successful than any other vertebrate ever – is due to the very fact that we have so much genetic diversity amongst us.

Consider this: every disease, every environmental hazard, every predator that has ever challenged our existence – we've overcome it because within our diverse genetic species there has always been those amongst us who resisted the disease, who could outsmart predators, those who could devise new hunting techniques, those who could tolerate the harsh environment we found ourselves living in, and those who could develop penicillin.

To give an example, in many parts of the world, both in the past and in the present, malaria killed and continues to kill in the millions. This year malaria will kill two million people globally. When it kills, it kills not just individuals, not just families, not just villages – but entire towns, cities and populations.

However, some amongst us have a high degree of resistance or even immunity to this deadly disease. Their HBB gene, located on the short (p) arm of chromosome 11 at position 15.5, is different from the rest of us. This genetic advantage is common among people living in areas that are, or have been, afflicted by malaria epidemics. If it was not for this genetic advantage, which is only found in people with the 'O' blood group, then malaria would have devastated, annihilated and made extinct many, many more communities.

The most serious form of malaria is known as plasmodium falciparum. This strain of malaria reached the southern part of Italy at about the time of Christ. About 450 years later it reached a small but beautiful town, Lugnano, which was just north of Rome. At this time, Roman scholars specifically mentioned that Lugnano was a zone of pestilence where people died of fevers. With modern DNA testing and detailed archaeological excavation, it has been established that this small town was wiped out by the arrival of malaria. We now know that not only was Lugnano's demise and ultimate death due to malaria – but to a large extent, the fall of the Roman Empire itself was due to this deadly parasite. If the Romans possessed the genetic advantage conferred by the version of the HBB gene that some O-type blood people have, then there would not have been such an epidemic and carnage – and very possibly the Roman Empire would have lasted for hundreds of years longer.

However, those with this version of the HBB gene, which protects them so well against malaria, suffer from another condition, namely sickle-cell. Many medical and genetic researchers now consider those carrying this version of the HBB gene genetically defective. This has given rise to mass screening programmes in many US states to identify and eradicate the condition. Here in the UK, the GPA has gone so far as to gazette the condition as a genetic defect.

The GPA has gazetted the condition and instituted a screening programme to detect and eradicate the condition, notwithstanding the fact that many of those with only a single copy of the HBB gene in question have no or only mild medical problems associated with the condition. Serious medical conditions only arise when a person has a copy of the HBB gene on both strands of their DNA.

Now in the twenty-first-century United Kingdom, in a time and place where malaria is not 'currently' a problem – you have the GPA not only espousing but gazetting that this version of the HBB gene is a genetic abnormality and that embryos are to be screened – and if an embryo has this version of the gene then the embryo should be terminated to prevent the occurrence of sickle-cell.

While malaria does not exist in the United Kingdom at the moment, with continued global warming, then it very well may be prevalent in these isles later this century.

In their attempt to eradicate sickle-cell, the GPA, rather than protecting or strengthening our genetic heritage, is actually damaging it by reducing the diversity in our population.

Reduced diversity equates to less ability to survive current and future diseases, current and future environmental hazards, and current and future predators – even if the predator can only be viewed through a microscope. Remember, malaria is still killing two million people a year – and the GPA is doing all in its power to eradicate the only known natural immunity that mankind has against this ferocious killer.

Let's now pause for one moment, and think about what society's position should be if there was no downside to having this version of the HBB gene, for instance, let's say that those with this version of the HBB gene did not have the sickle-cell side-effect. Would the GPA's position be that all those *without* this version of the HBB gene are genetically defective or inferior – as they do not have any resistance to the great killer malaria? If this was to be the GPA's position and we screened and terminated all embryos without this version of the gene – without any resistance to malaria – we would be left with a population where everyone had the same blood group, namely O.

Is this what we want? For everyone on Earth to have the malaria-resistant HBB gene – which would prevent two millions deaths each year due to natural resistance that HBB bestows on its carrier. Fantastic. If the GPA were to achieve this, wouldn't we all applaud it?

No, in fact we wouldn't applaud it at all. The HBB gene is only present in those with the blood group 'O'. Unfortunately, those with the 'O' blood group have no resistance to cholera – no resistance at all.

However, people with blood group 'A' have a high degree of resistance to cholera and to a lesser extent people with blood group 'B' have some resistance. Further, those people with blood group 'AB' are totally immune to the effects of cholera. But, they have no resistance to malaria.

So, by the GPA arbitrarily deciding what are defective genes and instituting screening processes to rid the population of these genes, it is in fact making mankind less diverse, weaker and more vulnerable to diseases and predators.

There are other similar cases: people with a single copy of a particular version of the CFTR gene located on the long (q) arm of chromosome 7, are protected against the worst effects of stomach infections and diarrhoeas caused by the typhoid bacteria, which today is still a major killer in many parts of the world. England is not immune from this killer, as evidenced on the 14 December 1861 when it killed Prince Albert.

Those who carry a single copy of this gene have a significant advantage over the rest of us – their immune system protects them against typhoid, whereas the rest of us are exposed to the debilitating effects of the disease. As our antibiotics are becoming increasingly less effective against bacteria and death rates from bacterial infections continue to increase – we as a species should be proud that some of us can withstand such a brutal bacterial onslaught.

However, because those who are unfortunate enough to carry two copies of this version of the CFTR gene develop cystic fibrosis, the GPA has gazetted it and is trying to eradicate all version of this gene from our gene pool. Again the GPA is actively reducing our genetic diversity, and by doing so reducing our ability to collectively survive our ever-changing environment and our current and future predators.

Similarly, carriers of one copy of a particular version of the hexosaminidase A (alpha polypeptide) gene – or as it is commonly referred to, the HEXA gene – have a high resistance to another mass killer, tuberculosis. Given that deaths caused by TB is on the rise throughout the western world – as the disease has become increasingly resistant to drugs and immunisation programmes – we should celebrate the fact that some amongst us have a natural resistance to this particularly insidious disease.

But again, the GPA in their flawed wisdom, have gazetted the disease as a genetic abnormality, because for those rare cases where a person has two copies of this gene – they develop Tay-Sachs disease.

Now, I doubt anyone in this court is advocating that we should not make prospective parents aware of the risks of having a child with two copies of these genes, i.e. a copy of the defective gene on both of their DNA strands, which gives rise to debilitating diseases. Neither is anyone questioning the need to provide a service to parents to inform them whether their unborn child has two copies of any of the three genes I just discussed. BUT, for the majority of the carriers, they only have a single copy of any one of these genes – which confers them a massive genetic advantage over the rest of us. They are resistant to diseases that have ravished our population and societies – and rest assured, these diseases will ravish us again.

But rather than taking a sensible approach to this issue and acknowledging that this genetic diversity is good for the population as a whole, as it gives us weapons against old adversaries, the GPA are doing all in their power to eradicate these versions of the genes altogether. Any embryo that the GPA screens in which they find either a single or double copy of these genes the GPA does all it can to have the embryo terminated.

So, every time we 'try' to strengthen our genetic heritage by removing genetic traits from our gene pool, we in fact do the exact reverse – we weaken our gene pool, we weaken our species, we collectively become more vulnerable to the elements, more vulnerable to disease, more vulnerable to current and future predators, more vulnerable to the harsh environment we live and will live in.

For homo sapiens to continue being the most successful vertebrate to ever walk this Earth – we need wide genetic diversity – not narrow mindedness.

FR   Mr Horowitz, how does this relate to the Bland Case?

BH   My Lord, there is no comparison between Tony Bland and my client. Tony Bland's genetic condition was never assessed, discussed or considered. The ruling of this court was based strictly on Mr Bland's sentient state at the time – or more correctly, the lack of it.

At this point Laurie Coulson abruptly stands up, with her emotional rage betrayed by her red cheeks and fiery facial expression

LC   He was sentient. He could hear me, he could understand me – he knew I was with him, he knew I loved him. He loved me.

        [Turns to face Judge Frederick Rogers.] And you gave permission to those barbarian quacks to kill him.

There is a long pause. The camera brings into view the shocked expressions of those present in the court. After a long silent deliberation, Judge Rogers eventually says:

FR   Counsellors, can I see you both in my chambers?

Scene 79 – The judge dresses down

10:30am, Friday, 7 June 2013

Setting: Judge Rogers Chambers

The scene opens in the familiar settings of Judge Rogers' chambers. Bill Horowitz and Laurie Coulson are both sitting on the same settee in a reasonably formal composure. Frederick is sitting on the opposite settee facing them, with his arm stretched out along the top of the couch, emphasising his confidence and control of the situation.

FR   You two are both highly regarded and experienced king's counsellors. Both of you are familiar with the proceedings and protocols of the High Court.

I will grant you that the case currently before the court is particularly sensitive. There are innumerable parallels that can be made with other cases that have been heard in this court – or in other jurisdictions or regimes. Notwithstanding the parallels that can be drawn or your degree of personal involvement in any of these cases – the purpose of this appeal is to make an objective assessment as to whether the GPA acted *ultra vires* in handing down its ruling.

Therefore, you shall confine your argument to the facts of the case before this court – and the extent to which current UK law governs such facts together with specific legal precedence that have been set.

Understand?

BH/LC Yes, Your Honour.

FR   If there are any further direct or implied personal attacks on myself, I will hold you in contempt of court – and have you taken off the case. Understood?

BH/LC Understood

FR   Last but not least, this is the High Court. I expect the King's Counsellors representing their clients to exercise a high degree of refrain and objectivity in the presentation of the legal basis of their arguments to this court.

Therefore, you will leave your emotional baggage at the door – it has no place inside my court. Any questions?

BH   Yes, Judge Rogers. Should you find in favour of the defendant, then you will be bring back the legal concept of 'outlawry' which was abolished in 1938 with the introduction of the Administration of Justice Act.

As you are aware, those unfortunates who had a judgment of outlawry bestowed on them were no longer protected by the laws of the land, i.e. they were outside the law – often referred to as outlaws. Outlaws had their human rights revoked – they couldn't own land or chattels and if anyone wronged or harmed them, they couldn't take them to court. Nor would the crown uphold any criminal deeds committed against them, including theft, assault and ultimately murder.

Should you find in the defendant's favour, then not only my client, but all dwarfs will be inflicted with this same unfortunate legal status. As soon as the media pick up on this, or individuals become aware of their dubious legal status, then it is likely to result in wholesale discrimination and assault against dwarfs.

Dwarfs' legal status as an outlaw will not be substantially different from the status of Jews under the Third Reich, where their legal and social status was changed, or degraded, to 'sub-human'. Once they were defined as a sub-human, they were subjected to terrible acts of violence, robbery and dispossession – and ultimately to the final solution.

So, I urge you to be very, very careful in arriving at your verdict.

FR   Counsellor Horowitz, I am aware of the legal principle of 'outlawry' and of the legal status of Jews under the Third Reich. I do not need a history lesson from you in order to arrive at a just verdict. Now, if there are no more questions, I'll see you both in court at eleven.

BH   Actually, I do have a further question. Part of the Ethics Ruling
        Committee's ruling included the following obiter dictum:

        *Future hearings hold the possibility of making rulings based on
        non-physical conditions, which can be objectively measured.*

        If you judge in favour of the GPA, then the Ethics Ruling Committee will
        be free to rule on non-physical genetic conditions

FR   Thank you, Counsellor, I am aware of the ruling handed down by the
        Ethics Ruling Committee. Is there anything else?

BH   Yes, for God's sake! Look, there are any number of pseudo psychiatric
        conditions that one day may be linked to specific gene sequences,
        which, if the GPA win this case, would allow them to terminate those with
        a propensity to develop such quack psychiatric diagnoses.

FR   Quack psychiatric conditions? Now you're refuting the validity of the
        entire psychiatric profession?

BH   I have here the latest edition of the US Diagnostic and Statistical Manual,
        [he opens his briefcase, removes a book and opens it up to tagged
        pages] which is the psychiatrist's bible. Among many others, it has
        categorised the following forms of psychosis:

        • Dissociative identity disorder.
        • Anti-social personality disorder.
        • Conduct and oppositional defiance disorder.

        And it was not so long ago that homosexuality was classified as a
        psychiatric disease – but it's now been dropped from this edition of the
        psychiatrist's bible. However, there is nothing stopping the psychiatric
        profession from bringing homosexuality back into their bible as a
        psychiatric disease!

        The ERC's ruling would allow the termination of a foetus if it contained a
        genetic sequence that can be linked to the conduct and oppositional
        defiance disorder. If this was to transpire, then every dissident will be
        terminated before birth. All the Martin Luthers, the Martin Luther Kings, the
        Malcolm Xs, the Noam Chomskys, the Michael Moores, the Suffragettes and
        French resistance of the world will be systematically killed off.

Are you really going to allow this to happen? Are you, Judge Frederick Rogers, going to go down in history as the man that sanitised the population of all diversity, all opposition and by default all of its energy?

FR   Counsellor Horowitz, as I said a moment ago, I am aware of the ruling handed down by the Ethics Ruling Committee and the implications of applying the three standard deviation rule to non-physical attributes. If there are no more questions, I'll see you both in court at eleven. And, please, act in a manner that dignifies both yourselves and your profession.

Insert Scene – 51

The discovery of the Jewish virus is one of the greatest revolutions the world has seen. The struggle in which we are now engaged is similar to the one waged by Pasteur and Koch in the last century. How many diseases must owe their origins to the Jewish virus! Only when we have eliminated the Jews will we regain our health.

Adolf Hitler

Scene 80 – The appeal – the final slog

11:00am, Friday, 7 June 2013

Setting: High Court

The court reconvenes and Judge Rogers takes his place on the bench.

FR   Counsellor Horowitz, before the recess I asked you how your discussion of genetic diversity related to Counsellor Coulson's argument relating to the late Tony Bland.

Can I ask you to continue your response – and please keep your arguments to the question at hand. How does your argument for greater genetic diversity relate to the case of Tony Bland?

BH   Certainly, Your Honour.

If my client was in a similar sentient state as the late Mr Bland, then we could have a similar discussion as to Mr Bland's condition. However, Mr Henry is fully sentient, he is tertiary educated, he is married, has a good professional job, pays taxes and contributes to society as much or more than those of us that do not have his particular genetic disposition.

There is nothing bad or wrong with my client – genetically or otherwise. He lives a full and fruitful life. Our society is socially, culturally and economically richer for having among its members those with the achondroplasia genetic makeup. This genetic condition provides us not only with genetic diversity but also cultural diversity.

We are decades away from fully understanding the complexity, interaction and interdependencies of the genes that define us as homo sapiens – such as those I highlighted before, namely:

- The malaria-resistant HBB gene.
- The Typhoid and diarrhoea-resistant version of the CFTR gene.
- The TB-resistant version of the HEXA gene.
- The cholera immunity properties of those with the AB blood group.

There may or may not be a downside to these conditions, but the upside is that this genetic diversity provides us with armaments to protect our species from current and future diseases, predators and environments.

However, there is a genetic condition that is closely analogous to the subject of this hearing, namely the Laron's form of dwarfism, which is found in an isolated community in Ecuador. From all accounts, those with the Laron form of dwarfism are immune from all forms of cancer. Further, their average life span is longer than both the average of their community and the global average as a whole.

A genetically defining aspect of their condition is that they lack the hormone 'insulin-like Growth factor 1' or IGF1 for short. Within the population as a whole, high levels of IGF1 can lead to the onset of early breast, prostate or bowel cancer. Laron dwarfs are spared these and other forms of cancer. There is promising research into the Laron form of dwarfism and IGF1, which has a strong potential to result in preventative cancer drugs and diagnosis and possibly later to cancer cures.

If this court rules against my client, then due to the short-statured nature of the Larons, they too will be extinguished. Is this a good result for humanity? I think not! Cancer is now the biggest killer in the world. To date, we have only found a single naturally occurring genetic defence against this wanton killer. And, now bizarrely, I find myself in court defending the right to life of those that are immune to cancer – who may very well hold the key to treatments for cancer victims.

When asked by all those suffering and dying from cancer, 'Why did you eradicate the only genetic immunity we have to cancer from the human gene pool?' Can the GPA, the Ethics Ruling Committee and this High Court all say in clear consciousness, 'Yes, they may have been immune from cancer, but they were short-asses, so their immunity didn't count. We would rather have a population of normal-heighted people dying of cancer than a cancer immune population with the odd short-ass.'

I think most people would rather be short than dead. Which is precisely my client's argument. To put this in perspective, is it really in our species' best interest to eradicate genetic diversity? Is it really in our species' best interest to eradicate achondroplasia before the condition, complexity and potential immunities are fully researched and understood? And, even if it is eventually found that there is no genetic advantage to those with achondroplasia – this completely ignores the huge cultural contribution that these folk offer our society. These folk should be cherished and admired, which outside of the GPA they mostly are.

On the other hand, Mr Bland was not in a state to reproduce, therefore he had no further genetic material to offer society or our species. His genetic material and diversity was terminated with his own death. In short, it is a spurious argument to compare someone in a PVS that has nothing to offer current or future generations – either culturally or genetically – with someone who has not only so much to offer – but is actively contributing on both of these fronts.

FR   Ms Coulson, do you wish to respond to our learned colleague's arguments?

LC   My Lord, yes I would. As a society, we accept that there is a balance between the right of the individual and the right of the population as a whole. The rights of the individual are enshrined in many decrees, conventions and in legislation, including the Magna Carta, which established the rights of freemen to a fair trial. Since the signing of the Magna Carta by King John, the rights of citizens in the UK have been enshrined in many other pieces of legislation and international conventions – including the six cited by the appellant earlier in this court.

Notwithstanding the rights of citizens, regardless of how those rights were obtained, bestowed or recognised, in cases where there is a conflict between the rights of the individual and the rights of the population at large within the United Kingdom – then the rights of the population takes precedence.

We see this basic principle of law in operation every day. Security checks at airports, surveillance cameras, mandated vaccinations, mandatory education, compulsory ID cards, conscription in the event of war. If there is not a conflict, then the rights of the individual prevail.

In the case of forced vaccinations, this is a classic case of conflicts between the population and the individual. We as a nation have managed to largely avoid the lethal avian flu pandemic that has swept the world over the last two years by mandating vaccinations against this disease.

The argument against the mandated vaccinations was that it was an individuals' choice whether to be inoculated or not. This totally disregarded the rights of everyone else the individual came into contact with – and with everyone they, in turn, came into contact with. Those countries that upheld the rights of the individual over the right of the population, collectively suffered a death toll of 113.8 million – with some countries suffering a 17% fatality rate, which has now devastated their economies leading to many more dying from starvation. A high price for respecting the rights of an individual over the rights of the population.

Mr Horowitz is suggesting this strategy was wrong. We also should have allowed individual choice as to whether or not an individual is inoculated, which would have left the UK with a death toll in the hundreds of thousands or quite possibly in the millions as opposed to the comparatively small number of fatalities that we have experienced to date, being a mere 2,168 deaths.

To illustrate this point further, namely the rights of the population vs the right of the individual, I'll cite another example. On the 2 September 1666, the Great Fire of London started at Thomas Farriner's bakery in Pudding Lane.

While the fire was still confined to the bakery, the firefighters were called. The firefighters quickly determined that the fire was going to spread to the adjacent buildings, so they sought permission of the owners to demolish them in order to halt the spread of the fire. However, the owners of the adjacent buildings refused.

Nearby householders, together with the firefighters, protested and called the Lord Mayor of London, Sir Thomas Bloodworth, to overrule the owners' decision and have the adjacent houses demolished. However, he refused, saying it was up to the owners to decide whether or not to have their house demolished, even though he did have the authority to order the demolition of these buildings.

The Lord Mayor's respect of the individuals rights of half a dozen or so property owners led directly to the destruction of 13,200 houses, 87 parish churches and St Paul's Cathedral. It is estimated that the fire destroyed the homes of 70,000 of the city's inhabitants.

However, as bad as it was, the fire could have been much worse. It was stopped by the action of James, the Duke of York, later to become King James II. After the fire had taken hold and already destroyed thousands of houses, he ordered and oversaw the demolition of hundreds of houses to create a firebreak – which eventually stopped the spread of the fire.

Had he sought the owners' permission prior to demolishing the houses the firebreak would never have been created – which would have resulted in the destruction of thousands more houses and the deaths of many more Londoners.

Who was right, the Lord Mayor or the Duke of York? Quite clearly KC Horowitz is siding with the Lord Mayor – whose efforts in managing the fire was described by the authoritative diarist of the time, Samuel Pepys, as:

> *People do all the world over cry out of the stupidity of my Lord Mayor in general; and more particularly in this business of the fire, laying it all upon him.*

Had the Lord Mayor understood the balance of rights between the individual and the rights of the population, as did the Duke of York, then thousands of houses would have been spared from the destructive fire.

We now find ourselves in an almost identical situation. We can take the Lord Mayor's approach and respect the rights of the few here and now, with total disregard to the rights of the future thousands that will have to contend with the consequences of the individual, selfish decisions made by the few today. Or we can take the approach of the Duke of York, and place the rights of future thousands over the rights of a few that are here today.

To put this in more specific context, let me turn to the source of genetic diseases. We know the presence of specific genes in an embryo directly leads to either a physical or psychological defect in either the child or the adult. This is not in dispute.

For those unfortunate to be missing a particular gene, WHSC1, on the distal short arm of chromosome 4, they suffer from a number of disorders including: severe growth retardation, mental retardation, microcephaly – or 'Greek helmet' faces – cleft lip or palate, coloboma of the eye and cardiac septal defects. Collectively, this is known as Wolf-Hirschhorn syndrome. Of those that have this genetic condition, 34% die within the first two years of their life.

To cite another example, we all have a repetition of a word within a particular gene, namely the genetic word, 'CAG'. The number of repetitions of this word varies in all of us. Where the repetition of this word occurs more than 38 times, by mid-life the carrier will slowly start to lose their balance, become unable to look after themselves and will ultimately die prematurely. This condition is known as Huntington's chorea. The more repetitions over 38 instances the younger the carrier will start suffering from the conditions. No medication, surgery, diet or exercise can change, stop, slow down, or reduce the symptoms of the disease. If you have the genetic defect – you get the disease; if you don't, you don't.

There are hundreds, if not thousands, of other genetically determined diseases. The human cost of these diseases is horrific. Those with children suffering from Wolf-Hirschhorn have to endure the torment of witnessing their child becoming progressively more ill – and then be subject to the premature death of their child. Those with either a spouse or a parent with Huntington's chorea go through unimaginable hell while the disease slowly consumes their loved one over a period of 15 to 25 years. Can you think of anything worse than having your loved one, your wife, your husband, your mother, your father deteriorating to such an extent that they can't even recognise you – or for that matter don't even know their own name?

They can't even remember where they should go to the toilet; doubtless remember where they live or how to get home.

For families with loved ones suffering from Huntington's chorea, this happens every day not just for a few days, a few months, a few years – but for decades. In short, it ruins not just the life of the carrier but the life of all their family. Additionally, there is a massive cost to the rest of us, in the form of taxes that we have to pay in order to support these unfortunate people – and we are the lucky ones.

Now, we have Mr Horowitz telling this court that this is a very fine thing and it has nothing to do with the state. He maintains that the state does not have the right to interfere when such a condition is detected in an embryo. He is saying the Lord Mayor of London was right to respect the rights of half a dozen property owners knowing full well that their selfish decisions would lead directly to the destruction of thousands of other homes. He is saying that those with genetic deformity have the right to spread the deformity to thousands of others in future generations.

Mr Horowitz, you are wrong.

The state not only has a right to become involved, but it has an obligation to the population as a whole to avoid the massive costs associated with the caring of these people, it has an obligation to the family members of these people to prevent their lives being wrecked by these detectable and preventable debilitating diseases. However, we have an even greater obligation to future generations. The world is a better place now that smallpox has been completely eradicated. Just because Wolf-Hirschhorn syndrome is due to genes not the environment, doesn't mean that we shouldn't make every effort to try and eradicate the disease.

Like smallpox, the world will be a better place without Wolf-Hirschhorn syndrome, without Huntington's chorea and without hundreds or thousands of other genetic diseases. It is the state's right and obligation to protect the population, both the current and future population, from the occurrences of diseases. This obligation covers both diseases that are caught from the environment and diseases that manifest as a result of a genetic abnormality.

As cited in the Ethics Ruling Committee Hearing, the condition of achondroplasia is not limited to just being short. There are numerous other medical conditions that accompany this disease. All have a cost to the carrier, the members of the carrier's family, the tax payers and to future generations. If the state can detect and then prevent this disease – it has an obligation to do so.

FR   Counsellor Horowitz, would you like to opportunity to respond?

BH   Yes, My Lord. My I ask my learned colleague if I understand the GPA's position correctly?

FR   I would have thought it was a little late in these court proceeding to be determining what the GPA's position is, but nevertheless, please proceed.

BH   Counsellor Coulson, can I ask you to confirm that my understanding of the GPA's position is correct? I understand it as follows:

> That defective people be prevented from propagating equally defective offspring is a demand of the clearest reason and, if systematically executed, represents the most humane act of mankind. It will spare millions of unfortunates undeserved sufferings, and consequently will lead to a rising improvement of health as a whole.

Have I understood your position correctly?

LC   Counsellor, while we could argue about the semantics of your understanding, yes as you are well aware from the court proceedings that we have gone through together thus far, this is broadly the GPA's position.

BH   Thank you, Counsellor, for confirming the GPA's position for me. If I may, I would like to remind this court of some recent history, where the same perverted rationale as the GPA is currently espousing was mercilessly pursued.

A little over one hundred years ago, in March 1907, the US State of Indiana ratified a bill which gave it the dubious honour of becoming the first jurisdiction in the world to legislate for the forced sterilisation of its mentally impaired patients, poorhouse residents and prisoners.

Over the following few decades, many other US states enacted similar legislation. This directly led to the forced sterilisation of at least 60,000 Americans. However, the true number is no doubt much higher than this, as at the time many records of such barbarianism were either not recorded at all or the records were destroyed.

Twenty years later, on 2 May 1927, after thousands had already been forcibly sterilised, the Supreme Court of the USA, in the case of Buck v. Bell, upheld the states' right to forcibly sterilise its citizens. Justice Oliver Wendell Holmes Jr wrote the opinion for the majority with:

> It is better for all the world, if instead of waiting to execute degenerate offspring for crime, or to let them starve for their imbecility, society can prevent those who are manifestly unfit from continuing their kind. The principle that sustains compulsory vaccination is broad enough to cover cutting the fallopian tubes.

> Three generations of imbeciles are enough.

The case was based on the assessment of Carrie Buck, her mother and her daughter – all three generations were assessed, by the state, as imbeciles. Carrie's daughter, Vivian, was only seven months old when the state examined and assessed her as an imbecile. Perhaps the extreme biasness of the medical profession, the social services, and the judiciary in assessing Vivian as an imbecile is best demonstrated by the fact that young Vivian not only went on to develop normally and went on to school, but she also earned herself a place on the school's honour roll.

Notwithstanding the tender young age that Vivian was falsely assessed as an imbecile, it was sufficient for the Supreme Court of the United State of America to declare that 'three generation of imbeciles were enough', which put the nail in the coffin, or scalpel in the fallopian, for Carrie. On losing the case, Carrie Buck was forcibly sterilised on 19 October 1927.

This stage-managed case in 1927 opened the flood gates for forced sterilisations in the US. A total of 29 US states enacted laws to forcibly sterilise the feebleminded, other mental patients, criminals, the moral degenerates, the poor and the medically unacceptable. By 1940, no fewer than 35,878 men and women had been sterilised or castrated – almost 30,000 of them after Buck v. Bell. However, again, due to the poor records maintained, or deliberately destroyed, the number is likely to be far higher.

And, just what was the definition of feeblemindedness? The short answer is 'pretty much anyone that the establishment didn't like'. To illustrate that I am not being emotive or exaggerating the prejudice of the 'establishment', I cite the example of the Sonoma State Home, where it viewed sexual activity by single women as evidence of mental deficiency, irrespective of whether or not a patient met medical or psychological standards of 'feeblemindedness'. If they were sexually active, they were sterilised.

The example of Sonoma State Home's unbelievable and unsupportable definition of feeblemindedness is far from an aberration in the abuse of defining – or not defining as the case may be – feeblemindedness. To illustrate how far the establishment abused the term 'feeblemindedness' to mount a war on anyone they didn't like, I shall relay to the court just one of many, many tragic stories where good, honest hardworking people were forcibly sterilised just because the establishment called them feebleminded.

One day during the 1930s, the Montgomery County sheriff in the State of Virginia, drove up unannounced to a white settlement on Brush Mountain and grabbed six brothers, and forcibly transported them to Western State Hospital in Staunton Virginia. The hospital did not have a clear definition of what feeblemindedness meant, but those in the hospital were pretty certain that the 'Hillbillies' that had just been dragged in fitted the description. They were all forcibly sterilised. They were sterilised without either a medical or psychological assessment, without a trial, without appeal, without recourse and without pity.

This story in itself is unbelievably sad. But, it is in fact much worse. On an earlier raid on this settlement, the brothers' sister was captured and sterilised, as were many of their cousins.

Every member of this family was forcibly sterilised for no apparent reason – certainly there was not any documented medical reason. I think everyone in this court would agree with me that this was an unbelievable and indefensible violation of these folks' civil liberties and human rights. If this story was confined to this one family alone, it would be an injustice of massive proportions. However, this family was not being singled out for special treatment – as they were just some of the victims of a campaign by the Virginian authorities to wipe out, what they referred to as 'white trash'.

A sense of the scale of this exercise can be gleaned from Howard Hale, the Montgomery County supervisor at the time, who said of the raids years later 'I don't know how many they took, but they were after a lot of them.'

The tragedy of this despicable state-endorsed genocide campaign was exacerbated by the misinformation given to these unfortunate individuals. Many, probably most, were not informed that they had been sterilised. It was only in later life, when they were married and trying to have a family, that they discovered exactly what had been done to them at Western State Hospital. Their inability to have children led many of their partners to divorce them.

These mountain folk were neither imbeciles nor feebleminded. The only crime, or more correctly, the only aspect of these folk that made them the target of the 'establishment' was their mountain accents and their lack of exposure to a formalised education system. They were not imbeciles, criminals or feeble minded. But, as the presiding establishment ran the courts, the police, the social services – collectively these institutions came together in an appalling attempt to eradicate the mountain folk from the American gene pool.

Perhaps, the prevailing attitude by the establishment at the time, was best expressed by HG Wells, who in his book *Anticipation of the Reaction of Mechanical and Scientific Progress upon Human Life and Thought* opines: 'The swarms of black, and brown, and dirty-white, and yellow people have to go.'

Appalling as the American Eugenics tale is, it gets worse, much, much worse. The American science of eugenics spread to Germany, where it caught the attention of Hitler and the Nazi movement. Upon adopting eugenic principles, the Nazis coined the following phrase, which became one of their mantras:

'National Socialism is nothing but applied biology'.

The zest with which the Nazis took to eugenics dismayed some American scientists and in 1934 the *Richmond Times-Dispatch* quoted Joseph DeJarnette, superintendent of Virginia's Western State Hospital and prominent American eugenicist, as saying 'The Germans are beating us at our own game.'

Clearly, the Americans wanted to sterilise more! In *Mein Kampf*, Hitler maintained that:

'The state must see to it that only the healthy beget children. The state must put the most modern medical means in the service of this knowledge. It must declare unfit for propagation all who are in any way visibly sick or who have inherited a disease and can therefore pass it on, and put this into actual practice.'

You may ask, in fact you should ask, was Hitler really influenced by the American eugenics movement when he wrote the above passage – and when he instituted his Nazi eugenics programme?

I shall read out a passage from a leading American scientist, also a leading eugenics advocate. Madison Grant was not only a leading scientist of his day, but also the trustee of the American Museum of Natural History. In his 1936 publication, 'The Passing of the Great Race', he wrote:

'Speaking English, wearing good clothes and going to school and to church do not transform a Negro into a white man.'

In *Mein Kampf*, Hitler wrote:

'It is a fallacy of thought to believe that a Negro or a Chinese, let us say, will turn into a German because he learns German and is willing to speak the German language in the future and perhaps even give his vote to a German political party.'

In *Mein Kampf*, Hitler went on to cite and praise the American racial policies:

'There is today one state in which at least weak beginnings towards a better conception of immigration are noticeable. Of course, it is not our model German Republic, but the United States, in which an effort is made to consult reason at least partially. By refusing immigrants on principle to elements in poor health, by simply excluding certain races from naturalization.'

Hitler went on to tell comrades:

'I have studied with great interest the laws of several American states concerning the prevention of reproduction by people whose progeny would, in all probability, be of no value or be injurious to the racial stock. But the possibility of excess and error is still no proof of the incorrectness of these laws. It only exhorts us to the greatest possible conscientiousness.'

While the above quotes from Hitler may have been mere talk and bravado, it led to the introduction of Germany's own eugenic legislation, which was modelled on the laws already introduced across America, upheld by the Supreme Court and routinely enforced.

On the 14 July 1933, less than six months after Hitler came to power, the first of Germany's eugenic laws was enacted, Reich Statue Part 1, No. 86, the Law for the Prevention of Defective Progeny. Based on the American equivalent, it was a compulsory mass sterilisation law. Nine categories of defectives were identified for sterilisation:

- Feebleminded.
- Schizophrenia.
- Manic depression.
- Huntington's chorea.
- Epilepsy.

- Hereditary body deformities.
- Deafness.
- Hereditary blindness.
- Alcoholism.

The American Eugenics movement was proud of the influence they had on Germany in enacting this legislation, as cited in their newsletter 'Current Record of Genetic News and Race Hygiene':

'The law recently promulgated by the Nazi government marks several substantial advances. Doubtless the legislative and court history of the experimental sterilisation laws in 27 states of the American union provided the experience, which Germany used in writing her new national sterilisation stature. To one versed in the history of eugenical sterilisation in America, the text of the German statutes reads almost like the "American model sterilization law".'

The article proudly goes on:

'In the meantime it is announced that the Reich will secure data on prospective sterilisation cases, that it will, in fact, in accordance with "the American model sterilization law", work out a census of its socially inadequate human stock.'

Later the publication boldly asserted:

'That in the 16,000 sterilisations performed in America over recent years, not a single 'eugenical mistake' has been made.'

And finally concludes:

'It remains for Germany in 1933 to lead the great nations of the world in the recognition of the biological foundations of national character.'

After its eugenic legislation was enacted in 1934, Germany was forcibly sterilising over five thousand hapless victims per month. The American eugenics movement was ecstatic with the Nazis' enthusiasm for sterilising so many helpless victims. The degree of ecstasy is evidenced by one of America's leading eugenics, the late Charles M Goethe, to this day a widely respected philanthropist, so much so that the Sacramento State University named part of their campus after him, the 'CM Goethe Arboretum'.

In 1934, after returning from a fact-finding mission to Germany, Goethe wrote to his friend Ezra Seymour Gosney:

> 'You will be interested to know that your work has played a powerful part in shaping the opinions of the group of intellectuals who are behind Hitler in this epoch-making program. Everywhere I sensed that their opinions have been tremendously stimulated by American thought, and particularly by the work of the human Betterment Foundation. I want you to know, my dear friend, to carry this thought with you for the rest of your life, that you have really jolted into action a great government of 60 million people.'

It is difficult to overstate the degree in which 'science' was used to support these racist eugenic views. To pick just one example, in 1933, the prestigious medical publication 'Journal of the American Medical Association' reported:

> 'The fact that among the Jews the incidence of blindness is greater than among the remainder of the population of Germany (the ratio is 63 to 53) is doubtless due to the increased danger of hereditary transmission resulting from marriage between blood relatives.'

And it went on:

> 'A foreign invasion, more particularly from the East, constitutes a menace to the German race. It is an imperative necessity that this menace be now suppressed and eliminated ... Radical problems and questions dealing with hereditary biology must receive special consideration ... Eugenics and the influence of hereditary must be the preferred topics at future medical meetings.'

Now, let me put the above indefensible campaigns in the context of the case that is before this court today. These two campaigns, the American and Nazi eugenic programmes, were carried out in the name of science.

The case before this court is being waged in the name of science. The State of Virginia used the façade of science to implement its ruthless racist policies. In addition to the 'hillbillies', Black people and Native Americans were also sterilised *en-mass* during this racist campaign. To stress the point – these outright and overt racist acts were justified and rationalised in the name of science.

Now, with our knowledge of race-specific genetic susceptibility to certain diseases, we again are opening the door to state-sponsored discrimination of minority groups, whether these groups are defined along ethnic grounds or some other equally repugnant classification scheme – like dwarfs, using the scientific name of 'achondroplasia'.

Naturally, you will be questioning my logic and asking whether I am overstating or exaggerating the issue. Well, consider this 'scientific' argument: two genes for breast cancer have been identified, namely BRCA1 and BRCA2. Those with either of these two genes are more susceptible to breast cancer than those without them. The, GPA, is currently in the process of having these two genes gazetted – on the same grounds that they have put forward in court today, to eradicate these defective genes from the human gene pool.

Let's consider this action for a moment. Neither of these two genes are deadly. Carriers of these genes do not necessarily develop breast cancer. Those that do, often have early treatment or surgery, and live an ordinary life with a life expectancy similar to their peers.

The point being that the carriers of these genes only have an increased risk of developing breast cancer. It is far from a certainty that the carriers will ever develop breast cancer. Furthermore, NOT having either of these two genes does not eliminate the risk of developing breast cancer. To stress this point further:

- Of all white patients with breast cancer, only 3.3% of them have either of these two identified genes. For Black people suffering from breast cancer, they never have either of the two genes.
- Those with either of these two genes have a 36% chance of getting breast cancer during their life time.
- However, 12% of all women will develop breast cancer sometime during their lifetime.
- Therefore, a carrier of either of the BRCA genes only has an increased risk of developing breast cancer by a factor of three – i.e. most carriers of either gene will never develop breast cancer.

It has to be asked why the GPA is so hell bent on eliminating these two genes that, at best, only have a marginal correlation with breast cancer? Eliminating these two genes will not eliminate breast cancer – at the most optimistic projection, the rate of breast cancer within the population would decrease by less than 2%.

It is irrational to screen for these two particular genes. That is, until a little more light is shed on some disturbing facts associated with these genes.

- The BRCA1 gene in question is pretty much isolated to Ashkenazim Jews.
- The BRCA2 gene in question is pretty much isolated to Icelanders.

We now have to ask – what is the GPA's real objective? Is it to eliminate breast cancer or to eliminate Jews? In the name of science, the GPA is attacking Jews and Icelanders, all the while maintaining the moral high ground that race has nothing to do with its screening programme. The GPA is arguing that it is strictly a scientific criterion that is being used for the forced termination of their embryos and foetuses.

Under the guise of eradicating a specific genetic related disease, an attack is being mounted on specific communities and races. This is a classic case of the modern day eugenics campaign – finding a scientific basis to mount a population-control programme against a defined racial population. The GPA and the broader establishment no longer has to expose its racial agenda, all it has to do is cite a genetic condition and call a race war in the name of science – just as the eugenics movements in America and Nazi Germany did last century.

> If you are under the impression that this is an isolated race/genetic combination – then think again. There are literally hundreds of race-specific genes – or at least where one race has a higher propensity of carrying a disease-related gene than others. To illustrate this point, consider the following examples, Duchenne muscular dystrophy for north-eastern British people, adult lactase deficiency for African-Americans and the Chinese, cleft palate for North American Indians and the Japanese, or cystic fibrosis for Northern Europeans.

In 1933, the American Medical Association, in the name of science, espoused eugenic intervention to preserve race and culture. They even openly supported the Nazi eugenics campaign against Jews, by citing a higher hereditary blindness rate in Jews compared with the rest of the population. These campaigns were not waged in the name of racism; they were waged in the name of science.

Now, a mere 80 years later, we have the GPA espousing a near identical political and social philosophy, again in the name of science, that unborn Jews should be terminated, citing a higher rate of breast cancer in Jews compared with the rest of the population.

Now, bear in mind, the above example of the two BRCA genes are instances of specific genetic conditions that are about to be gazetted. This example demonstrates the abuse that the gazetting process allows – by allowing specific ethnic or other groups to be targeted.

The case before the court today is asking the court to rule on a human condition, which is outside the controls associated with the gazetting process – remembering the gazetting process itself has totally inadequate controls. What essentially the GPA is demanding is for it to have the right and authority to unilaterally decide who can propagate and who cannot. It is seeking this authority without any pre-determined criteria or controls over who will be allowed to have children and who will not.

The definition that the GPA is asking for, the three standard deviations from the human norm rule, is so much broader and open to interpretation and abuse than the 'feebleminded' rule used by the USA and Germany. And the narrower US and Nazi definitions were abused beyond measure and beyond all conscience.

The American and Nazi eugenic movement of the twentieth century and the GPA eugenic movement in the twenty-first century were not and are NOT science. It is racism and fascism. Hitler would be proud of the work that the GPA is undertaking.

If you think I have taken a step too far in saying that Hitler would be proud of the GPA, then pause and reflect for a moment on the GPA's position that Counsellor Coulson affirmed a little earlier. As a reminder, the position she agreed with was:

> That defective people be prevented from propagating equally defective offspring is a demand of the clearest reason and, if systematically executed, represents the most humane act of mankind. It will spare millions of unfortunates undeserved sufferings, and consequently will lead to a rising improvement of health as a whole.

This position that the GPA agreed with, is a direct quote from Hitler's *Mein Kampf*.

My Lord, Winston Churchill described it as our nation's proudest moment when we defeated the Nazis. In excess of 70 million people died during that brutal war, stopping that tyrant's racist, brutal, murderous policies and exterminations. Do not let these 70 million lives be lost in vain. My Lord, do not go down in history as the man that let Hitler into Britain through a back door called GPA genetic screening.

I rest my case.

FR   A little earlier in these proceedings, I was on the receiving end of a thinly veiled accusation of being a murderer and now, Counsellor Horowitz, you are comparing me with Hitler. You have sailed dangerously close to being held in contempt of court. One more such attack, inference or innuendo from anyone in either party will be held in contempt of court. Now, for the remainder of these proceedings, I remind legal counsel to stick to the facts of the case in accord with this court's proceeding.

Do I make myself clear?

Judge Rogers looks at Bill Horowitz.

BH   Yes, My Lord.

Judge Rogers looks at Laurie Coulson.

LC   [Begrudgingly.] Yes, My Lord.

FR   I have now granted each party sufficient opportunity to present their case to this court, in which both sides have presented very robust arguments supporting their respective cases.

I shall now adjourn the court until 3:00pm Monday, 10 June 2010, whereupon I shall hand down my judgment.

Court adjourned.

Court Stewart   All rise

The judge rises, turns and walks straight out of the courtroom through the back door. Laurie Coulson and Bill Horowitz race to the bench in an attempt to bring him back to discuss the case and the sudden abrupt adjournment. But this is to no avail, as the judge ignores their calls and walks straight out.

The scene fades out on Laurie and Bill at the bench with the look of dismay and possibly dejection on their face.

Scene 81 – The appeal – the Club discussion

1:00pm, Sunday, 9 June 2013

Setting: Judge Rogers' Chambers

The scene opens in Judge Rogers' chambers, where on the sideboard half a dozen birthday cards are on display. Frederick is sitting at his desk reading John Milton's 'Areopagitica', when his secretary, Clarissa, buzzes the intercom to inform him that he has a number of visitors.

CD   Judge, eight visitors have just arrived asking to see you. Shall I see them into your chamber?

FR   Thank you, Clarissa, yes I am expecting them, so please see them in.

CD   Certainly, Judge.

Frederick gets up from his chair and walks to the door of his chamber and arrives just as there is a knock on the door and, without waiting for a reply, Clarissa opens the door and delivers Frederick's guests to his chamber. The eight guests are the members of the Country Club that meet at Claydon House, namely: Sir John Poo Beresford, Lord Thomas Denman, Sir Ronald Lawe-Davies, Oscar Williamson, Sebastian McKibben, Chris Braithwaite, Max Lyford and Angus Le Bon.

The party walk in and exchange greetings with Frederick.

FR   Please, do take a seat. I have ordered sandwiches for lunch, which should be here in a minute or two.

As the party gather around the centre coffee table and position themselves to take a seat, Lord Thomas looks up and notices the birthday cards on the sideboard.

LTD   Frederick, have you had a birthday recently?

FR   Well, yes, in fact I turned 67 today. If I wasn't a judge, I would now be up for retirement.

LTD   Well congratulations, young man. You should have told us, and we could have brought you a little surprise.

All the others join and wish Frederick a happy birthday.

FR   Thank you, but, I have had enough surprises over the past few weeks, so there really is no reason to surprise me again.

At this moment, there is a knock on the door. Frederick looks up, assuming it is Clarissa coming in with the sandwiches.

SRLD Too late, my dear chap, we caught wind that it was your birthday and thought we should honour you with a little surprise. And, why not, you more than deserve it – working on Sundays deserves special commendation.

Clarissa walks in pushing a drinks trolley with two chilled bottles of Krüg Champagne and nine Loreley range of Edmee Champagne flutes with a birthday cake in the middle. Without waiting for instructions, she starts to open the bottle of Krüg. At this point Oscar comes to her aid.

OW   Thank you very much, Clarissa, but if you like I will take over from here.

CD   Sure, if you need anything, then please call. I am just on the other side of the door.

OW   Thank you, Clarissa. This is terrific, and a real sign of dedication to give up your Sunday to help out the judge.

CD   My pleasure – and he is worth it!

FR   Clarissa, yes, thank you for all your assistance, it is very much appreciated.

CD   Any time.

Oscar immediately opens the Krüg and starts pouring everyone a glass of Champagne. The scene fades out as Oscar passes everyone their glass while the others are engaged in general conversation about Frederick's birthday – and how long he has been in his job.

Insert Scene – 52

The supreme natural aristocrat is the genius, and it is the shining example of genius that makes clear the baseness of the mass and the folly of parliamentary democracy. The creative act of genius is always a protest against the inertia of the mass. Democracy, by vesting power in the dunderheaded multitude flies in the face of the aristocratic principle of nature.

Mein Kampf *by Adolf Hitler.*

Scene 82 – Ivan talks, while Greg incites

1:30pm, Sunday, 9 June 2013

Setting: Auditorium at City University London

The scene is set in a tired auditorium/seminar room at City University London. The paintwork is dull and flaky, the seating and benches are made up of dull, tired, used dark wood, the windows made of cheap aluminium single-glazed frames – where the window frames no longer properly close.

The auditorium is full of dwarfs, all quite excited with very concerned looks on their faces – all whispering and chatting to each other. While there is no one at the lectern, there is the odd look up by those present to see if anyone is there.

The chatter suddenly reduces to next to nothing.

The camera takes a new aspect showing the front of the auditorium, where Ivan is walking in from the side door, immediately followed by Andy and Rob. Ivan is dressed in a checked flannelette shirt and tightly fitting jeans. Rob is dressed in a business suit, shirt and tie, complete with black shoes. Andy is dressed in a black suit, white shirt, black tie, dark sunglasses and black fedora hat and black violin case – aside from his physical size, he looks very much like a bouncer-come-gangster.

Ivan walks up to the lectern, and just before stepping into the lectern stops and waits motionless. Without pause, Andy places his violin case on the front bench of the auditorium, flips it open and removes a contraption made up of a series of small poles – the diameter of thin curtain rods. With a hint of showmanship, Andy elegantly unfolds the contraption, which folds into a small stand with a step, which Andy places by the lectern. Ivan climbs the step onto the top of the stand, which makes him visible over the lectern to the rest of the gathering.

Ivan places his hands either side of the lectern and stands tall and authoritative. Andy and Rob position themselves each side of Ivan, so that they too are visible to those in attendance. Ivan waits until there is total silence in the room. The wait escalates the degree of tension in the room.

Slowly but purposefully, Ivan reaches for the mic and moves it towards him in a manner that reinforces his authoritative stance.

IH   Ladies and gentlemen, I have called this emergency meeting today, as we are faced with a great danger. I now speak to you for the last time as a human.

Pause.

I now speak to 'you', as humans, for the very last time.

Long pause.

AUD   What are you telling us – that you are about to toss yourself? I got better things to do on a Sunday than listen to a suicidal short-ass looking for empathy!

IH   Believe me, if suicide was the answer to my problems, to your problems, I'd gladly do it. Unfortunately, our problems are a little more intractable.

AUD   Ivan, quit with the melodrama, why did you call us here today?

IH   As I said, I speak to you now, as a human, for the last time. You see, tomorrow at 3:00pm, I will be, you will be, animals.

Long pause, with the audience all looking very quizzical and alternatively looking at Ivan then their neighbour, seeking an explanation for the absurd remark that Ivan just made.

During this prolonged pause, Ivan maintains his authoritative poise and stares intently at the crowd without focussing on anyone in particular, but maintaining a very intense expression. Andy and Rob survey the room with a barely visible nod, showing their endorsement of Ivan's statement.

After a minute or so passes, the chattering noise from the audience has built up quite a bit – as has the tension.

AUD   Ivan, are you taking the piss or what?

This is followed by a number of others shouting to Ivan to clarify his position.

IH   [In a very solemn and very authoritative voice.] I would like to say that I am taking the piss.

He pauses – and there is a slight relief of tension in the audience, but replaced by confusion.

IH   As much as I would like to say I was taking the piss, I can't – because I'm not!

The level of tension and confusion within the audience again rises.

AUD   Ivan, what the fuck are you saying, spit it out or fuck off and let us get back to our weekend.

IH   Tomorrow, at 3:00pm, Judge Frederick Rogers will be making his judgment as to whether or not, I, as a dwarf, meet the criterion that defines what it is to be human. If his judgement goes against me – then officially, I will no longer be a human. [Long pause.] If I am judged not to be a human, then the only thing that I can be is an animal. [Long pause.]

      You see, Judge Rogers will decide whether I meet the statistical definition of what constitutes a human, by sole reference to my height. If Judge Rogers so decides that, due to my height, I'm a statistical outlier – i.e. outside of the 'human norm', then it means that I am not a human. [Long pause – and a lot of consternation within the audience.] And, by the anxiety I see in you, you have all realised that if I am judged to be an animal, then you too are an animal.

      Yes, all of us in this room, every dwarf in this country, will be classified as an animal. We will no longer be protected by British law. We will have no more rights than an ordinary animal. Animals do not have the right to own property, animals do not have the right to work, animals do not have the right to reproduce or have families. Animals, at best, are considered stock or chattel.

      If an animal is killed, however intentional, the killer cannot be charged with murder. The crime of murder is the preserve of humans – not animals, not dwarfs. Tomorrow, at 3:00pm, if the judgement goes against me, against us, against you, we will be free game. Anyone will be able to kill us – knowing that they cannot be charged with murder because they will have killed a dwarf, an animal, not a human.

Pause. Angry looks take shape on all the dwarfs in the crowd – all turning to each other and expressing their outrage and indignation at such a prospect.

AUD   [Shouting to Ivan] Nobody can do that – we have the same rights as everyone else does.

IH   If tomorrow's judgment goes against me, against us – it means that the government has the right to determine who is human and who isn't. And the government will have ruled that we, as dwarfs, are not human.

AUD   This is ridiculous, Ivan, you're definitely taking the piss now. No court in the country would uphold such a law. If they did, then it would never stand up in the High Court.

IH   Unfortunately, I'm not taking the piss. And, for your information, it is the High Court that will be making the judgment at 3:00pm tomorrow. This is it! Whatever the judgment is tomorrow, the judgment will seal our fate forever.

AUD   Explain, I don't understand what this means for the rest of us?

IH   What does this mean for the rest of you? Indeed, this is the question. This is why I'm here. This is why you are here! As I said at the beginning, you may very soon find yourself legally classified as an animal. Because, if you are not classified as a human, then there is only one other option – you are an animal.

AUD   They can't do that to us. That's inhumane.

IH   That's the point – inhuman, non-human. In the eyes of the law and the eyes of the court, we will not be human.

AUD   So, what legal rights will we have?

IH   Last time I checked, I didn't find dwarfs on the list of protected species.

AUD   Don't be ridiculous, the law will not allow people going around shooting us.

IH   The law on homicide only relates to humans. In anticipation of your disbelief of what we're facing, I brought with me some film footage from a prior generation, of a people that were also deemed to be non-human, or in their case 'sub-human'. Please watch, learn and prepare yourselves for a similar fate starting at three pm tomorrow.

At this point, Ivan nods to Andy, who touches his smartphone, which is wirelessly connected to a projector via Bluetooth, and film footage of Jews in Germany starts to be projected on the whiteboard at the front of the lecture theatre.

The footage is of Nazi Germany, taken on 10 November 1938 during the Krystalnacht, or the Night of the Broken Glass, where mobs smash Jewish shops, burn down Synagogues and mercilessly round up and beat up Jews.

As the footage plays, Ivan narrates:

IH   In January 1933, an act was passed in Germany which defined Jews as 'Untermenschen', or sub-human. From this moment onwards, Germans were prohibited from shopping in Jewish shops – which was enthusiastically enforced by Nazi thugs. On buses, trains and park benches, Jews had to sit on seats marked for them. A few years later in 1935, the Nuremberg Laws were passed which revoked Jews' rights to be German citizens and prohibited marriage between Jews and non-Jews.

        Influenced by propaganda and Nazi pressure, many German shops refused to sell food or medicine to the sub-human Jews. The campaign against the Jews reached a pre-war peak in November 1938 when Hitler ordered a seven day campaign of terror against the Jews, known as the Krystalnacht, or the Night of the Broken Glass.

        On the tenth of November 1938, 10,000 shops owned by Jews were destroyed and their contents stolen. Homes and Synagogues were set on fire and left to burn. The fire brigades showed their loyalty to Hitler by assuming that the buildings would burn down anyway, so why try to prevent it? Many Jews were rounded up and mercilessly beaten by anti-Semitic mobs.

        No German was arrested or charged in connection with the violence, looting or destruction of property. No German was charged – as they had not committed a crime against a human, only a Jew, a sub-human, an animal.

The footage stops.

IH   We are now in danger of being similarly defined as sub-human. If we are so defined, then crimes committed against us will likewise not be considered as crimes. If the law does not recognise us as humans, then nobody can be charged with murder if they kill us. The best hope that we would have is to be put on the protected species list.

AUD   What about our homes, our jobs, our possessions?

IH   I have no idea. But, if the judgement goes against us, then all our civil rights and liberties may be lost. If we lose the case, we may well find ourselves with the same rights – or more correctly – lack of rights, that the Jews had under the Third Reich. In the UK, this is definitely unchartered legal territory. So anything and everything is possible.

AUD   Is it really this bad – or are you exaggerating the issue?

IH   At the very minimum [he points to two pregnant women in the audience who are accompanied by their partners], you, and you – and everyone in this room in all probability –will never be allowed to have children.

AUD   What? That's insane, nobody can stop us from having babies and having a family.

IH   Sorry, guys. If you are a dwarf and you have an unborn child that will be likewise a dwarf, well as you do not have the legal rights of a human then the state will be in its rights to forcibly terminate your pregnancy.

You may be thinking that a way around this unfortunate situation would be to have a non- dwarf, i.e. a human, to have your kids. This could work as, at least at the moment, the government cannot legally force the termination of your non-dwarf wife's pregnancy.

However, if the judgement goes against us tomorrow, then government actively encourages the termination of any pregnancy where the embryo has the genetic traits of a dwarf. Now, you may be thinking, the government can do all the encouraging they like, but I'm still going to have my baby. But, the government is pretty persuasive in its encouragement to terminate dwarf babies being carried by normal-heighted mothers. Just for starters, this is how it encourages the termination:

The paternal rights of the father, in regards to any decision to continue with the pregnancy, are revoked.

However, the father's financial obligations to support the child, should it be born, are not revoked – nor for that matter are the mothers' financial obligations. And, by financial obligations, these are considerable, or more correctly overbearing or crushing. The reason the financial obligations are so crushing is that the government removes all financial, social, educational and medical support and aid from the child and parents. To rub salt into the wound, the withdrawal of financial assistance is for life – including the death and burial of your child.

The effect of this is that the parents have to pay for all education, medical, health support. If the parents cannot or do not pay for something, then the government will seize and sell the parents assets – their home, car or anything else that they may have. So, no one will be able to afford to have and raise a dwarf child, therefore they will be forced, financially, to terminate the pregnancy.

Ivan pauses.

IH   Tomorrow, if the judgment goes against me, against us, then the blood line of everyone in this room will die with us. Should we lose this case, if that's all that happens to you, then you will be lucky! Truth is that we are likely to be treated like animals, like the Jews under the Nazis.

AUD   [Black dwarf partner of one of the white dwarf pregnant women.] That's preposterous – nobody has the right to kill my baby. Just who the hell do these guys think they are? Tell you what, if anyone dared come near Sheryl and tried to abort our baby, I'd fucking kill the bastard. And I mean that, they try and kill my baby, I kill them. I don't give a fuck who it is, or who authorised it, I'd fucking kill them. So, Ivan, what do you want me to do? Whatever it is, wherever it is, I'll be there and I'll do it!

IH   I am not sure what we can do. But, I think sheer numbers and a show of strength will help – to show the judge that he is not just dealing with me – but he is dealing with all of us here and more.

At this point, a 'rough' looking dwarf (Greg O'Leary) dressed in worn black leather, who had been sitting quietly on the side of the seminar room, grabs a large blackboard ruler (1 metre) that was lying on his bench, picks it up and starts slamming it into the bench – making a massive racket.

Everyone in the seminar room stops and looks at him.

GO   I've heard enough of this shit. I'm no fucking animal. If anyone thinks they can treat me like one – they are sorely mistaken. I don't give a shit who they are, judge, pig, polly or civilian. If they want to kill off my kids, then it's over my dead body.

        I think it's time for us to show all those fuckers out there exactly who they are dealing with. They need to know that, if they think they can class us as animals, then we ain't going to just roll over and let them piss on us. It's time that we stood up to all those cunts who have constantly treated us like second class citizens – who now want to degrade us even further and classify us as animals.

IH   Greg, I think we need to be a little careful as to what we do now.

GO   Why, in case they condemn us to death? Isn't that exactly what you've just told us those wankers are about to do? For fuck's sake, now is the time for action, to show the world exactly who they are dealing with – and what they can expect if they go ahead and class us as fucking animals.

At this point Greg climbs onto the bench where he had previously been sitting and takes control of the meeting

GO   Are you sick of those wankers constantly putting us down?

AUD   [Moderate.] Yeah.

GO   I didn't hear you. Now, tell me, are you sick of those wankers constantly putting us down?

AUD   [Louder.] Yes.

GO   For fuck's sake, your very existence is at risk, if those cunts get their way, they are going to kill your kids. Now, tell me, are you sick of those wankers constantly putting us down?

AUD   [Loud.] Yes.

GO   Are you sick of them constantly insulting you?

AUD   [Loud.] Yes.

GO   Are you sick of being the butt of every fucking joke?

AUD   [Loud.] Yes.

GO   Are you sick of being looked over for every fucking promotion?

AUD   [Loud.] Yes.

GO   Are you sick of our women constantly being harassed to appear in porno movies?

AUD   [Loud.] Yes.

GO   Is this stupid court case, which is threatening your very existence, the very last fucking straw?

AUD   [Very loud.] Yes.

GO   Are you going to come with me to the High Court and those stupid fuckers at the GPA and give them a little of their own macabre fucking medicine?

AUD   [Very loud.] Yes.

GO   And are you going to come with me NOW?

AUD   [Very loud.] Yes.

IH   Guys, we really need to think about this – I'm not sure storming the High Court is such a good idea.

GO   Fuck you, Ivan, you got us into this mess – but you've got no idea how to get us out of it.

       What the fuck have we got to lose by showing those wankers at the GPA and the High Court that we mean business and that we're a force to be reckoned with? [Turning to the audience.] What do you say, short-asses, let's storm the GPA offices and the High Court and show those cunts exactly what we're made of?

AUD   Yes, let's do it.

With this, Greg jumps off the bench and charges out of the door screaming a deafening war cry. As he runs through the seminar room (with the exception of Ivan, Andy and Rob) all the other dwarfs get swept up in the heat of the moment and run out following Greg, all screaming their own virgin war cries.

The scene fades out on the disconcerted expressions on Ivan, Rob and Andy – not knowing what they should do.

Insert Scene – 53

> *The cross between a white man and an Indian is an Indian; the cross between a white man and a Negro is a Negro; the cross between a white man and a Hindu is a Hindu; and the cross between any of the three European races and a Jew is a Jew.*
>
> *Madison Grant, Trustee of the American Museum of Natural History, 1936*

494

Scene 83 – The birthday boy

2:00pm, Sunday, 9 June 2013

Setting: Judge Roger's Chambers

The scene fades back in on the meeting in the court chambers, where Frederick and his colleagues are debating the merits of the case. It is evident some time has passed since the last scene in the Judge's chambers, as the two Champagne bottles are empty and the empty flutes are neatly stacked on a drinks trolley in the corner, and there are now various legal books open on the coffee table that they are sitting around.

ML   Laurie put in a truly magnificent performance. She clearly addressed the points of consideration in the appeal and made a compelling legal and moral argument as to why the state needs to intervene in cases of foetal abnormality.

Based on her good work, Frederick, you are in a sound position to make a judgment in favour of the GPA based entirely on the facts and the legal arguments that she presented. This alleviates you from having to invent new legal precedence to rule in the GPA's favour.

SJPB   I must say I have to agree with Max. While Bill put in arguments, they were all emotionally based, not based on the facts and circumstances before the court. Now, in all clear conscience, you can rule in favour of the GPA. In fact, I would go further and say, that your moral and legal conscience would compel you to rule in the GPA's favour.

ALB   It is interesting that each of the arguments that Bill put up Laurie was able to totally refute – especially all people being equal before the law due to the international treaties we are signatories to. What a load of rubbish. The only argument not totally demolished by Laurie was the reference to the American and Germany eugenics programmes of last century, which from a legal standpoint, is totally irrelevant to this case.

Frederick, Bill has left it wide open for you to rule in the GPA's favour. There is not a single legal argument amongst all his ranting and raving which needs to be considered before you rule in favour of the GPA.

FR   I'm sorry, I must disagree. Of the criteria I set at the beginning of the hearing, Laurie has not made a compelling legal case for each of the criteria.

ML   Frederick, I have considered the criteria you set, and Laurie did a sterling effort in systematically addressing each criterion. There are no loose ends.

FR   Max, that simply is not the case, let's go through the criteria. Does the state have the right to determine what constitutes a human or a person? As much as I hate to admit it – Laurie did establish that the state does have this right, and routinely exercises such rights.

At this point, Frederick reaches into his pocket and pulls out his mobile phone, which is vibrating. Without checking to see who is calling, he kills the call, puts the mobile back into his pocket and continues his conversation.

FR   Sorry for the interruption. Now, if the state does have the right to determine what constitutes a person, under what circumstances can a state make such a ruling? Again, Laurie defined precedence where this very court, this very judge made such a ruling. The criterion has been defined under what circumstances the state can make such a ruling. In regards to the third criteria, what controls are in place to prevent arbitrary or discriminatory practices?

At this point, Frederick again reaches into his pocket to withdraw the vibrating mobile. Without checking who the caller is, he switches the mobile off and puts it back into his pocket.

FR   Apologies again, at least it won't happen again.

      Anyway, this is where I have a problem: mainly, the lack of controls to prevent abuse. Bill highlighted that discriminatory practices have been used in the past, albeit by the Americans and Germans. Nevertheless, Laurie failed to demonstrate that the GPA has implemented any controls to stop similar practices being adopted by the GPA.

      All that the GPA had as a defence was that there is an objective measurement of three standard deviations from the human norm. This is wide open to interpretation and systematic abuse.

ML   Frederick, that is the whole point, isn't it? For Pete's sake, the whole country is being overtaken by imbeciles with IQs of 80 and less, and since no one dies of a hereditary disease anymore – because the state keeps them artificially alive to go forth and reproduce more genetically impaired offspring – our whole population is heading for a genetic meltdown.

It has taken five million years of evolution since we split from the chimpanzees to get to this elevated state of evolutionary superiority. Now, we are on track to undo five million years of work in just five generations. If we do not act now to clean up our genetic inheritance, it will be too late. Our genetic capital will be all but spent.

If you do not make a judgment in favour of the GPA there will not be another chance to correct the genetic decline for at least another generation. A generation we cannot afford. For the sake of humanity, you need to make an objective, unemotional decision. We as a proud species have already allowed ourselves to erode, weaken and diminish the very thing that makes us human, makes us special – our genes. We cannot afford a further decline, otherwise there simply will not be enough smart and healthy people out there to run our society.

At this point, Frederick's desk phone starts ringing. It rings five times then stops.

FR   Someone is keen, trying to phone me in my chambers on a Sunday afternoon.

Look, Max, I capitulated on the Bland judgment, something I still have reservations about. But, in that case, and the cases that followed, it involved single individuals on a case-by-case basis. So, if it were to be argued that it was an unsafe decision, unfortunate as it may be, only a few individuals would have been impacted by the decision. However, this case, involves whole classes of people.

If I rule in favour of the GPA, then thousands, potentially an order of magnitude more, will be impacted – none of whom will have the right of appeal. How can the state that upholds the values of a democratic and free society, that cherishes the civil rights of the individual, endorse the forced termination of all embryos that have a peculiarity that the state does not like – regardless of how the parents feel – and regardless of how others with the same peculiarity feel.

This is a clear case of the state taking a step too far. The Roland Barthes quote that the short guy paraphrased was right on the button. I took a copy from the hearing's transcript [with this, Judge Rogers picks up a sheet of paper on the table in front of him]:

> 'We are all potential Ivans, not as inferiors but accused as such, deprived of our right to be human, or worse, rigged out in that of our accusers, humiliated and condemned by it. To rob a man of his humanity in the very name of humanity: this is the first step in all legal genocides.'

If I rule in favour of the GPA, I'll be explicitly depriving hundreds, thousands or more, of their right to be human. I cannot, in all conscience, make such a judgment.

Insert Scene – 54

Improvements of the human race can probably be effected only by understanding and applying these methods. How appalling is our ignorance, for example, concerning the effect of a mixture of races as contrasted with pure breeding; a matter of infinite importance in a country like ours containing numerous races and subspecies of men.

Charles Davenport, Director Cold Springs Harbor Laboratory,1903

Scene 84 – Gough starts to make amends

2:15pm, Sunday, 9 June 2013

Setting: Edgar Wallace Pub

The scene opens with Gough sitting at a table in the Edgar Wallace pub, with a half-empty pint of lager on the table right beside a box wrapped up in birthday paper, with an envelope containing a birthday card fixed on top. The envelope is simply addressed to 'Dad'.

In an effort to try and relieve the high level of anxiety Gough is feeling, he leans forward, picks up his beer, leans back with his legs stretched out and has a long mouthful. He rests his glass on his chest and gazes intensely at the ceiling. After a few moments, he sits up straight, looks out the window and stares at the High Court.

He whispers to himself, 'Better luck this time'.

With that, he draws in a deep breath, and dials a number into his mobile phone.

Scene 85 – A father's dream comes true

2:20pm, Sunday, 9 June 2013

Setting: Judge Roger's outer Chambers, inner chamber and Edgar Wallace pub

The scene switches back to Frederick's Court Chambers, where Frederick is still debating the merits of the case with his colleagues. Then there is a knock on the door. Frederick looks up as his secretary, Clarissa, comes in.

CD Judge Rogers, you have a phone call that sounds urgent.

FR Thank you, Clarissa, but at the moment, I am rather busy – and I can't foresee any urgency that is so important that it should interrupt me at this point. Can I ask you to please take a message and I will call them back when I get the opportunity?

CD It did sound very urgent.

FR It can't be that urgent.

CD Okay, I will inform Mr Gough Rutherford that you cannot take his call.

There is a long, deep silence as Clarissa gazes at Frederick and then she slowly starts to close the door. Frederick looks quite puzzled – like trying to remember a long-lost name. Then, suddenly he peers at a photo on a sideboard near his armchair, which is the same photo that Gough had on his desk. His eyes suddenly flare open with astonishment and deep misgivings. His fazed demeanour lasts several long moments, as the others stare at him in question – as who could possibly call Frederick and cause him this level of consternation.

FR Clarissa, did you say Mr Gough Rutherford?

CD Yes, that's the name the gentleman gave me.

FR Oh, well, in that case, I think I ought to take his call.

CD Do you want me to put him on hold or transfer the call to your desk?

FR Um, no, can you transfer the call through to my inner chamber?

CD   Certainly, judge.

The others all look at each other with a sense of disbelief that Frederick is leaving the discussion at such a critical point to take a call.

SJPB Really Frederick, we do not have much longer to discuss the current case. Can't you get Clarissa to take the number and then call him back in your own good time? Surely, they would be aware of your position and would understand that you are very busy – and that you need to call them back when time permits.

FR   Yes, yes, I'm sure. Sorry gentlemen, I do need to take this call in my office. Do please excuse me.

Frederick gets up clumsily and anxiously makes his way across the room to the door on the opposite side of the room from which Clarissa and his guests have used. He opens the door to his 'inner chamber', walks in and closes the door behind him. The camera pans around the room until it focuses on the desk. The office is very stylishly furnished in Jacques-Emile Ruhlmann's art deco furniture. He walks to the desk and just as he sits down his phone starts to ring. He takes a big breath, hesitates for a moment, the suddenly picks up the phone.
The Church's 'An Unguarded Moment' starts to play.

FR   Ah, eh – this is, ah, Frederick Rogers speaking.

There is a long pause on the phone. The scene changes to Gough at the Edward Wallace pub. Gough is dumbfounded and unable to speak – trying to get something out but unable to make a sound. The scene changes back to Frederick, who is listening intensely for anything from the other end of the call.

As the silence grows longer, a sense of frustration and sadness starts to replace the previously anxious face of Frederick. A few moments of silence more and he starts to remove the phone hand piece from his ear and looks at it with contempt – as though he had been set up for a really sick joke.

Frederick's disappointment is overwhelming and he starts to move the phone piece to its base station to finish the call. At the very cusp of hanging up, he hesitates and brings the handset back to his ear.

FR   Gough, is that you?

GR   Dad ...

Tears roll down the cheeks of both father and son, both paralysed by the intensity of the emotional outpouring they're experiencing – the emotions that they have locked up deep inside themselves for the past three decades. After another intense long pause …

GR   Happy birthday, Dad.

FR   Gough, you remembered, thank you so very much. How are you, where have you been, where are you?

GR   Actually, I'm just across the road, in the Edgar Wallace pub.

FR   What are you doing there?

GR   Well, I tried to phone you at home – but your housekeeper told me you were at work. So, I came over to this side of town and have been trying to call you ever since. Anyway, the reason I'm here, is that, well, I've got you a little present – and I was wondering whether I could bring it to you and wish you happy birthday.

FR   Jesus, Gough you have caught me in a terrible moment – I'm right in the middle of a very important meeting. Can I ask you to come a little later – or maybe I can come to you – or take you out for tea – or something.

Long pause …

GR   Dad, just forget it. I just wanted to wish you happy birthday in person but, I understand, you are far too important and busy to see me. I understand, I'll just go away and never bother you again …

FR   NO, NO – no, please, please don't go. Please come and see me now – so that I can see my long-lost son. Yes, yes – please Gough, please come now.

GR   I thought you said that you were in the middle of an important meeting – and too busy to see me.

FR   I am busy, but never, ever too busy to see my son. Come over to the courts and I'll be waiting for you – okay?

GR   Are you sure?

FR   Yes, I'm very sure. When you come in, go to the reception on the ground floor, and tell them your name and that you have an appointment with me. I'll notify them so they will be expecting you – and they will give you directions to my chambers, which are on the fifth floor.

GR   Okay Dad, I'll come over and see you in fifteen minutes or so.

Frederick hangs up the phone looking as pleased as a kid who had just won a prize at a fun fair. He gets up purposefully, strolls across to the door leading to his reception room where his guests are seated. Closing the door behind him, he enters his outer chambers. Then in a confident and authoritative pose he announces:

FR   Gentlemen, I must sincerely thank you all for your assistance and counsel in assessing the merits and implications of the case before my court. Your advice and input has been invaluable. However, at the end of the day, it falls on my shoulders to actually make the judgment and provide the *ratio decidendi* in support of my judgment.

        Now, if you will excuse me, a rather important matter has just arisen that needs my immediate attention. Therefore, unless there is any other business that you need to discuss, I will ask Clarissa to see you out.

ML   I beg your pardon, Frederick. What could possibly be more important than the case before us right now. We have worked tirelessly for decades to get to this point …

FR   I did not say it was more important – it is just that I have now had the advantage of receiving your counsel on this sensitive case, and I do not believe that there is much more to be gained by discussing it any further.

ALB   Frederick, settle down, most of us have travelled quite a way to be with you now to discuss the case, and there are still many facets and implications of the case that have yet to be fully discussed and digested.

FR   Angus, my dear chap, I'm sure you are fully aware of the 80/20 rule – 80% of the facets can be covered in 20% of the conversation. I'm sure that we have covered more than 20% of the conversation and we certainly have covered more than 80% of the issues.

        And, I do not think there are any nuances of law or social welfare within the remaining 20% that are so significant that they are likely to change my mind.

ML   And what, may I ask, is your mind?

FR   I am minded to rule against the GPA.

ALB   Now, now, that is a little rash. Frederick, please take the time now to consider the implications of such a judgment. You will be creating misery for countless generations to come. That's just not right, is it?

FR   Gentlemen, as I said, I am minded to rule against the GPA, but I still have a little time to contemplate the issues at hand. To reiterate, I am responsible and accountable for making the judgment – and so I shall. Now, if you will excuse me, I really do have to prepare for a rather urgent matter that has just arisen.

At this moment, Clarissa opens the door, and the entourage reluctantly leave, visually showing their disquiet with Frederick – at both his decision and for asking them to leave.

The scene fades out with ALB frowning displeasingly as he is ushered out of the judge's reception room.

Insert Scene – 55

'Finally perish!' That is the exact alternative which confronts the white race … If white civilisation goes down, the white race is irretrievably ruined. It will be swamped by the triumphant colored races, who will obliterate the white man by elimination or absorption … Not today, nor yet tomorrow; perhaps not for generations; but surely in the end. Of the present drift be not changed, we whites are all ultimately doomed.

We now know that men are not, and never will be, equal. We know that environment and education can develop only what heredity brings.

The Rising Tide of Color Against White World Supremacy *by Lothrop Stoddard, American Eugenic Leader, 1926*

Scene 86 – The start of the Second Great Fire of London

2:20pm, Sunday, 9 June 2013

Setting: London Bridge, the Monument and the GPA offices

The scene opens with a view of London Bridge, similar to scene 1, but as it is a Sunday, it is mainly tourists leisurely strolling over the bridge rather than thousands of city workers marching across during the morning crush hour. The camera slowly swings around so that 'The City' end of the bridge comes into view and proceeds to travel along the bridge until 'The Monument' tube station entrance is in central view.

As the camera steadies on one of the tube station's exits, three dwarfs, Greg O'Leary and his two sidekicks, Peter Giles and Paul Firth, come charging out, each with a knapsack on their back. They reach the top of the stairs, walk out onto the footpath and look around until they spot 'The Monument'.

GO   [Pointing to the Monument] This way.

The three dwarfs walk towards, then pass, the Monument as they continue walking towards Pudding Lane. Upon reaching Pudding Lane, they search for identifications on the buildings.

PG   [Peering through an entrance door of the building on the corner of Pudding Lane and Monument Street, he spots a sign on the reception desk, 'Genetic Protection Authority'.] This is it!

The other two dwarfs join him and peer into the closed building and see the reception sign for the GPA offices.

GO   Yep, this is it. Let's do it!

The three dwarfs walk onto the crossroads of Pudding Land and Monument Street, take off and open their knapsacks and each retrieve three 568ml Magners Cider bottles. Each bottle is full and sealed, but with six inches of damp protruding from the bottle cap. They each put two of the bottles on the ground and hold the third. Greg reaches into his trouser pocket, retrieves a cigarette lighter and ignites the flame.

GO   Okay boys, this is it – this will show those fuckers just who they're dealing with!

Greg nods to Peter, who then holds out his bottle. Greg duly lights up the moist cloth dangling from the cap of the bottle. He nods to Paul, who holds out his bottle, which Greg lights, and then he lights up his own bottle.

GO   Take your time from me, on three we throw. One, two, three.

Each of them hurls their Molotov cocktail at the GPA offices windows. The windows smash and a fireball erupts within the GPA reception area. The three light their remaining two bottles and target windows on the first, second and third floors of the building. Flames leap from the building as the fire engulfs the building.

The three dwarfs stand back and a look of accomplishment is evident on their face.

PG   Wow, that is pretty impressive. Way better than I was expecting.

PF   Pretty fucking good. That will show those bastards who they're dealing with.

GO   Good work, boys. Now, let's get the fuck out of here before the filth come and arrest us.

PG   Okay – let's hit the High Court.

As the dwarfs make their getaway, the burning building remains in focus. The following text is displayed:

> *On this fateful day, the second Great Fire of London started – at the very spot that the first Great Fire of London started.*

The scene fades out on the text and the burning building.

Scene 86(b) – The dwarfs riot

2:20pm, Sunday, 9 June 2013

Setting: Tube stations and the Strand

The scene opens with a shot of the Thames, then moves back to the north bank, then keeps moving back until Temple tube station comes into view.

The camera keeps moving slowly backwards bringing more of Temple tube station into view. Shortly after the tube station comes into view, Greg O'Leary emerges from the tube station – all fired up and very energetic. Upon reaching the top of the tube stations stairs, he runs out of the station as though on 'a mission'. He is quickly followed by another two dwarfs, equally fired up, who run out of the station following Greg. Then another quickly follows, then a whole stream of dwarfs swarm out of the underground – all with a vivid determined expression, walking/running with a sense of deep conviction and purpose.

The scene fades out and fades back in on Holborn tube station – which repeats the scene of a swarm of dwarfs emerging from the station lead by Peter Giles.

The scene fades out and fades in on Embankment tube station – which again shows a repeat scene of bunches of dwarfs, led by Paul Firth, all emerging angrily from the tube station. They march up Villers Street, turn right and continue their march up the Strand towards the High Court.

The scene swaps between these three tribes of dwarfs emerging from the three different tube stations, all angry and marching determinedly for a cause.

The dwarfs from Temple march up Arundel Street. The dwarfs from Holborn march down Kingsway then turn left into Aldwych and keep marching.

The scene changes to a shot taken outside the High Court looking down the Strand towards the direction of Trafalgar Square. In the distance, the tribe of dwarfs from Embankment can be seen marching up the Strand. As they pass the corner of Aldwych and the Strand, the dwarfs from Holborn march around the corner and join up with them, and across the road the dwarfs from the Temple station march up from Arundel Street and turn right into the Strand, joining the other two tribes.

The large mass of dwarfs is so numerous, so worked up and so confident in their sheer numbers that they deliberately spill over from the footpaths onto the streets. The traffic becomes overwhelmed with the number of dwarfs taking to the streets – which brings the traffic to a standstill.

All the drivers and other pedestrians are in a state of disbelief in what they are witnessing, which on all accounts appears to be the brink of a dwarf riot.

With the traffic still, some of the dwarfs start walking on the road. With added confidence that comes with number, combined with the pumping adrenaline that comes with a mission, some of the dwarfs start scaling the cars and walking over their bonnets, roofs and boots. They start jumping from car to car, causing minor dents to vehicle bodyworks. This, causes some of the drivers to become quite annoyed, and in some cases abusive and hostile towards the dwarfs. The attitude of the drivers riles the dwarfs, creating high tension with the dwarfs who start to shout obscenities back at the drivers and change from merely scaling the cars to deliberately kicking and damaging the cars.

With the increase in tension between the dwarfs and drivers, several of the drivers get out of their cars to 'tackle' the dwarfs that have damaged their cars. This act incenses the dwarfs, who ascend en-mass on these drivers and tackle them to the ground, where they begin to kick and punch.

A few of the drivers fight back and start hitting and kicking the dwarfs very hard, causing considerable pain and probable broken ribs. The level of violence again increases as more dwarfs dive on those drivers that dared to retaliate, bringing them brutally to the ground, where they are subjected to sustained kicking and punching.

The violence against the drivers that dared get out of their car deters other drivers straying from their cars. Worse, many of the drivers now feel insecure and intimidated, which the dwarfs pick up on. This is the first time in their lives that normal-heighted people have treated them in any way other than with contempt or as inferiors. The dwarfs like the feeling. They like this first ever feeling of power, their ability to intimidate, their ability to impose their will, the first time ever that they have been able to call the shots.

With the new feeling of power and superiority, they turn their attention to those drivers still in their cars. They walk past drivers' windows and peer in. For those drivers or passengers that do not show total submissiveness by looking scared and downward, the dwarfs eye them up and start jeering them:

What the fuck are you looking at?

It's a trap. If the driver looks away and fails to answer, or they do provide an answer, then the jeering questioning continues:

Aren't I good enough to talk to – ah? You consider yourself too good to speak to a short-ass midget do you? Well fuck you.

And with this, bricks, bars and whatever else is produced and used to smash car windows – allowing the driver to be pulled from their vehicle and subjected to what Alex DeLarge, from Clockwork Orange, would contentedly call 'a bit of the old ultra-violence'.

The scene becomes very ugly, with groups of dwarfs going from car to car and randomly selecting victims to taunt, then forcefully breaking into their car, dragging their victims out and viciously assaulting them.

Fortunately for their victims, due to the time pressure the dwarfs are under, they do not spend too long assaulting any one victim. After the victims are dragged out of the car and forced to the ground, the beatings only go on for a minute or so, just sufficient time to bloody the victims' head and badly bruise them all over.

However, their leader, Greg O'Leary, is significantly more violent than the others.

As the assaults start, Greg climbs onto the back of a plumber's pickup truck, and finds a four-foot length of copper pipe. As he picks up the piece of tubing, he holds it up to the sky and gazes at it with sinister admiration. He then slowly turns his gaze onto the two occupants of the pickup, who he can see through the cab's rear window. The occupants turn and stare at him – then with a swiftness of movement that startles them Greg brings down the piping and smashes the rear window. With the window smashed, Greg positions the pipe horizontally, clasps it with both hands, draws the pipe back then with both hands spears the pipe through the smashed window. The driver sees the pipe coming straight for him and has just enough time to turn his head, before the full force of the thrust hits him on his ear. As blood gushes from his head, he brings his hands up to assess the damage he sustained and to protect him from further attack, shouting 'Stop it, that fucking hurt.'

With this, Greg lines himself up for a second joust. The driver realises his predicament and tries to unfasten his seat belt – but his blood soaked hands keeps slipping off the seatbelt latch. In desperation he leans forward on the steering wheel, with both hands raised to protect the back of his head. Greg eyes the gap between the upside down 'V' formed by the drivers hands, and rams the copper tubing into the base of the skull up into his brain. The driver's hands drop and his body flops into a state of lifelessness.

Greg twists the pipe and, with a degree of macabre curiosity, slowly removes it from his victim's skull. When the four inches of pipe are extracted from the victims head a large blob of brain remains attached to the end of the pipe. Greg brings the pipe up to his face for a closer look – and gives a nod of depraved satisfaction.

The passenger in the pickup, having just witnessed the horror, opens his door and attempts to escape the violent madness of the scene. Unfortunately for him, after stepping out, he immediately trips over a short dwarf and falls to the ground. A pack of dwarfs immediately surround him and start accusing him of deliberately kicking the short dwarf.

The passenger apologises profusely and declares his innocence of any malicious intent. However, the dwarfs vent their anger and start kicking and punching him.

Above this racket, from the back of the pickup, Greg shouts:

GO   Just hold him down and I'll do the rest.

The camera pans back to Greg, who very casually reaches over to the oxy-acetylene kit that is secured to the tray of the pickup truck, he picks up the cutting nozzle, opens the acetylene valve, ignites the flame using the flint lighter attached to the gas bottle harness, then slowly turns on the oxygen valve until an intense blue flame shoots out from the nozzle.

With an astonishing degree of co-ordination, while holding the oxy-acetylene flaming torch in one hand and the copper pipe in the other, Greg wistfully climbs down from the back of the pickup and casually walks up to the terrified passenger being held on the ground by the five dwarfs.

GO   [Brings the end of the pipe up to his nose and takes a deep smell of the glob of brain still skewered to the end of the pipe.] Well, it smells pretty damn good to me!

        [He glances first at the glob of brain, then to the passenger, then back to the brain] So, how would you like your brain – cooked or sushi style?

Pass   Really, I don't want any brain.

GO   That option is not on the menu – it is either sushi or BBQ. How would you like it?

Pass   I can't eat that, it's my father's.

GO   Well, if you have a little snack, then maybe your father's memories will somehow get passed onto you. Not many people have that opportunity – so, best to take advantage of it, don't you think so?

Pass   Please, don't make me eat it.

GO   As I said, that option isn't on the menu. As you're not ordering anything from the menu, allow me to order for you. Now, let me see. Brain sushi or flame grilled? I really cannot decide. The only reasonable thing to do is to give you a taste of both. Okay guys, hold him down for the first course!

The other dwarfs hold his head to the ground and force his mouth open.

Greg lines the copper pipe up and jams the brains into the passenger's mouth – including several inches of the pipe, which takes out several of his teeth and rips his palate open.

The passenger recoils in pain with blood spilling out of his mouth and running all over his face and neck.

GO   Like the sushi?

Greg looks down on the face of the passenger who is in extreme pain and indignation.

GO   I guess you didn't. I should have known a red-neck like you wouldn't have appreciated the finer things in life. So, I'll do you a favour, and give it a little flame grilling – okay? Hold him down for the second course.

With this, the dwarfs again bring the passengers head to the ground and hold it there by pushing on his forehead and pulling his hair. Once the passenger is secured, Greg walks over him, and then comes to a halt with his feet located close to each side of the passenger's armpits. The acetylene torch is clutched menacingly in his right hand.

GO   This should be delicious – flame grilled brain. Now, open up.

With this, Greg bends over and slowly starts to move the flaming nozzle towards the passenger's mouth.

Pass   [Spluttering through his blood filled mouth.] Jesus Christ, what the fuck are you doing! Please, please, don't do this, please.

GO   Well, I guess you now regret deriving sinister satisfaction from watching all those dwarf pornos – hey?

Pass   I swear, I have never watched a porno that had a dwarf in it.

GO   Well, maybe your dad did. So, this is for your dad.

Pass   [With intense pain and discomfort due to his torn palate, ripped mouth and broken teeth.] Jesus, my dad doesn't even own a video player, doubtless an internet connection – so, how the fuck could he watch midget porn?

GO   Well, did you ever do anything to stop dwarfs being exploited?

The passenger hesitates, as he doesn't know how to respond. With this, Greg brings the nozzle over the passenger's mouth – where the flame has direct contact with his lips and teeth.

Within a second of this 'burning' of the passenger, Greg pushes the pure oxygen valve of the cutter nozzle – which sends a stream of pure oxygen through the middle of the flame. With this, the flame extends all the way through the passengers mouth and neck and into the road tarmac.

The passenger, now totally mutilated, dies.

GO   Talk about ungrateful, I give him the best cuisine in the world – freshly grilled brain – and he gets up and dies on me. Fuck it; I guess I won't get a tip now. Cheap arse bastard.

As Greg steps back from the body, small flames from the tarmac become visible, set alight by intense heat of the oxy-acetylene cutter. In the distance, police sirens become audible – becoming progressively louder as the vehicles approach the Strand.

With the sound of the police sirens, Greg O'Leary starts shouting at the herd of rioting dwarfs:

GO   Come on, we have to get to the High Court, can't afford to be caught out here.

The assaulting immediately ceases and all the dwarfs start moving forward – running onward up the Strand towards the High Court, with Greg at the head closely followed by Peter and Paul. As the dwarfs stampede towards the High Court, the mutilated burning passenger remains in focus. The following text is displayed:

> *The fire spread from Pudding Lane to the Strand.*

The scene fades out on the text and the burning body.

Insert Scene – 56

> *They exist in tens and hundreds of thousands; they are one of the characteristic by-products of the modern world … This is part at least of what industrialism has done for us … This is where it all lead – to labyrinthine slums and dark back kitchens with stickly, ageing people creeping round them like blackbeetles.*
>
> Down and Out in Paris and London *by George Orwell*

Scene 87 – Low people in the High Court

2:45pm, Sunday, 9 June 2013

Setting: High Court

The scene opens up with Gough near skipping as he enters the High Court, stopping in the foyer to assimilate the grandiosity of the building – the whole time with a big grin on his face. After a few moments of being awe struck with the building he sights the 'information desk' and heads towards it. The attendee at the information desk, the same lady that served Ivan when he was placing his injunction, as before is well attired with a confident demeanour.

Upon reaching the desk, Gough asks the receptionist:

GR   I am here to see Judge Rogers – can you let me know where his chamber is?

Recep Are you Mr Gough Rutherford?

GR   Indeed, I am that very person.

Recep Very good – Judge Rogers just phoned and requested that a security pass be made up for you.

The receptionist looks up at Gough – then studies him for a moment.

Recep My word, you have a very strong family resemblance to Judge Rogers. Are you related?

GR   Do you really think I look like him?

Recep Yes, I can spot family resemblance a mile away.

GR   Well, yes, I am sort of related – he's my father.

Recep I thought so. With your square jaw line, high cheek bones and arched eye brows – you look just like a younger version of him.

GR   Well, I haven't seen him for a wee while – so, I don't know if that is a compliment or not. But, as you are such an attractive dish and, after all, he is my dad, I will take it as a compliment.

Recep And so you should – your old man is still quite a catch.

GR   In that case, you obviously must think that I am just a little bit tasty?

Recep [Giggling.] You wish. Now dear, here is your security card. The lift you need to take is the one marked 'visitors' over to the right. When you get into the lift, before you press the button for level five, you will need to swipe the card on the card reader inside the lift. If you don't swipe the card you will not be able go to level five and see your father. Once on the fifth floor, you will be met by Clarissa, who will take you to Judge Rogers', or should I say, your Dad's chambers.

GR   Thank you very much. [Then with a cheeky grin] If you are ever looking for a date on a Saturday night – well here is my business card. Just give me a ring.

Recep [Smirks and takes the card.] Well, young man, as I've been singularly unsuccessful in bedding your father, I may just take you up on that offer and give you a call.

GR   [With a warm grin.] You do that – I will be waiting!

Gough walks off to his left, walking towards the public lift bank. Just as Gough disappears from view, Greg, Peter and Paul come into view, entering the High Court through the public main entrance.

The three dwarfs progress into the reception area – their heightened level of bravado come neo- mobster poise, so apparent when they enter the building, dramatically fades when they find themselves in the middle of the grand foyer – where they are surrounded by opulence and a grandeur that none of them have ever witnessed before. They draw to a halt in the middle of the foyer, betraying their lack of exposure to 'high culture', all gazing bewilderedly at the unfamiliar surroundings that they have now found themselves in.

However, their 'fish out of water' syndrome abruptly finishes when Greg's commanding personality re-emerges, provoking him to bark out the order:

GO   Let's get on with it!

The three compose themselves, look around the vast near empty foyer, as being a Sunday, only a skeleton crew is on duty, then in perfect synchronisation they all spot the bank of lifts. They give each other a look and then all set off to the lifts.

They gait with purpose towards the lifts – then spot the information desk. They change their direction and head for the receptionist.

Recep [Under her breath] Oh my God, not more dwarfs.

The three dwarfs reach the information counter, and look upwards to the receptionist.

GO   We're here to see the Judge Rogers. What floor is he on?

Recep I don't believe the judge is expecting you?

GO   Good, so he is in his office then.

Recep I didn't say that he was in his chamber.

GO   You didn't have to – your language gave it away. Where's his office?

Recep Well, as he is not expecting you, then there is not much point in me telling you where his chamber is.

GO   Look bitch, for your own welfare, I suggest you tell me now where his fucking office is.

Recep Gentlemen, I'm afraid I am going to have to call security. It would be advisable for you to leave the building before security arrives.

While the exchange between Greg and the receptionist is taking place, Paul sneaks behind the receptionist and watches her from behind.

The receptionist clicks on her computer to bring up the corporate directory and types in 'security'. As she reaches for her phone to call the number displayed on the computer screen, Paul forces his way between her and the receptionist desk, picks up a pair of scissors from the desk, grabs the phone and cuts through the cable of the hand piece.

The startled receptionist looks down on Paul, only to find that he has raised the open blades of the scissors against her throat, at which point he whispers to her:

PF   Don't make a move or say a fucking word! Do you understand?

The receptionist nods her understanding and brings her hands up in a surrender pose.

PF   Good, just obey and be quiet – and all will be okay. Understand?

Recep [Whispers] Yes.

Paul then types 'Rogers' into the computer and a list of four names appear on the screen. The corporate directory listing displays the full name, number and location of those displayed – one of the four listed is designated as 'Judge Frederick Rogers', which shows that he is on level five.

PF   He's on level five.

GO   Let's go.

The three dwarfs head towards the bank of lifts.

Recep: [Shouts out in a loud voice.] Security.

Gough anxiously strolls up to the bank of six lifts – presses the button – and nervously waits for a lift to arrive. After an edgy wait of 10 or so seconds, the lift bell rings and a light on top of one of the lifts illuminates. Gough hastens over to the illuminated lift and impatiently waits for the doors to open.

An eternity passes in the five seconds it take for the doors to finally open. As the doors open, Gough positions himself to enter the lift. Just as he is about to step into the open lift, three dwarfs rush past him, roughly pushing him aside as they forcefully enter the open lift. As soon as the dwarfs enter the lift Greg turns and pushes the button to the fifth floor – then presses the 'Close Door' button and the doors immediately start to close. Greg then notices that the button to the fifth floor failed to illuminate, so he presses it again and it still fails to illuminate.

Meanwhile, Gough is still somewhat startled by the mad rush of dwarfs into 'his' lift, is jolted into action as he realises that the doors are closing. He swings his arm through the closing doors. The lift sensors detect the movement of his arm, stop and start to open again.

Once there is a sufficient gap between the lift doors, Gough joins the dwarfs in the lift. Once there, the three dwarfs all glare at him.

GR   You guys in a bit of a hurry, hey?

The three dwarfs give him a glance – then glance at each other – but say nothing.

Gough notices that none of the lift buttons are illuminated, pauses for a moment wondering why, then takes out the security card that the receptionist gave him, swipes it over the security sensor and presses the fifth floor button – which now illuminates.

The dwarfs note that their lift passenger managed to illuminate their floor lift button, and give each other a 'that was lucky' look.

The doors now fully close – and there is another eternity of three seconds for the lift to slowly start to ascend. The atmosphere within the lift is thick with tension – with a never-ending series of subtle glances being passed around the confines of the dimly lit lift.

Gough, a little perplexed that he has found himself sharing a lift with three dwarfs, starts to discretely study them. In particular, he becomes intrigued by their bodily dimensions – how they have common features, fat stocky hands, big heads, flat noses, stumpy legs and stumpy arms – then he turns his observation powers to their buttocks, and notes that they all have disproportionately large buttocks.

Gough, being in a jovial mood, finds the level of tension too high, too awkward and unnecessary. He reverts to his usual manner in dispelling social tension by cracking a smart arse joke.

GR   You guys may be short, but you sure have great asses.

With this, in a flash, Greg reaches into his coat pocket and pulls out a 5" flick knife and flicks it open.

GO   Great asses huh?You faggot bastard. So, I guess you want to make a faggot porno with great arsed midgets being fucked senseless do you. At this very moment, the only arsehole that is going to get fucked is you, you fucking arsehole. Now, get on your fucking knees so I can start punching that stupid fucking head of yours. NOW, get on your fucking knees or I swear I'll cut your fucking knee caps out.

GR   [Very startled] Sorry guys, no offence meant. I guess it was a bad joke, and I guess I took a step too far. I'm really, really sorry.

GO   Not as sorry as you are going to be – now, fuckwit, get on your fucking knees.

At this point, Greg presses the emergency stop button in the lift, and the lift comes to an abrupt halt. As Gough still hasn't started to kneel, Greg visually indicates to him that he is serious and that he had better get down on his knees or he will start cutting him.

GR   Okay, okay let's be reasonable – okay – it was just a slip of the tongue – I was just trying to make light conversation.

Greg maintains his savage look – and again visually demands that he gets down on his knees.

Gough now gets the message that the dwarf is serious, so he very slowly crouches down and rests on his knees.

GO   Not so tall now are ya? You stupid fuck!

At this point Greg notices a package under Gough's arm.

GO   [Sarcastically.] So, what do you have in that beautifully wrapped package?

GR   It's nothing really.

GO   Well, if it is nothing – then I guess you don't mind giving it to me.

GR   By nothing – I mean it is worthless, it just has a little sentimental value.

GO   Really, a sentimental present. Isn't that so fucking sweet? Who is it for?

GR   It doesn't matter who – it's just an old piece of crap – it's worthless.

GO   Don't tell me what and who matters. Who's the fucking present for?

GR   My father.

GO   [Snatches the present off him – and immediately whisks his switchblade in front of Gough's face to stop Gough from coming after it.] Let's see now. [He tears open the card.]

'Dear Dad,

I still remember when I was a wee little boy, how I would sit on lap and beg you to read me more from your favourite boyhood book 'The Champion Book for Boys'. I must confess that I can't remember much of our time together, but those times were good times – the times that I treasure more than any other.

Thank you for never giving up on me – and I'm so sorry it has taken me until now to accept you back into my life.

Now, after all these years, I think it is high time I returned your book – so that once again, I can beg you to read it to me.

Love, Gough'

Isn't that just so sickly sweet. I bet when your old man reads this he will get a hard on. Sitting on his lap – how so very naughty. You faggot bastard.

Gough winces towards Greg, but his move was anticipated by Greg, who rests the point of his knife in his neck, which ceases Gough's advance. Greg then waves the wrapped present in front of Gough.

GO   So, I guess this is that lovely book of your daddy's, *The Champion Book for Boys*?

Greg passes the present to Peter and demands.

GO   Peter open the fucking present and give it back to me.

PG   Sure.

Peter rips the wrapping paper off and passes the book back to Greg, a First Edition of The Champion Book for Boys.

GO   Would you look at that? *The Champion Book for Boys*. So, tell me, Gough, what's the going rate on eBay for this piece of crap, ah?

GR   I don't know.

GO   Of course you know – don't tell me you haven't looked it up. If it was worth anything you would have hocked it by now, wouldn't have ya?

GR   Alright, it is worth about €4:50. As I said, it's worthless, just sentimental value.

GO   Not even worth a fiver.

With this, Greg starts to tear the book up.

GR   [Gough launches at Greg, shouting.] You little prick, that was for my father.

Greg had anticipated the launch and braced himself, so that as Gough came falling on top of him, he extended his knife so that the knife pierced him between his left third and fourth ribs – whereupon the long blade went straight into his heart.

Gough falls to the lift floor and starts convulsing.

After a few moments, Gough's convulsing reduces, and he slowly opens his eyes. He looks at Greg and the other two dwarfs and utters:

GR   Is this it?

GO   Well, I guess it is the last 'short ass' joke you're going to make.

GR   It wasn't a 'short ass joke'; it was a 'big fat-assed fact'.

With this, Greg brutally kicks Gough's head, at which point Peter and Paul join in the kicking frenzy. Peter pauses for a moment to press the lift button for level three – which causes the button to illuminate.

The dwarfs continuing their kicking fest as the lift comes to a halt and the lift doors begin to open. As the doors start to open, the following text is displayed:

> The fire spread from the Strand to the High Court.

The scene fades out with the dwarfs starting to exit the lift, but before Greg exits, he climbs up onto the lift hand rails, jumps and lands on Gough's head with both feet, then scampers out of the lift.

Insert Scene – 57

From the view of human comfort and happiness, the increase in population that occurs at each advance in human security is the greatest evil of life.

A Modern Utopia *by HG Wells*

Scene 88 – Feeling low in the High Court

3:30pm, Sunday, 9 June 2013

Setting: Judge Roger's inner and outer court chambers

Frederick Rogers is anxiously waiting in his 'inner chamber', nervously walking between his desk and office table. Periodically, he stops to gaze at a photo of Gough and himself on a sideboard. He frequently looks down at his watch with a petulant expression then glances towards the door.

FR   [Speaking to himself] Jesus Gough, where the hell are you? How long does it take to cross Fleet Street and catch a lift?

He then walks over to the window and peers out, and while he 'sees' a lot of commotion and police presence in the street below he is oblivious to it – all he can do is to search the faces below to see if anyone of them belong to his long-lost son. The intercom in his chamber chimes, whereupon he hastens over to his desk to take the call.

FR   Judge Rogers speaking.

CD   [In quite a distressed voice.] Judge – it is Clarissa speaking.

FR   Yes, Clarissa?

CD   Judge, there are two police officers here to see you.

FR   What?

CD   Yes, Judge, there are two police officers here to see you.

FR   What on Earth for – can you ask them to come back later? As you know, I do have a very pressing meeting that I need to attend, which is going to start imminently.

CD   Yes Judge, I did inform them of your meeting, but they are very insistent that they see you now.

FR   Really, they must be able to wait for an hour or so, so please ask them to come back at, say, 5:00pm.

CD   Judge [with her voice croaking, but managing to hold a striking degree of authority], you do need to see the police officers, you need to see them now.

FR   Clarissa, are you okay? You sound terrible?

CD   I'm fine, but I will be bringing the police to your chambers – so, please be ready to receive them.

FR   Really …

The intercom hangs up. Frederick looks very bothered and confused.

FR   Need to see me now – what on Earth for?

He walks over to the window again and peers out, waits a few seconds, looks at his watch, then despondently walks to his door, opens it and walks through to his main chambers. He anxiously waits while staring around his chambers and sneaks the odd glance at his watch. The door opens, and Clarissa shows the two police officers into the judge's chambers, a male inspector and a female chief inspector.

CD   Judge Rogers, this is Inspector Cheng and Chief Inspector Banerjee – and this is Judge Rogers.

Clarissa and the two officers all look very solemn, with Clarissa betraying her teary eyes. Frederick spots the teary eyes and the solemn look of the police officers.

FR   Clarissa, are you in some sort of trouble?

Clarissa looks down, shakes her head and walks out – leaving the three standing and staring at the closed door.

FR   Well, I'm not sure what this is all about, but please take a seat, and let's get through this as quickly as possible, as I do have a very pressing appointment that I do need to keep.

At this moment, Frederick notices a torn book in a clear plastic bag in Chief Inspector Banerjee's hand. He studies it for a second and a 'moment of recognition' crosses his face.

FR   How very odd, I used to have a copy of the *Champion Book for Boys* when I was a wee lad – God only knows what happened to it.

JB   [Very sternly and authoritatively] Judge Rogers, please sit down.

Frederick, taken by surprise by the forcefulness of the chief inspector's directive, proceeds to sit down.

FR   Well, what can I do for you?

JB   This is your book – the very one you used to read to your son when he was a youngster.

FR   [A very puzzled look comes over the judge's face – and a long pause ensues before he can even compose a reply.] Is this some sort of joke? Look, I really do not have time for this now, can I ask you to leave? As, coincidentally, I am expecting a visit from my son any second now.

JB   Judge, Gough was on his way to return this book to you.

FR   [Stunned at this announcement] I am sorry, then what in heaven's world are you doing with it?

JB   Judge, there has been an incident and, unfortunately, Gough will no longer be able to visit you.

FR   Oh damn, what has he done, where have you taken him? Does he require bail? If so, then I can certainly put up the bail.

JB   [There is a long pause.] Judge, your son was murdered.

FR   [A long agonising pause transpires – while the judge tries to digest what has just been said to him.] I really do not know what you are on about – but the joke is up. You see, I just spoke to Gough on the phone not fifteen minutes ago. And he is definitely not dead – he will be here any minute, whereupon you will be able to see him with your own eyes.

JB   Yes, I have checked his phone log and I am aware that he phoned you around 45 minutes ago – at 2:20. However, there was … an incident in the public lift of this court building.

FR   An incident? In the lift? What on Earth are you talking about?

JB   He caught the lift from the foyer – the public lift – and pressed the button for the fifth floor on his way to see you. However, there were three others in the lift with him. We do not know what happened in the lift, but by the time it had reached the fifth floor, your floor, Gough was dead from a stab wound to the heart and ferocious kicks to his head.

FR   What? He was stabbed and kicked? In the High Court lift? Through the heart? How preposterous! Come now, the joke or whatever you are playing at is up. Now please tell me why you are here or please leave at once. I really do not have time for poor taste pranks at the moment.

JB   I am sorry, but this is not a prank. It appears that the three suspects stopped the lift between the second and third floor by pushing the emergency stop button, and during the time the lift was stopped between the two floors, a scuffle of some sort broke out and your son was stabbed in the heart and received a series of violent kicks to the head. The three suspects then exited the lift on the third floor, descended the fire stairs and left the building.

Meanwhile, the lift continued up to the fifth floor. When the doors opened, a court security guard spotted a body and contacted Central Court Security, who phoned for an ambulance and called the police. The paramedics rushed him to the A&E at St Bartholomew's Hospital where he was pronounced 'dead upon arrival'.

FR   No, no, no … NO, this just does not make sense. You must have the wrong guy. Gough wouldn't incite so much hate in people that within a few seconds of meeting them in a lift that they would resort to killing him. He may not be perfect, but he is certainly not that objectionable.

NC   Judge, from the CCTV footage, we know that four people entered the lift on the ground floor. We know that one of them was your son. We know that one of them is dead. And we know that none of the other three passengers were your son.

Judge, your son is dead from a fatal stab wound to the heart and violent kicks to the head.

FR   How can you be so certain that one of the other three passengers wasn't my son? You do not even know what my son looks like.

NC   Did your son suffer from any obvious birth defects, unusual genetic conditions or physical abnormalities?

FR   Sorry, I don't understand the question – why are you asking such a wayward question?

NC   The three lift passengers that exited the lift on the third floor, all share a common physical abormality. If your son does not have this abnormality – then he is the victim of this atrocious attack.

FR   He did have very fuzzy hair.

NC   Nothing else?

FR   Not to my knowledge – but I have not seen him for some years now.

NC   How tall was he?

FR   I think he was just on 6 foot tall.

NC   Hmmm – well that does rule him out from being one of the three other passengers, as none of them were that tall.

FR   Well, I don't know, as I said I have not seen him in years – maybe he is only, I don't know, maybe he is only 5'5".

NC   Judge, our estimates from viewing the CCTV footage, is that the tallest of the other three passengers was only 4'2".

FR   [There is a very long pause. On several occasions, the judge starts to form a question, then stops and reflects – goes to ask another – again stopping. As he thinks through what he has just been told he finally sinks back into his chair and brings his hands up to his face in despair. After several moments, he positions his hands back on his lap.] Dwarfs?

NC   Yes, Judge.

FR   Three of them?

NC   Yes, Judge.

FR   Three dwarfs killed my son in a lift, while he was on his way to visit me for the first time in 25 years?

NC   I can't say how many were involved in the incident – and as yet they are only suspects. They are yet to be apprehended and charged. However, we are confident of apprehending them within a few hours.

FR   The little pricks! How could they do this to me after everything that I have done – and am doing – for them. That's the gratitude I get for helping them – they go and kill my son.

Jesus Christ, how in God's name did they think this would help their cause? The little shits!

JB   Judge, we will need to keep these for evidence [holds up the plastic bags with the card and book inside them], but before we take them away and secure them, I thought you may wish to have a look at the book that Gough was returning to you and the card he had written.

But, you have to wear gloves so that the evidence is not destroyed or contaminated [hands the judge a pair of latex gloves].

Without another word being uttered, the judge takes the gloves and puts them on. Chief Inspector Banerjee hands over two evidence bags, one containing the book and the other the card.

JB   Judge, we will step outside and leave you with these for ten minutes. Then, I am afraid, we have to take them back and secure them for evidential purposes. I am sure you understand.

FR   Hmmm – thank you.

The two police officers show themselves out of the Judge's chambers. Frederick, removes the card out of the clear plastic bag and reads it. Gough's voice does a 'voiceover' as Frederick reads the content of the letter. As the voiceover progresses, Frederick's memories of having Gough sitting on his lap while reading him stories from the book fades into the picture.

Dear Dad,

I still remember when I was a wee little boy, how I would sit on your lap and beg you to read me more from your favourite childhood book 'The Champion Book for Boys'. I must confess that I can't remember much of our time together, but those times were good times – the times that I treasure more than any other.

Thank you for never giving up on me – and I'm so sorry it has taken me until now to accept you back into my life.

Now, after all these years, I think it is high time I returned your book – so that I can beg you to read it to me once again!

Love Gough

After the voiceover finishes, the scene fades back to Frederick sitting on his couch – the card pressed against his stomach with both hands while his head is flopped back over the couch as he gazes unfocusedly on the ceiling with streams of tears flowing down his cheeks. The scene fades out on this image.

The scene fades back in on the judge being disturbed by soft knocking on his door. There is a pause while the judge gathers his composure. Another soft knocking on the door is heard. The judge gets up, walks to the door, opens it and lets Chief Inspector Banerjee and Inspector Cheng into his chambers.

FR   Chief Inspector Banerjee and Inspector Cheng. Please do come in.

JB   Thank you.

Chief Inspector Banerjee and Inspector Cheng quietly enter his chambers.

FR   Yes, you have come to collect the evidential material from the crime. I have left it on the sideboard over there – and I assure you that I didn't touch the evidence without wearing gloves.

NC   Thank you, Judge, very much appreciate it.

JB   We'll just collect the material and leave you in peace.

FR   Before you go, there is a little formality that I need to impose.

JB   Sorry Judge, what would that be?

FR   I'm currently presiding over a case that is quite sensitive. If news was to get out that three dwarfs violently killed my son, then it may well jeopardise the whole case – as it could be asserted that I was no longer disinterested in the case, that my independence may have been compromised.

JB   Yes, Judge. And what is the formality that you were speaking of?

FR   I have no intention of calling the whole trial off – merely on groundless arguments that my judgment may be impaired.

Therefore, I am placing a legal embargo on both of you, the Metropolitan Police and the media. Should anyone speak of this incident, publish anything about this incident or cause others to do likewise, then they shall be held in contempt of court and charged as such.

Picking up a piece of paper from his desk and handing it to Chief Inspector Banerjee.

I have written up and signed the embargo and am now handing it to you in person. So, as of now, you will be held criminally liable should you disclose anything about this case to anyone – other than your direct superiors at the Metropolitan Police. Your superiors shall also be getting similar formal notification.

JB   Well, thank you for your time. We will leave you in peace now.

FR   I apologise for having to insist on this formality, but I cannot afford for this case to collapse due to media coverage and speculation.

Inspector Cheng finishes retrieving the book and places it in an evidence bag.

NC   We understand. Thank you for your time. And, again, our commiserations.

The scene fades out on the two police officers closing the door behind them as they leave the Judge's chambers.

Insert Scene – 58

*Can we build a wall high enough around this country so as to keep out
these defectives and cheaper races, or will it be a feeble dam leaving it to
our descendents to abandon the country to the defectives, blacks,
browns and yellows and seek an asylum in New Zealand.*

Charles Davenport, Director Cold Springs Harbor Laboratory,1920.

Scene 89 – At the morgue

10:30am, Monday, 10 June 2013

Setting: City morgue

The scene fades in with Frederick Rogers already inside a morgue building talking to morgue staff (MS) member.

MS   Judge, I will take you into the visiting room.

FR   The visiting room?

MS   Yes, we were expecting you, so we moved the cadaver from the cold room to a bed in the visiting room. This will allow you a little time with your deceased in a more dignified setting.

FR   Thank you.

MS   This way.

They walk down a short corridor – and stop outside a door.

MS   Okay, your son is in this room. I will come in with you – and turn down the sheets.

FR   Thank you.

MS   Now, I must warn you, your son was subjected to a savage attack. He sustained a number of powerful kicks to his head. This, as you would expect, has damaged his face.

FR   Yes, I understand.

MS   Yes, I am sure you do understand. However, you do need to prepare yourself – as the extent of facial damage is significant.

FR   Thank you for your caution. Shall we proceed?

MS   Certainly, Judge.

The two enter the visiting room. There is a bed in the middle of the room, a stool next to the bed and a settee in the corner of the room. There is another door in the wall opposite to the one they entered. The lighting is soft.

The judge positions himself on one side of the bed while the morgue staff member positions himself on the other side of the bed. The staff looks up to the judge and, with his eyes, questions whether the judge is ready for him to turn down the sheets. The judge nods back to him. The staff member reaches up and carefully turns down the sheets.

Gough's face comes into view. It is horrifically bashed, with huge black and purple bruises and swellings all over it. His lips are swollen and split. His mouth is slightly open, revealing several broken teeth. One eye has been pushed deep inside his skull – so much so that it looks as though it is missing.

FR   Oh my God!

With this, it is evident that the judge is so horrified by the injuries that he is about to be physically sick. The morgue staff had anticipated this – and motions him towards a bucket that is next to the wall by the head of the bed. The judge moves towards the bucket leans over and vomits. After the judge has finished vomiting, the morgue staff member continues.

MS   Judge, there is a basin in the en suite [motioning towards the other door] where you will find a toothbrush and toothpaste. I'll now change your bucket and leave you alone with your son.

       When you are ready, please call me [points to a phone on a table next to the settee] – just press the speed-dial labelled 'Assistance'. If you do not call me, then I'll come back in an hour. Is that okay?

FR   Yes, yes, that is fine. Thank you for your assistance.

The scene fades out with the staff member changing the bucket and exiting the room.

It fades back in with the judge looking over Gough, caressing his bruised and battered face with a stream of tears rolling down his cheeks.

The scene fades out and then back in where the judge is sitting on the settee, leaning forward with his head stooped, with a very slow movement of his head from side to side.

The scene fades out and back in on the judge leaning back on the settee, with his head on the headrest, with him staring unfocusedly at the ceiling.

The scene fades out and back in, with the judge back over the bed looking at his son.

The scene fades back in with the judge in the settee looking intently across the room at his son – when there is a knock on the door. The judge looks up to the door as it slowly opens.

MS   Judge, are you okay?

FR   Yes, thank you.

MS   Judge, an hour has passed. Unfortunately, your visiting time has come to an end. Can I get you anything?

FR   Unless you can bring my son back to life, then no.

MS   I'll leave you for five more minutes – then you will have to leave. Apologies.

FR   No, it's quite okay, I understand. Thank you, another five minutes is very much appreciated.

The scene fades out on the staff member leaving the room – and fades back on the judge pacing distressedly up and down the room, with the demeanour of a person who has the weight of the world on their shoulders.

The scene fades out and in with the staff member knocking on and opening the door. The judge had obviously anticipated the arrival of the staff member as he has his coat on and is standing, waiting, at the foot of the bed. The staff member enters the room – and walks to the bed – the judge walks to the other side of the bed. Together they turn the sheet up to cover Gough's face.

FR   Rest in peace my sweet child. I love you, I always have and always will.

With this, the judge starts sobbing.

MS   Are you okay Judge?

FR   Yes, yes, I'm fine. I'm ready to leave now. Thank you for being so patient with me.

The scene fades out on the two of them leaving the visitors room.

The scene fades back on the two of them as they walk down the morgue corridor.

FR   As you are no doubt aware, an embargo has been placed on the morgue – preventing all staff members from discussing or disclosing anything about my son or myself.

The reason for this is that I am currently presiding over a trial that is very sensitive – and, should information be leaked to the press about my son, the subsequent press coverage could jeopardise the trial.

MS   Yes, my supervisor had informed me that I am not allowed to discuss your son with anyone, including other employees here at the morgue.

FR   Yes, that is the case. Thank you very much for your assistance, it is very much appreciated – but, please, can I ask you to strictly observe the embargo and speak to no one on this matter.

MS   Certainly, I understand.

The scene fades out on the backs of the two of them as they walk down the corridor in deafening silence.

Scene 90 – Judgment Day

3:30pm, Monday, 10 June 2013

Setting: High Court

The scene opens in the courtroom where, with the exception of Judge Rogers, all the key players are present – all looking anxious. The camera pans around the courtroom – and, aside from Ivan, Andy and Rob, there is not a single dwarf present. However, for the first time, Valentina Henry is in the gallery. The camera zooms in on Ivan and his team. Ivan looks back into the public gallery, spots his mother and is visibly surprised, if not shocked, to see her there. Ivan recovers from spotting his mother in the gallery, checks his watch and turns to Bill.

IH   Where the hell is he? He's 25 minutes late.

BH   Stay calm – it is not unusual for a judge to be a little late. They have a lot of shit to do – particularly in a complex case like this.

AW   He may have got caught up in the investigation into yesterday's commotion outside of the court buildings.

BH   Speaking of the commotion – what on Earth did you guys do?

       I can understand that you may have felt the need to get a little support – possibly even asking them to get a little media attention about your plight. Albeit, at this late stage, I can't see how that would have influenced the judgement. But, rather than getting a little positive media attention, you incite a pack of dwarfs to firebomb the GPA offices then riot down Fleet Street. Just what on God's Earth do you think you were doing? And, do you really think that having two plumbers, a father and son team, murdered is in anyway going to help your cause?

AW   That strife was not inglorious, though the event was dire, As this place testifies, and this dire change

       Hateful to utter: but what power of mind
       Foreseeing or presaging, from the depth
       Of knowledge past or present, could have feared,
       How such united force of gods, how such

As stood like these, could ever know repulse?

BH   Andy, now is not the time for reciting quirky quotes, as you guys are in serious trouble.

AW   [Without acknowledging Bill or anyone else] John Milton, Paradise Lost.

IH   [Ignoring Andy and looking very distressed and embarrassed.] All I did was ask the guys to come down and support us in the gallery today. But, this mad midget got up and provoked the meeting into a riot. It got out of hand – beyond my control. Certainly, I – or we – had nothing to do with the murdering of the two plumbers. I condemn those responsible for the murder as much as anyone can.

BH   But it was you who called the special meeting of the Dwarf Society, didn't you? You did get up and deliver a raging address to them, telling them that their very existence is at stake – didn't you?

IH   Yes, yes, yes – but I didn't expect any violence. I mean, due to our size we always steer clear of violence. We always come off second best – we hate violence.

BH   Coming off second best? Well on this occasion you managed to reverse the trend – your mates and kinship have managed to stay pacifists for thousands of years. Then, on the day before you have to prove that you are good, decent, normal people – you decide to riot and go on a killing spree.

Jesus Christ, what was in your head? And, what have you actually achieved? Is there a single dwarf in the gallery supporting you today? No, they've all been arrested! The Bill has packed them all up in paddy wagons and taken down to them lockup. Not a great moral endorsement of your 'genetically defined social minority' is it?

Well, my boy, I think you have come off second best again. Personally, I wouldn't be surprised that, after this case is over, you are arrested for the crime of 'Incitement of Hatred'.

IH   You're not serious.

BH   I'm very serious – I mean, you go and whip up a crowd of dwarfs into a frenzy, they burn down the GPA offices and then charge down Fleet Street vandalising cars, dragging innocent people out of their cars to kick the shit out of them. Then just to top it all off – one of your mates sticks a copper pipe through one guy's head and cuts his son's head off with a blow torch.

Yes, I think you are in serious trouble.

IH   Do you think the riot will affect the outcome of this case?

BH   Judge Rogers is a good and fair judge. So, hopefully he will separate his thoughts on the riot from his thinking on this case. But, who knows, as it sure does damage your case that dwarfs actively contribute to and advance the nation's arts and culture.

At this point Judge Rogers enters the courtroom.

Sheriff All rise for Judge Rogers.

All attendants rise. The judge enters the court, with a very stern and unforgiving face, does not look at anyone, rather walks straight to his chair and sits down abruptly. The attendees then sit.

FR   I have considered all the arguments that have been put forward during this appeal. As I stated in the opening address of this appeal, this court will not be revisiting the GPA's ruling. Rather, this court will determine whether or not the GPA had the right to make such a ruling. The criterion in judging whether the GPA acted *ultra vires* was defined at the outset of this case. To refresh our memories, I defined it as follows:

a) Does the state have the right to determine what constitutes a human or a person?
b) If it does, then under what circumstances can a state make such a ruling?
c) What controls are in place to prevent arbitrary or discriminatory practices?
d) Given the above, were these controls observed when the GPA made its ruling?

If the above four conditions are satisfied, then the GPA was within its rights to make the ruling. The legal positions put forward during this appeal have satisfied the following criteria:

a) The state does have a reserved right to determine what constitutes a person.

b) The state can exercise this reserved right where public health issues are at stake, whether in the present – or in future generations of its citizens.

c) The parliamentary act that established the GPA has sufficient safeguards in place to prevent arbitrary discrimination practices – which includes hearing and appeals to the GPA's Ethics Ruling Committee and to this very court.

d) The controls and safeguards were observed by the GPA in arriving at its ruling.

Given that the above four conditions have been satisfied, the GPA was within its right to rule that dwarfism – or achondroplasia – satisfies the criteria that those with the condition are in excess of three standard deviations from the human norm.

As the foetus being carried by Ms Sandra Small has been ruled as being outside the human norm, the state has the right to revoke all paternal rights that Mr Henry has over the embryo or foetus. Further, the state has the right to encourage the mother to terminate the pregnancy. Encouragement includes withdrawing all state aid for the care, schooling, health, and benefits from the child from birth through to burial.

As the judge finishes pronouncing his judgment, the following text is displayed:

The fire spread from the High Court to consume London and the entire United Kingdom.

The judge gets up – belatedly followed with an 'All rise' from the sheriff, caught off guard as to how quickly the judge wrapped things up – and swiftly leaves the courtroom.

The camera cuts over to Ivan and his team, who are all shell shocked and speechless. The camera cuts over to the GPA team, who are as equally stunned by the sheer swiftness and brutality of the judgment.

The camera focuses on Sandra, who is first stunned, then an incredible anger erupts within her, at which point she stands up and hurls abuse and insults at the GPA team, all the while with tears rolling down her cheeks. Bill stands up to both comfort her – and to stop her protests – but Sandra turns on him and starts physically hitting him. Ivan then transforms himself out of his shock into a tyrant and starts to abuse Bill for losing the case, insulting him with Nazi connotations.

The camera focuses in on Jon Raney – who has his face in his hands and is slowly shaking his head in disbelief.

The camera pans the courtroom – where it picks up on Max, who is leaning back in his seat with a very smug look on his face, barely perceptibly nodding in delighted agreement.

As the pandemonium rages on, Jon Raney quietly gets up, still obviously distressed by the outcome of the judgment and slowly starts walking down the aisle to leave the courtroom. As he passes the bench where Valentina is sitting he stops and looks at her, and with a barely perceptible gesture, asks her to join him.

Valentina, seemingly unfazed by the commotion or judgment, picks up on Jon's non-verbal invitation, and stands up and walks to the aisle to join him.

As she nears Jon, he puts out his arm and Valentina places her hand in it – and they proceed to walk out of the courtroom together.

As they walk down the aisle, Ivan momentarily looks up from his torrential abuse of Bill and sees Jon and his mother arm in arm, which catches him totally by surprise and dumbfounds him to the point he ceases his rantings to Bill. He is left standing on his bench, at the centre of a chaotic scene, totally motionless and expressionless.

At this point the scene fades out.

Insert Scene – 59

The day will certainly come when the whole of mankind will be forced to check the augmentation of the human species ... Nobody can doubt that this world will one day be the scene of dreadful struggles for existence on the part of mankind.

Mein Kampf by Adolf Hitler.

Scene 91 – Gloating at the Club – as they join the readers

10:30am, Sunday, 16 June 2013

Setting: Claydon House

The scene opens in the familiar setting of Claydon House, with the exception of Frederick Rogers, all the usual members of the Country Club are assembled in the sitting room enjoying afternoon tea. All of those present have a very solemn expression.

LTD   Yes, very, very unfortunate. Frederick had waited so long and done so much to be re-united with his lad, then, just as it was about to happen – well, those brutes murder his son without even a glimmer of compassion or sympathy. Terrible shame.

ALB   The CCTV footage showed just how inhumane those little monsters are. It does go to show that America has at least one thing right – the death penalty. It's a travesty of justice, not to mention a complete waste of state resources, to have those little beasts imprisoned for the next 30 years rather than solving the problem with capital punishment.

CB   Very true. However, it was a stroke of good fortune that those dwarfs picked that very moment to murder Frederick's son – say, rather than a day or so later.

SB   It is extremely unfortunate what happened, but since it did happen, then yes – the timing was impeccable. It achieved what we seemed incapable of, namely to get Frederick to change his perspective on the case before him – to convince Frederick that those little beasts are not human.

ML   Indeed, now that we have won our equivalent of Donoghue v. Stevenson, we now have a precedent that the GPA has the necessary vested authority to determine who is human. Those that are deemed not human will have their rights to reproduce severely reduced.

However, now is not the time for complacency or recklessness. To cleanse our society, to quote Chris, will require 'gradualism'. While we can cleanse the midgets from our gene pool now, we still can't make a ruling on the Blacks and Arabs immediately. We need to gradually build up the case by identifying race-specific genetic disorders or abnormalities.

OW   Quite true, Max. However, an area I think we can immediately focus on is IQ. The GPA could rule within the next year or so that those with low IQ fall outside the three standards deviation threshold. This will allow us to classify anyone with an IQ of, say, less than 80, as non-human.

Getting rid of that class of 'very dull' people would be a worthy achievement in its own right. Such a ruling would have an added benefit. Herrnstein and Murray firmly established that more blacks than whites fall into the low IQ bracket. This gives us a great opportunity to kill two birds with one stone, the feebleminded and blacks.

ML   Exactly. Providing that we can demonstrate a scientific and objective manner in arriving at a ruling, and that the condition is generally perceived by the public as undesirable, the public would then support, or at least accept, a ruling to stop the propagation of imbeciles.

CB   Excellent. Shall we join the others?

ALB   Indeed, otherwise we will be seen as impolite and I would rather avoid such a suggestion.

With this, the gentlemen all stand up and leisurely stroll through the smoking room in which they had been sitting.

Insert Scene – 60

It is evident that a people which is endowed with high creative powers in the cultural sphere is of more worth than a tribe of negroes.

Mein Kampf *by Adolf Hitler.*

As the child finishes reading the above passage, the camera pans around the room showing the many applauding parents – and during this applause, the members of the Country Club stroll into the room and heartily join the clapping.

542

Scene 92 – The Aryans

8:30am, Friday, 9-June-2113

Setting: London Bridge

The scene opens as the first scene – on London Bridge, with sub-text showing that it is Friday, 9 June 2113 – One hundred years since the judgment handed down by Judge Frederick Rogers.

Narrator: The Great Fire of London in 1666 rid the city of its deadly bubonic diseases. The Great Fire of London in 2013 rid the city of its deadly genetic diseases. Just as London came back stronger after the Great Fire of 1666, the human race came back stronger after the Great Fire of 2013:

No more achondroplasia. No more dwarfs.
No more feeble minded. No more schizophrenia. No more bipolar disorder.
No more Huntington's chorea. No more epilepsy.
No more hereditary body deformities. No more hereditary deafness.
No more hereditary blindness. No more alcoholism.
No more cystic fibrosis.

No more sickle-cell anaemia. No more diabetics.
No more tuberculosis. No more cleft pallet.
No more colour blindness. No more dyslexia.
No more dysgraphia.

No more dissociative identity disorder. No more anti-social personality disorder.
No more conduct and oppositional defiance disorder. No more geniuses.
No more giants.

No more arrogance. No more shyness. No more dissidents.
No more troublemakers. No more religious fanatics. No more weaklings.

As the narrator speaks the camera is focused on London Bridge during the morning rush hour with hordes of workers walking over the bridge. The scene eerily shows the absolute 'sameness' of everyone:

All the men are around 6'1", all the women are around 5'10". All have blue eyes.

All have a tanned white skin. All have the same athletic build. All have blonde hair.

All Aryans.

The narrator's voice slowly starts to fade as the traffic noise fades in

Narrator No more criminals. No more liars.

> No more adulterers. No more sinners. No more atheists. No more agnostics.

> No more heretics. No more anarchists.

The scene fades out with the camera picking up that all the people crossing the bridge are carrying the same umbrella, wearing the same coat, and all reading/carrying the same newspaper.

There is a distinct lack of any 'skip' in anyone's step. They are all bored and have nothing unique and nothing to live for. The scene fades out on the masses crossing London Bridge, with the narrator continuing his ever-fading mantra:

> No more homosexuals. No more blacks.

> No more yellows. No more browns. No more Jews …

With this the scene fades out over London Bridge arching over a Thames low tide.

The End

Lightning Source UK Ltd.
Milton Keynes UK
UKHW031819010922
408167UK00005B/250